BANKRUPT
REPRESENTATION
AND PARTY SYSTEM
COLLAPSE

BANKRUPT REPRESENTATION AND PARTY SYSTEM COLLAPSE

JANA MORGAN

THE PENNSYLVANIA STATE UNIVERSITY PRESS
UNIVERSITY PARK, PENNSYLVANIA

Library of Congress Cataloging-in-Publication Data

Morgan, Jana, 1977– .
   Bankrupt representation and party system collapse /
Jana Morgan.
      p.   cm.
Includes bibliographical references and index.
Summary: "Explores the phenomenon of party system
collapse through a detailed examination of Venezuela's
traumatic party system decay, as well as a comparative
analysis of collapse in Bolivia, Colombia, and Argentina
and survival in Argentina, India, Uruguay, and Belgium"—
Provided by publisher.
ISBN 978-0-271-05062-1 (cloth : alk. paper)
ISBN 978-0-271-05063-8 (pbk. : alk. paper)
1. Political parties.
2. Representative government and representation.
3. Comparative government.
4. Political parties—Case studies.
5. Representative government and representation—
   Case studies.
6. Political parties—Venezuela.
7. Venezuela—Politics and government—1974–1999.
I. Title.

JF2051.M67 2011
324.2—dc22
2011013378

FOR MY PARENTS, *who always believe*

AND FOR NATE, *who helps make dreams come alive*

CONTENTS

FIGURES AND TABLES

FIGURES

TABLES

ACKNOWLEDGMENTS

In the course of developing the ideas and gathering the data reflected in this project, I have accrued numerous intellectual and personal debts. While it is impossible to recognize all who have contributed in some way to this book, I acknowledge here many of those who offered me support on the journey.

My academic skills and scholarly identity have been profoundly shaped by Evelyne Huber's wise guidance and incisive feedback. Evelyne pushes me to ask important questions, while encouraging me to care about issues that have repercussions for people's lives. This attitude toward scholarship has imbued my approach to research, instilling in me a passion for my work and making the work more meaningful. Evelyne also helped equip me to discover answers to the questions I ask, and she remains a deep reservoir of valuable advice. She has read drafts of this manuscript more times than I could count, and her comments have motivated me to refine the argument and strengthen the evidence. Most of all, Evelyne's unflagging encouragement through the process of writing this book gave me confidence in the project and in my ideas, creating space for me to think.

Jonathan Hartlyn has also been a constant source of advice and support. Jonathan offered candid and insightful feedback on multiple drafts. His suggestions frequently raised tough questions, urging me to clarify or flesh out less developed portions of the manuscript, and some elements of the book surfaced as significant parts of the argument in response to the constructive criticism he offered. Jonathan always accompanies his critiques with steadfast confidence and enthusiasm about my work, and working with him has been an important source of intellectual and professional growth.

In addition to Evelyne and Jonathan, several other people on faculty at the University of North Carolina at Chapel Hill provided valuable advice at various stages of this book's development. Lars Schoultz helped clarify my writing, challenged me to develop portions of the theoretical argument further, and recommended strategies that strengthened my evidence concerning policy unresponsiveness. Jim Stimson offered important methodological advice, and Graeme Robertson asked questions that helped me refine the logic underpinning case selection.

Many other colleagues have contributed to the development of this manuscript by facilitating access to crucial sources of data or providing comments on various portions of the manuscript. David Myers connected me with numerous contacts in Venezuela, offered guidance concerning the political landscape in the country, and was always willing to give advice as the project developed. Kirk Hawkins generously shared a wealth of insights that helped orient me as I began my Venezuelan field research, and his contacts proved invaluable. Kirk also read large portions of the manuscript, offering detailed comments that significantly improved the final product.

Thanks are also due to Bob Barr, Henry Dietz, Ian Down, Scott Mainwaring, Erika Moreno, Tony Nownes, Carlos Pereira, Omar Sánchez, Andrew Schrank, Joel Selway, Andrew Stein, Sue Stokes, Liz Zechmeister, and especially Juan Pablo Luna and Steve Wuhs, who offered helpful comments that strengthened the conceptual and theoretical framework developed in part 1 and later reviewed in part 3 of the book. I also benefited from important clarifications and corrections concerning the comparative cases in part 3 offered by Bob Barr, Ian Down, Jonathan Hartlyn, Liesbet Hooghe, Anirudh Krishna, Juan Pablo Luna, Sara Niedzwiecki, Eswaran Sridharan, and Dhirendra Vajpeyi. In addition, José Vicente Carrasquero, Brian Crisp, Luis Pedro España, Marino Gonzalez, Michael Kulisheck, José Molina, Daniel Ortega, Adolfo Vargas, and Friedrich Welsch each graciously provided access to data they had collected or archived. Indira Palacios helped with some translations and read portions of the manuscript, and Jenny Wolak gave feedback on grant proposals.

I have presented work related to this book in various venues, where I received helpful comments and suggestions: Michigan State University, Missouri State University, Texas Tech University, UCSD, University of North Carolina at Chapel Hill, University of Oregon, and the University of South Carolina Political Research Workshop. I appreciated the opportunity to vet my ideas in each of these contexts, and I am particularly grateful for the feedback I received from Gary Cox, Phil Roeder, and Peter Smith at UCSD, Dennis Galvan at Oregon, and Chuck Finocchiaro at South Carolina.

My colleagues at the University of Tennessee have also supported the development of this book. They commented on portions of the manuscript presented in different fora. John Scheb and David Feldman helped me obtain financial and other sources of research support, including a Professional Development Award and a summer Graduate Research Award through the Chancellor's SARIF program. Pat Freeland has been a constant source of advice and encouragement. The University of Tennessee Library has also been an amazing resource. I especially extend my thanks to Kathleen Bailey in Interlibrary Services for facilitating my access to countless reels of microfilm and rare books; to Ellie Read, our data librarian, for efficiently obtaining data I needed to make some of the final revisions to the manuscript; and to the Digital Media Services department for digitizing some of the newspaper data, which facilitated coding.

Several other entities supported this research financially. The Pew Foundation Younger Scholars Program supported three years of graduate study, including time for field research and writing. A Fulbright-Hays Doctoral Dissertation Research Abroad grant financed ten months of field research in Venezuela. The University of North Carolina Graduate School provided additional funds for field research and dissertation writing through the Off-Campus Dissertation Research Fellowship and the Dissertation Completion Fellowship. Tinker Foundation awards, administered by the University of North Carolina's Institute for Latin American Studies and the University Center for International Studies, supported preliminary fieldwork in Peru, Venezuela, and Argentina. A Library Travel Research Grant from the University of Florida's Center for Latin American Studies allowed me to gather data from its extensive Latin American collection. A Professional Development Award from the University of Tennessee financed field research in Venezuela during summer 2006. I am also grateful to the Latin American Studies Association for granting me permission to reprint portions of my 2007 *Latin American Research Review* article; extracts from the article appear in chapters 4 and 8.

Gathering and analyzing the data underpinning this book was a collective effort. Student research assistants compiled cross-national election returns and legislative composition data and also coded newspapers for the legislative responsiveness analysis. Thanks especially to Ole Forsberg as well as Maiba Belisario, Beth Wilson, Amber Sheets, Samantha Powell, James Trimble, Gaby Maldonado, Katie Gunter, and Alissa Ralph. Furthermore, the graduate students in my spring 2008 Latin American politics seminar read early drafts of some chapters; their comments pushed me to clarify my ideas and their presentation.

Much of the data analyzed in this book was collected during extended periods of field research, including nearly a year and a half in Venezuela, as well as four months of archival research in the United States at the Library of Congress and the University of Florida. Many of the ideas articulated here emerged during my time in the field, and this book would not exist without the gracious support and collaboration offered by numerous Venezuelans, who unreservedly gave their time, candidly discussed their experiences as politicians and party leaders, provided access to political party and think tank archives, opened their personal papers, and offered access to other data sources. I am especially grateful to the eighty-nine Venezuelans who agreed to be interviewed and willingly offered hours of their time to engage in frank conversations about the collapse of their party system. While confidentiality requirements prevent me from naming these participants here, I acknowledge their contributions because their ideas and reflections helped me gain a deeper understanding of the country's political landscape and enabled me to develop more meaningful analyses.

Many other Venezuelans facilitated access to important resources for my research. The Universidad Simón Bolívar provided me with an institutional home during my longest stint in Caracas, offering access to its library and other campus resources. José Vicente Carrasquero, Friedrich Welsch, and their student María de Pilar Canprubi gave me numerous contacts in Venezuela and even offered to share their office space. I am also grateful to the Venezuelan pollsters and academics who provided access to their public opinion data archives, including Adolfo Vargas, who manages the Universidad Simón Bolívar Banco de Datos Poblacionales, Felix Seijas of IVAD, Roberto Zapata and Luis Christiansen of Consultores 21, José Antonio Gil Yepes of Datanalisis, and Edmond Saade, José Rondón, and Mario Acuña of DATOS. Alfredo Torres and Argelia Rios also helped me gain access to important sources of public opinion data, and Alfredo provided advice and encouragement throughout my time in Venezuela.

I am also appreciative of the invaluable array of contacts I was able to make with the help of Irma Blanco, Toby Jiménez, and Calixto Ortega. Several current and former AD and COPEI party leaders opened portions of their personal archives to me, and Luis Coronado oversaw my unfettered use of the IFEDEC archives. Thais Maingon facilitated my access to the CENDES library, and Miriam Kornblith, Margarita López Maya, Michael Penfold Becerra, and Aníbal Romero each helped shape my thinking at various critical points during my field research. Robert Bottome opened the *VenEconomía* archives, and Jhoany Pérez at the *El Nacional* archive efficiently and cheerfully fulfilled my numerous requests, even after I had left Caracas. In the United States, the staffs at the Library of Congress Newspaper and Current Periodical Reading Room and the University of Florida Library helped me fill large gaps in my legislative output and newspaper data sets.

During my time in Venezuela, Caracas came to feel very much like home. Ángel, Irma, Ángel Eduardo, and their entire family welcomed me and my family as their own. They included us in an array of activities, such as birthday parties, trips to the beach, and debates around the kitchen table, which made us feel like we belonged. On one return trip to Caracas, Magaly and José allowed us to use their apartment for several months, and after leaving Venezuela, Irma even gathered some missing data for me. These friendships made life in Caracas richer and gave me an appreciation for the fun that comes with salsa dancing, drinking whiskey, and watching Venezuelan baseball. *¡Un abrazo fuerte!*

Friends in Knoxville and elsewhere have provided encouragement, enthusiasm for my work, and welcome diversions from long hours of writing. Mary, Jeremy, and Jewel are the best friends and neighbors I could imagine; they make life more beautiful and help me live it intentionally. Kathy makes me think and evaluate life from new perspectives. Travetta, David, Ashley, Levon, Rebecca, Steve, Doug, Laurens, Polly, and many others encouraged me throughout the long journey to completing the book and loved me no matter what.

My dear family cares for me well. My sister Alyssa always has a listening ear and an encouraging word. Ethan makes me smile whenever I see his precious face. Milt and Connie have confidence in me and treat me like their own daughter, celebrating life's joys and mourning the sorrows. My aunts, uncles, cousins, and siblings-in-law have taken an interest in my work and are understanding when it takes me away from family.

My parents, Kathy and Harry Morgan, taught me a love for learning and thinking, instilled me with faith, and always believed in me. They have provided profound love and support through life's ups and downs. Their words of encouragement, their open door, and their comprehension of my passions were indispensable to me as I researched and wrote this book. I feel unusually fortunate to have such supportive parents.

Nate Kelly is my partner, my colleague, and my best friend. As I worked on this book, he helped me in innumerable ways. Nate traveled with me to collect data and even wrote much of his own dissertation in Caracas. He helped code data, scanned endless pages of microfilm, offered methodological advice, commented on several drafts of the manuscript, and engaged in countless conversations with me as I puzzled out the dynamics of party system collapse in Venezuela and elsewhere. In Caracas as I collected data and in Knoxville as I pushed to complete the manuscript, he cheerfully assumed far more than his share of household duties. But perhaps most importantly, Nate helps me remember why I do this work, understands when it is time-consuming and difficult, and knows with considerable conviction that what I contribute is valuable. His love, his thoughtfulness, his laughter, and his confidence in me are priceless gifts. I dedicate this book to Nate and to my parents.

ABBREVIATIONS

ABP	Alianza Bravo Pueblo (Venezuela)
AD	Acción Democrática (Venezuela)
ADN	Acción Democrática Nacionalista (Bolivia)
AN	Alleanza Nazionale (Italy)
ANDI	Asociación Nacional de Industriales (Colombia)
ANUC	Asociación Nacional de Usuarios Campesinos (Colombia)
AP	Acción Popular (Perú)
APRA	Alianza Popular Revolucionaria Americana (Perú)
ASP	Asamblea por la Soberanía de los Pueblos (Bolivia)
BJP	Bharatiya Janata Party (India)
BSP-PSB	Socialist Belgian Workers' Party
BTV	Banco de los Trabajadores de Venezuela
CDN	Comité Directivo Nacional (Venezuela)
CEN	Comité Ejecutivo Nacional (Venezuela)
CEPB	Confederación de Empresarios Privados de Bolivia
CGIL	General Confederation of Italian Labor
CISL	Italian Confederation of Free Trade Unions
CN	Comité Nacional (Venezuela)
CNE	Consejo Nacional Electoral (Venezuela)
CNE	Corte Nacional Electoral (Bolivia)
COB	Confederación Obrera Boliviana
COMIBOL	Corporación Minera de Bolivia
CONDEPA	Conciencia de la Patria (Bolivia)
CONIVE	Consejo Nacional Indio de Venezuela
CONV	Convergencia Nacional (Venezuela)

COPEI	Comité de Organización Política Electoral Independiente (Venezuela)
COPRE	Comisión Presidencial para la Reforma del Estado (Venezuela)
CPI	Consumer Price Index
CPN	Comité Político Nacional (Venezuela)
CTC	Confederación de Trabajadores de Colombia
CTV	Confederación de Trabajadores de Venezuela
CVP-PSC	Christian Democratic Party (Belgium)
DC	Christian Democratic party (Italy)
EMU	Economic and Monetary Union (European Union)
ENP	Effective number of parties
FA	Frente Amplio (Uruguay)
FCV	Federación de Campesinos de Venezuela
FEDECAFE	Federación Nacional de Cafeteros de Colombia
FEDECAMARAS	Federación de Cámaras y Asociaciones de Comercio y Producción (Venezuela)
FIDES	Fondo Intergubernamental para la Descentralización (Venezuela)
FREPASO	Frente País Solidario (Argentina)
FRG	Frente Repúblicano Guatemalteco (Guatemala)
IDB	Inter-American Development Bank
ILO	International Labour Organization
IMF	International Monetary Fund
INC	Indian National Congress (India)
ISI	Import-substitution industrialization
IU	Izquierda Unida (Perú)
JAC	Juntas de Acción Comunal (Colombia)
JD	Janata Dal (India)
LCR	La Causa R (Venezuela)
LN	Lega Nord (Italy)
LPP	Law of Popular Participation (Bolivia)
MAS	Movimiento al Socialismo (Venezuela and Bolivia)

MEP	Movimiento Electoral del Pueblo (Venezuela)
MIP	Movimiento Indígena Pachakuti (Bolivia)
MIR	Movimiento (de la) Izquierda Revolucionaria (Venezuela and Bolivia)
MNR	Movimiento Nacionalista Revolucionario (Bolivia)
MNRI	Movimiento Nacionalista Revolucionario de la Izquierda (Bolivia)
MR	Movimiento Reformador (Guatemala)
MVR	Movimiento Quinta República (Venezuela)
NF	National Front (Colombia)
NFR	Nueva Fuerza Republicana (Bolivia)
NPE	Nueva Política Económica (Bolivia)
OPEC	Organization of Petroleum Exporting Countries
PAN	Partido Acción Nacional (Mexico)
PAN	Partido de Avanzada Nacional (Guatemala)
PCB	Partido Comunista de Bolivia
PCI	Communist Party of Italy
PCV	Partido Comunista de Venezuela
PDS	Democratic Party of the Left (Italy)
PDS	Partido Social Democrático (Brazil)
PDVSA	Petróleos de Venezuela, S.A. (Venezuela)
PFL	Partido da Frente Liberal (Brazil)
PJ	Partido Justicialista (Argentina)
PJ	Primero Justicia (Venezuela)
PLI	Liberal Party of Italy
PLRA	Partido Liberal Radical Auténtico (Paraguay)
PMDB	Partido do Movimento Democrático Brasileiro (Brazil)
PODEMOS	Poder Democrática y Social (Bolivia)
PP	Partido Patriota (Guatemala)
PPI	Partito Popolare Italiano
PPT	Patria Para Todos (Venezuela)
PRD	Partido de la Revolución Democrática (Mexico)

PRI	Partido Revolucionario Institucional (Mexico)
PRI	Republican Party of Italy
PSDI	Social Democratic Party of Italy
PSI	Socialist Party of Italy
PSN	Partido Solidaridad Nacional (Guatemala)
PSUV	Partido Socialista Unido de Venezuela
PV	Proyecto Venezuela
PVV-PLP	Liberal Party (Belgium)
RC	Refounded Communists (Italy)
UCR	Unión Cívica Radical (Argentina)
UCS	Unidad Cívica Solidaridad (Bolivia)
UDP	Unión Democrática y Popular (Bolivia)
UIL	Union of Italian Labor
UNE	Unión Nacional de la Esperanza (Guatemala)
URD	Unión República Democrática (Venezuela)
UTC	Unión de Trabajadores de Colombia

PART 1

UNDERSTANDING PARTY SYSTEM COLLAPSE:
CONCEPTS AND THEORY

1

INTRODUCTION: THE CATASTROPHE OF COLLAPSE

Political parties created democracy and . . . modern democracy is unthinkable save in terms of political parties. As a matter of fact, the condition of the parties is the best possible evidence of the nature of any regime.

—E. E. Schattschneider, *Party government*

In the 1970s, prospects for democracy in Venezuela seemed limitless. Competitive elections installed political leaders. Control of government peacefully changed hands from one established political party to another. By 1973, the militant left laid aside its weapons and entered electoral politics, and two parties consolidated their positions as the primary actors linking society and the state. These parties, Acción Democrática (AD) and COPEI (Comité de Organización Política Electoral Independiente), and the party system they formed were widely regarded as pivotal for Venezuelan democracy. In the 1970s and 1980s, over half the population identified with AD or COPEI, and nearly 85 percent of voters cast their ballots for them. At the same time, the economy prospered. Oil prices more than tripled in the 1970s, nearing $10 per barrel (OPEC 1999), and government revenue and GDP per capita increased significantly (Karl 1997; Baptista 1997).

Today, however, Venezuela's political and economic landscape is almost unrecognizable. Virtually no traces of AD or COPEI remain; they hold only 13 percent of seats in the legislature. In their place stands the personalistic, hegemonic government of Hugo Chávez, who has cultivated an impressive following but increasingly disregards democratic norms and practices. Elections are held regularly, but Chávez's opponents insist that fraud is rampant despite close international scrutiny. The control that Chávez exercises over the National Assembly, Consejo Nacional Electoral, Tribunal Supremo de Justicia, and many other institutions raises concerns about horizontal accountability. The left has gained substantial influence; moreover, some of Chávez's most loyal supporters, including governors, National Assembly deputies, and cabinet officials, were once members of the militant left, which was supposedly incorporated into the regime decades ago. Rather than relying on support from unions and professional associations, as AD and COPEI had done, Chávez has cultivated support among the historically marginalized.

The economic situation has also changed radically since the 1970s boom. Although oil prices rose in the mid-2000s, they had hovered around $5 per barrel for over a decade (adjusted for inflation; OPEC 2001); GDP per capita is down over 40 percent from the 1970s.[1] Inflation is in the double digits, although this is an improvement from its 1996 high of 100 percent.[2] Debt service is more than twice what it was thirty years ago.[3] And the portion of the population in poverty has nearly doubled since the 1970s, increasing from 33 to almost 60 percent (CISOR 1975, 2001).

What has happened in Venezuela since the 1970s? Given the institutionalization of the party system and the oil wealth the nation enjoyed, Venezuela seemed to be safely on route to democratic consolidation. But as the economy deteriorated and the parties did little to respond, people began defecting from the party system. A strong signal of mounting frustration came in the 1989 Caracazo, when violent protests erupted in response to President Carlos Andrés Pérez's neoliberal program. In 1992, factions of the military attempted two unsuccessful coups, and Pérez was impeached in 1993. By the early 1990s, new parties had begun to appear and contested the 1993 elections, which were won by former COPEI leader Rafael Caldera, who ran as an independent supported by a diverse set of parties. But during his presidency, Caldera found his strongest ally in AD—his longtime nemesis. As the traditional parties closed ranks, Venezuelans found no meaningful alternatives in the party system and turned elsewhere for representation. The prolonged crisis also provoked radical social change, which undermined the parties' bases of support and increased the numbers of the poor and unemployed, who were excluded from the party system. As a result, the parties lost ties to large swaths of society, encumbering stressed

---

1. Data are for 1974 and 2003, expressed in constant 1984 currency units. Source: Banco Central de Venezuela.

2. Inflation was 14.4 percent in 2005. Source: Banco Central de Venezuela.

3. Debt service equaled 16 percent of export earnings in 2004. Source: World Development Indicators.

clientelist networks with greater pressure to deliver votes. When financial scarcity and political reforms limited the parties' resources, clientelist capacities contracted, further weakening their draw.

By the end of the 1990s, the party system collapsed. First, a volatile multiparty system emerged, but Hugo Chávez gradually solidified a near-hegemonic hold on power. Chávez's repeated reelection and his efforts to restructure institutions and society suggest that Venezuela made a complete break with its history as an institutionalized party democracy.

While particularly severe and surprising in Venezuela, the dynamics and traumatic consequences of party system collapse seen there are not unique. In Italy, the Christian Democrats (DC) dominated post–World War II politics, controlling government with their frequent allies, the Socialists, for over four decades. Italy's postwar economic resurgence was touted as a miracle. But in the 1980s, public debt escalated and unemployment rates reached double digits. International commitments limited the parties' ability to address these problems, and patterns of coalition government discredited all the viable system alternatives. Class and religious cleavages lost salience, and economic realities and political reforms strained clientelist resources. By the mid-1990s, the DC and the Socialists had almost evaporated, and the permanent opposition party, the Communists, splintered. In the aftermath, uncharacteristic upheaval, even for Italy, plagued politics, and media baron Silvio Berlusconi monopolized power.

The Venezuelan and Italian systems faced challenges from economic crisis, social change, and political reform, while constraints hindered adaptation, causing collapse. Alternatively, other party systems in countries like 1990s Argentina, which was beleaguered by severe crises, and 1970s Belgium, which faced intractable ethnic divisions, managed to adapt and survive. Why do some party systems collapse when faced with considerable pressures while similar systems confronting seemingly insurmountable obstacles endure? Why do people reject not just the incumbent but the entire menu of options in a party system? What are the implications of this rejection for democracy? This book answers these questions, explaining how breakdowns in party politics occur and examining the ramifications of collapse.

PARTY SYSTEM COLLAPSE AND DEMOCRACY

Political parties are pivotal players in contemporary democracies, serving as vehicles for representation, accountability, and governability, and the system of interactions they form (Sartori [1976] 2005) shapes political contestation and government outcomes. A party system collapses when the parties decay and the structure of the system changes. As a result, patterns of representation, accountability, and governability are likely to change, and processes of contestation are prone to restructuring. The collapse of an entire party system, therefore, marks the complete reshuffling of the democratic order. Explaining this phenomenon, then, is crucial not only for illuminating party system dynamics but also for understanding democratic politics.

Parties are the primary agents of representation and often the only actors with access to elected positions in democratic systems (Hagopian 1998). By channeling the pursuit of interests into an institutional structure, parties peacefully frame competitive politics and allow divergent interests in society to participate through democratic means (Morales Paúl 1996; Przeworski et al. 1995). Parties also help voters hold elected officials accountable, providing heuristics at the polls and facilitating identification of those responsible for government outputs (J. Aldrich 1995). Significant changes in parties, especially the deterioration associated with collapse, may threaten the fulfillment of the crucial tasks that parties perform in democracy.

Changes in party *systems* likewise have important implications. Party systems organize contestation, shape which interests are articulated and how, and direct government outputs. It follows that modifications in party system structure will have important ramifications, reconfiguring contestation and reshaping policy outcomes. The volatility associated with change may also increase conflict and weaken accountability.

The potential impact of party system *collapse* is even more profound. The rupture in a party system's structure and the disintegration of its component parties, which together constitute collapse, have substantial consequences. When collapse occurs, the tasks typically performed by parties, such as promoting accountability and governability, may go unfulfilled. Meanwhile, as interparty interactions undergo dramatic restructuring, the regime may be exposed to instability and conflict. Most ominously, collapse may make the democratic regime vulnerable. The instability of the collapse period makes democracy more tenuous, at least in the short run, as citizens are caught in uncertainty. Collapse also opens the door to new and at times unpredictable actors. Although new groups may address previously unanswered clamor for access, their jockeying for position is likely to elevate conflict. Some emergent actors may directly undermine regime survival by disrespecting democratic norms or threatening entrenched interests. Given the significance of collapse for democracy, analyzing the factors that cause this outcome and examining its consequences provide important insight. Moreover, understanding what causes party systems to be susceptible to collapse may allow policy makers and party leaders to avoid some of the pitfalls that precipitate such catastrophe.

THEORETICAL FOUNDATIONS

Many have explored the reasons for and implications of changes in parties and party systems. Scholars have examined the emergence of new parties (Kitschelt 1995), adaptation efforts of existing parties (Kitschelt 1994; Levitsky 2003b), electoral shifts between parties (Dalton, Flanagan, and Beck 1984; Miller and Schofield 2003), and party failure (Lawson and Merkl 1988), among other types of change. Despite this plethora of scholarship on party dynamics, it is not clear whether these arguments, which were largely developed to explain individual party performance, may be directly extended to explain party system collapse. While explanations of collapse may draw inspiration from studies of party dynamics, a successful theory must explain why all the system parties fail simultaneously with changes in the system structure. Nevertheless, much of the existing research on party system collapse emphasizes the features and behavior of individual parties without considering how the entire party system is made vulnerable, neglecting theoretical advancements that account for the system-level features of collapse.[4]

To understand the processes that produce disintegration across entire party systems, I develop a theory of collapse.[5] Based on insights from research examining changes in individual parties and party systems and from studies that have theorized about party system structure, I argue that a system will collapse when it fails to fulfill its primary role in democracy— linking society to the state. Such failure is caused when a party system faces challenges to its core linkage strategies and when specific institutional and environmental constraints limit the ability of the system and its component parties to respond appropriately to these challenges. The party system's resulting inability to perform the critical task of linkage causes its collapse.

---

4. Work by Dietz and Myers (2007) provides an exception. Coppedge (2005) and K. Roberts (n.d.) take a system-level approach in examining the related issue of democratic decay in Venezuela and Peru; however, their work does not seek to explain party system collapse but rather examines regime-level processes.

5. I expound the theory much further in chapter 3.

Studies on individual party change demonstrate that for parties to survive, they must channel public concerns (Levitsky 2001b; Panebianco 1988b). Research analyzing electoral shifts within stable system structures argues that failed responsiveness leads voters to abandon one party and embrace another (Dalton, Flanagan, and Beck 1984). Studies explaining continuity and change in system structures suggest that for a system to be effective, it should mirror the demands and configuration of society (Lipset and Rokkan 1967). Jointly, then, the literatures on party dynamics and party system structure suggest that the extent to which a party system provides linkage affects its ability to survive.

Building on these literatures, I argue that for party systems to survive, they must channel and respond to public concerns; without linkage, the system will collapse. To explain why party systems cease to provide adequate linkage, I contend that a system is at risk when structural changes challenge its core linkage profile, demanding a response. If the challenges emerge in a context that limits the parties' ability to maneuver and address them, linkage deteriorates. The theory synthesizes sociostructural and institutional approaches, delineating how conflicting pressures generated by structural changes and by contextual constraints undermine ties between parties and voters. Unlike more deterministic explanations that view collapse as a natural outcome of threats like economic crisis or corruption (Hillman 1994; Molina and Pérez 1998), my focus on decaying linkage acknowledges the pressures that such challenges present but also analyzes the party system's response. By examining exactly how the ties between voters and politicians deteriorate in the period leading up to collapse, I illuminate the process through which threatening structural changes generate mounting demands for linkage and how specific constraints restrict the system's ability to respond to these pressures.

As countries change and evolve, party systems face countless challenges to their ability to provide linkage. Economic crisis, social change, and political reform may complicate a party system's job. But according to their specific linkage portfolios, different party systems are threatened by distinct challenges and find specific constraints especially difficult to overcome. To explore how particular challenges and constraints make different linkage strategies vulnerable to decay, I consider three main avenues through which party systems respond to demands for linkage: programmatic representation, incorporation of major social interests, and clientelism. In chapter 3, I detail the specific challenges and constraints expected to undermine each type.

I trace how structural changes amid contextual constraints led to severe linkage decay and produced party system failure across a diverse group of collapse cases. First, I carry out a detailed examination of Venezuela as a least-likely case. Then, I conduct a cross-national analysis, comparing Venezuela and three other instances of collapse with four cases in which party systems survived despite serious threats. Throughout, I employ large-N statistical analysis, quantitative content analysis, qualitative analysis of interviews and documents, and comparative historical analysis. The data include public opinion surveys, legislative archives, news reports, interviews with party elites, election returns, and government and party documents, as well as secondary sources.

I analyze the Venezuelan collapse in greatest depth because the institutionalized nature of its party system made collapse due to failed representation improbable and surprising. Although Venezuela is not the only long-standing party system that has encountered the trial of collapse, the quality and complexity of the linkage mechanisms in Venezuela rendered complete failure more unlikely there than in the other countries that have experienced collapse.[6] Furthermore, collapse has been particularly challenging for the stability and quality of Venezuelan democracy, making it an excellent case for understanding the ramifications of party system failure.

Explaining complex processes like party system collapse requires detailed analysis, and my treatment of Venezuela constitutes such an approach. But collapse is not a distinctively Venezuelan phenomenon. Therefore, I expand the analysis to consider a broader set of cases that includes instances of both collapse and survival. I conduct comparative analysis of other instances of collapse, demonstrating how the patterns present in Venezuela are replicated in other cases. Linkage failure, caused by particular structural challenges in a context of specific constraints, led to collapse in cases as diverse as Bolivia, Colombia, and Italy.

I also show how other at-risk party systems avoided collapse. I pair each of the four cases of collapse with a similar party system that managed to survive serious threats, matching them on linkage profiles, party system features, and important shared pressures on linkage.[7] I contrast Venezuela to Argentina, Bolivia to India, Colombia to Uruguay, and Italy to Belgium. Analyzing these matched cases of survival clarifies how countries facing

6. See chapter 2 for more details concerning the selection of Venezuela.
7. See chapter 9 for a detailed discussion of case selection.

some similar challenges avoided collapse by providing at least one form of linkage. In these instances of survival, I find that either the challenges facing the party system did not seriously undermine all components of the system's linkage profile or the context did not impede the system's capacity to adapt. When systems failed, foundational threats and limits on appropriate accommodation were present. When systems averted disaster, one of these conditions was absent.

OUTLINE OF THE BOOK

The book is organized into three parts. In the rest of part 1, I lay the book's theoretical foundation. Chapter 2 addresses conceptual issues. I distinguish between party system collapse and other sorts of party or party system change, placing collapse within the broader literature and spelling out how collapse is distinct. I conceptualize collapse as involving the concurrent decay of the major parties and a fundamental transformation in the structure of an established system. Operationalizing this idea, I identify all collapse cases in Europe and Latin America from 1975 to 2005. Then, I explain my rationale for focusing the most detailed analysis on Venezuela's party system collapse. This chapter will be especially useful to scholars concerned with how collapse fits into the broader panorama of party system change and to those interested in classifying cases of collapse.

In chapter 3, I develop the book's central theoretical argument. Collapse occurs when structural challenges and constraints on adaptation cause entire party systems to fall short of performing their central task of linkage. I specify three major strategies that parties might employ in fulfilling this task: programmatic appeals, interest incorporation, and clientelism. Then, I develop specific expectations concerning the structural changes that threaten each type of linkage and the constraints that limit the system's response. If all facets of linkage encounter core challenges that the parties are together unable to address, the system collapses. Readers interested in understanding the theoretical foundations of the causal process underlying collapse will find this chapter particularly valuable.

Those who are most interested in deciphering the Venezuelan case may wish to focus on part 2, which presents the empirical analysis of Venezuelan collapse. Throughout this portion of the book, I draw on considerable original data collected during fifteen months of field research in Venezuela. The data include interviews with eighty-nine political elites, thirty years of public opinion surveys, all laws passed from 1974 to 2004 and news coverage for the same period, documents from party and government archives, election returns, and social and economic data. I elaborate on the collection and analysis of these data in chapter 4, other portions of part 2, and the data appendixes.

Chapter 4 sketches the Venezuelan party system's founding and evolution. I outline the system's linkage portfolio at its apex in the 1970s, revealing a multifaceted strategy that included programmatic representation, interest incorporation, and clientelism. But by the late 1980s, rising pressures complicated linkage, and support for the traditional parties began to wane. Then, as chapter 4 describes, in 1988 the system collapsed. The subsequent chapters in part 2 explain this collapse, analyzing decay in each linkage type and showing how linkage failure caused collapse in Venezuela.

In chapter 5, I examine programmatic decay. Economic crisis heightened pressure on the parties to provide a policy response to worsening conditions. However, analysis of an extensive database I compiled, which details the quantity and significance of policy making on important issues, reveals that responsiveness declined considerably in the late 1980s and 1990s.[8] Rather than responding to the crisis, the parties froze, succumbing to constraints imposed by conflicting incentives that pitted historical legacies of state-led growth against international pressures toward neoliberalism. At the same time that responsiveness failed, the major parties ceased to offer meaningful programmatic alternatives. Patterns of interparty agreements produced ideological convergence among the parties and made it impossible for voters to find alternatives to the status quo within the system. The absence of policy responsiveness and lack of ideological differentiation between major parties produced programmatic discrediting across the entire system.

Chapter 6 explores how incorporation deteriorated in the face of dramatic social change. In the 1990s, the formal sectors of the economy, around which the traditional party system had been built, shrank, while the ranks of the poor, unemployed, and informal sector expanded to over half the population. However, the parties' incorporation strategies were strongly rooted in the decaying social structure, and conflict between the goals and organizational structures of new and entrenched interests made innovation risky.

8. I use public opinion data to identify important national problems, and then I assess the amount and significance of policy outputs dealing with these issues. I determine contemporaneous significance by analyzing news reports at the time policies were passed and identify retrospective significance using expert analysis. See appendixes B and C.

As a result, they did not pursue the political potential of these burgeoning groups, allowing incorporation to wither.

Chapter 7 shows that clientelism likewise crumbled as the parties faced growing demands, resource shortages, and clientelism-constraining reforms. Increased poverty and uncertainty motivated more Venezuelans to seek clientelist benefits. But the economic situation also limited resources available for political distribution, and the party apparatuses were increasingly shut out of patronage opportunities as technocrats took control of the state and fiscal decentralization rerouted resources to smaller, local or regional networks. At the same time, the introduction of separate, subnational elections increased the number of electoral processes for which clientelist resources were needed and undermined interdependence between the parties' geographical units, thereby increasing clientelist demand while reducing the gains achieved through each exchange.

By 1998, programmatic representation, interest incorporation, and clientelism were all floundering. Representation was bankrupt. Chapter 8 brings together the components of the previous three chapters to chronicle the system's collapse in the 1998 elections and provides a summary of the central arguments concerning the Venezuelan case. By using survey data to analyze Venezuelans' (lack of) support for the traditional parties at the time of these pivotal elections, I show that the absence of programmatic appeals, failure to incorporate new groups, and clientelist decay were together instrumental in producing the exodus from the old party system.

Part 3 extends the analysis beyond Venezuela, comparing instances of collapse and survival and exploring the ramifications of collapse. The material in this part will be especially relevant to those interested in a broader test of the theoretical argument or in the specific dynamics of the seven cases analyzed here. Chapter 9 outlines the rationale behind the selection of the four sets of paired comparisons between cases of collapse and survival: Bolivia-India, Venezuela-Argentina, Italy-Belgium, and Colombia-Uruguay. Chapter 10 examines Italy, Bolivia, and Colombia, assessing how threats and constraints produced system collapse in each. Through these comparisons, I demonstrate how the patterns in Venezuela were replicated in other cases of collapse. Chapter 11 contrasts the collapse cases with the paired survival cases. As opposed to the collapse cases, in which structural changes threatened core linkage strategies and constraints limited the parties' response, in the survival cases either significant threats were absent or the pattern of constraints did not impede all successful adaptation, and at least one type of linkage was sustained, enabling the systems' endurance.

Finally, chapter 12 provides a summary of the book's major insights and explores the aftermath of collapse. Using evidence from the four collapse cases analyzed here, I detail how post-collapse party systems make up for the representational failings of their predecessors, and I discuss how collapse poses a variety of challenges to democracy, including personalism, de-institutionalization, instability, and conflict. I conclude by suggesting some ways in which future episodes of collapse might be averted.

2

WHAT IT LOOKS LIKE: SYSTEM CHANGE, TRANSFORMATION, AND COLLAPSE

Party system change occurs when a party system is transformed from one class or type of party system into another. . . . The importance of the appearance or disappearance of a party . . . relates to [its] systemic role.

—Peter Mair, *Party system change*

Party system collapse is abrupt and catastrophic, presenting exaggerated challenges to the democratic system. But while collapse is rare and momentous, similarities exist between collapse and other, more ordinary party system dynamics, which often leads to confusion. This murkiness makes defining collapse and placing it in a broader context important, but the disparate research on party and party system change often renders conceptual clarity elusive (Langston 2009).

This chapter defines party system collapse, situating it within the broader literature on party system change and spelling out the core features of collapse in order to distinguish it from other sorts of change. Specifying how collapse is both distinct from and related to other, more common forms of change provides opportunities for theoretical leverage and for advancing understanding of why some systems fail and others do not. Delineating the intension of the collapse concept and identifying its essential elements clarifies its meaning and also enables me to develop a portable operationalization of collapse that is in line with the concept (Goertz 2006). I then employ this operational definition (Sartori 1970, 1045) to identify each collapse case in Europe and Latin America from 1975 through 2005. I conclude the chapter by discussing why I opt to focus the most in-depth analysis on Venezuela, as a case well suited for theoretical advancements in understanding the problem of collapse.

DEFINING PARTY SYSTEM CHANGE

A sizeable body of literature explores various facets of change in parties and party systems, ranging from studies of organizational change in individual parties to analyses of shifts in the mass electorate (Kitschelt 1995; Lawson and Merkl 1988; Levitsky 2003b; Mair 1997). In part, such diversity is useful and provides empirical and theoretical insight. But it also renders the concept vague, making cumulative theoretical and empirical advancements difficult because different types of dynamics are often grouped together or confused (Sartori 1970). Unifying theories about disparate phenomena may be sensible if they share common essential characteristics. However, in the party system change literature, different studies often explore distinct phenomena, failing to justify their treatment as analyses of the same basic concern. For example, realignment studies examine the causes behind electoral shifts that occur between parties within a *stable* system structure (Burnham 1970; Hurley 1989; Key 1955), while studies of major party decline often involve implicit analysis of changes in the system structure itself (Burgess and Levitsky 2003; Greene 2007), and other analyses consider dynamics that do not necessarily have electoral manifestations, like deinstitutionalization or organizational adaptation (González 1995; Kirchheimer 1966). These contrasts are just a few of the many divergent dynamics joined under the broad banner of party system change. The empirical diversity and conceptual confusion that characterize this literature make theory building difficult. Here I resolve some of this lack of clarity, particularly as it relates to our understanding of party system collapse.

Elucidating the idea of party system collapse and how it relates to party system change more broadly first requires specification of the core concept—the party system. I follow Sartori in conceptualizing a party system as "the *system of interactions* resulting from inter-party competition" ([1976] 2005, 39; emphasis in original). This conceptualization has become a standard in the literature (Mainwaring and Scully 1995a; Mair 1997) because it acknowledges that a party system is not just the sum of its parts but is also constituted by the structure of interparty competition. Party systems are not simply composed of individual parties operating independently, unaffected by competition and coalitions with other organizations in the system. Rather, the parties and their behaviors are interdependent, such that the system "displays properties that do not belong to a separate consideration of its component elements" (Sartori [1976] 2005, 39). This view of a party system as consisting of its constituent parties as well as the patterns of interactions between them becomes especially significant in conceptualizing and theorizing party system collapse, because the collapse of a system involves more than decay in its component parties and must also include foundational changes in the structure of the system.

With this definition of party system in hand, I turn to identifying fundamental similarities and differences among patterns of party system change. The party system concept I employ suggests that system change can be broken into two essential types: system-maintaining change, which primarily involves changes in the component parties, and system-transforming change, which extends beyond the parties alone to encompass shifts in the basic structure of interactions in the system.[1] System-maintaining changes occur within the system, without disrupting the overarching framework of interparty interactions or altering the essential structure of the system. System-transforming changes involve shifts in the structure of interparty interactions, which occur when a party system moves from one major type of structure to another. Internal changes and structural changes are likely to be produced by different kinds of causal processes. Thus, demarcating the two types enables greater accumulation of knowledge about the causes and consequences of party system change, because analyses will not suffer from the muddling of distinct processes.

Both types can be properly understood as changes in the system because they involve modifications in interparty interactions, but only system transformations involve restructuring the overarching framework in which these interactions occur. Many of the most important or fundamental changes occur when a system transforms, and transformation has wide-ranging implications. Other less momentous, but not necessarily trivial, changes that do not restructure the system fall into the category of system maintenance. Modifications in nondefining facets of the system, like party organizations or platforms, are qualitatively different from changes in the structure of the system itself (Mair 1997). But because even these sorts of changes have

1. This distinction is in part inspired by Mair's (1997) recommendation that party system analyses should differentiate between electoral stability and system stability, which can be achieved by distinguishing between changes to a party system and changes to the parties within the system. Confusion between these different phenomena led to the mistaken view that many European party systems underwent radical transformation in the 1980s and 1990s, when in practice the *systems* were stable.

ramifications for system features like representation and competition, they are appropriately treated as instances of system change, albeit of a different sort than transformations in structure.

When the internal characteristics or components of a party system vary but the system structure remains constant, we are observing system-maintaining change. Often it is precisely the changes made within the system—be it in organization, ties with voters, or policy positions—that enable the system structure to remain intact. This sort of change includes adjustments in individual parties or in the interplay between parties, as long as these changes are not part of a fundamental restructuring of the entire system.

System-maintaining change may entail shifts in the electoral fortunes of existing parties or the emergence of new parties that replace or augment existing options without challenging the basic structure of the system. System-maintaining changes may also manifest outside the electoral arena. Parties frequently change ideologically and organizationally (Kirchheimer 1966), and this type of change may actually sustain the parties and promote electoral stability (Dittrich 1983; Mair 1997).[2] Essentially, system-maintaining changes involve internal modifications and adaptations that do not reshape the system but instead occur within the structure already in place.

The second type of change, system transformation, involves a fundamental shift in system structure that "occurs when a party system is transformed from one class or type of party system into another" (Mair 1997, 52). Changes involving significant restructuring of the basic patterns of system interactions are qualitatively distinct from changes that take place in the context of a stable structure, as system-transforming changes reorder the core logic and principal incentives of interparty competition and cooperation. Transformations in party system structure may be less common than system-maintaining changes, but their impact is likely to be more significant. Transformation may carry ramifications for policy, stability, governance, and representation.

CONCEPTUALIZING COLLAPSE: SIMULTANEOUS SYSTEM TRANSFORMATION AND PARTY DECAY

Clarifying the distinction between system-maintaining change and transformation is important because I view party system collapse as an especially

---

2. For instance, in the Irish case, apparent electoral stability between the 1930s and 1980s masked dramatic changes in the parties' ideologies and organizations as well as increased interparty competition (Mair 1987, 1997).

dramatic kind of transformation in system structure. Some scholars have set forth a view of collapse that only requires the sustained deterioration of major parties (e.g., Seawright 2003). While collapse naturally involves party decay, I consider it to be more than just the decline of individual parties. Approaches to conceptualizing collapse that are exclusively concerned with party decline fail to recognize that party *system* collapse transcends the fortunes of individual parties and necessarily involves the fate of the whole system in which the parties interact. If we conceive of party systems as the set of interactions created by patterns of competition and cooperation between parties, then we must view collapse as more than mere party decay and develop a definition of system collapse that looks for changes not only in the parties themselves but also in the structure of the relationships between them.

To align our understanding of collapse with this view of party systems, I specify the intension of the collapse concept as including both party deterioration and transformation in system structure. *Collapse occurs when an established party system changes in type (transforms) concurrently with decay in the system's major parties.*[3] An entire party system, both its components and its structure, is democratically dissolved and gives way to a different system type with new parties (Dietz and Myers 2007). In this sense, collapse is a particular subtype of transformation. It is not simply a system-maintaining change that entails parties decaying in an undisturbed structure, but also involves fundamental alterations in the system structure itself.[4]

For change to constitute collapse, then, it must satisfy two necessary and sufficient conditions:[5] the system must simultaneously experience (1) a significant decline in its major component parties and (2) a transformation in the established system structure. If the components of the old system decay but the system structure does not transform at the same time, we do not have *system* collapse, but only the decay and replacement of old parties within a stable system structure.[6] Conversely, if the system transforms but

3. Name changes and divisions or mergers of existing parties do not constitute instances of party decay.

4. This approach to conceptualizing collapse also has ramifications for theoretical development, because accounts of collapse must explain not only the decay of individual parties but also the disintegration of the entire system. I briefly discuss these implications later in this chapter and expand and act upon them as I develop the theory in chapter 3.

5. See Goertz (2006, 35–39) for a discussion of necessary and sufficient concept structures like that applied here.

6. This distinction is important, as it is possible for some or even all the parties in a system to fail without precipitating the breakup of the system. Consider Ecuador, where the two largest parties in the 1979 and 1984 elections, Concentración de Fuerzas Populares and Izquierda Democrática, declined dramatically by the 1990s. Despite party decay, the system's structure was

the traditionally significant parties remain important players within the new structure, transformation has occurred, but without major party decay, this change likewise fails to meet the requirements for collapse.

Context and timing are also important elements of the collapse concept. As stated in the definition above, only established party systems can experience collapse. By established systems, I mean those that have some regular patterns of interaction, as opposed to emerging or highly volatile systems where dramatic fluctuations in system structure are commonplace and do not reflect a significant break with existing patterns. By restricting collapse to established systems, we avoid confusing it with generalized patterns of volatility. Furthermore, the idea of collapse implies that a fairly consistent pattern of interparty interactions is in place and that the major parties are identifiable, so that we can recognize fundamental shifts in the structure of these interactions and point clearly to decay in the system's core parties. This is *not* to say that a system must be institutionalized or entrenched for it to experience collapse, but only that the structure of interparty interactions and the major parties must be in place for enough time so that transformation constitutes a significant break with existing patterns.[7] Timing is also pivotal. The two necessary processes that constitute collapse, system transformation and party decay, must happen over a short period. They cannot be separated by an extended stretch of time and still be properly viewed as a single event.[8] Temporal distance implies two disconnected processes, not a unified incident of collapse.

Taken as a whole, then, this approach to conceptualizing collapse reflects the idea that party systems are composed not only of parties but also of the structure in which the parties interact. Because collapse constitutes an extreme sort of transformative change, rather than system maintenance, it is likely to be most closely linked empirically and theoretically to other sorts of transformation. In the next chapter, I theorize about collapse, drawing from existing studies on party system maintenance and transformation, with an emphasis on the latter. I take care to treat collapse as a systemic problem so

---

unaffected, preserving an extended multiparty system. Although the Ecuadorian system experienced volatility and replacement of its component parties, its basic structure remained unchanged (Conaghan 1995). Ecuador, therefore, provides an example in which major party decay was not part of a collapse incident, as the decline of individual parties altered interparty interactions but did not produce a fundamental transformation in the structure of those interactions.

7. Below, I operationalize this element of the concept by requiring that a system structure with the same major parties must be in place for at least two complete election cycles before the system can experience true collapse.

8. In the operationalization section below, I specify that transformation and decay must occur within one full election cycle to meet the requirements of collapse.

that the theory explains individual party decay as well as the system-level failure inherent to collapse. But first, in the rest of this chapter, I operationalize the collapse concept and identify cases of the phenomenon.

OPERATIONALIZING PARTY SYSTEM COLLAPSE

To differentiate between cases of collapse and other sorts of party system change, I determine whether a case satisfies the two facets of collapse: transformation of the system and substantial decline of the major parties. If both of these elements occur concurrently within an established party system, the observed change can be properly treated as collapse.

Distinguishing System Transformation from System-Maintaining Change

Identifying instances of transformation requires us to determine when a party system shifts from one structure to another, thereby distinguishing transformations from system-maintaining changes. While both types of change may have implications for interparty interactions, only transformations involve the kind of dramatic shifts in the structure of these interactions that are an essential element of collapse. To determine when a party system crosses from one structure to another and thus transforms, we must be able to differentiate clearly between major types of party system structures.

Isolating system transformations, then, demands a categorization of party system structures, which allows us to pinpoint instances in which a system shifts from one system structure to another. Given that the purpose of this categorization is to identify system transformations, a necessary component of collapse, the typology should be parsimonious, measurable, and broadly relevant. The goal is to develop a classification strategy that captures the major patterns and structures of interparty interactions within a manageable, portable scheme that is neither overly complex nor indeterminate, qualities that might render reliable measurement unattainable. Various strategies for classifying party systems have been developed (Blondel 1968; Duverger 1954; Mainwaring and Scully 1995a; Mair 2002; Rokkan 1970; Sartori [1976] 2005; Siaroff 2000).[9] The typology I employ builds on this literature with an eye toward capturing the essence of the major structures in which parties interact, while still retaining enough simplicity to

9. See Mair (1990, 1997) and Wolinetz (2006) for more detailed accounts of different classification systems.

make categorizing systems and identifying transformations clear and feasible. Ultimately, I identify five major types of party systems or frameworks that structure interparty interactions, which I discuss below.

In developing a classification of major types of party system structures, Sartori's ([1976] 2005) typology, which has been the standard in the field for several decades, provides a logical starting point. His approach combines simplicity with some nuance, thereby satisfying at least some of the requirements I have set forth for a categorization strategy designed to identify system transformations. Furthermore, my conceptualization of party systems mirrors that of Sartori, making his classification scheme a good foundation.[10] However, Sartori's approach has some weaknesses, which I remedy in my final typology.

Sartori built his typology on two facets: fragmentation and polarization. Fragmentation is measured using the number of relevant parties and considers parties' roles in coalitions and policy making when counting, thereby highlighting that this facet is more than mere numbers and that it successfully encapsulates meaningful features of interparty competition. Polarization, which is reflected in the distance between parties, sheds light on the potential for conflict in the system.

On its face, this two-dimensional scheme might seem excessively complex, potentially generating numerous combinations and complicating the task of categorizing party systems. But in practice, the classification remains simple because Sartori sees fragmentation and polarization as highly correlated. As a result, he identifies only four major types of competitive party systems: predominant party systems, two-party systems, moderate pluralism, and polarized pluralism ([1976] 2005). The predominant party system has very low fragmentation and polarization, and the two-party type, which is reminiscent of Duverger's (1954) categorization, also possesses relatively low fragmentation and polarization. Only when we come to the multiparty category does Sartori's scheme create some complexity, but it does so in a place where it is sorely needed. Even a cursory review of party systems around the world demonstrates considerable substantive differences in the structure of interparty interactions among those that would nevertheless fall into the same catchall multiparty category. In response to this now obvious insight, Sartori divides the multiparty group based on ideological

10. Mair (1997) also relied on Sartori's definition of party system when distinguishing between changes in party system structure and other sorts of change—the same distinction upon which I build the concepts of system-maintaining and system-transforming change, which I am seeking to differentiate here.

polarization, calling systems with moderate to high fragmentation but low polarization "moderate pluralism" and those with high fragmentation and more extreme ideological differences "polarized pluralism." He also goes to great lengths to identify the "distinctive features" of polarized pluralism, which in practice extend well beyond his two initial criteria ([1976] 2005, 117–23). These features paint a rather stylized picture of polarized pluralism that closely resembles the peculiar features of party systems that possessed significant communist parties around the time of Sartori's writing. And as Mair has pointed out, the decline of traditional communist parties has made it "more and more difficult to find any sustained cases of polarized pluralism" (2005, xvii), raising questions about the utility of this category.

Sartori's typology of party system structures meets the goals of parsimony and measurability and is also widely regarded as successful in capturing the most significant patterns of interparty interactions. But his approach to dividing the multiparty category constricts the relevance of that component of the classification system to a specific, bygone historical era and limits the typology's portability. Additionally, the empirical overlap between fragmentation and polarization raises questions about the purchase we gain from Sartori's exact strategy for separating the multiparty grouping, because the only category where polarization comes into play is the now obsolete polarized pluralism, which possesses high scores on both dimensions.[11] On the other hand, Sartori's intuition to divide the multiparty category based on different structures of interparty interactions remains perceptive and aligns with my goals and conceptual premises concerning party systems and system-transforming change. In light of the diminished relevance of polarized pluralism and the decreasing number of systems fitting the two-party category (Mair 2002; Wolinetz 2006), innovations in differentiating systems within the diffuse multiparty category remains a pressing issue, which my typology addresses.

My typology begins by recognizing the continued purchase of portions of Sartori's approach, especially its ability to join simplicity and nuance in identifying some major, recognizable system structure types. Specifically, I employ Sartori's predominant party and two-party system categories.[12] In

---

11. Empirically, systems with low fragmentation are treated as having low polarization, while high fragmentation accompanies high polarization. Systems with five or fewer parties are in the moderate pluralism category; those with six or more tend to fall into the polarized pluralism group. Sartori views this as an empirical artifact, but the overlap between criteria suggests that the number of parties actually tells us a lot about interparty interactions (Wolinetz 2006).

12. Like Sartori, I exclude one-party systems, in which there is only one legal party, and hegemonic systems, in which parties that are secondary to the dominant party do not compete on a

predominant systems, one party consistently wins a majority of legislative seats in competitive elections, and in two-party systems, two parties typically control at least 95 percent of seats. Both types have low fragmentation, but there are important differences in the levels of competition and the nature of interplay between parties, which clearly distinguish the structures of inter-party interactions between the two categories.

To create the rest of the typology, I break down the common multiparty category, aiming to create more nuance in order to encapsulate major structures of interparty interactions while still maintaining a straightforward approach that is amenable to measurement. The few post-Sartori innovations in party system typology development have produced excessively compli-cated schema and/or employed continuous measurement strategies.[13] These approaches blur distinctions between types and impede identification of significant shifts from one category to another, which is essential in dis-tinguishing between system maintenance and transformation—the central purpose of the typology employed here. Because Sartori's approach to divid-ing the multiparty category based on polarization has lost leverage over time and more recent efforts to typologize party systems are overly complex and

---

level playing field, because these types do not meet the basic requirement that a party system in a democracy include free and fair competition among its components.

13. For instance, Siaroff (2000) considers the relative size and strength of parties and specifies eight categories of party systems. But under his typology, classifying party systems and identify-ing changes in type becomes quite messy, as his approach creates the appearance that some clearly stable systems endure for only one election before giving way to another, slightly different type (Wolinetz 2006). This classification strategy does not identify *major* changes in system structure. Mainwaring and Scully (1995a) have classified systems based on institutionalization. Party system institutionalization had previously gone unexamined in the party system typology literature, which developed with reference to advanced democracies where institutionalization was often taken for granted. But in other contexts, institutionalization varies. Despite the utility of understanding institutionalization particularly in new democracies, I do not include this dimension in my typology for assessing transformation. This decision is based on several con-siderations. First, adding institutionalization would make the typology extremely complex, with at least ten potential types, even if institutionalization were treated as dichotomous. If institu-tionalization were measured more finely, then the typology would expand beyond utility. Second, determining institutionalization is difficult and entails analyzing multiple dimensions of a party system. Assessing shifts in institutionalization may be feasible in a single country over time or in several countries at a fixed point in time. However, using institutionalization to identify sys-tem transformation in numerous countries would require evaluating dozens of party systems in a comparable way over a thirty-year period. Such a task would be daunting if not impossible (Hartlyn 1996). The difficulty of arriving at valid assessments of institutionalization over time puts such an approach at odds with the goals for the typology stated above. Finally, institutional-ization is likely to be a process that occurs over a long time period. Identifying the transformation of a system from inchoate to institutionalized would therefore be a complex and contested deci-sion. Thus, while institutionalization is important, I view this characteristic as descriptive, rather than definitive of party system type.

difficult to operationalize, I propose an alternative that builds upon some of the intuition of previous scholarship but that also clarifies how the categories capture important differences in the structures of interparty interactions.

The multiparty categories I include are 2.5-party, moderate multiparty, and extended multiparty.[14] In creating these three types, I distinguish party systems based on the amount of competition, the need for cooperation and coalition building, and the nature and complexity of dealings among parties—all important elements that structure interparty interactions. I treat the 2.5-party system as a discrete type because multiple parties compete but two large parties dominate, typically winning 75 percent of legislative seats and controlling the executive. The logic of interparty competition in such a system is unmistakably distinct from that of multiparty systems in which several equal-sized parties compete and from that of pure two-party systems (Blondel 1968). The 2.5-party systems possess unique patterns of competition and cooperation, with two powerful parties regularly at odds with each other, but with governing coalitions often requiring support from smaller parties. In the moderate multiparty type, party power is more evenly distributed. Fragmentation and the complexity of interparty interactions are moderate, and competition is high but not intense.[15] In this system type, where three to five relevant parties typically compete, coalitions are frequently necessary, but only a couple of parties are required to form them. In extended multiparty systems, fragmentation is high, with the relevant parties typically exceeding five. This fragmentation complicates interparty interactions, requires coalitions among multiple parties, and intensifies competition.[16]

The complete typology, then, includes five categories: predominant party, two-party, 2.5-party, moderate multiparty, and extended multiparty systems. This approach distinguishes between the major structures of system dynamics, capturing the central features of interparty interactions. It also produces a manageable classification system that facilitates precise distinctions between types based on observable and measurable features, enabling

14. The term "extended multiparty system" is suggested by Wolinetz (2006, 60) as a neutral alternative to the more common term "extreme multiparty system," which has negative connotations.

15. This type aligns in some ways with Sartori's moderate pluralism, but I am agnostic as to the level of polarization. However, in practice, as fragmentation increases, polarization typically does as well (Mair 2005).

16. This type has some similarities with Sartori's polarized pluralism but does not require high polarization, even though the extent of fragmentation makes polarization a likely outcome. Additionally, I have endeavored to rehabilitate his category by taking a more open approach that does not treat the specific features Sartori associated with polarized pluralism, like centrifugal competition and antidemocratic oppositions, as essential elements of extended multiparty systems.

clear identification of the structural changes that constitute transformation. Furthermore, the categories are neither unique to nor principally significant in a particular place or time, which promotes the broad relevance of the typology. Overall, then, this classification of party system structures meets the aforementioned goals of parsimony, measurability, and portability, while still capturing the most important patterns of interparty interactions.

Table 2.1 lists the five party system types with examples of each. They were categorized based on Sartori's strategy for counting relevant parties, which views the number of parties as an indicator of the amount of competition, need for cooperation, and complexity of interactions in a system. I also report Laakso and Taagepera's effective parties in the legislature measure (ENP) to provide a rough approximation of system structure, but ENP is not used to identify type.

The typology I have developed forms the basis for identifying system transformations and for distinguishing them from system-maintaining changes. Transformative changes in the structure of interparty interactions are marked by a party system shifting from one major system type to another. Using the five-category typology, I am able to identify transformations in party system structure by examining changes in the number of relevant parties in the legislature, which allows me to operationalize the first component of collapse. Table 2.2 displays some empirical instances of system transformation.

Table 2.1 Examples of party system types

Party system type	Country	Date	ENP in the lower house
Predominant party	India	1984	1.68
Two-party	Colombia	1982	1.98
2.5-party	United Kingdom	2005	2.47
	Venezuela	1983	2.42
Moderate multiparty	Chile	2005	5.60
	Sweden	2002	4.23
Extended multiparty	Belgium	2003	7.02
	Brazil	2006	10.19

Note: Dates reflect a specific election in which the party system fit the type. ENP is not used to determine type, but only to give readers a general sense of system structure.

Source: Author's classification of party system type using relevant number of parties (Sartori [1976] 2005) and author's calculations of ENP (Laakso and Taagepera 1979). Based on data from Payne et al. (2002), Electoral Commission of India, Ministerio del Interior (Chile), Tribunal Superior Eleitoral (Brazil), Political Database of the Americas, Consejo Nacional Electoral (Venezuela), and *European Journal of Political Research*.

Table 2.2 Examples of party system transformation

Country	Date	Type of transformation
Austria	1990–94	2.5-party system transforms into moderate multiparty system
Belgium	1978	Moderate multiparty system transforms into extended multi-party system
Brazil	1990	2.5-party system transforms into extended multiparty system
Costa Rica	2002	2.5-party system transforms into moderate multiparty system
Paraguay	1993	Predominant party system transforms into 2.5-party system
Portugal	1987	Moderate multiparty system transforms into 2.5-party system
Venezuela	1973	Extended multiparty system transforms into 2.5-party system

Source: Author's calculations based on data from Payne et al. (2002), *European Journal of Political Research*, and Consejo Nacional Electoral (Venezuela).

Identifying Major Party Decay

To operationalize the second element of collapse, I must determine whether the major system parties decayed. There are two steps in making this assessment: identifying the parties that are major components of a system and determining whether these core parties have decayed sufficiently to constitute collapse. The impact of individual party decay varies according to a party's role in the system. So pinpointing a system's central parties is crucial for distinguishing system decay from the decline of other, less crucial elements of the system (Mair 1997).

Identifying the major parties in predominant, two-party, and 2.5-party systems is straightforward. Predominant systems have only one major component—the party that consistently wins a supermajority of legislative seats. Two- and 2.5-party systems have two major components—the two large parties that dominate the system.

Isolating the major parties in moderate and extended multiparty systems is slightly more complicated. I consider a party to be a major player in these systems if it holds a significant share of seats in the legislature. Substantial legislative representation suggests that a party's presence is important in elections and policy making, and using legislative seat share, rather than vote share, to identify major parties mitigates the potential effect of different rules for translating votes into seats and facilitates cross-national and cross-temporal consistency. Exactly how many seats parties must hold to meet the criteria of having a significant block will vary from one system to the next. If seats are divided among only a handful of parties, a party would need to hold a larger percentage to be a major player than if the seats were distributed among a dozen parties. To establish a threshold separating major parties from minor ones, I divide the number of seats in the legislature by one plus the average effective number of parties in the lower house (ENP+1). Parties, which on average hold at least this number of seats over the system's lifespan, meet the criteria for being a major component of the system.[17] This approach accounts for the number and relative size of parties in establishing the percentage of seats a party must hold to be classified as a significant element of the system. This logic may be expressed as follows:

Definition 1: M_i is a major component party iff $s_i \geq S/(1+\text{ENP})$
      where M_i is a political party
             s_i is the percentage of seats in the legislature held
               by M_i
             S is the total number of seats in the legislature

$$\text{ENP} = 1 \; / \sum_{i=1}^{n} P_i^2$$

    and   and P_i is the proportion of seats held by the ith party
             in the lower house

If a legislature has 100 seats (S) and ENP is four, then party M_i would be considered a major component of the system if it holds at least 20 (100 ÷ 5) seats. This definition consistently identifies the parties that experts consider to be the most important in a system. For example, the major parties in contemporary Mexico identified by this approach are the PRI (Partido Revolucionario Institucional), PAN (Partido Acción Nacional), and PRD (Partido de la Revolución Democrática).

The next step is to develop a decision rule for evaluating when a system's major parties have decayed significantly. By definition, the major component parties will together control a substantial portion of legislative seats. Therefore, I determine when the major parties have decayed based on their loss of legislative impact. Specifically, if the joint seat share of these parties drops below a majority, then they have clearly lost influence. When this condition obtains, the major component parties have decayed sufficiently to satisfy the second criteria of collapse:

---

17. To identify major parties in a system over its lifespan, I use the average ENP and a party's average seat share to determine whether a party meets the threshold.

Definition 2:   The major parties have decayed when

$S_{m1} + S_{m2} + \ldots S_{mn} < (S/2)+1$

where M_i is a major component party

S_{mi} is the percentage of seats in the legislature held by M_i

and S is the total number of seats in the legislature

Accounting for Timing and Scope Requirements

Identifying collapse also requires determining whether transformation and party decay occurred concurrently in an established party system. Neither transformation followed after some time by party decay nor party decline followed much later by transformation should be treated as an instance of collapse. To operationalize this intuition, I specify that transformation and party decay must take place within the span of one complete legislative election cycle for the case to constitute collapse. At the limit, then, a party system undergoes collapse if transformation occurs in one legislative election and the major parties lose control of the legislature in the subsequent election, or, alternatively, if the parties decay during the first election and the system transforms in the succeeding election. Of course, system transformation and major party decay also constitute a collapse event when they occur simultaneously in a single election.

Finally, as detailed above, collapse can only afflict somewhat established systems, such that change marks a significant and clear break with old parties and set patterns of interactions. We should not confuse collapse with ordinary volatility that characterizes new or unpredictable systems. To identify collapse and distinguish it from other sorts of system change, I specify that the momentous break with the past that defines collapse is only possible in established systems. By established systems, I mean those that have been intact, both in system structure and in major component parties, for at least two complete legislative election cycles before beginning the transformation and decay that constitute collapse. In this way, we differentiate between collapse and other forms of change. If political volatility, stemming from a democratic transition, endemic patterns of instability, or some other source, causes such uncertainty that the system changes in structure and components before it has been in place for two election cycles, then this change cannot be properly treated as collapse because the system was not remotely stable at the outset. Instances of transformation and decay that do not satisfy this requirement, whether as a result of a recent regime transition when system dynamics and major parties are in flux or due to ongoing volatility that prevents any stable system from forming, do not satisfy the concept of collapse. The complete operational definition of collapse can thus be stated as follows: *Collapse occurs when an established party system transforms from one major type into another at the same time that the main component parties of the old system together lose control of the legislature.*

IDENTIFYING INSTANCES OF PARTY SYSTEM COLLAPSE IN EUROPE AND LATIN AMERICA

With this definition, I identify instances of party system collapse, assessing the utility of the concept and its operationalization while also clarifying the universe of cases for analysis. I applied the definition to all democratically elected legislatures in Latin America and Western Europe from 1975 to 2005.[18] I examined 19 European and 18 Latin American countries—nearly 300 legislatures.[19] In this context and time period, there have been eight events in which a party system transformed concurrently with major party decay. Of these cases, four occurred in established systems. The cases that fully satisfy the definition of collapse are detailed in table 2.3. They are Bolivia (2005), Colombia (2002), Italy (1994), and Venezuela (1998). Instances in which a system transformed and its parties decayed but the system was not intact for at least two complete election cycles include Brazil (1990), Guatemala (2003), Paraguay (1993), and Peru (1990). These cases of decay and transformation in less established party systems are detailed in table 2.4.

18. I focused on Europe and Latin America because the party literature on these regions is more developed, which facilitated case selection and analysis. Also, as the history of democracy is limited in Africa, Asia, and the Middle East, leaving them out is unlikely to have excluded many suitable cases. Democratic elections are those held when the Polity IV score was seven or higher (Marshall and Jaggers 2009). For countries that had authoritarian regimes over the past thirty years, I consider only the democratic period since the most recent transition.

19. The European countries are Austria, Belgium, Czech Republic, Denmark, Finland, France, Germany, Greece, Hungary, Ireland, Italy, the Netherlands, Norway, Portugal, Slovak Republic, Spain, Sweden, Switzerland, and the United Kingdom. The Latin American countries are Argentina, Bolivia, Brazil, Chile, Colombia, Costa Rica, Dominican Republic, Ecuador, El Salvador, Guatemala, Honduras, Mexico, Nicaragua, Panama, Paraguay, Peru, Uruguay, and Venezuela. The data for Europe were compiled from the *European Journal of Political Research*. The data for Latin America through the mid-1990s were taken from Payne et al. (2002). The most recent Latin American data were compiled by the author from individual countries' electoral tribunal and legislative websites and the Political Database of the Americas. Information on party splits, mergers, and name changes was compiled from various country-specific sources. Party divisions or mergers do not constitute decay of the parties involved.

Table 2.3 Collapse of established European and Latin American party systems, 1975–2005

Country	Date	Transformation	Major party decay
Bolivia	2005	Transformed from a moderate multiparty to a 2.5-party system in 2005.	The major parties of the old system were the center-right Nationalist Revolutionary Movement (MNR), the right-wing Democratic and National Action (ADN), and the center-left Movement of the Revolutionary Left (MIR). Following the 2002 elections, these parties barely held on to a majority in the lower house, and in 2005 their support dropped precipitously. Even including the new electoral movements spawned out of the old parties, the traditional political elite retained only 44 percent of seats (without the "new" movements, 5 percent).
Colombia	1998–2002	Transformed from 2.5 parties to an extended multiparty system over 1998–2002.	The major parties of the old system, Liberals and Conservatives, lost control of both houses of Congress in 2002. Their decline continued in subsequent elections.
Italy	1992–94	Transformed from a moderate to extended multiparty system over 1992–94	The dominant Christian Democratic party (DC) won only 11 percent of the vote in 1994 under its new name, the Italian People's Party (PPI). The Communist Party (PCI) split in two in 1992, and its remnants, the Refounded Communists (RC) and the Democratic Party of the Left (PDS), received only 23 percent of seats in Parliament in 1994. Even the Socialist Party (PSI), which typically held about 10 percent of seats and was an important DC coalition partner, dropped to 2 percent of seats in 1994 and disappeared completely in 1996.
Venezuela	1993–98	Transformed from 2.5 parties to a moderate multiparty system in 1993 and then to an extended multiparty system in 1998.	In 1998, the two major parties of the traditional system, Acción Democrática (AD) and COPEI, decayed and no longer held a majority of seats in Congress. Hugo Chávez's Movimiento Quinta República (MVR) emerged as the main challenger.

Note: Only democratic elections, when a country's Polity IV score is seven or higher (Marshall and Jaggers 2009), are included.

Source: Author's calculations based on data from Payne et al. (2002), *European Journal of Political Research*, Consejo Nacional Electoral (Venezuela), Corte Nacional Electoral (Bolivia), and Political Database of the Americas.

Table 2.4 Transformation and major party decay in less established party systems, 1975–2005

Country	Date	Transformation	Major party decay
Brazil	1990	The transitional 2.5-party system shifted toward an extended multiparty system in 1990.	In the 1986 elections, the two major parties of the 2.5-party system were the Partido do Movimento Democrático Brasileiro (PMDB) and a break-off group from the Partido Social Democrático (PDS)—the Partido da Frente Liberal (PFL). After the 1990 elections, these two parties held only 38 percent of seats in the lower house.
Guatemala	2003	Transformed from a 2.5-party system to a moderate multiparty system.	The two major parties of the 2.5-party system, the Partido de Avanzada Nacional (PAN) and Frente Repúblicano Guatemalteco (FRG), together controlled only 37 percent of seats after the 2003 elections. They gave way to Unión Nacional de la Esperanza (UNE) and a coalition of the Partido Patriota (PP), Movimiento Reformador (MR), and Partido Solidaridad Nacional (PSN).
Paraguay	1993	Transformed from a predominant party to a 2.5-party system in 1993.	The dominant Asociación Nacional Republicana (Colorados) lost control of both houses of Congress in 1993 with the increasing electoral strength of the Partido Liberal Radical Auténtico (PLRA).
Peru	1990	In the post-transition period, transformed from a 2.5-party system to a moderate multiparty system in 1990.	APRA (Alianza Popular Revolucionaria Americana was clearly a major party in the 2.5-party system. The second major party in the first five years was Acción Popular (AP), but Izquierda Unida (IU) took over as the second major party in the second half of the decade. After the 1990 election, APRA and IU held only about 38 percent of seats in the lower house of Congress.

Note: Only democratic elections, when a country's Polity IV score is seven or higher (Marshall and Jaggers 2009), are included.

Source: Author's calculations based on data from Payne et al. (2002), *European Journal of Political Research*, and Tribunal Supremo Electoral (Guatemala).

Distinguishing transformation and decay in established versus more transitory systems facilitates theoretical and empirical clarity. The causal processes that produce party system collapse in established systems are more likely to share common patterns and are therefore more suited for developing and assessing theoretically motivated explanations. Given the early stages of theoretical development concerning party system collapse, I focus my analytical efforts on the set of cases that satisfy all elements of the concept of collapse: simultaneous transformation of and major party decay in an established party system. Therefore, the potential cases for analysis are the collapses of established party systems in Bolivia, Colombia, Italy, and Venezuela. Theoretical explanations of collapse in these cases may also illuminate the processes underlying transformation in cases that meet some but not all the criteria for collapse, but I reserve efforts to extend the scope of the analysis for future research.[20]

RESEARCH DESIGN FOR EXPLAINING PARTY SYSTEM COLLAPSE

To explain why some party systems collapse while others avert failure, I conduct an in-depth examination of one case, as well as cross-national comparisons of collapse versus survival. Part 2 of the book presents a detailed analysis of a critical case, Venezuela, the selection of which I discuss below. Then, in part 3, I compare Venezuela and other collapse cases with instances in which party systems survived despite serious challenges. Given the nature of the collapse phenomenon and the state of the existing literature on collapse, in-depth case analysis is particularly suitable, as it enriches our theoretical understanding of the factors that cause the rare and complex process of collapse. At the same time, by testing the applicability of the theory in several cases, I strengthen the argument, demonstrating the power and generalizability of the explanation.

Identifying the incidences of collapse in Latin America and Europe over the past thirty years indicates that it is a relatively rare event. But in each case, the party system's collapse was momentous, shaping the nature and stability of democratic politics. Because party system collapse is a significant,

---

20. Research on momentous processes like party system collapse often necessitates restricting the analytical scope to cases most likely to yield theoretical insight. Once causal processes have been assessed based on these cases, then it is possible to extend the analysis (George and Bennett 2005; Mahoney and Rueschemeyer 2003).

large-scale event, it is unlikely to be the result of a simple process (Eckstein 1975, 80). Rather, when an entire system gives way, a number of factors jointly precipitate collapse. In-depth case analysis is well suited to parse out the multiple and conjunctural causation likely to characterize collapse processes (Ragin 1987; Tilly 1997).

Additionally, as I discuss further in chapter 3, theoretical advancements in understanding party system collapse have been limited. Most of the hypotheses that can be set forth to explain collapse must be either extended indirectly from the literatures on party dynamics and on party system structure or drawn from more descriptive accounts of individual collapse cases. In-depth case analysis facilitates the development and deepening of theories in research areas that are not yet highly sophisticated, enabling clear specification and testing of hypotheses and identification of causal mechanisms (George and Bennett 2005).

Parts of the case analysis, most notably the statistical analysis of public opinion data in chapter 8 and the content analysis of legislation and news coverage in chapter 5, employ quantitative techniques and follow the oft-repeated recommendation of increasing the number of observations in order to engage in hypothesis testing (King, Keohane, and Verba 1994).[21] Although collapse is rare, it is possible to creatively expand relevant data within collapse cases and apply quantitative analysis to assess portions of the theoretical argument. Applying large-N techniques within a comprehensive case study and pairing them with qualitative analyses of interviews, news reports, and archival data, as well as cross-national comparisons, permits me to draw theoretical expectations from existing literature, further develop these ideas by examining the causal process in a critical case, and then test the hypotheses with numerous new observations from various data sources.

The comparative analysis in part 3 allows me to assess the applicability of the theory beyond the original case, extending the test to other contexts and different data. I analyze the other established party systems that experienced collapse—Bolivia, Colombia, and Italy—testing the theoretical argument across these diverse systems. By analyzing all four collapses, I consider each relevant case and am able to assess the extent to which the explanation accounts for every instance of the phenomenon (Ragin 1987). Furthermore, as I elaborate in chapter 9, the four collapse cases have important differences with regard to several potential explanatory factors, including electoral rules,

---

21. The universe of cases of collapse identified here is only four, making statistical analysis at the macro-process level difficult. But I expand the N by engaging in more micro-level analyses that test observable implications of macro-level theories.

type of government, and party system features, which casts doubt on these variables as alternative explanations (Przeworski and Teune 1970).

In addition to examining each relevant case of collapse, the comparative analysis also considers four relevant negative cases—instances in which collapse did not occur but seemed possible (Mahoney and Goertz 2004). I evaluate cases of survival in which systems confronted challenges similar to those that contributed to collapse elsewhere. These cases are Argentina, Belgium, India, and Uruguay. I pair each case of survival with one collapse case, matching them on key characteristics, including party and party system features, linkage profiles, and challenges faced. Analyzing negative cases strengthens the theoretical argument, demonstrating the importance of each aspect of the causal process and emphasizing how specific conjunctions of causes lead to collapse. This comparison also enables consideration of strategies for promoting system survival.

SELECTION OF A CRUCIAL CASE

Employing a research strategy that incorporates in-depth analysis of causal processes as one important component makes case selection important. Specifying instances of collapse, as I have done in table 2.3, isolates cases of the phenomenon and allows selection of the case that provides the greatest leverage on my explanation of collapse (Eckstein 1975; George and Bennett 2005). The rest of this chapter details the rationale for focusing the detailed analysis on Venezuela's party system collapse.

The decay of the once well-established and widely respected party system in Venezuela provides a particularly interesting opportunity for analysis. In part, the suitability of the Venezuelan case stems from its status as a least-likely case for the theory of collapse that I seek to test. Analysis of a least-likely case provides a particularly tough test of the proposed theory. A theory that is substantiated by evidence from a case in which it is least likely to be true has found strong validation (George and Bennett 2005), and the more crucial the case, the easier it is to draw strong theoretical inferences from the analysis (Eckstein 1975, 127).

In essence, my theory argues that the failure of the party system to provide linkage between society and the state causes collapse. Core challenges to linkage and constraints that limit party system capacity to confront these threats undermine linkage, and without linkage the system fails. I flesh out this argument and the nuances of the causal process that produces collapse thoroughly in the next chapter. For our purposes here, demonstrating that linkage failure was unlikely to have been the cause of Venezuelan collapse positions Venezuela as a least-likely case for the theory posited here and strengthens the theoretical implications of the analysis that follows.[22]

Several features of Venezuela and its party system make it a particularly demanding test for the theory that bankrupt representation produces collapse. First of all, the level of institutionalization in the Venezuelan party system suggests that linkage failure would have been unlikely. Certain types of party systems are advantageous for representation (Diamond, Hartlyn, and Linz 1999), and leading scholars have argued that institutionalized systems are particularly effective because they offer benefits such as stability, governability, and accountability (Mainwaring and Scully 1995a). A strong party system with institutionalized and popularly supported parties is vital for the "institutional resilience of democracy" and "long-term consolidation of broad-based representative government" (Dix 1992, 489). Institutionalized systems have strong ties to society, and parties in these systems are viewed as legitimate and have stable and meaningful organizational structures. These factors should work to promote programmatic responsiveness as well as interest representation for major groups in society, leading to the expectation that an institutionalized party system would provide strong linkage.

The old Venezuelan party system was widely recognized during the golden years of the 1970s and 1980s as highly institutionalized (Kornblith and Levine 1995). The two main parties, AD and COPEI, and the system they formed were perceived as pivotal in the establishment and endurance of Venezuelan democracy, even as nearby countries succumbed to authoritarianism (Karl 1986; Kornblith and Levine 1995). The parties had close ties with important social groups, including unions, peasant organizations, and business associations. Party members constituted an unusually high portion of the population—more than any other country in the world (Coppedge 1994a, 30). The level of institutionalization in the system, with its stability, longevity, meaningful elections, and close ties to society, makes linkage failure an unlikely cause of this system's collapse.

Institutionalization was stronger in Venezuela than in the other cases of collapse, making the other countries more vulnerable to linkage failure and

---

22. Cases that are not least likely for a theory can also provide considerable theoretical insight, particularly when paired with in-depth process tracing or compared to other cases, as I do here. Therefore, the significance of the insights from the Venezuelan analysis does not hinge entirely on its status as a least-likely case, but this status does serve to further enhance the theoretical impact of the analysis.

positioning Venezuela as a least-likely case. The Italian party system had some elements of institutionalization, such as legitimacy and low electoral volatility. But stagnant governing coalitions led to ideological uncertainty and undermined the parties' roots in society (Farneti 1983). In Colombia, the old party system possessed some elements of institutionalization, like stability in interparty competition, but fell short of Venezuelan levels because of factors like organizational incapacity and lack of party discipline (Archer 1995; Boudon 2000; Pizarro Leongómez 2006). In the case of Bolivia, scholars generally agreed that the party system was not at all institutionalized (Gamarra and Malloy 1995).[23] Mainwaring and Scully classified the system as inchoate, languishing among other historically weak party systems, like those in Ecuador and Brazil (1995a, 17).

Another feature that makes it unlikely that linkage failure caused collapse in the Venezuelan context is the multifaceted nature of the parties' ties to society. Although the parties' linkage capacity ultimately failed, at its peak the party system employed a diverse and successful linkage profile. Some voters were attracted to the parties through policy-based appeals, others through ideological affinity, some through membership in well-integrated sectors of society, and still others through direct, material appeals.[24] This complex, multilayered portfolio allowed the parties to reach different sectors of society with successfully targeted appeals, thus attracting broad and stable support.

In essence, we would not expect the Venezuelan system to collapse as a result of failed linkage. Venezuela's party system was highly institutionalized. The system's major component parties did not rely exclusively on nonprogrammatic linkages but also made programmatic and interest-based appeals. Although Venezuela was clearly not perfect before the system collapsed, the nature of the party system and the linkage options it provided make it an unlikely context for bankrupt representation to have caused collapse. Venezuelan party system collapse, therefore, presents an excellent opportunity to test the theory that linkage failure causes collapse because it serves as a particularly challenging case.

Other considerations also make Venezuela's collapse an appealing focus for analysis. Venezuela's party system decay marked a precipitous and surprising decline from a highly institutionalized party system in a prosperous polity to a failed system in a tenuous democracy. Although some scholars

23. However, see Mayorga (2005) for a divergent view.
24. See chapter 4 for a full discussion of the linkage strategies at the height of the traditional Venezuelan system.

observed cracks in the system and expected change or slow decay (Coppedge 1994a; Karl 1986; Myers and Martz 1986), complete collapse was largely unanticipated and caught many observers off guard. Venezuela, then, presents a puzzle: Why did unexpected, dramatic decay occur in what seemed to be a felicitous context for survival? Additionally, the traumatic failure of the Venezuelan party system had profound consequences, including the absence of institutionalized parties and the rise of Hugo Chávez—a personalist leader with increasingly questionable democratic commitments. These processes heighten theoretical and empirical interest in the case and create pressing implications for understanding its dynamics. The next chapter turns to the task of developing a theory that explains why collapse has occurred, in Venezuela and in other contexts.

3

THEORIZING COLLAPSE:
CHALLENGES, CONSTRAINTS, AND DECAYING LINKAGE

Parties in Latin America have not thus far responded to the challenges of representing the interests of citizens being discarded by decaying networks of representation.

—Frances Hagopian, "Democracy and Political Representation in Latin America in the 1990s"

The central task of parties and party systems is to provide linkage between society and the state. Parties that fail at this essential undertaking lose their reason for existence and become empty vessels without a base of support. If an entire party system is unable to provide sufficient linkage, it will collapse. Challenges to linkage, stemming from crises, social change, and political reform, threaten the system, while contextual constraints limit capacity for response. When challenges outstrip the system's ability to cope, linkage fails and the party system with it. This chapter elaborates how demands and constraints cause the linkage failure that produces collapse.

LINKAGE: THE TASK OF PARTY SYSTEMS

Research on parties and party systems repeatedly emphasizes that parties in democratic societies exist to serve as intermediaries between society and the state. Linkage provision is central for party and system survival, and linkage failure is pivotal in the theory of system collapse that I elaborate. By linkage, I refer to the various means by which parties connect society and the state— the strategies employed by political actors and people to exchange support and influence (Barr 2009, 34; Lawson 1980).[1]

1. I opt for the linkage terminology because it carries less conceptual baggage than the more common term "representation." While the two terms are sometimes used interchangeably,

Successful links between society and the state take varied forms (Kitschelt and Wilkinson 2007a; Lawson 1980; Magaloni, Diaz-Cayeros, and Estévez 2007; Stokes 2005). Although programmatic ties are generally regarded as the most prized form of linkage because of the representational quality and electoral stability that tend to accompany them (Luna and Zechmeister 2005; Lyne 2008; Mainwaring and Torcal 2006; Mishler and Hildreth 1984), other linkages may also provide connections between society and the state (Kitschelt 2000; Levitsky 2007). The literature suggests three basic types of linkage: programmatic representation (J. Aldrich 1995; Budge et al. 2001; Erikson, MacKuen, and Stimson 2002; Sartori [1976] 2005), interest incorporation (Collier 1995; Crisp 2000; K. Roberts 2002a; Schmitter and Lehmbruch 1979), and clientelism (Auyero 2000; Brusco, Nazareno, and Stokes 2004; Calvo and Murrillo 2004).

These linkage types range from universal policy appeals to excludable goods directly exchanged for votes (Kitschelt 2000; Luna n.d.). Programmatic linkages are the unconditional offerings parties extend to voters through ideological commitments or policy responsiveness (Kitschelt et al. 1999; K. Roberts 2002a). Clientelism, on the other hand, entails conditional exchanges in which support is traded for excludable incentives (Kitschelt 2000; Magaloni, Diaz-Cayeros, and Estévez 2007, 182; Piattoni 2001a). Incorporation, which may follow pluralist or corporatist patterns, normally involves integration of major societal interests by extending group-oriented benefits or identity-based appeals that attract support from specific sectors (Kitschelt and Wilkinson 2007a).

The primary factor distinguishing the different linkage types is the level of conditionality attached to the benefits that the parties offer.[2] Programmatic links provide indirect, unconditional benefits that are available to all or most people in society, regardless of who they support at the polls

representation carries positive normative connotations associated with accountability and responsiveness (Mainwaring, Bejarano, and Pizarro Leongómez 2006; O'Donnell 1999; Pitkin 1967), and scholars often reserve the term for those links considered supportive of liberal democratic ideals, most notably programmatic linkage (Eulau and Prewitt 1973; K. Roberts 2002a). Less frequently, representation is also applied to group-based linkages (Lipset and Rokkan 1967; K. Roberts 2002a). The term "linkage," on the other hand, is more neutral, facilitating its generic application to diverse types of state-society ties (see, for example, Kitschelt 2000; Lawson 1988; Levitsky 2003a; Lyne 2007; K. Roberts 2002a). I use "linkage" to refer to all strategies for connecting society and the state, reserving the term "representation" for programmatic ties only. For variety, I also use the terms "appeals" and "ties" interchangeably with linkage.

2. The linkage types may also be distinguished based on the nature of the beneficiaries, with programmatic appeals being universal in nature, incorporation being group based, and clientelism targeting individuals or families.

(Kitschelt 2000; Magaloni, Diaz-Cayeros, and Estévez 2007). Clientelism entails direct, conditional exchanges that offer excludable benefits in return for party support (Medina and Stokes 2007; Stokes 2005). Incorporation falls between clientelism and programmatic linkage in the level of conditionality in the relationship. Incorporating ties restrict benefits to those aligned with a particular social group or interest and are, therefore, somewhat conditional. But parties that use these encapsulating linkage strategies (K. Roberts 2002a) cannot control benefit distribution within the targeted group, making incorporation a less direct and less conditional linkage form than clientelism (Kitschelt and Wilkinson 2007a; Magaloni, Diaz-Cayeros, and Estévez 2007).

Incorporation may include tactics associated with clientelism, like distributing material benefits based on membership in a targeted group. It may also involve strategies associated with programmatic links—for instance, policies aimed at helping certain sectors, such as labor laws that only protect unionized workers. In this way, targeted programs or clientelist exchanges may be designed to appeal to specific groups, thereby bolstering interest incorporation. The literature refers to these kinds of targeted programmatic appeals and group-based clientelist benefits as club goods (Kitschelt and Wilkinson 2007a, 11–12; Kitschelt et al. 2010).

But incorporation goes beyond just employing programmatic or clientelist strategies to attract core constituencies. Incorporation is distinct from these other linkage types in terms of the level of conditionality as well as the nature of the target. Furthermore, while incorporating important societal interests may be partly achieved by implementing policies designed to benefit certain constituencies or by distributing material benefits based on group membership, other strategies for accomplishing incorporation are not captured within the dichotomy of programmatic and clientelist linkages. Tactics such as fostering the formation of organizations designed to promote specific interests, reserving spaces on party lists for representatives of targeted social groups, providing certain sectors guaranteed seats on party governing boards, allowing groups to shape administrative rule making in particularly relevant arenas, or protecting special channels of access for important interests may all be important elements of interest incorporation. However, these and many other strategies that aim to build linkage around group identities and interests are not captured empirically or conceptually by our typical understandings of programmatic and clientelist linkage. Rather, these incorporating strategies achieve linkage by creating organizational ties or identity-based appeals that involve neither the policy promises associated with programmatic appeals nor the material exchanges associated with clientelism. So while interest incorporation overlaps somewhat with other linkage strategies in terms of certain tactics, all facets of group-based linkage cannot be subsumed under these two categories. Treating incorporation as a third type of linkage is therefore conceptually sound and empirically sensible. Furthermore, by considering incorporation as well as programmatic appeals and clientelism, we are able to construct more complete pictures of systems' linkage practices.[3]

Each of these linkage types provides something substantive to supporters, whether it is unconditional ideological appeals or policies such as better policing, guaranteed representation for core constituencies in party leadership, or direct clientelism like jobs or food. Using these strategies, parties fulfill their task of linking society to the state. How parties and systems combine programmatic, incorporating, and clientelist strategies in pursuit of support from different segments of the electorate constitutes a system's linkage portfolio or profile (Luna n.d.; Magaloni, Diaz-Cayeros, and Estévez 2007).[4]

3. Also, as we will see below, including all three types is important for understanding how complete linkage failure occurs because by using this conceptualization of linkage, the theory and empirical analysis are able to explain the deterioration of programmatic appeals based on ideology or universal policies, the declining linkage capacity of appeals to core constituencies, and the decay of clientelism, which are each crucial elements of linkage failure.

4. While some scholars also consider charisma to be a form of linkage (Kitschelt 2000; K. Roberts 2002a), others explicitly exclude charisma (Barr 2009). In my view, charisma plays a role in *enhancing* a sense of connection between people and government, but unlike the three types of linkage outlined here, it is not rooted in substance or strategic exchange but rather draws support based on rhetoric and emotion. Charismatic leadership, when operating within a party system, may strengthen the bonds formed by policy offerings, incorporation, and clientelism. However, without some substance to linkage, charisma does not strengthen party ties but only builds personal followings that compete with party organizations (Knight 1998; Weber 1978). Charisma fluctuates over time with leaders' rise and fall. Even individual leaders themselves may find that their ability to use charisma varies with the success of their substantive linkage efforts. Think, for example, of how Carlos Andrés Pérez's charisma fluctuated. It was very high in his first term and second campaign, but then became extremely low during his second term as he championed unpopular economic policies. Without some substantive appeal, charisma loses its power, and it explains little about systematic factors that underlie system change (Kitschelt and Wilkinson 2007a). To understand the processes of linkage failure and collapse, I focus on substantive linkage as composed of programmatic appeals, incorporation, and/or clientelism. Charisma remains outside the analytical framework. There is precedent for treating charisma as unique and transitory, tending to operate outside the party system. Some of the literature on populism treats charisma as being in direct competition with or serving as a temporary replacement for substantive linkage (Knight 1998; K. Roberts 1995). Others go further, treating charisma as an anomaly that necessarily lies outside systematic analyses of linkage (Kitschelt 2000; Müller 2007). Both views acknowledge the need to exclude charisma from a central role in systematic analyses of party systems. I view charisma as having the potential to multiply the draw of other linkage forms but unable to generate ties by itself. Charisma cannot substitute for substantive linkage.

Linkage portfolios take many forms. Each party system possesses a different linkage structure, depending on the tactics of its component parties and the interactions between parties in the system. The purest portfolios are found in systems that rely on one linkage type. In an important theoretical work on linkage, Kitschelt (2000) even argues that it is difficult for a party to pursue multiple linkage strategies simultaneously. Specifically, he contends that there is a trade-off between programmatic and clientelist appeals, such that provision of one type necessarily undermines capacity to deliver the other. But other authors have shown that in practice parties often minimize the theoretical trade-offs between linkage types and pursue a diverse portfolio (Levitsky 2003b; Luna n.d.; Piattoni 2001a; Stokes 2005).[5] Parties appeal to different constituencies with distinct forms of linkage, making mixed strategies theoretically possible and empirically desirable, particularly in countries with high inequality or at intermediate stages of development (Brusco, Nazareno, and Stokes 2004; Coppedge 2001; Levitsky 2007; Luna n.d.). In this context, parties may employ a complex linkage portfolio, appealing to wealthier or more educated voters with programmatic appeals while attracting the working class with club goods and the poor with clientelism. However, at the extreme, excessive reliance on clientelism might make policy-based appeals ring hollow, particularly among voters who would prefer meaningful programmatic solutions and view clientelism as part of a corrupt system that gets in the way of these goals. But such contradictions are only likely to surface as a serious problem when linkage is already decaying and programmatic demands are going unmet at the same time that the parties' clientelist networks are under stress.[6]

In addition to individual parties pursuing mixed strategies, different parties in the system may employ distinct tactics, with some extending broad programmatic appeals while others rely on incorporating core constituencies or offering conditional material exchanges. Interactions between parties also shape the linkage profile of the entire system. For instance, programmatic linkage is frequently achieved when various parties in the system advocate distinct ideologies, thereby offering a range of policy visions that provide meaningful options to voters. Moreover, when different parties advocate on behalf of groups representing opposing sides of a salient social cleavage, together these parties provide linkage via interest incorporation to

5. Kitschelt himself implies as much in later work (see Kitschelt and Wilkinson 2007b).

6. I flesh out the ramifications of this potential negative feedback in my discussion of clientelism below. I credit an anonymous reviewer for the Pennsylvania State University Press with highlighting this point.

wide swaths of society on both sides of the divide. The ways in which individual parties build support and the interactions among parties that generate state-society ties together shape a party system's overall linkage profile.

CHALLENGES TO AND CONSTRAINTS ON LINKAGE MAINTENANCE

Because a party system's primary function is to provide linkage, failure to fulfill this task raises doubts about the system's effectiveness and foments pressure for change. Studies of individual party change (J. Aldrich 1995; Kitschelt 1994; Levitsky 2001b; Panebianco 1988a; Rose and Mackie 1988) and analyses of system-level change (Dalton, Flanagan, and Beck 1984; Lawson 1988; Mair 1997) suggest that for parties and party systems to survive, they must provide linkage. When demands on the system remain relatively constant, sustaining linkage is easy. But all systems eventually face threats to linkage. Responding to these challenges and sustaining adequate linkage enables a system to survive, while failure to adapt lets linkage atrophy, making the parties and the system vulnerable to decay (Lawson 1988).

The importance of adaptation in the face of challenges to linkage is a significant and persistent theme in research seeking to explain continuity and change in parties and party systems (Burgess and Levitsky 2003; Dalton, Flanagan, and Beck 1984; Lipset and Rokkan 1967; Panebianco 1988b). Party systems frequently face shifting demands. Typically, when confronted with such challenges, existing parties will respond and channel them into the system, perhaps requiring some adjustments but not demanding dramatic adaptive efforts. These are common, system-maintaining changes. But sometimes, representational challenges require more, necessitating a restructuring of the system—that is, transformation. At the extreme, if challenges test the existing system's capacity to respond, unmet linkage demands may cause the entire system to buckle under the strain. Why are some parties able to adapt to address changing pressures for linkage single-handedly, while in other cases linkage demands require system transformation? Why, in a few rare cases, is adaptation inadequate, abandoned, or never pursued, undermining the entire system as it fails to sustain linkage?

To answer these questions, studies of party system continuity and change typically either emphasize sociostructural changes that threaten to undermine linkage or focus on constraints that limit party or system adaptation. Research that examines the demand side of linkage argues that party systems change because the pressures on the system shift. These studies emphasize threats to linkage as the primary motivator for change and focus their explanations on sociostructural factors such as economic challenges or social transformations, which demand adaptation or innovation for linkage to persist (Degregori and Grompone 1991; Hagopian 1998; Kenney 2000; Lipset and Rokkan 1967; Morlino 1996; K. Roberts 2002a).

In the Venezuelan context, many scholars have pointed to structural factors and the challenges they posed as essential to understanding the crisis generally and party system collapse specifically. According to a common line of thinking in this literature, the threat posed by the country's severe economic crisis in the late 1980s and 1990s was too great for the parties to overcome—economic decline exposed the parties to increasing public frustration, which produced disenchantment with the entire party system and led to its collapse (see, for example, Borges Arcila 1996; Molina and Pérez 1998). Karl's (1997) work on the politics of petro-states follows a similar vein but specifies a more nuanced causal logic in which the structures and incentives stemming from the oil economy are pivotal in explaining Venezuelan politics. Although her work does not specifically tackle the issue of party system collapse, Karl's claim that the peculiar nature of the petro-state caused government and its clients to become addicted to oil rents suggests that linkages between society and the state were tenuous and highly susceptible to economic misfortune. Because the parties used petroleum income to distribute benefits and appease competing constituencies, sustained downturns in oil prices, like those endured from the mid-1980s through the 1990s, arguably made satisfying these interests unsustainable and triggered threats to linkage. Karl's argument therefore points to structural changes, particularly those related to shifts in the oil economy, as posing serious challenges to the party system.

Kenneth Roberts (2003a, 2003b, n.d.) also suggests that economic changes were important in the decay of traditional patterns of representation. However, his emphasis is not on the economy per se but rather on the social restructuring that occurred in the aftermath of economic crisis and neoliberalism. Roberts (2003a) argues that the Venezuelan economic crisis undermined the formal sector and increased informality and unemployment, which challenged traditional linkage patterns and opened the door to Chávez's populist appeals. In this articulation of the structural argument, economic crisis undermined linkage indirectly by eroding established linkage strategies and by demanding that the parties accommodate new and competing interests.

These sociostructural analyses emphasize challenges to linkage by underlining the major threats posed by crisis and societal restructuring. The literature on Venezuela that favors structural explanations provides insight that clarifies why it was imperative for the party system to adapt and adjust its linkage strategies in order to sustain ties between society and the state. But although these arguments explain why sweeping and exhaustive revisioning of linkage was necessary, they do not account for the parties' inability to respond appropriately to these challenges, nor do they explain the absence of system-level changes that could have refreshed linkage to avert collapse. These studies illuminate the severity of the threat facing the party system, but we must look elsewhere to decipher why the reaction to these threats fell short.

Assessing the capacity of a party system to meet the challenges posed by linkage threats is the strength of the second major strand of research on party system dynamics, which emphasizes factors that limit or aid adaptation. Prominent in this literature are explanations that stress how institutional patterns and organizational features facilitate or impede the adjustments necessary for linkage maintenance (Levitsky 2007; Mair 1997; Pasquino 1997; Tanaka 2005). For instance, in his account of Peru's party system decay and attendant crisis of democracy, Tanaka (1998, 2005) rejects structural explanations related to economic crisis and the growth of informality. Instead, he argues that intraparty factionalism and the run-off system for presidential elections caused the traditional parties to make grave mistakes, which opened the door for Alberto Fujimori's rise to power (2005, 270–71). Other studies of party system change that accentuate constraints on adaptation point to international institutions or commitments, like treaties or IMF agreements, as confining parties' flexibility in their linkage maintenance efforts (Barr 2005; Bohrer and Tan 2000; Carter 1998).

Some scholarship on Venezuela follows this emphasis on constraints, pointing to institutional or international factors as central in accounting for the parties' lack of response to the mounting crisis of representation. For example, in drawing comparisons between Argentina's Peronists (PJ) and other labor-based parties, like Venezuela's AD, Levitsky and Burgess argue that organizational flexibility enabled populist parties like the PJ to adapt while the institutional routinization of AD constrained its ability to adjust and maintain linkage (Burgess and Levitsky 2003; Levitsky 2001b, 2003b). Coppedge (1994a) also accentuates party organizational features in explaining decaying party and democratic legitimacy, arguing that AD's hierarchical structure coupled with presidentialism created rigidity, which undermined the quality of democracy.[7] Likewise, Crisp (1996, 2000) stresses institutional features in explaining Venezuela's economic and political crisis. He emphasizes a restricted policy-making process that privileged traditional interests while limiting flexibility, which presumably undermined linkage. But Crisp also acknowledges that Venezuela's political crisis can only be understood fully if the challenges posed by the economic downturn are also taken into account.

The general argument of this approach, regardless of the specific institutions emphasized, is that the rigid nature of Venezuelan institutions made adaptation difficult. Why these institutional features became liabilities when they did and how they led to party system collapse are issues that remain undeveloped in most of these analyses.[8] Additionally, while Venezuela's institutional framework was inflexible, other countries with more malleable institutions, like Bolivia, also experienced system collapse. Understanding institutional constraints offers insight into the way parties (fail to) respond to pressures for linkage, but cannot explain the source of these pressures.

Much of the existing research on Venezuelan party system dynamics, as well as political party and party system change in other contexts, focuses on either challenges to linkage or constraints on adaptation, with the first type favoring sociostructural variables and the second stressing institutional and international factors. Rather than privileging one set of factors over the other, I join the two perspectives, deploying the strengths of each to gain insight into the aspects of collapse that each is best suited to explain. Analyzing challenges to party system survival, like economic crisis and social change, suggests why linkage is placed at risk and when adaptation is imperative. Exploring how constraints, like organizational patterns or international commitments, limit adaptation or create incentives for seemingly poor choices helps us understand why maintaining linkage in the face of these challenges is sometimes unattainable.

Some previous studies of party and system change have employed a similar analytical lens that considers challenges and constraints. In explaining individual party change, Panebianco (1988b), Aldrich (1995), and Kitschelt (1994) all argue that parties change when external pressures produce a crisis, which results in a mismatch between a party's organization and its

7. Coppedge's work was written well before the system's collapse. He was concerned with the general process of decaying support for the parties and the political system, as opposed to the specific collapse outcome.
8. None of the institutional analyses in the preceding paragraph specifically sets out to explain collapse.

goals. If the old structure is inadequate and not amenable to appropriate adaptation and if associated elites do not address the crisis, they are discredited and replaced—theorizing, in essence, that crisis and an inability to respond together produce changes within parties (Panebianco 1988b). Coppedge (2001) follows a similar synthesized logic in his work on Latin American party system evolution. He contends that the nature of demands, the extent of accommodation these pressures require, and the structural and institutional constraints parties face shape how systems change. The logic of this general argument is that party system change is shaped by challenges that require adaptation and by constraints on parties' responses to these demands.

However, these studies are primarily concerned with explaining change, not collapse. Aldrich, Kitschelt, and Panebianco analyze party change, and Coppedge examines the death or survival of individual parties. None of them offers an argument to explain total system failure. Here I follow this basic framework, exploring the nexus between structural challenges and contextual constraints, but extend it to the system level, detailing the processes by which individual parties' failures aggregate to yield linkage decay in an entire system, causing collapse. For the survival of an entire system to be at risk, serious threats from structural changes must undermine the primary linkage tactic(s) employed, and the parties as well as the system must be constrained such that appropriate adaptation is not possible and linkage decays across the entire system.

Different linkage profiles are placed at risk by distinct kinds of challenges. For instance, a party that utilizes policy-based appeals to attract supporters would not necessarily be affected by changes in the size of the electorate, whereas a party dependent on clientelism would be seriously threatened by exponential growth in the number of voters, as new participants demand material exchanges for their votes (Lyne 2008). The types of structural changes that challenge a party system are contingent on the parties' linkage strategies. When escalating pressures imperil the core linkage strategies of the major parties, the need for adaptation is especially intense, because normal tactics are no longer adequate (Hannan and Carroll 1995).

As pressures on linkage mount, parties have incentives to adjust their strategies to address new demands and thereby stay in power (Downs 1957). But rational political actors encounter considerable constraints imposed by organizational inertia—entrenched patterns and interests that impede innovation (H. Aldrich 1999; Arrow 1974; Kitschelt 1994). Leaders who try to adapt face considerable risk, because it is difficult to predict future developments and because efforts to change may not have the intended effect. These complications, combined with an organizational equilibrium in which powerful ensconced interests are threatened by reorganization, make adaptation both risky and disruptive (Hannan and Carroll 1995). Challenges that threaten parties' central linkage efforts demand considerable adaptation, which is often difficult to achieve because of contextual features that impede modifications.

When the extent of new demands or the nature of the pressure on the parties requires them to change in ways that threaten core identities or that are highly constrained, their ability to provide linkage flounders. If the system as a whole is unable to adjust its linkage strategy to accommodate pressures for representation, linkage decay may occur across the system. The process of party system collapse, therefore, entails an onslaught of new demands that challenge the system's core linkage strategies. When these foundational demands develop amid constraints that cripple the system's capacity to adapt or that produce incentives for misadaptation, the party system's response to mounting pressures is inadequate and linkage fails. When linkage fails across the entire system, collapse results. This general model of party system collapse is illustrated in fig. 3.1.

This model provides an overarching framework to explain why linkage fails and causes party system collapse. But to understand collapse fully, it is important to specify the precise kinds of challenges and constraints that cause the failure of each type of linkage in a system's portfolio. What sorts of threats challenge a system's core linkage features, demanding considerable adaptive efforts? What constraints conflict with these specific demands,

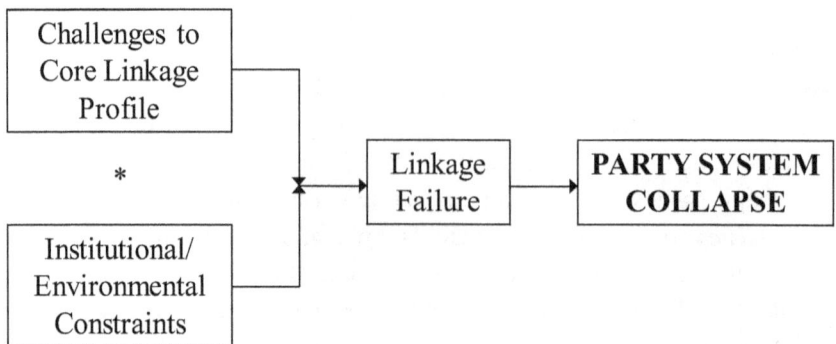

Fig. 3.1 General model of party system collapse

Note: * stands for the logical AND. Joint arrows indicate a conjunction of necessary causes. Notation follows Goertz and Mahoney (2005).

rendering adaptation risky or infeasible? The answers to these questions will depend on a system's specific linkage profile, because different strategies are vulnerable to distinct challenges and the threat posed by those challenges is heightened by particular constraints that limit appropriate adaptation. To explore the combinations of challenges and constraints that are likely to threaten different linkage tactics, I detail the challenges expected to undermine each form of linkage and spell out the precise contextual features that limit the adaptations needed to respond to these challenges and maintain linkage. Furthermore, because I am concerned with explaining the system-level phenomenon of collapse, rather than the decay of individual parties, I focus on the mechanisms by which these factors threaten linkage maintenance across the entire system. For each strategy, I specify how linkage failure aggregates and infects all the parties, producing system-wide decay.

DIVERSE PORTFOLIOS: EXPLAINING WHAT CAUSES EACH LINKAGE STRATEGY TO FAIL

Because linkage failure involves the inadequacy of all forms of linkage, it is important to spell out exactly how each type decays across the entire party system. A complete model of party system collapse should specify the threats that pose particular challenges to each linkage type and detail the sorts of constraints that especially limit or undermine the adaptations necessary to address these challenges. I embark on this task below. By enumerating the process through which each linkage type fails and becomes broadly ineffective for all the major parties, I construct a general but detailed explanation of why entire systems collapse, which can be applied to different party systems according to their linkage profiles.[9]

Programmatic Decline

Programmatic representation, which may involve ideological appeals or valence policy responsiveness, has been traditionally regarded as a superior linkage form. Programmatic parties aggregate interests and implement

---

9. The following discussion focuses on challenges and constraints and how they threaten linkage across the entire party system. I do not consider explanations that only account for linkage decay in individual parties because one party's decay is not equivalent to system collapse. Instead, I focus on factors that contribute to system-level decay.

unconditional policies that seek the general interest or balance competing demands for the best aggregate outcome (J. Aldrich 1995; Lyne 2008;
Piattoni 2001b). As a result, party systems that extend appeals rooted in policy or ideology are more likely to achieve what Hanna Pitkin has lauded
as representation in which parties "look after the public interest and [are]
responsive to public opinion" (1967, 224). Programmatic representation
also promotes the development of long-standing partisan ties, which make
linkage less vulnerable and promote stability (Kitschelt and Wilkinson
2007a; Mainwaring and Torcal 2006).

Despite their many benefits, programmatic linkages can be difficult to
build and costly to maintain, and a variety of factors may weaken parties'
programmatic appeals (Grzymala-Busse 2002; Kitschelt 1994; Kitschelt and
Wilkinson 2007a; Stokes 2001). My primary concern here is not to explain
individual parties' programmatic shortcomings; rather, my goal is to specify
how entire party *systems* lose programmatic linkage capacity. While this
distinction may seem trivial, it is in fact quite significant. Given the unconditional nature of programmatic appeals, if the governing party fails to provide satisfactory policy responsiveness, other parties in the system may step
in to fill the void, offering meaningful programmatic alternatives (Kitschelt
et al. 2010). So the programmatic failings of one party simply provide opportunities for opposing system parties to strengthen and expand their programmatic appeals, producing ordinary ebbs and flows in support for different
parties from one election to the next (Remmer 1991). Only when all the parties neglect programmatic responsiveness and none of the system parties
offer meaningful alternatives to the failed status quo do we have system-
level programmatic decay.

To explain this kind of system-wide decline in programmatic linkage, it
is necessary to develop an explanation that demonstrates how *all* the system parties become programmatically discredited. I argue that generalized
crises, which call into question the viability of a system's established policy
patterns, seriously threaten programmatic linkage. If such crises occur amid
international constraints, which limit viable crisis responses to policies that
conflict with the governing parties' ideological commitments or to solutions
that are unpopular, policy responsiveness decays. System-level programmatic
decline results if all the parties are implicated in this failed responsiveness.
The joint discrediting of all system parties occurs when programmatic differences between the parties are blurred and voters no longer view opposition parties as providing meaningful alternatives to the failed programmatic
offerings of the incumbent. When the system parties are programmatically

indistinguishable from one another and their policy solutions are widely deemed to be deficient, programmatic linkage capacity decays across the entire party system.

Programmatic appeals require a party to develop an ideology and policies. Then, in the face of change, policy offerings must be adjusted to respond to new pressures while remaining consistent with established ideological legacies and entrenched patterns of policy making. If the contours of the policy arena remain constant, preserving programmatic linkage requires routine maintenance; major innovations or departures from ideological legacies are not needed. However, during crisis, sustaining programmatic linkage involves extensive ideological work and significant restructuring of policy appeals (Dalton, Flanagan, and Beck 1984; Kitschelt et al. 2010). Parties risk becoming programmatically irrelevant if they cannot update programmatic offerings in ways that provide relevant solutions to pressing problems while staying within their established ideology or policy-making framework.

Shocks to the policy-making arena demand that parties exert substantial effort in order to provide adequate answers, and crisis conditions therefore pose serious challenges to programmatic linkage (Borges Arcila 1996; Hagopian 1998; Kitschelt et al. 2010; Mainwaring and Scully 1995b; Molina and Pérez 1998; Myers 1995). Profound economic or social crises, like recession, hyperinflation, or escalating violence, threaten programmatic representation for two main reasons. First, crises necessitate a policy response. Issues such as rampant crime, widespread insecurity, and deep recession cannot be ignored or outlasted. Such problems, which hurt broad swaths of society, demand a programmatic response—policy solutions that help alleviate the crisis for the many citizens affected. Second, crises frequently demand answers that go beyond ordinary policy making, challenging parties to move outside their comfort zone in search of innovative solutions for the problems at hand. In crisis circumstances, programmatic adaptation becomes both extremely important and especially difficult, requiring more drastic measures, an accelerated policy-making process, greater productivity, innovation, and more effective policy outputs.

Crises are especially threatening to programmatic linkage when pressures for dramatic, innovative policy responses stem from the exhaustion or inherent shortcomings of an old policy model. In this context, normal policy tools become useless. For instance, if a crisis entails high unemployment, informality, and poverty, parties accustomed to following neoliberal principles, which are not focused on addressing these sorts of social problems, will be hard-pressed to resolve such issues using their ordinary repertoire of responses. On the other hand, problems such as hyperinflation, fiscal deficits, and onerous foreign debt burdens often stem from the shortcomings of Keynesianism or import-substitution industrialization, making it particularly difficult to address these issues in contexts where such strategies have been habitually utilized. In other words, crises that threaten established policy-making patterns or call into question the viability of favored policy strategies pose especially strong challenges to programmatic linkage, because governing parties face formidable hurdles to identifying and implementing effective policy responses, which necessarily reside outside their normal repertoire. Where crises stem from the exhaustion of established programmatic models, parties are "compelled to embark on the arduous trajectory of devising new programmatic appeals . . . or quit the game of programmatic party competition altogether" (Kitschelt et al. 2010, 38–39). Thus, I argue that maintenance of programmatic linkage is seriously threatened when the party system confronts crisis conditions that call into question the viability of established ideological positions or customary policy-making patterns.

The struggle to sustain programmatic linkage in the face of these kinds of crises is exacerbated when boundaries imposed by international commitments or pressures limit policy options and constrain adaptation efforts. The demands of the global economy or the restrictions imposed by technocratic recommendations may undermine parties' opportunities to enact responsive policies (Bohrer and Tan 2000; Mainwaring and Scully 1995b; Mair 1997). Specifically, the policy adjustments necessary to provide responses to important problems may be out of reach when the governing parties face international constraints that insist on a limited set of policies, which are either unpopular or contradict the parties' ideological commitments.

Thus, the constraints imposed by the international context are especially strong when the party's ideological identity or patterns of decision-making conflict with external incentives or pressures. A party's legacy limits the range of policies it can credibly pursue, especially when its ideology or organizational patterns are well established (Coppedge 2001; Dalton, Flanagan, and Beck 1984; Kitschelt 1994; L. Roberts 2007). When international pressures constrain responses to those that contradict a party's values, the party faces a lose-lose situation. It may attempt a response and thereby abandon its identity and risk alienating supporters, or it may stay true to its legacy but not address the crisis and thus frustrate people for having failed to deal with the country's problems. Regardless of its choice, a party faced with this dilemma will experience decay in the success of its programmatic appeals. If it takes the first path, people will choose not to support the party because of ideological inconsistencies. If it opts for the second, programmatic appeals lose their attractiveness due to unresponsiveness. In either case, programmatic linkage capacity decays. So, where the international context conflicts with ideological or policy-making legacies, the adaptation needed to sustain successful programmatic appeals becomes extremely difficult.

This dynamic played out among Latin American left parties in the 1980s, which were particularly ill-suited to handle the inflationary crisis that confronted the region because the policy response prescribed by international financial institutions directly contradicted these parties' ideologies (Coppedge 2001, 174). In countries where left parties followed neoliberal prescriptions, they violated their ideological legacies, saw programmatic capacity decline, and increased their reliance on other forms of linkage (Levitsky 2001b; Morgan 2007). Alternatively, where left governments attempted to reject neoliberalism, they faced severe retribution for failing to act and not alleviating the crisis (Cotler 1995; K. Roberts 1995).

When crisis conditions demand a policy response but international constraints conflict with party legacies, successful adaptation seems out of reach, as parties in government confront strong impediments to providing a solution to the crisis. Of course, decay in the valence policy responsiveness offered by the party/parties in power does not directly translate into the programmatic failure of the whole system. Only when all the system parties are implicated in this failed responsiveness is loss of programmatic linkage across the entire system likely. Therefore, aggregating the logic of programmatic decay to the system level requires specifying how all the parties are discredited.

System-level programmatic decay occurs when people reject the status quo and at the same time cannot find meaningful alternatives to the current state of affairs because they do not see distinctions among the policies or ideologies of any of the viable governing parties in the system.[10] When there are no pro-system parties offering alternatives that credibly promise to rectify the status quo of failed policy responsiveness, all the parties' policy appeals lose credibility. The absence of programmatic differentiation between parties indicates that none offers meaningful alternatives to the incumbent, and all the parties' promises to resolve the crisis ring hollow because they simply offer more of the same. Without programmatic differentiation between incumbent and opposition, all the parties are implicated in the

10. This logic does not apply to systems in which only one party employs programmatic linkage, and the loss of programmatic appeals by one party would constitute an absence of such linkage from the entire system. In such cases, party-level explanations of programmatic decay may be adequate.

failed status quo, and programmatic discrediting infects the entire system (Kitschelt et al. 2010, 45).

Such system-level discrediting is most likely to occur when interparty agreements, like grand coalition governments or pacts, include all the pro-system parties and thereby incriminate every viable governing option.[11] These arrangements obscure ideological differences between parties and eliminate meaningful alternatives from the system. When the parties collude in power, the programmatic and ideological distinctions between them are diluted. The policy failure of one party indicates that the others, and by extension the system, are also unable to provide programmatic representation. In this context, people transfer one party's policy failing to the other parties, and all share the blame. Interparty agreements undermine meaningful alternatives and therefore allow the contagion of programmatic decay to affect the entire system, as none of the parties are insulated from the failed response to the crisis (Borges Arcila 1996; Colazingari and Rose-Ackerman 1998).

In summary, when crisis conditions challenge established policy tactics and international constraints limit responses to those that contradict governing parties' legacies, policy responsiveness decays. If all the parties are discredited through programmatic convergence, most likely created by interparty agreements that undermine differences between the parties and eliminate meaningful alternatives to the failed status quo, programmatic linkage deteriorates across the entire system. Fig. 3.2 illustrates this programmatic decay process: a crisis of the policy model demands that the parties in power make herculean adaptations to provide a response, while international constraints in conflict with established patterns limit their ability to introduce necessary policy innovations, and interparty convergence and collaboration blur programmatic distinctions and undermine the credibility of viable pro-system alternatives, weakening the pull of programmatic appeals across the whole system.

Limited Interest Incorporation

Parties may also furnish linkage by incorporating major interests, offering semi-conditional benefits to important sectors of society. As long as the

11. Loss of differentiation between the parties could also theoretically occur when all the parties pursue similar policies during a sustained crisis that remains unresolved even after party control of government changes hands (Kitschelt et al. 2010; K. Roberts 2003a). But typically, when such extended crises occur, the parties also enter into pro-system coalitions to help them weather the storm. I found no evidence of extended crises and common policies across all the major system parties where interparty agreements were not also in place.

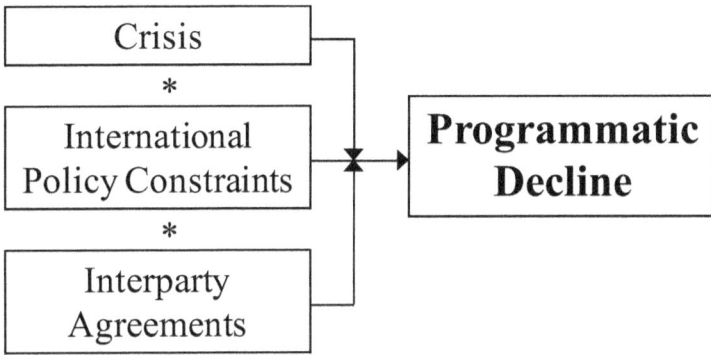

Fig. 3.2 Programmatic linkage decline

Note: * stands for the logical AND. Joint arrows indicate a conjunction of necessary causes. Notation follows Goertz and Mahoney (2005).

structure of societal interests does not change drastically, incorporation provides a steady base of support due to the strong ties often forged between significant sectors and the parties that give them access and voice (Rose and Mackie 1988). Interest integration may take the form of corporatism in which important sectors like labor or business are granted special access. Alternatively, different groups may compete more openly in a pluralist system.[12] Both corporatist and pluralist systems aggregate interests and tend to involve significant sectors in policy making (Collier 1995; Piattoni 2001b; Schmitter 1974). Regardless of its precise form, incorporation affords linkage to much of society while also providing a stable base for parties.

In fact, in their classic work on party system formation and structure, Lipset and Rokkan (1967) argue that major societal interests, or cleavages, form the foundation of party systems. Although the specific details and implications of their argument have been debated, many scholars agree that the structure of salient social cleavages and their transference into the political sphere play important roles in shaping party system dynamics.[13] Depending on which cleavages are politically salient, parties and systems that employ interest incorporation tend to prioritize certain kinds of interests over others.

12. In practice, systems often fall between pure corporatism and pure pluralism (Collier and Collier 1979).

13. Even work that emphasizes the impact of electoral rules suggests that salient social cleavages, together with the strategic incentives of electoral institutions, determine party system structures (Cox 1997; Ordeshook and Shvetsova 1994). In essence, these works argue that electoral institutions generate a limit on the number of parties in a system, but the cleavage structure determines whether the system reaches this limit.

Rarely are all potential concerns politicized as relevant cleavages. As a result, incorporation strategies frequently favor certain interests and neglect those that do not fit dominant incorporation patterns (Diamond 1999; Piattoni 2001b). For instance, where incorporation is based on class, ethnic interests may be neglected or vice versa. As long as parties tap politically significant interests and the system as a whole represents the main facets of salient social divides, then incorporation is effective in linking much of society with the state.

But because this strategy bases linkage on the structure of society and the nature of politically significant interests, incorporation faces challenges from changes in salient cleavages. If social changes simply entail shifts in the relative size of already integrated interests, then dynamics within the system may be altered, increasing the appeal of parties that represent growing interests and weakening the draw of parties that base their support on shrinking groups. But the relative waxing and waning of existing salient interests does not challenge the fundamental logic of incorporation in the system. While individual parties may be unable to sustain successful incorporation if their traditional social base declines, the entire system is unlikely to lose incorporating capacity as long as other parties already accommodate the concerns of groups on the rise. For example, if a system's incorporation strategy is based on traditional class cleavages, with one party appealing to the working class and another attracting support from white-collar professionals, then declines in the industrial sector and growth in the service sector are likely to weaken support for the worker party and increase support for the professional party. But because these changes do not challenge the logic of incorporation, while individual parties may lose ground, the entire system does not see incorporating linkages decay.

However, some social transformations threaten the very logic upon which party systems structure incorporation and therefore pose serious challenges to the maintenance of such linkage throughout the whole system (K. Roberts 2003a). Significant transformations that threaten incorporation at the system level, instead of just weakening individual parties, are manifested in two possible ways. First, realignments of societal interests around new *kinds* of concerns menace incorporation because they alter the types of group identities that are salient, demanding that all parties in the system drastically reshape how they construct incorporating appeals. For example, in a system where incorporation was historically based on functional interests, the escalating salience of an ethnic divide may wreak havoc with established patterns of integrating interests based on class. Because the system as a whole traditionally worked to incorporate competing functional groups, the declining significance of the class cleavage and the reorientation of interests around a newly activated ethnic divide calls for all the parties to engage in dramatic restructuring of incorporation. The adaptations necessary to adjust to a shift in the nature of relevant cleavages are traumatic, requiring new types of appeals based on different identities and directed toward altered constituencies. Social transformations in which traditionally significant interests lose salience and previously inconsequential concerns take on new political relevance threaten the very structure of incorporation and expose the entire party system to linkage decay.

Second, social transformations that stem from changes in the *structure* of the dominant cleavage may also threaten incorporation at the system level. Effective incorporation strategies integrate most sectors of society but are not exhaustive in integrating every potential interest produced by the dominant cleavage. Frequently, party systems do not incorporate smaller, unorganized, or less influential groups. If these excluded interests do not constitute a significant portion of society, their omission from incorporation does not dangerously undermine linkage. However, if society changes such that previously neglected sectors grow or gain political significance, their exclusion undercuts the system's incorporating capacity. For instance, if a party system traditionally targeted interests based on the worker-owner cleavage but disregarded the concerns of a small or politically immaterial informal sector, the rapid growth of informality would require the system to reconfigure its incorporation strategy in response to mounting pressure from this group. The emergence or growth of previously neglected interests, therefore, necessitates innovation in the party system, requiring either adjustments by existing parties or the introduction of new parties in order to capture emerging demands. Each of these potential avenues for accommodating new concerns requires considerable adaptation. In the face of a restructured dominant cleavage in which previously excluded groups grow and become politically relevant, the party system must rethink how competing interests are effectively integrated.

Fundamental societal changes that threaten the party system's conventional structure of incorporation expose a significant vulnerability of this linkage strategy. If a party system does not respond to challenges posed by significant social transformations in the *kind* of salient interests or in the *structure* of the dominant cleavage, incorporation will cease to provide meaningful linkage because growing sectors of society are no longer linked through traditional incorporation mechanisms.

When confronted with dramatic social transformations that threaten existing patterns of incorporation, party systems must adapt their strategies to accommodate new or growing interests. However, there is considerable risk and uncertainty associated with investing the resources necessary to build incorporating links to new interests. Contextual factors alleviate or intensify these risks, influencing whether a party system rises to the challenge posed by social transformation or falters and allows linkage to deteriorate. In the case of incorporating linkages, the party organizational context plays a central role in shaping parties' incentives and capacity to adapt and respond to new demands stemming from changes in the type or structure of the dominant social cleavages.

A large body of literature has emphasized how organizational flexibility enhances parties' ability to adapt to pressures for linkage, while highly routinized organizations constrain party latitude in adjusting to new demands and thus have more difficulty making the adaptations needed to reach out to new kinds of interests (Burgess and Levitsky 2003; Coppedge 1994a; Levitsky 2001b, 2003b). This literature would suggest that when existing patterns of incorporation are highly entrenched and the goals or organizational structures of emerging groups directly threaten the interests of already integrated sectors, the risks and challenges associated with adapting to social change are exacerbated. In this kind of organizational context, parties face especially high obstacles to adapting their incorporation strategies and run aggravated risks associated with failed efforts. Therefore, I argue that parties' capacities to respond effectively to social transformation and accommodate new interests are severely constrained when well-established structures and the entrenched interests they represent conflict with the organizational patterns and concerns of emerging sectors.

If emerging interests cannot be accommodated through existing strategies and instead demand innovation, the effort required to integrate new concerns is strenuous, involving considerable resource expenditure in exchange for uncertain outcomes (Levitsky 2001b; Navarro 1995). Existing system structures tend to privilege certain types of interests and patterns of incorporation. If new interests are structured in ways that follow traditional incorporation configurations, their integration into the system simply requires the extension of existing arrangements. For instance, parties accustomed to incorporating traditional agricultural interests through centralized peasant associations could potentially reach out to the organized working class through national labor federations, as both sets of interests follow common hierarchical patterns that can be accommodated through similar strategies and mechanisms. But when social transformations produce emergent interests that are not easily slotted into established patterns, the parties must engage in more extensive and inventive adaptations. For example, the proliferation of grassroots social movements based on ethnic identities fundamentally challenges incorporation strategies built on hierarchical and centralized, class-based organizations. Parties with established incorporation patterns designed to integrate class-based peak associations find that their old strategies cannot be easily translated into the context of identity politics, forcing these parties to step outside their comfort zone and get creative if they are to integrate ethnic movements (Barr 2005; Domingo 2001; Yashar 1999). Thus, when parties' conventional incorporation strategies do not align with the organizational structures of emergent interests, they face considerable obstacles to achieving the adaptations they must implement in order to maintain this form of linkage.

Parties also carry considerable inertia in their structures. Institutions tend to take on a life of their own, reinforcing established patterns and discouraging innovation. This inertia often makes adaptation difficult and risky (Hannan and Carroll 1995).[14] Organizational inertia is especially likely to impede the incorporation of new groups if their concerns conflict with the goals of powerful entrenched interests already integrated into the system (Greene 2007; Levitsky 2001b). The stronger entrenched interests are and the more threatened they feel by new groups, the more dangerous adaptation becomes, as reaching out to new groups might alienate important elements of parties' existing support bases (Levitsky 2007). Rather than adapting to incorporate new but potentially conflicting interests, parties may opt to protect old allies, hoping to sustain the status quo and avoid upsetting the political equilibrium within their organizations (Hannan and Carroll 1995). Furthermore, if emergent interests are unorganized or diffuse, trading established (albeit shrinking) incorporated sectors for a flimsy new base of support poses very high risks in exchange for what seem to be few potential rewards, thereby creating a disincentive for making the adaptations needed to accommodate new interests. Party systems will have particular difficulty accommodating new or burgeoning groups when they do not fit the dominant channels of representation or when they have goals in competition with entrenched interests, especially when incorporation patterns are well established (Diamond 1999; Levitsky 2003b; Piattoni 2001b).

---

14. These challenges are heightened when organizations are internally institutionalized (Levitsky 2001b).

In summary, when confronted with extreme social disjuncture, party systems must adapt to include emerging interests or risk declines in the linkage capacity of interest incorporation. Adaptation, however, is a precarious proposition, one that is particularly risky if organizations are highly routinized and emerging interests either cannot be absorbed through existing channels or their concerns threaten already established groups. Uncertainty about the potential contributions that new but unorganized groups might offer for the system's support base further complicates adaptive attempts. Even less institutionalized or newer parties may find it difficult to innovate beyond tried and true incorporation patterns in such a context. The costs and risks associated with overcoming the collective action problem and inventing new incorporation strategies discourage all parties in the system from trying to represent emerging groups. Established parties control patterns of representation and may erect barriers to entry for pioneering parties, whereas a new party that mimics common strategies does not threaten the existing system. These incentive structures make innovation perilous even for new organizations.

Fig. 3.3 illustrates the process through which social transformation and organizational constraints together cause the deterioration of incorporation. Transformations in the structure or kind of salient cleavages pose serious challenges to the entire system's linkage strategies by menacing the very logic of incorporation. If emergent groups challenge powerful existing interests or entrenched patterns of integration, the party system may find it especially costly to expand or reinvent incorporation in order to accommodate them. If social change persists or escalates and the system does not respond, incorporation narrows, such that it is no longer a viable form of linkage for the great majority of the population.

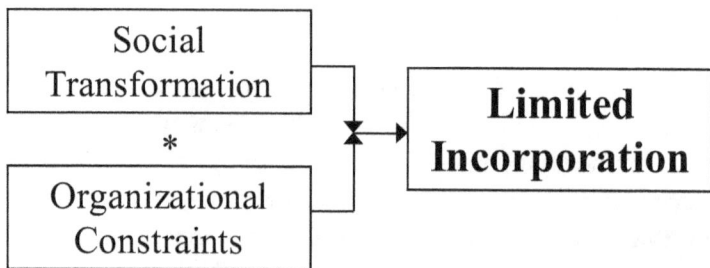

Fig. 3.3 Narrowing of interest incorporation

Note: * stands for the logical AND. Joint arrows indicate a conjunction of necessary causes. Notation follows Goertz and Mahoney (2005).

Decay of Clientelism

Clientelism is usually considered the least desirable form of linkage (Landé 1973; Shefter 1994). But despite its atomistic nature and potential for weakening accountability (Lyne 2008; Piattoni 2001b), clientelism still involves satisfying certain demands, enabling parties to provide some linkage between people and the state (Kitschelt 2000; Levitsky 2007; Richardson 1997).

As long as the system possesses sufficient resources to meet demand for benefits in exchange for votes, clientelism may persist for some time. But clientelist linkage is fragile and vulnerable to failure when demands cannot be met, especially when other linkages that promote more general public interest, like programmatic and incorporating ties, are absent. Unlike these other linkage strategies, which typically foster strong partisan ties, clientelism is highly contingent on recent performance. Absent a programmatic or interest-based foundation, clients are not loyal partisans. Rather, they look out for individual or familial interests and tend to have short time horizons. Without a recent investment, clients withdraw their support. When parties lack sufficient benefits to satisfy demand, people become suspicious about misuse of resources (Kitschelt and Wilkinson 2007a). Therefore, clientelist parties must sustain the benefit flow to attract votes, and as a result, they are vulnerable to pressures from increased demands and dwindling resources, which threaten their capacity to buy support (Landé 1973; Magaloni, Diaz-Cayeros, and Estévez 2007; Piattoni 2001b).

The central challenges to clientelist linkage stem from structural changes that escalate demand for direct exchanges, while limits on the resources available for partisan ends constrain parties' ability to adapt and satiate these increased demands. Specifically, certain kinds of social changes and electoral decentralization heighten pressure for clientelist benefits, even as economic crisis and restrictions on partisan manipulation of state resources limit parties' clientelist capacity. Together, challenges from increased demand and constraints on resources undermine the system's ability to sustain adequate clientelist linkage.

Social changes that expand the ranks of those seeking party-based material benefits in exchange for their vote pose a considerable challenge to clientelist linkage, pressuring parties to find a way to meet growing demand (Kitschelt and Wilkinson 2007a; Levitsky 2003a; Magaloni, Diaz-Cayeros, and Estévez 2007; Piattoni 2001a). For instance, when parties rely on clientelism to attract support, growth of the electorate through the extension of suffrage, population booms, or dramatic episodes of immigration stresses linkage, because the parties must invest in additional material exchanges in order to build linkage with new voters (Lyne 2008).[15] Other social changes, such as increased poverty or uncertainty, also heighten demand for benefits, because desperate people turn to clientelism in an effort to satisfy immediate needs (Auyero 2000). People living in conditions of poverty or uncertainty are much more inclined to seek the immediate, tangible benefits offered in clientelist exchanges, rather than hope for future programmatic improvements that may never be implemented or that may not help them in a meaningful way (Piattoni 2001a). If the poverty rate escalates, the masses seeking clientelist benefits will expand, as more people are unable to wait for the fulfillment of programmatic promises (Hale 2007; Levitsky 2007; Magaloni, Diaz-Cayeros, and Estévez 2007). Likewise, uncertainty about the future due to economic crisis or security threats may push people to opt for immediate clientelist exchanges instead of risking the ambiguity of potential long-term solutions (Hopkin and Mastropaolo 2001; Kitschelt and Wilkinson 2007a; Piattoni 2001b).

In a similar way, social restructuring that destroys traditional networks increases the number of individual clients seeking direct exchanges from parties. When old networks built on community ties, social class, or ethnic identities crumble, parties are no longer able to deliver benefits efficiently to many people through a single hierarchical network. Instead, as each voter or family pressures parties for clientelist exchanges outside these traditional avenues, the efficiency of old distribution patterns deteriorates and the number of claims on the parties expands (Escobar 2002; Gutiérrez Sanín 2007; Yashar 1999). Furthermore, if a party has a strong reservoir of support based on a tradition of linkage provision, people may be willing to overlook a temporary inability to furnish clientelist benefits, delaying the effects of resource shortages. But as the reserve of goodwill dries up, a party is much more vulnerable to escalating demands. Overall, then, social changes that increase the number of voters seeking material exchanges threaten the core logic of clientelist linkage, pressuring parties to find new resources to meet demand.

Reforms that create inefficiencies in clientelist delivery and thus necessitate more resources are another cause of strain on clientelism. In particular, political decentralization that proliferates the number of separate electoral

---

15. Such expansions of the voting population do not threaten systems able to integrate new voters through established programmatic or incorporating linkage mechanisms. But where new voters can only be accommodated with conditional exchanges, their entrance requires additional clientelist inputs from the parties.

contests at the subnational level requires more clientelist inputs and undermines the mutual dependence fostered under hierarchical clientelist delivery systems. I argue that these reforms threaten clientelism, and therefore party system survival, because each separate election requires provision of a new benefit, which delivers a vote for just one or two candidates and does not serve the party as a whole (Dávila and Delgado 2002; Gutiérrez Sanín 2007; Kitschelt and Wilkinson 2007a; Luna 2004, 2007).

These expectations concerning the consequences of political decentralization for linkage maintenance may seem to contradict conventional wisdom about the impact of these reforms. Many scholars have emphasized the positive, intended consequences of decentralization, making the case that it creates openings for participation (Blair 2000; Grindle 2000; Huther and Shah 1999), provides a civic training ground (Fox 1994; Tocqueville [1848] 1988), promotes efficiency (Artana and López Murphy 1994; Oates 1972; Rondinelli, McCullough, and Johnson 1989; Tiebout 1956), and fosters accountability and responsiveness (Abers 1996; Fox 1994; Nickson 1995; Selee 2011). Some have even equated political decentralization with democracy, arguing that electing subnational leaders is crucial for the deepening of democratic regimes (Diamond and Tsalik 1999; Fox 1994; Grindle 2000; Huther and Shah 1999). Decentralizing reforms were frequently advocated by the development community as a strategy for moving "government closer to the people" and promoting laudable and seemingly innocuous goals such as efficiency, accountability, and transparency (BID and PNUD 1993; Blair 1996; Campbell 1993; Dillinger 1994; Faguet 2001; Huther and Shah 1999). Moreover, politicians across the developing world who sought to overcome governance and legitimacy crises and to please international lenders or donors often turned to decentralization, perhaps hoping that it would foster support at home and abroad (Grindle 2000; Kornblith 1998b; Myers 2004; O'Neill 2003). Frequently, this scholarship focused on general indicators of democratic quality and did not explore the potential ramifications that decentralization might have for parties and party systems, except to suggest that the reforms might eliminate particularism, vote buying, and corruption (Borja 1989; Fox 1994; Huther and Shah 1999).

However, a growing body of research has begun to suggest some potentially destabilizing effects that decentralization may have on parties and party systems, shifting focus to unintended consequences of the reforms (Goldfrank 2011). This scholarship suggests that corruption and clientelism are actually more prevalent locally than nationally and that decentralizing to lower levels of government only exacerbates these problems (Prud'homme

1995; Ryan 2004; Samuels 2003). Decentralization also undermines the nationalization of party systems, promoting regionalization and fragmentation, especially in emerging democracies (Brancati 2008; Harbers 2010; Lalander 2004; Ryan 2004; Sabatini 2003; Stepan 2001). To the extent that decentralization promotes dispersion and parochialism, political instability is likely and national goals and accountability may be more difficult to achieve (Chandler 1987; Harbers 2010; Sabatini 2003).

Decentralization is particularly threatening to party systems that employ clientelism to attract support (Harbers 2010). Political decentralization, which occurs via the establishment of separate subnational elections, intensifies demand for clientelist exchanges because parties must unearth enough benefits to mobilize voters and activists in order to win electoral support, not only in occasional national contests but also in numerous subnational races across the country. Unlike other forms of linkage in which people vote based on general policy positions or interest-based appeals, under clientelism people use their votes as leverage to extract something tangible. Because clients repeatedly seek to trade their vote for material benefits during each trip to the polls, more elections mean more demands (Dávila and Delgado 2002).

Furthermore, the introduction of separate subnational elections decouples local and national politics (Luna 2007; Ryan 2004). Locally elected officials are increasingly autonomous, with their own bases of support (Falleti 2010; Kitschelt and Wilkinson 2007a; Luna 2008; Sabatini 2003). This disconnect between the central party apparatus and subnational elites undermines traditional pyramidal patterns of exchange and heightens clientelist demand (Luna 2004). When nationally elected politicians appoint subnational officials or when centralized concurrent elections determine local political outcomes, support for the party organization across all territorial levels is purchased with a single material exchange furnished by the central party and distributed by loyal local leaders. These hierarchical networks reinforce interdependence across different levels of the party apparatus (Grindle 2000). Local politicians rely on the central party for continued access to political positions, and national party leaders depend on subnational affiliates to deliver votes for the party organization. However, as decentralization promotes local leaders' autonomy, these mutually reinforcing ties disintegrate (Falleti 2005; Harbers 2010; Ryan 2004; Sabatini 2003). Instead of national networks efficiently delivering support that enhances the electoral fortunes of the entire party and all its candidates, we observe the emergence of "parallel clientelistic structure[s]" (Ryan 2004, 88) in which empowered local leaders build their own personal networks. These parallel networks serve the political ambitions of individual politicians rather than the goals of the party (Crook and Manor 1998; Grindle 2000; Luna 2008).

As political decentralization causes the parties to lose control over their local agents, they face increased pressures for clientelist resources, not only from the voters but also from empowered subnational elites seeking to further their own purposes. And because the parties are no longer able to exercise effective control over these leaders, the central apparatus cannot ensure that the benefits it channels through subnational networks are used effectively to benefit the party across all levels (Kitschelt and Wilkinson 2007a; Luna 2007; Sabatini 2003). Frequently, political decentralization undermines the efficiency of resource distribution, necessitating more inputs in order to purchase support comparable to levels achieved with fewer resources in the pre-decentralization period. Thus, like social change, political decentralization heightens demand for clientelism.

For parties to maintain clientelism in the face of these threats, they must unearth adequate resources to satisfy pressures for direct exchange, or risk the decay of clientelism as an effective linkage strategy. As Scherlis notes, "Parties in which material benefits constitute the prime inducement for participation become reliant on the availability of those resources for their stability and survival" (2008, 580). Without sufficient resources to meet escalating demand, clientelism deteriorates. Two main factors affect parties' ability to distribute enough benefits to sustain clientelist linkages: economic conditions and the parties' ability to access state resources.

Economic crises reduce both public and private resources available for clientelism (Hopkin and Mastropaolo 2001; Kitschelt and Wilkinson 2007a; Lyne 2008). State resources are likely to dry up during economic downturns. As the tax base shrinks, export income declines, or the debt burden grows, funds available for parties to politicize for clientelist distribution dwindle. Parties that appeal to private donors may also find that their funding slows to a trickle during crisis, constricting the resource base. Even membership dues, which are especially relevant in mass parties, are likely to decline during hard times as unemployed or impoverished party supporters may allow their memberships to lapse.

Political reforms that limit party control of state resources also constrain the supply of fuel for clientelist machines. Efforts to professionalize the bureaucracy take many government jobs off the patronage rolls, as people are hired based on their qualifications rather than their political connections. Reforms associated with neoliberalism, which rationalize the allocation of state benefits and may place social programs and other public funds beyond the reach of partisan manipulation, hamper parties' access to resources they would customarily trade for votes (Hale 2007; Warner 2001). Fiscal decentralization may also reduce resources available to the central party, especially when the national party organization cannot exercise control over local elites who now manage the decentralized funds and programs. Frequently, autonomous subnational politicians do not use these resources in service to the party apparatus, but channel them to reward their own supporters and build their personal clientelist networks (Crook and Manor 1998; Harbers 2010; Luna 2007; Sabatini 2003). Alternatively, if parties are able to protect their access to state funds, maintain patronage distribution of jobs, or sustain discretionary distribution of public goods and services, they can sustain or even expand their resources for clientelism (Hopkin and Mastropaolo 2001; Kitschelt and Wilkinson 2007a).

Reforms that limit parties' capacity to monitor clientelist exchanges also strain their resource base. Monitoring tactics like party-printed ballots and highly disaggregated election returns enable parties to identify people who violate their end of the clientelist bargain, limiting the potential for misspent funds (Kitschelt and Wilkinson 2007a; Medina and Stokes 2007). If reforms weaken parties' monitoring capabilities, voters are more likely to shirk their promise to a party, undermining the efficiency of distribution and exacerbating resource strain (Lyne 2008).

If economic crisis and political reforms constrain resources at the same time that demand escalates, a party's clientelist capacity decays. When one party cannot sustain clientelism, clients seeking material exchanges will readily turn to other parties in search of some benefit, because clientelism does not foster strong and stable partisan affinities. Of course, this process only heightens the demands placed on other parties, thereby spreading the effects of increased pressures for clientelism to all the parties in the system. One party's inability to deliver on promises for clientelist linkage, therefore, ripples throughout the entire system, threatening the maintenance of adequate clientelist linkage at the system level. If limitations on resources produce shortages for all the parties, then these demands will go unmet. Thus, social change and political reforms heighten the demand for clientelism across the whole system, while economic crisis, bureaucratic professionalization, and other reforms that limit access to the state undermine the ability of all parties to furnish enough benefits to satiate this demand. In this way, individual parties' failure to deliver clientelism can easily infect the linkage capacity of the entire system.

When there are not enough resources to satisfy escalating pressure for exchange-based linkage and none of the system parties furnish the benefits that voters seek, people become frustrated with the entire system. Paradoxically, in the absence of meaningful programmatic and incorporating linkage, parties' desperate efforts to satiate clientelist demand escalate (the appearance of) corruption, and those voters who disdain the clientelist elements of parties' linkage profiles are ever more likely to condemn the entire system as corrupt (Kitschelt and Wilkinson 2007a). Furthermore, as fewer potential clients receive the benefits they seek, they also become frustrated and vilify the clientelist system, from which they have been excluded. If clientelism cannot meet the demands of many and if other forms of linkage are absent, people reason that the explanation for the parties' failure to deliver must be corruption. Among those who do not receive benefits, clientelism loses its acceptance because it ceases to provide widespread linkage between society and the state, and instead enriches the select few who benefit. The decay of clientelism, therefore, provokes mounting disenchantment with the whole system (Hopkin and Mastropaolo 2001).

The process by which proliferating demands and resource constraints produce the decay of clientelism is portrayed in fig. 3.4. Social changes and political decentralization heighten petitions for clientelism. Increased demand challenges the parties to find enough resources to continue furnishing linkage, but crisis conditions and political reforms that limit party

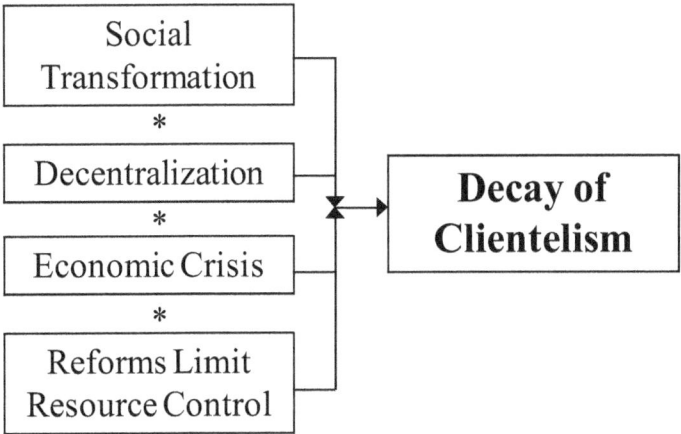

Fig. 3.4 Decay of clientelism

Note: * stands for the logical AND. Joint arrows indicate a conjunction of necessary causes. Notation follows Goertz and Mahoney (2005).

control over state funds shrink resources, widening the gulf between pressures for material exchange and the parties' capacity to deliver. If resources do not meet demand, clientelism decays.

LINKAGE FAILURE AND PARTY SYSTEM COLLAPSE

Different factors provoke the failure of each kind of linkage, but the general causal pattern underlying linkage decay involves new demands, which stem from structural changes that threaten the core logic of the linkage strategy and require significant adaptation. If these challenges arise amid specific contextual constraints that restrict the latitude for response, the system is unable to answer pressures for linkage. When threats to linkage emerge and constraints impede appropriate adaptation, linkage decays. If all the linkage strategies employed deteriorate across the entire party system, collapse results. Systems that rely on one type of linkage fail if that form is exhausted, unless the system can develop other linkage strategies to replace what was lost. Systems with mixed linkage profiles must experience the decay of all their strategies in order for the system to collapse. Having outlined the general process through which linkage failure produces party system collapse and detailed the structural changes that challenge each linkage type, as well as the specific contextual constraints that limit adaptation in the face of these challenges, I bring these elements together in a two-level theoretical framework in fig. 3.5.

The figure depicts the overarching theory of party system collapse, which stipulates in the core model that the failure of all three types of linkage produces collapse. The secondary level of the model identifies the specific challenges and constraints hypothesized to undermine each linkage strategy. Crises, specifically those that stem from the exhaustion of established policy models, threaten programmatic representation. When international constraints limit parties' policy options for addressing the crisis to those that contradict their ideological or policy-making legacies, then the governing parties face a lose-lose situation and policy responsiveness deteriorates. If all the parties are programmatically discredited because ideological distinctions between them are blurred, likely as a result of interparty agreements, all the parties are implicated in this failed policy responsiveness and programmatic linkage deteriorates throughout the whole system. Incorporation suffers if the structure or kind of salient cleavage changes, challenging the logic by which interests were traditionally integrated. If the parties'

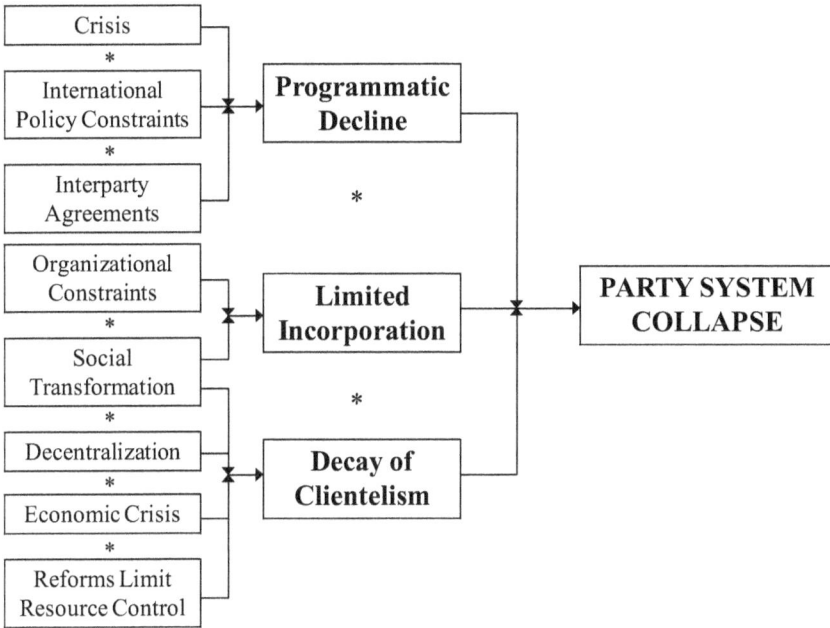

Fig. 3.5   Full model of party system collapse

Note: * stands for the logical AND. Factors in bold are part of the core theoretical model; factors in standard font are part of the secondary model. Joint arrows indicate a conjunction of necessary causes. Notation follows Goertz and Mahoney (2005).

organizational structures make reaching out to new groups risky or infeasible because routinized incorporation patterns are not easily translated to new groups or because new and old interests conflict, then adaptation flounders and incorporation narrows. Finally, clientelism loses the capacity to win support when social changes and electoral decentralization heighten demand for direct exchanges at the same time that the parties lose resources for distribution as a result of economic crisis and reforms that constrain partisan manipulation of the state. Without sufficient fuel to feed their hungry machines, clientelism decays.

Structural changes endanger linkage and require a response. If these challenges occur in a context that constrains adaptation, linkage fails. When a party system is unable to sustain meaningful programmatic appeals, does not incorporate major societal concerns, and cannot satisfy clientelist demands, the system collapses. This is the argument that I examine throughout the rest of the book, assessing the threats to linkage and the limitations on adaptation that produced bankrupt representation and party system collapse in

Venezuela as well as Bolivia, Colombia, and Italy. In the analysis that follows in parts 2 and 3, I find that collapse occurs when all linkage strategies fail across the party system. Furthermore, the analysis of cases of collapse as well as instances of survival suggests that the combinations of structural challenges and contextual constraints outlined here effectively explain the decay of each linkage type.[16] Where the hypothesized causal patterns are present, linkage decays; where the patterns are not complete, linkage persists and the party system survives.

16. Note that I am only examining whether these hypothesized combinations of causes account for the system-level linkage decay that leads to collapse. Because I am primarily concerned with explaining collapse, as opposed to analyzing linkage decay as an end in itself, I do not test the theory in every instance where any sort of linkage deterioration has occurred. Testing the general applicability of the hypothesized causes of causes to all cases of linkage decay is beyond the scope of this project, and I leave this task for future research.

PART 2

LINKAGE FAILURE AND VENEZUELAN COLLAPSE

4

THE PARTY SYSTEM AT ITS PEAK

Having delineated the process through which challenges to linkage and constraints on adaptation produce bankrupt representation and party system collapse, in this part of the book I examine the theory in Venezuela. This chapter begins the story by detailing the Venezuelan collapse. I discuss the development and consolidation of the institutionalized 2.5-party system and describe the system's linkage profile at its zenith in the 1970s and 1980s. Analyzing the system during a time when it did not display much indication of impending collapse provides a baseline for comparison with later periods of crisis in subsequent chapters. Chapters 5, 6, and 7 trace the processes that led to decays in programmatic, incorporating, and clientelist linkage, respectively. Chapter 8 concludes the analysis of Venezuelan collapse by showing how linkage failure led to the exodus from the party system, which climaxed with collapse in the 1998 elections.

PORTRAIT OF VENEZUELAN COLLAPSE

In the 1960s and 1970s, while many of its neighbors experienced extended bouts of authoritarianism, Venezuelan democracy thrived. Throughout the 1970s, Venezuela enjoyed political stability and economic prosperity, and the development of an institutionalized party system was central to democratic politics. However, in the 1980s, this unassailable image began to crumble, and by the late 1990s, the country faced mounting threats to its political, economic, and social order, which ended in party system collapse in 1998.

When Venezuela transitioned to democracy in 1958, the parties, which had begun to develop over the previous thirty years and had contested democratic elections during the *trienio* from 1945 to 1948, reemerged as pivotal actors.[1] To protect democracy and avert the trienio's failed dynamics of conflict without compromise, the parties formulated rules of the game that encouraged conciliation (Karl 1986; Levine 1973). The three major noncommunist parties—AD, the Christian democratic COPEI, and URD (Unión República Democrática)—demonstrated support for the new system by signing two formal agreements: the Pact of Punto Fijo and the Minimum Program of Government, which together formed the basis for Venezuela's pacted democracy (Borges Arcila 1996; López Maya, Gómez Calcaño, and Maingón 1989).[2] The pacts empowered the participating parties, solidifying their role as the primary intermediaries between society and the state (Martz 1966). To reassure conservative interests in society, the pacts excluded left parties like PCV (Partido Comunista de Venezuela) and MIR (Movimiento Izquierda Revolucionaria), which responded with militant opposition to the regime for over a decade (Alexander 1969; Ellner 1988).

Following the transition, multiparty competition between AD, COPEI, URD, and some smaller parties prospered from 1963 until 1973. But with the 1973 elections, the multiparty system shifted to a 2.5-party system in which AD and COPEI were the dominant players and MAS (Movimiento al Socialismo) emerged as the most significant third party.

The two major parties' electoral dominance continued through the 1980s, and by almost all accounts, the party system from 1973 to 1983 was successful. The militant left was subdued, and government control alternated between democratically elected civilian leaders who generally respected citizens' political and civil rights. The economic model of state-led growth propelled by oil revenues seemed to be functioning well. And the party system

1. See Karl (1986), Levine (1973), and Martz (1966) for detailed discussions of party and party system development.

2. The agreements committed signatories to respect elections, to party alternation in government, to sharing responsibility and patronage, and to defense of the Constitution (Borges Arcila 1996; Karl 1986; Martz 1966). The pact set aside irreconcilable differences and focused on areas where consensus could be reached (Levine and Crisp 1999). Furthermore, the Church and the military, which had been threatened by the radical democracy of the trienio and were instrumental in the coup that led to the Pérez Jiménez regime (1948–58), received assurances that their interests would be protected and their major demands met. The parties also pledged themselves to a common economic program, which emphasized state-led growth while still encouraging foreign and domestic capital and industry. Finally, the parties committed to a prudent approach to social reform while promising benefits to labor, peasants, and the middle class. Later, with the 1970 Institutional Pact, the practice of giving government positions and power to the opposition was formalized (Borges Arcila 1996).

was highly institutionalized (Dix 1992; Kornblith and Levine 1995). Research conducted during the party system's heyday, especially U.S. scholarship, was generally favorable (Coppedge 1994a). While scholars acknowledged some weaknesses, such as the lack of programmatic renewal and an inability to incorporate growing urban sectors, they generally emphasized positive features, like the organized and programmatic parties that helped manage conflict and change (Baloyra and Martz 1979; Herman 1980; Levine 1973; Martz 1966). Linkage during the height of the party system, which I discuss in detail below, was multifaceted, attracting voters with programmatic, incorporating, and clientelist appeals (Karl 1997; Martz 1966; Martz and Myers 1994; McCoy 1989; Powell 1971).

Despite its multilayered linkage strategy, the party system began to show signs of decay in the mid-1980s, and over time, assessments became more critical. Of course, recent research benefits from the advantage of hindsight, but negative evaluations began appearing in the 1990s, well before the 1998 collapse. Scholars criticized the parties for lacking transparency (Morales Paúl 1996), responsiveness (Borges Arcila 1996), flexibility (Coppedge 1994a), and inclusiveness (Crisp 2000; Hillman 1994), among other issues.

Voters became increasingly dissatisfied, and shifts in partisanship depict drastic decay in party support (fig. 4.1).[3] The parties did not begin to lose support until the late 1980s, but in 1989 traditional partisanship dropped rapidly. Affiliation with AD plummeted after Carlos Andrés Pérez's reelection in 1988. The timing of this decline is significant, as it occurred simultaneously with Pérez's abandonment of the state-centric development for which he had become famous in his first term. In early 1989, he announced unpopular reforms that embraced orthodox neoliberal policies, including privatization, trade liberalization, and deregulation (Naím 1993). In February, concerns about increased transportation fares provoked a largely spontaneous protest, the Caracazo, which lasted for several days and ended only when Pérez called out the military to stop the violence. The Caracazo played an important role in revealing a growing disenchantment with the linkage options provided by the party system and frequently served as a symbol of the system's decay. Despite the unrest, Pérez proceeded with implementing his agenda, albeit in scaled-back form (Karl 1997; Naím 1993). Neither

3. I assembled these data from dozens of nationwide face-to-face surveys from Baloyra, Batoba, Consultores 21, DATOS, and IVAD. The typical question battery treated members and sympathizers as partisans; those with no partisan sympathy are independents. The data are three-year moving averages of annual partisanship, constructed by averaging all surveys in a given year. In years when no data were available (1974, 1976–78), I fill the gaps by averaging adjacent years' frequencies. Data from different sources track together, indicating cross-firm reliability.

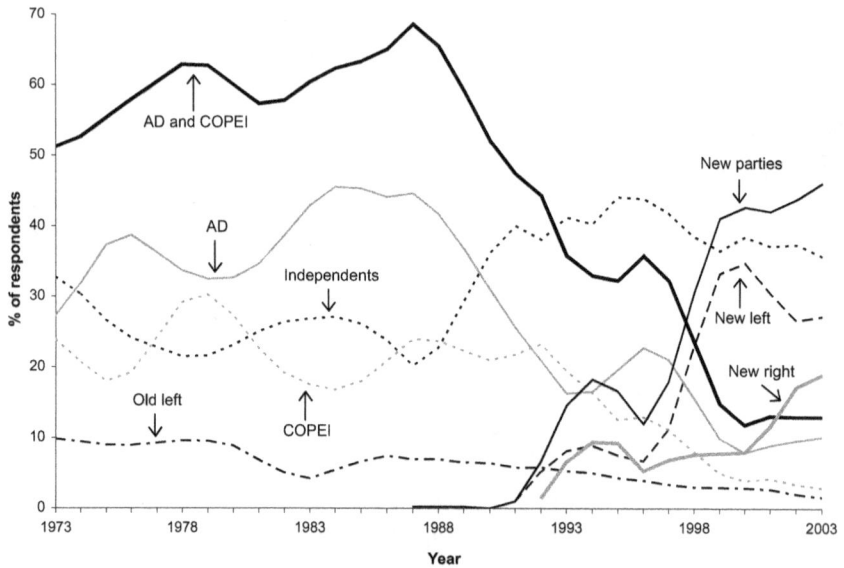

Fig. 4.1 Partisan identification in the old and new party systems, 1973–2003

Note: Data displayed are a smoothed version of the annual average frequency of survey respondents who identified with each group. The old left includes Movimiento al Socialismo (MAS), Movimiento Electoral del Pueblo (MEP), Movimiento Izquierda Revolucionaria (MIR), and Partido Comunista de Venezuela (PCV). The new right includes Convergencia, IRENE, Proyecto Venezuela (PV), Primero Justicia (PJ), and Gente de Petroleo. The new left includes La Causa R (LCR), Movimiento Quinta República (MVR), and Patria Para Todos (PPT).

Source: Morgan (2007), using data compiled by the author from Baloyra, Batoba, Consultores 21, DATOS, and IVAD. Figure printed with permission from the *Latin American Research Review*.

COPEI nor the old left capitalized on the widespread rejection of AD. The old left decayed slowly, beginning in the late 1980s, while COPEI's decline was precipitous, starting in the early 1990s and intensifying when former president and COPEI founder Rafael Caldera abandoned the party and won reelection in 1993 as an independent. Independence grew to 40 percent by 1991.

Growing electoral abstention also evidences party system decay. After years of high participation rates, abstention increased in the late 1980s and dramatically expanded in 1993, when nearly 40 percent of eligible voters did not participate (fig. 4.2). Compulsory voting laws were relaxed to remove sanctions for non-voting in the 1993 elections, which complicated voter mobilization, but the extraordinary increase in abstention cannot be entirely rooted in this rule change, indicating that citizens felt dissatisfied with their electoral options and chose to abstain rather than vote for any of

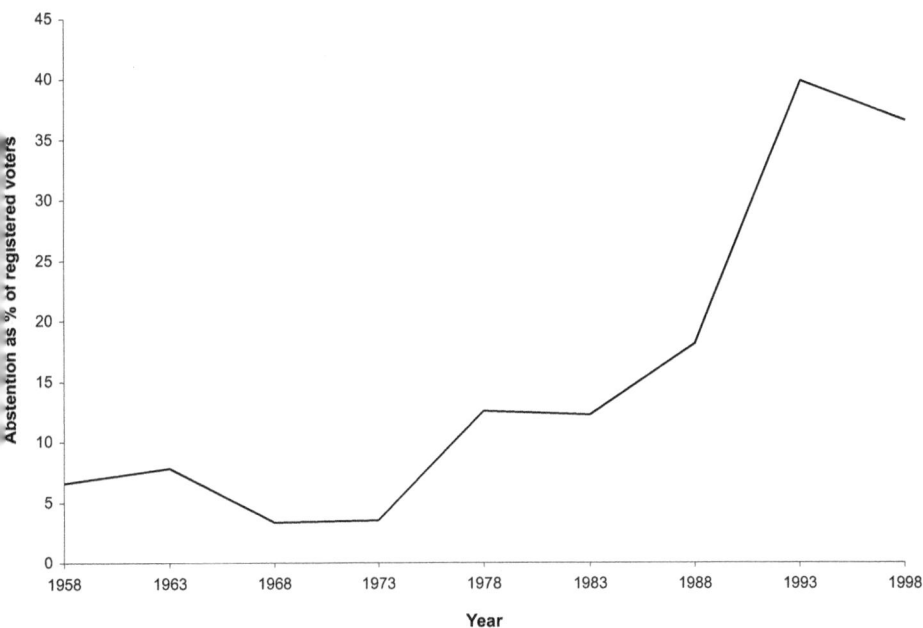

Fig. 4.2   Abstention in presidential elections, 1958–98

Source: Data from Venezuela's Consejo Supremo Electoral.

the available parties (Molina and Pérez 1995, 2004).[4] Blank and spoiled ballots also tripled from 2.1 percent of votes cast in 1978 to 6.5 percent in 1998.

Support for the old parties and participation in the party system evaporated in the 1990s. Moreover, the transformation of the established 2.5-party system into a multiparty system concurrent with the major parties' drastic decay meets the definition of collapse outlined in chapter 2. In the 1970s and 1980s, two major parties dominated while a handful of smaller parties also competed, constituting a 2.5-party system. But in the 1993 elections, the dominance of AD and COPEI waned. They faced stiff competition, and the number of effective parties surpassed five, reflecting a shift toward a moderate multiparty system.

This transformation occurred in conjunction with considerable decay in the major components of the old system. AD and COPEI controlled the

4. Voting was compulsory until the passage of the 1999 Constitution. Sanctions for non-voting, which had always been minor and rarely used, were removed in 1993 (Kornblith 1998b). Research on compulsory voting suggests that eliminating sanctions results in a six- to seven-point increase in abstention (Fornos, Power, and Garand 2004; Franklin 1999). Given that abstention in Venezuela jumped about 20 percentage points between 1988 and 1993, it is unlikely that this sudden spike could be entirely attributed to removing sanctions (Molina and Pérez 2004).

presidency and won about 80 percent of the seats in the legislature through-out the 1970s and 1980s (fig. 4.3). But after this period of relative stability, the proportion of seats held by AD and COPEI dropped. In 1994, only 60 percent of senators and 53 percent of deputies were *adecos* or *copeyanos*. By 1998, the party system's collapse was complete, as the two parties lost control of the legislature, holding only 48 percent of the seats in the Senate and 43 percent in the Chamber of Deputies. Thus, all elements of the definition of party system collapse were satisfied, as an established system transformed from one type to another while the major components of the old system lost their majority in the legislature. The once venerated and supposedly stable Venezuelan party system was no more. Instead, the parties' decay continued into the twenty-first century as Hugo Chávez consolidated power.

LINKAGE IN VENEZUELA'S 2.5-PARTY SYSTEM

I have theorized that a party system will collapse when linkage fails due to challenges that threaten its core strategies and constraints that limit appropriate adaptation. In this chapter, I lay a foundation for the analysis by detailing linkage in the 2.5-party system from 1974 through 1983, thus establishing a benchmark for comparison. In the eyes of all but the most pessimistic analysts, the system functioned satisfactorily in this decade. Delineating the system's linkage profile during these stable and prosperous years allows me to specify the different mechanisms used by the parties to link society and the state. Hindsight makes it easy to deride the old party system, but at its peak, it had beneficial features that have been overlooked in the aftermath of collapse. The parties employed a diverse linkage portfolio, attracting support through programmatic appeals, incorporation of major societal interests, and clientelist benefits. By assessing linkage at the system's height, I am able to trace in subsequent chapters why and how it faltered.

Data for Analyzing Linkage

To outline linkage during the party system's peak and to later illuminate how linkage decayed, I analyze an array of data mostly collected during fifteen months of field research. I conducted a series of semi-structured interviews with Venezuelan political elites in May 2001, April to December 2003, and May to August 2006. I interviewed eighty-nine elites, including current and

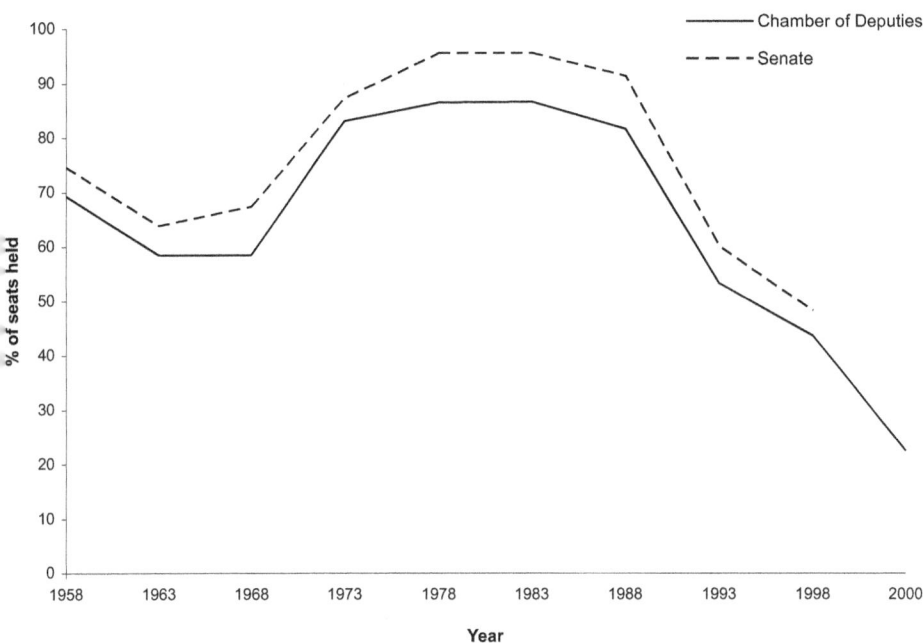

Fig. 4.3 Legislative seats held by AD and COPEI, 1958–2000

Source: Data from Venezuela's Consejo Nacional Electoral and Consejo Supremo Electoral.

former party leaders and legislators from all of the traditional as well as many new parties. Participants were selected based on positional and reputational sampling strategies. In the interviews, participants discussed the parties' shortcomings and miscalculations, the challenges they faced, and the constraints within which they operated. To facilitate forthright responses about sensitive topics surrounding the parties' failures, I promised confidentiality to the participants. Thus, throughout the book, I refer to them by interview number and indicate their areas of expertise without revealing their identities. Appendix A contains details about the interviews and information concerning the selection and qualifications of the respondents.

Other data sources used throughout the book include news reports,[5] documents culled from party archives,[6] election returns, and social, economic,

5. I analyzed hundreds of stories from *El Nacional, El Universal, El Globo, Tal Cual,* and *VenEconomía* concerning parties, policy responsiveness, incorporation, informality, clientelism, and other themes.

6. Party documents were procured from AD and COPEI headquarters and ideological foundations, as well as interview respondents' personal archives. The CNE provided access to party legal records held at its library.

and demographic data. To analyze programmatic linkage here and in chapter 5, I aggregate dozens of public opinion surveys from academic and reputable professional survey organizations to identify the issues that Venezuelans considered to be most important during each presidential administration. Then I analyze the content and significance of all legislation passed in each five-year term from 1974 to 2004 to assess the extent to which parties in government enacted policies in response to public concerns. I use news reports to identify the contemporary significance of this legislation and expert evaluations to assess retrospective importance. Together, these techniques allow me to determine the quantity and significance of legislation responding to important national problems.[7] To analyze incorporation and clientelism in chapters 6 and 7, I use interview data, news reports, party documents, socioeconomic data, and secondary sources. Throughout part 2, I also analyze data from nationwide public opinion surveys conducted from the 1970s through the 2000s. I frequently draw upon Baloyra 1973, Batoba 1983, CIEPA 1993, and RedPol98, all of which were nationwide surveys overseen by academics.[8] In addition, I use data from dozens of other surveys conducted by the firms Consultores 21, DATOS, IVAD, and Datanalisis.

Meaningful Programmatic Appeals

Programmatic representation is an important linkage mechanism that builds support through unconditional appeals such as universal policy outputs and ideological position taking. Programmatic linkage takes two possible forms: policy responsiveness by parties in government and ideological or programmatic alternatives provided by competing parties at the polls. Throughout the system's heyday, the Venezuelan parties consistently offered both types.

During this period, the parties in government enacted policies that responded to citizen concerns, implementing several important elements of their platforms. In the first presidency of adeco Carlos Andrés Pérez (1974–79), an AD-led Congress passed laws that nationalized oil and gave the

---

7. The legislative data were collected from the *Gaceta Oficial* and legislative archives. Contemporary significance was determined using news coverage in the most widely circulating national daily, *El Nacional*. Retrospective importance was assessed by experts. See appendixes B and C for details on the public opinion and legislative data.

8. The UNC Odum Institute facilitated access to the Baloyra 1973 survey, designed by Enrique Baloyra and John Martz and administered by DATOS (N=1521) (Baloyra and Martz 1979). Batoba 1983, also designed by Baloyra, was provided by the USB Banco de Datos Poblacionales (N=1789). The CIEPA 1993 survey was supplied by José Molina of La Universidad de Zulia (N=1499). RedPol98 was designed by a network of Venezuelan scholars and conducted by DATOS. The survey was provided by the USB Banco de Datos Poblacionales (N=1200).

government power to set prices on items of necessity. Another major law empowered Pérez to enact decrees aimed at equalizing wealth and protecting workers. Pérez used these special powers to establish Venezuela's first minimum wage, which raised income for nonunionized workers by 50 percent, and to implement a progressive pay increase for all employees (Karl 1997, 132). These and other significant policy initiatives addressed the major concerns raised in public opinion surveys at the time, namely cost of living, poverty, and unemployment. During the subsequent term, under copeyano president Luis Herrera Campíns, policy responsiveness continued. Laws addressing important problems increased in raw numbers and in the proportion of total legislative output, and significant legislation relating to the important issues of unemployment, the economy, and debt remained constant.[9] Reforms promoted development and extended workers' rights, granting severance protection and other benefits. Overall, legislation produced during the height of the party system reflected voters' concerns.

Venezuelans themselves viewed government as moderately responsive to national concerns. The Baloyra and Batoba surveys conducted in 1973 and 1983, respectively, asked people whether they felt that politicians were concerned with solving the country's problems. Only 46 percent of respondents in 1973 and 38 percent in 1983 disagreed with the view that politicians were responsive to national issues, indicating a modest level of satisfaction with the policy activity of government.

From 1973 to 1983, the parties also offered ideological choices between AD, COPEI, and smaller left parties. Although the left never threatened to control government, making its ideological offerings less viable, AD and COPEI provided meaningful options. AD advocated social democratic ideology, and COPEI Christian democracy. With regard to the system's heyday, a former COPEI president explained, "Venezuelan political parties were very ideological, and the social democratic and Christian democratic ideologies they espoused had a lot of weight" (Interview 37). Other elites whom I interviewed agreed that although these distinctions decayed over time, at their height AD and COPEI presented different visions of society. Voters also viewed the two parties as offering discernible ideological options. In surveys conducted in 1973 and 1983, Venezuelans consistently placed COPEI significantly to the right of AD, and they placed AD and COPEI significantly right of the left parties. Thus, at its zenith, the traditional system furnished meaningful ideological alternatives.

9. Chapter 5 and appendix C detail the responsiveness analysis thoroughly and discuss the focus on joint legislative-executive action in the form of laws.

By the 1980s, Congress had passed many laws that addressed early policy promises, including efforts at land reform, infrastructure development, and petroleum nationalization. Unfortunately, once these original ideas were implemented, the parties seemed content to rest on the laurels of past achievements. Little doctrinal renewal occurred, and few innovative policies were proposed. The parties were not proactive in addressing new problems, making them vulnerable to traumatic changes. Therefore, although the system provided ideological options and policy responsiveness, by the 1980s the parties showed declining evidence of creative contemporary responsiveness.

Successful Incorporation of Major Social Interests

Another tactic used by parties to promote linkage is interest incorporation. Under this strategy, parties reach out to major sectors of society with partially conditional appeals in which benefits offered are available to anyone within a particular group but are not accessible by those outside the targeted sector. As we will see below, in Venezuela, incorporating linkage may include sectorally targeted policies or group-based material benefits, but it also involves distinct strategies aimed to promote and integrate important interests, such as giving them privileged positions or special representation in party and government decision making. At the Venezuelan system's peak, the parties maintained close ties to major functional groups, incorporating their interests and subjecting them to party influence. The parties did not integrate all sectors, but in the 1970s and early 1980s, those that were incorporated constituted a substantial majority of the population.

Venezuela's system of interest mediation did not perfectly reflect pluralist or corporatist patterns, but the strong and institutionalized ties between the parties and specific groups reveal a tendency toward the more structured configuration common to corporatism.[10] Elements of pluralism were present, as various organizations with different levels of attachment to the parties were allowed to voice an array of interests. But the parties favored certain groups, especially organized labor and domestic capital, privileging them in terms of access and influence. The parties even played an active role in founding many functional organizations and promoted their development.

10. For a more detailed discussion of pluralism versus corporatism, see Schmitter and Lehmbruch (1979). Crisp (2000), who discusses the patterns of interest influence in Venezuela, also views the system as having elements of both corporatism and pluralism, but he emphasizes its pluralist features and takes a pluralist approach to analysis.

Through the party system, these advantaged interests maintained direct formal ties as well as more informal channels for influencing government.

The advantages of such a system of interest aggregation include easing communication between parties and major social groups, promoting stability by limiting overt pressure tactics, and providing benefits to group members. However, the corporatist strategy of granting special access to some groups virtually necessitates excluding others. As long as society's most significant groups are incorporated and social structure does not change, omitted interests do not pose a serious threat to linkage. However, if the excluded increase in size or power, then their omission may limit the utility of incorporation.

In Venezuela's system of incorporation, the most influential interests corresponded with the traditional class cleavage. The parties cultivated bases of support among functional sectors: business, labor, peasants, and professionals. These interests were initially included through the transition pacts. As the 2.5-party system solidified, the parties created a variety of mechanisms specifically designed to incorporate these groups, including representation in party structures, input in policy making, and overlapping leadership between parties and functional groups. The parties also offered policies and material benefits targeted toward members of important sectors in order to strengthen their ties to the system.

Formally, the major functional groups found voice in party organizations. In AD, the national party organization initially included secretaries of labor and agriculture, who held seats not only on the Comité Ejecutivo Nacional (CEN) but also on the Comité Político Nacional (CPN), "regarded as the very heart of AD leadership" (Martz 1966, 156). In 1972, AD added a secretary of professionals and technicians; though never as strong as labor and peasant interests in the party, this position nevertheless gave middle sectors a voice (Martz and Myers 1994, 16). In all three cases, members of the group itself—labor, peasants, or professionals—typically selected their own secretary. The positions gave the groups access to the pinnacle of party leadership. Most other parties followed AD's successful incorporation strategies and had similar organizational configurations in which these same groups held privileged status, with party functional bureaus incorporating their interests. From its founding, COPEI incorporated labor (COPEI 1948) and later gave peasant and professional wings representation via secretaries on the Comité Nacional (CN), the party's most influential executive authority, and on the National Secretariat, which oversaw everyday activities (COPEI 1991; Herman 1980). Even MAS, which drew most of its support from the middle class and in principal advocated a less corporatist approach (Ellner 1988), included functional representation of workers, peasants, professionals and technicians, and also teachers in its national organization (MAS 1989).

Furthermore, the major class interests wielded influence through direct participation in the policy process. These functional groups controlled most of the nongovernmental seats on advisory consultative commissions and decentralized public administration boards. Particularly important were domestic capital interests, represented by FEDECAMARAS (Federación de Cámaras y Asociaciones de Comercio y Producción); labor, represented by CTV (Confederación de Trabajadores de Venezuela); and professionals, who offered technical expertise (Crisp 2000).[11]

The parties also maintained ties with these socioeconomic interests through overlapping leaderships between the peak organizations representing each group and the parties' functional wings. Peak organization elections were based on partisan slates, and sectoral leaders were often in the upper echelons of one of the parties. Using data gathered in the mid-1980s, Coppedge found that three-quarters of adeco CTV leaders were members of the party's Labor Bureau—revealing a strong intermingling between the two organizations' leaderships (1994a, 32). The peasant movement displayed a similar pattern, with nearly all of the national leaders of Federación de Campesinos de Venezuela (FCV) also holding positions in a party (Powell 1971, 121).

Programmatic and material incentives targeted toward functional group members were other important mechanisms for incorporating sectoral interests. Peasants and organized labor depended on the parties to enact government policies promoting their welfare. Middle-class professionals and domestic capital interests expected the parties to foster favorable economic and business conditions in exchange for their support. The parties, therefore, walked a difficult line in trying to satisfy these diverse and at times competing demands, but oil wealth helped smooth over potentially opposing concerns. The parties used the 1960 land reform law and the agricultural subsidy to maintain peasant support, with distribution mechanisms favoring peasants loyal to the parties and the FCV (Martz 1966; Powell 1971). For workers, minimum wage laws guaranteed incomes, the social security system provided benefits, and price controls kept consumer

11. Several other types of groups were also represented on these commissions and boards, but each of these functional groups alone had greater representation than the other groups combined.

goods affordable. The parties also used the Venezuelan Workers' Bank (BTV) to distribute benefits to union leaders and members (Crisp 2000; McCoy 1989). The CTV itself was highly dependent on government subsidies, with nearly half its income coming from the state (McCoy 1989, 59). In conflicts between labor and capital, government mediated between the two constituencies through tripartite commissions, protecting each group's ties to the system. Even capital sought policies that guaranteed favorable exchanges rates and protected domestic industry (Herman 1980). In the professional *colegios*, advancement and access to government jobs and contracts frequently depended on partisan affiliation (Martz and Myers 1994). These incentives, whether they were targeted policies or group-based material benefits, solidified the major functional groups' support for the party system.

The connections between the parties and society's major functional interests provided opportunities for the groups to shape government and party decisions, offered policies targeted to benefit incorporated interests, and furnished material incentives to members. But to imply that these benefits came without costs would be misleading. In return for access and influence, the groups, particularly workers and peasants, sacrificed autonomy, and their leaders often held primary allegiance to the party, not their functional group.

The patterns of incorporation possessed another potentially more threatening shortcoming—the complete exclusion of some interests from the system. While business, labor, peasants, and to a lesser extent the professional middle class were incorporated into the system, other groups did not find linkage this way. Most significant among the unincorporated were those laboring in the informal sector of the economy. Unlike the influential functional groups, the informal sector lacked opportunities to shape and benefit from party and government decisions. They were not incorporated into party organizational structures, they lacked influence over policy making, and they did not receive group-targeted material benefits. The informal sector was without a voice. The parties' secretariats for municipal and neighborhood affairs could have been a vehicle for their representation, but in practice this was not the case. The parties did not have barrio or informal sector organizations, and there were no influential groups advocating for their interests (Ray 1969, 141; various interviews).[12] Thus, the parties' incorporation

---

12. In addition to excluding the far left and the informal sector, the traditional parties made little effort to incorporate the small, isolated indigenous population and did not recognize the largely "invisible" population of Afro-Venezuelans (Colmenares 2004). The primary means through which the parties appealed to these excluded sectors was through clientelist exchange.

strategies included traditional functional interests to the detriment of the informal sector, the urban poor, and the unemployed.

Despite neglecting these interests, however, incorporation included a large portion of the population at the party system's peak. Estimates by the International Labour Organization (ILO) suggest that Venezuela had one of the highest unionization rates in the region in the early 1980s. Between 30 and 40 percent of the economically active population was unionized—about the same as Argentina and Chile (ILO 1987a, 11). Moreover, agricultural employment accounted for about 15 percent of the economically active population in the early 1980s (ILO 1987b). Peasants and organized labor alone made up a majority of the workforce. Their integration—along with those connected through professional or business associations, groups for which precise data are not available—clearly indicates that incorporating linkage captured significant swaths of society.

Another way to compare incorporated and unincorporated sectors is to examine rates of formal versus informal sector employment. Those working in the formal sector found their interests voiced through several well-integrated organizations, including FEDECAMARAS, CTV, and professional colegios, whereas informal and unemployed workers lacked such representation. During the 1970s and early 1980s, about 65 percent of the non-agricultural workforce was employed in the formal economy, while the unincorporated informal sector remained much smaller at 30–35 percent (OCEI, various years). Unemployment was also fairly low during the party system's peak years, generally hovering around 5 percent.

Whether we consider unionization rates or the formal sector's size, the clear conclusion is that incorporating linkage reached a majority of the population at the party system's peak. Despite the hierarchical nature of this kind of linkage in Venezuela, and the marginalization of some sectors, the parties channeled the major interests reflecting the traditional class cleavage and thereby integrated most of society.

Clientelism as a Linkage Strategy

In addition to cultivating programmatic representation and ties to major functional interests, the Venezuelan parties used direct clientelist appeals. Clientelism reached those who were neither interested in nor appeased by the parties' programmatic appeals, nor incorporated through interest integration. At the height of the traditional party system, clientelist exchanges were prevalent, but they constituted only part of the system's overarching linkage profile. Some voters, particularly the informal sector and the urban poor, were exclusively tied to the system through material exchanges, while for many others, programmatic or incorporating linkages were decisive. Given the less dominant role of clientelism at the party system's height as well as the tendency of literature from this era to idealize the system and emphasize its more favorable features, data on clientelism during the system's golden years is more limited than our knowledge of programmatic representation and incorporation. But drawing on existing relevant literature and my interviews with party leaders, I sketch a portrait of clientelism here.

Clientelism during this period was manifested in a variety of ways. Oil income enabled spending on social programs, which the parties manipulated to deliver in conditional ways that promoted clientelist ends. Petroleum enabled "the economy [to become] a populist tool" and promoted the clientelist system that the parties used to buy support (Interview 68). When oil prices increased, as they did in 1974 and 1979, the state experienced windfall profits that the parties employed to shore up loyalty. Clientelism thus became a vehicle to ensure that everyone shared in state oil funds (Karl 1997). In exchange, the parties expected support from the beneficiaries.

Oil income also facilitated the delivery of patronage jobs. In a study examining the presence of oil rents, Baptista (2005) estimated that in the 1970s and 1980s Venezuelan public employment was over 60 percent higher than it should have been, given the country's level of development. By the end of the 1980s, the state employed more than 1.2 million Venezuelans (Baptista 2005, 104), many of whom received their jobs as a reward for party loyalty (Interview 4). The overgrown public sector was also an important mechanism that enticed lower- and middle-class party organizers and neighborhood leaders to work on behalf of their party, effectively turning parties into "employment agencies" (Interview 30).

Additionally, the parties developed distribution networks via party offices throughout the country. The common saying that the parties maintained *casas* (offices) in every village and barrio was not much of an exaggeration during the system's heyday. A variety of party functions, such as civic education, local party meetings, and ideological training, occurred in these offices. But the local casa also served as a distribution point for clientelist benefits. Both AD and COPEI endeavored to meet people's basic needs through their local headquarters, offering services like job training and medical care (Interviews 44, 50). Party members with specialized skills, such as doctors and teachers, donated their expertise by providing services on behalf of their party. Other party activities served the specific goal of turning out the vote during elections. The parties transported supporters to campaign rallies and created incentives to get them to the polls, offering material goods like T-shirts, caps, and alcohol as enticements.

In particular, the parties used clientelism to attract support from people not linked through programmatic ties or incorporation. Conditional exchanges were especially important in capturing votes from elements of the popular classes not represented through traditional corporatist linkages, and direct benefits dominated the parties' efforts to reach excluded groups like the urban poor and indigenous (Interviews 31, 33, 41, 49, 51).[13] The daily pressures of fulfilling basic needs often led the poor to prioritize immediate benefits that met an urgent physical concern over long-term policy goals. So the poor relied on party largesse merely to subsist, looking to the party to provide even "the boards for their roofs and the cement for their houses" (Interview 41). The otherwise marginalized supported the traditional parties only because they satisfied some material concern; the possibility of programmatic representation or interest incorporation was not decisive in their political choices (Ray 1969).

Representation Portfolio During the System's Heyday

The preceding discussion shows that during its heyday, the Venezuelan party system employed what Kitschelt and Wilkinson have termed "menu diversification," strategically mixing different linkage forms (2007a, 30). Their diverse portfolios enabled the parties to reach different kinds of voters by targeting appeals or benefits to suit their goals and concerns. The parties provided programmatic representation through policy responsiveness and meaningful ideological options, particularly attracting the more educated and informed segments of the population, who preferred to cast their support behind ideas and policies. The party system also integrated the interests of the most significant groups in society—peasants, organized labor, and business. In addition, the parties offered clientelist exchanges to garner support from the excluded, especially the urban poor and informal workers. Each type of linkage was important in building party support. In a 1973 survey,

13. The parties also appealed to incorporated groups, such as peasants and organized labor, through the use of material benefits, as discussed above. But the sorts of benefits provided to incorporated organizations were group-level offerings, which targeted members of major functional organizations and were typically more valuable than the kinds of material inducements offered in direct, conditional exchanges with individuals. Also, group-based benefits were part of an overall incorporation strategy, not the sole basis for linking integrated sectors.

party members were asked why they joined their party.[14] Of the 498 party members in the sample, 13 percent said that they had joined because of a material appeal, specifically that they had received party help in finding employment. Alternatively, 26 percent responded that they had enlisted in the party because of its ideology or doctrine, and another 21 percent had joined because of the party's work in government. Clientelist appeals certainly played a role in gaining support, but the parties' programmatic offerings were weighted as more important by most members.

Although not perfect, linkage during the system's heyday was sufficient for the economic and social climate of the time. Legislative activity in policy areas that were important to Venezuelans was not extremely abundant, but about 16 to 18 percent of important laws from 1974 to 1983 addressed issues people considered significant, and a minority of survey respondents thought that government was not responsive to the country's problems. Venezuelans also found meaningful ideological options at the polls. People who belonged to one of the major functional groups associated with the traditional class cleavage found linkage through interest incorporation, and the parties offered clientelist exchanges to those not otherwise connected.

To demonstrate how this multifaceted linkage profile deteriorated and caused collapse, I analyze the process through which each type of linkage decayed and show how lack of linkage resulted in abandonment of the party system. The next three chapters analyze the striking deterioration of programmatic appeals, interest incorporation, and clientelism, respectively. I explain how each strategy faced grave challenges to linkage maintenance, even as contextual constraints limited adaptation. As a result, each linkage type decayed significantly. Then, in chapter 8, I show how this linkage failure caused Venezuelans to exit the traditional party system.

---

14. The question read, "¿Por qué se hizo Ud. miembro de ese partido político?"

5

POLICY UNRESPONSIVENESS AND IDEOLOGICAL CONVERGENCE

When we entered the [economic] crisis, an enormous discontentment was created because the parties did not resolve the problems of the country.

—COPEI party vice president, *interview with author, June 2006*

In the end, AD and COPEI were exactly the same.

—Former AD CEN member, *interview with author, December 2003*

By the end of 1998, the Venezuelan party system collapsed completely. The major parties—AD and COPEI—had been decimated at the polls, and the once stable 2.5-party system disintegrated. How does a seemingly established, flourishing democracy with institutionalized parties fall into the personalism and uncertainty that characterizes contemporary Venezuelan politics? In chapter 3, I theorized that linkage failure causes party system collapse. Such breakdowns occur when the parties' primary linkage mechanisms are threatened by dramatic structural changes and their capacity to respond effectively to these threats is limited by specific contextual constraints. In Venezuela, the old party system encountered serious challenges to programmatic, incorporating, and clientelist linkages, and the constraints facing the system limited the parties' ability to adjust their linkage strategies to confront these threats.

This chapter demonstrates how programmatic linkage in Venezuela deteriorated over the fifteen years preceding collapse. Economic crisis stemming from the exhaustion of the oil-led development model intensified programmatic pressure in the 1980s and 1990s. However, analysis of policy responsiveness indicates that the parties did not rise to meet this challenge. Instead,

international constraints conflicted with the parties' ideologies and customary policy patterns, undermining their capacity to provide answers and resulting in policy stagnation. This failure extended to the system level as
all the parties were discredited by interparty agreements. Patterns of interparty conciliation and intraparty conflict encouraged politicians to form
cross-party alliances, making it difficult for the parties to sustain ideological
differences and removing meaningful alternatives from the system. In a
context of shared governance and ideological uniformity, the major system
parties were associated with the objectionable status quo and were discredited, weakening programmatic representation throughout the entire system.

THE PROCESS OF SYSTEM-LEVEL PROGRAMMATIC DECLINE

At the level of the party, programmatic representation may be provided via
a policy response to important problems confronting the country. This
aspect of programmatic linkage entails valence representation in which the
party (or parties) in government addresses common concerns. As long as
people believe that the ruling party is providing answers to pressing issues,
voters are likely to return it to office. However, if policy responsiveness falls
short in voters' eyes, they will look outside the governing party for resolution of their concerns.

Here is where the second facet of programmatic linkage, which involves
the provision of meaningful alternatives within the party system, comes into
play. If a system contains parties that offer different ideologies and distinct
strategies for resolving the country's challenges and that have a legitimate
chance of controlling the governing apparatus, then the system provides
programmatic options to voters, allowing them to choose the vision of society
they prefer. If responsiveness falls short, the presence of meaningful alternatives in the system enables voters to hold the governing party accountable
and to select a distinct option from within the system.

A party system may sustain programmatic linkage through policy responsiveness and/or meaningful ideological options. For such linkage to
deteriorate, the parties in power must fail to furnish adequate responses to
important problems, and voters must see no viable alternatives to the status
quo within the system. When the governing coalition faces international
constraints that limit its ability to address pressing, commonly held concerns, responsiveness fails, and voters typically hold the parties in power

responsible for this breakdown. If the other major parties in the system have entered into interparty agreements that blur distinctions between those in power and those supposedly in opposition, all the system parties are discredited. Thus, programmatic representation is likely to fail when a system is confronted with crisis conditions that demand an answer at the same time that international commitments limit responsiveness and interparty agreements undermine ideological options, eviscerating the programmatic capacity of the entire system. Below, I explore these processes in Venezuela.

CRISIS CONDITIONS THREATEN PROGRAMMATIC REPRESENTATION

Part of the story behind the Venezuelan party system collapse is tied to escalating challenges, including stagnant oil prices, mounting debt and inflation, and shrinking international reserves, which demanded a policy response. These problems stemmed from exhaustion of the oil-led development model, which had been the dominant economic strategy for decades. In the 1970s, the oil boom and petroleum nationalization deepened and solidified this trajectory (Karl 1997). As oil prices plummeted in the mid-1980s, government relied on foreign borrowing. But international reserves were depleted by the late 1980s, and oil prices remained stagnant, failing to provide the influx of cash that the parties had come to rely on. Meanwhile, inflation soared in the late 1980s and then fluctuated, reaching nearly 100 percent in 1996. Unemployment also grew through much of the 1990s (fig. 5.1). Under these conditions, the old strategy of using oil income to support the economy, sustain the exchange rate, and provide employment opportunities was no longer viable, as prices languished at or below $20 per barrel through the 1990s and financial reserves were depleted. By the time the party system collapsed, the economy had spiraled out of control and experienced stagflation, making this old model virtually defunct.

By the late 1990s, people's economic and social well-being had deteriorated notably. Average real wages in 1998 had fallen to one-third of their level in 1982, indicating that the limited macroeconomic successes achieved by neoliberal reform efforts of the 1990s were not reaching ordinary Venezuelans (CEPAL 2008). The proportion of the population in poverty more than doubled from 25 percent in the mid-1980s to over 60 percent by the end of the 1990s (CISOR 2001). Social ills escalated. From 1980 to 1998, the

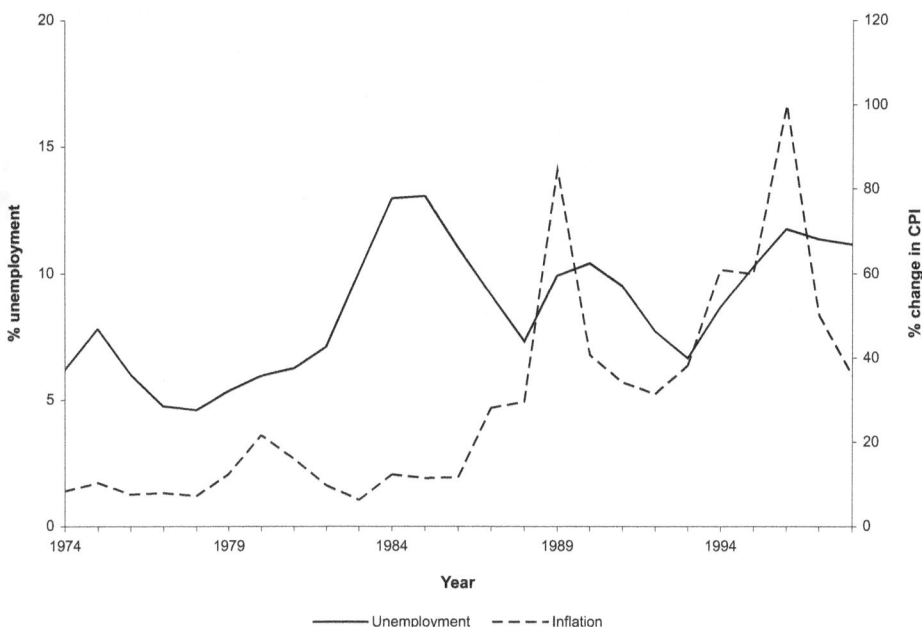

Fig. 5.1 Annual unemployment and inflation rates, 1974–98

Source: Data from World Development Indicators and the Instituto Nacional de Estadística (Venezuela).

homicide rate per 100,000 people rose from 12 to 22 (Arriaga and Godoy 2000), and Venezuela had one of the highest crime victimization rates in all of Latin America (Gaviria and Pagés 1999).

The crisis presented increasing challenges for the party system. In interviews, numerous traditional party leaders identified the pressures generated by the mounting economic and social crisis as significant threats to the sustainability of representation and to the party system. Several pointed to the crisis and the parties' failure to respond as the most important causes of collapse (Interviews 38, 39, 46, 56, 58, 66, 71). As a former COPEI leader put it, "Without the crisis, the party system would not have failed" (Interview 39). Economic and social problems demanded a response, and the parties needed to redouble their efforts to fulfill their duties to the people and address the issues confronting the country. However, "government did not answer the economic problems that were clearly developing" (Interview 15). Moreover, because the crisis stemmed from the deterioration and long-term negative ramifications of Venezuela's model of state-led development based on petroleum revenues, conventional policy tools in the parties' standard repertoire were rendered useless. Responding to this crisis demanded that they step outside their comfort zone and engage in innovative policy making that still remained true to their character. The crisis itself, which demanded a response, and its specific contours, which reflected the exhaustion of established policy-making patterns, posed a serious challenge for the Venezuelan parties as they struggled to maintain programmatic ties.

DETERIORATION OF POLICY RESPONSIVENESS

Had the parties in power been attempting to provide valence responsiveness, we would expect to see a flurry of policy activity addressing significant issues during this time of crisis. Alternatively, stagnant or decaying responsiveness to important problems indicates a lack of valence representation. To assess the extent to which parties in government failed to address intensifying challenges, I examine whether policy making responded to problems that many Venezuelans considered serious. I use public opinion surveys to identify the most important problems during each presidential administration. Then I analyze all legislation passed during the term to evaluate government's response to these concerns. Together, these data reveal if, when, and how parties in government took steps to address significant problems.

Identifying Important, Pressing Problems

To identify the issues that Venezuelans considered important, I employ data from nearly one hundred surveys conducted between 1974 and 1998 by Consultores 21, DATOS, and IVAD. Each survey asked respondents to name the most important problem facing the country. Based on the surveys, I created a five-year average to rank order the most pressing problems of each legislative term and concurrent presidential administration.[1] Table 5.1 presents the top four problems in each term from Carlos Andrés Peréz's first (1974–79) through Rafael Caldera's second (1994–99). In each term, the four principal problems together account for about 60 to 70 percent of responses, suggesting that the overwhelming majority of Venezuelans desired answers to these concerns.

1. For details about samples, question wording, response categories, and creating five-year averages, see appendix B.

Table 5.1 Four most important problems by presidential administration, 1974–99

Carlos Andrés Pérez 1974–79		Luis Herrera Campíns 1979–84		Jaime Lusinchi 1984–89		C. Pérez/R.Velásquez 1989–94		Rafael Caldera 1994–99	
Problems	% naming	Problems	% naming	Problems	% naming	Problems	% naming	Problems	% naming
Cost of living	45.6	Unemployment	27.9	Cost of living	24.6	Cost of living	22.6	Cost of living	20.4
Poverty/scarcity	11.4	Economy	15.7	Unemployment	23.7	Corruption	13.2	Crime	19.3
Unemployment	8.2	Debt	14.1	Crime	14.8	Crime	12.9	Unemployment	13.8
Crime	8.0	Cost of living	11.5	Debt	5.3	Unemployment	10.2	Corruption	12.7
Total	73.2	Total	69.2	Total	68.4	Total	58.9	Total	66.2

Source: Author's calculations based on surveys conducted by Consultores 21, DATOS, and IVAD.

The issues that citizens identified as important also correspond with objective assessments of the country's problems. For instance, in line with Venezuelans' perceptions, crime escalated between the 1970s and 1990s, with the homicide rate nearly doubling; at the same time, crime became a more salient issue. Likewise, economic issues were significant challenges to which people sought a response, and the relative significance of different types of economic challenges waxed and waned in the eyes of the public along a pattern similar to that of objective economic indicators. For instance, unemployment, not cost of living, was considered the most significant issue during the Herrera presidency, as unemployment passed 12 percent while inflation remained under control. Alternatively, inflation was the most pressing problem in the late 1980s and throughout the 1990s in both perceived and real terms. In fact, inflation's trajectory in the 1990s closely mirrors changes in the percentage of respondents who identified cost of living as the most important problem.[2] Thus, citizens' perceptions of the problems facing Venezuela reflected issues that were truly matters for concern, and the relative importance of different issues among respondents varied in ways that paralleled changes in the problems' severity. Responsive parties would have addressed these concerns.

Measuring Policy Activity

To evaluate the parties' responsiveness to important problems voiced by the people, I assembled a team of researchers to analyze government activity in the form of bills passed by the legislature and signed into law by the executive. Law activity incorporates action by both the legislature and the executive and is, therefore, a good overall measure of efforts to address important issues. I consider legislative activity, as opposed to policies enacted unilaterally by the executive, because Congress was the clearest avenue through which the parties as organizations could shape policy. Parties were influential actors in legislative policy making in Venezuela, where party discipline was high and legislative action was routinely subjected to the will of party leadership. In fact, Congress often acted as the parties' mouthpiece, and committee chairs were almost uniformly held by members of the parties'

2. Cost of living/inflation was ranked the number one problem in every year during the 1990s except 1993, 1995, and 1998, when it dropped to number two or three on the list. Indeed, inflation remained a serious problem throughout the entire period, meriting mention by survey respondents. But 1993, 1995, and 1998 were all years in which inflation declined relative to the rest of the decade, and it was precisely during these years that other issues superseded inflation on citizens' lists of pressing issues.

central directorates (Coppedge 1994a). Alternatively, presidents were typically freed from party discipline and oversight during their term in office. The parties' limited influence over executive policy making suggests that unilateral presidential action is a less suitable measure of policy responsiveness than legislative activity, which taps party efforts more directly. Furthermore, many of the most important presidential decrees are also accounted for in the legislative responsiveness analysis, which includes the enabling laws passed by Congress to grant special presidential decree powers in specified policy areas.[3] The parties' influence and discipline in the legislature should have allowed them to use Congress as a vehicle to enact policies addressing pressing problems. In practice, however, policy responsiveness on important issues decayed in the face of the escalating crisis.

I analyzed all laws enacted in Venezuela, beginning with the consolidation of the 2.5-party system in 1974 and extending through the system's collapse in 1998.[4] Each law was assessed in terms of its substantive content as well as its significance. Thus, I was able to evaluate both the quantity and the importance of the legislative response to pressing problems. Based on a careful reading of each new law as well as a comparison to existing legislation affected by it, I summarized the goals of every law and categorized each according to the major policy areas it addressed.[5]

I identified significant legislation by coding laws based on retrospective and contemporary assessments of importance (Epstein and Segal 2000).

3. Executive decrees issued under ordinary constitutional powers are not included in the analysis, but ordinary decree authority was weak. As Crisp notes, "[Venezuelan presidents] never receive binding legislative powers unless the Congress delegates it to them. So, presidents are always operating within bounds set for them by the legislative branch" (1998b, 142). The one exception to generally weak decree powers was presidential authority to issue decrees as a result of suspending the constitutional guarantee to "economic liberty." The right to economic liberty was nearly permanently restricted from the implementation of the Constitution in 1961 through 1991, when Pérez reinstated the right. Caldera suspended the right again briefly in 1994 and 1995. Significantly, however, the pattern of decrees issued under the restriction of the right to economic liberty generally followed the patterns of legislative activity. In the 1970s and early 1980s, the decrees were used as a means for state intervention in the economy. But beginning with the second Pérez administration, presidents made much less use of this type of decree authority (Crisp 1998b).

4. The database actually extends through 2004, to include the first six years of the Chávez government. But here I focus on the pre-collapse period. The data were culled from the daily government publication, La Gaceta Oficial, which publishes records of all government activity, including legislation. I verified all the Gaceta data in the Dirección de Información Legislativa, the archives of the National Assembly.

5. To test for reliability, a secondary expert coder also read, summarized, and coded 11 percent of the laws. Reliability rates were high, with agreement nearing 99 percent on the content of the laws. More details about coding for substantive content and the development of content categories are found in appendix C.

Retrospective assessments, identified through the lens of time, tap sustained perceptions of significance determined by experts who evaluate the importance of past government actions. Contemporaneous significance is determined based on assessments of laws when they were passed and requires analyzing archives or news reports that reveal perceptions of legislation at the time of passage.

To assess retrospective and contemporaneous significance of Venezuelan legislation, I used two phases similar to Mayhew's (1991) two sweeps for identifying important laws in the United States, the first based on retrospective assessments and the second on contemporaneous evaluations. In coding each law for retrospective significance, I analyzed the law and its relationship to other legislation to determine whether it promised to have a significant impact on policy or affect a large portion of the population.[6] Then, in the second phase, I analyzed news reports in Venezuela's most widely read daily, El Nacional, to identify laws that the media deemed significant enough to cover and that the public was most likely to know about, thereby measuring contemporary importance (Fan 1988; Hertog and Fan 1995; Krippendorff 2004).[7]

Finally, to assess the overall level of important legislation, I created a joint measure of significance, incorporating retrospective expert evaluations and contemporaneous news analysis. All laws identified as significant under either approach were coded as important. Thus, the full measure of significance captures how contemporary Venezuelan news media evaluated legislative activity and how experts retrospectively assessed the intended impact of legislation.[8] Coupled with the survey data on the country's most important problems in each legislative term, this data on the content and significance of legislation enable me to evaluate the extent to which legislation dealt with issues of concern to Venezuelans.

6. A second coder with a Ph.D. in political science and knowledge of Venezuela followed the same guidelines and evaluated the significance of 11 percent of the legislation. Intercoder agreement was 93.5 percent, well over the 70 percent considered acceptable (Neuendorf 2002, 143). Appendix C contains more details about retrospective significance. A total of 134 laws passed between 1974 and 1998 were identified as retrospectively significant.

7. According to surveys that asked respondents about their news sources, El Nacional was typically the most widely read paper throughout the period, and as a major daily, its coverage was likely representative of other newspapers. See appendix C for details concerning the twophases and news coverage coding. We identified 116 contemporaneously important laws in the pre-collapse era. Intercoder agreement was high at 97 percent.

8. This joint measure produced a total of 188 important laws passed between 1974 and the end of Caldera's term in early 1999. This process identified 70 laws as both retrospectively and contemporaneously significant, 68 as only retrospectively significant, and 50 as only contemporaneously significant.

Assessing Policy Responsiveness to Important Problems

To examine whether policy responded to public concerns, I analyze the level, proportion, and significance of legislative activity in important policy areas over time, contrasting responsiveness at the height of the old party system with unresponsiveness as the system decayed. Policy activity under the first two administrations of the consolidated 2.5-party system (1974–84) provides a baseline for comparison with later periods, allowing me to assess the extent to which responsiveness increased, stagnated, or decayed in the years preceding the system's collapse.

Fig. 5.2 displays the number of laws that addressed one of the four most important problems in each legislative period. The policy response to national concerns shows a general pattern of deterioration leading up to collapse. The total number of laws that dealt with important problems increased in the 1970s and through the Lusinchi administration (1984–89), but then dropped off markedly in the late 1980s and early 1990s. Only three laws

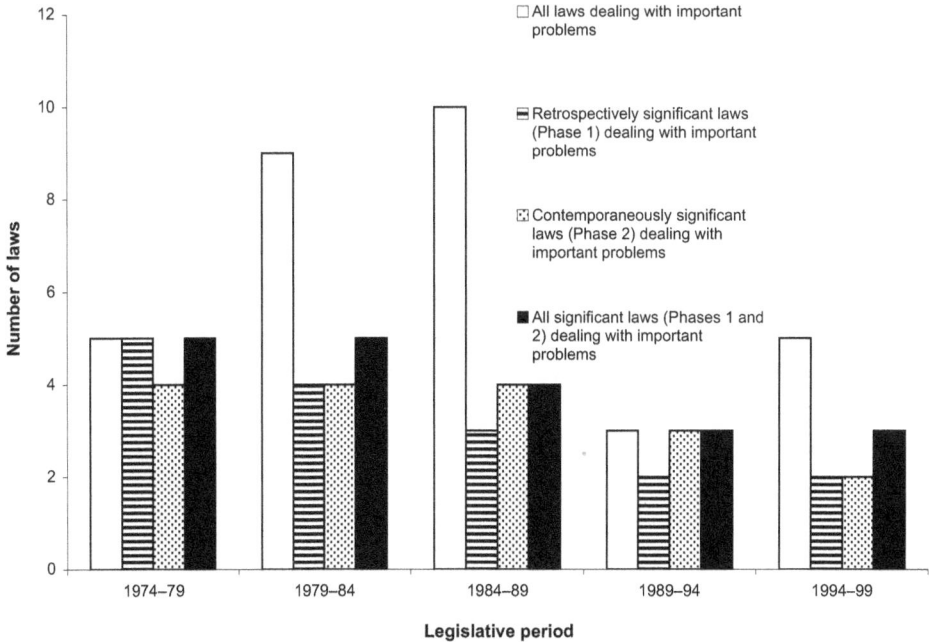

Fig. 5.2 Number of laws addressing important problems, 1974–99

Source: Author's analysis of legislative output, news coverage in *El Nacional,* and public opinion data from about one hundred surveys conducted by various firms.

addressing important problems were passed during the term spanning from 1989 to 1994.

Major legislation in these policy areas also decayed. Retrospectively significant legislation addressing pressing issues declined almost monotonically. In the first Pérez administration (1974–79), parties in government passed five retrospectively significant laws dealing with important problems, but in each of the two terms preceding collapse, only two such laws were enacted. Responsive legislation that was contemporaneously significant also saw a marked decline from its 1970s levels, when the party system was at its peak. The measure combining retrospectively and contemporaneously significant laws shows the same pattern. Responsive, influential legislation was at a high when the party system crested from 1974 to 1984, and then it deteriorated beginning in the late 1980s and continuing through the system's 1998 collapse.

Fig. 5.3 provides more evidence of decaying responsiveness. The figure displays the proportion of all enacted laws dealing with important problems, depicting a pattern of decline from one term to the next, with a notable drop-off in the late 1980s and early 1990s. The most dramatic decline occurs in all laws addressing important issues. At the system's height from 1974 through 1984, a total of 300 laws were passed by Congress and signed by the president, of which 4.7 percent responded to important problems. In the last two legislative terms before the system's collapse, 378 laws were enacted, but only 2.1 percent dealt with significant concerns.[9]

The three measures of significant legislation addressing important problems also show a steady decline in responsiveness. The measure incorporating both retrospectively and contemporaneously significant laws shows the steepest decline. The share of all laws that were significant pieces of legislation (Phases 1 and 2) and responded to pressing concerns was reduced by more than half between the first Pérez administration, beginning in 1974, and the second Caldera administration, ending in 1999. This constituted a drop from 3.6 percent to 1.4 percent. Deteriorating responsiveness is also evident in the two phases separately.

9. While one possible explanation for unresponsiveness could be declining majorities in the legislature, in practice this argument does not fit the data. First of all, we see here that overall productivity actually increased between the 1970s and the 1990s, suggesting that lawmaking was not more difficult in later periods. Instead, the legislature simply did not act on issues of importance. Secondly, while policy responsiveness decayed considerably beginning in the late 1980s, the share of seats held by the president's party did not show a pattern of decline until the 1993 elections. In fact, AD had a larger seat share from 1984 to 1994 than COPEI had under Herrera (1979–84), indicating that coordinating amid declining majorities was not the main impediment to responsiveness.

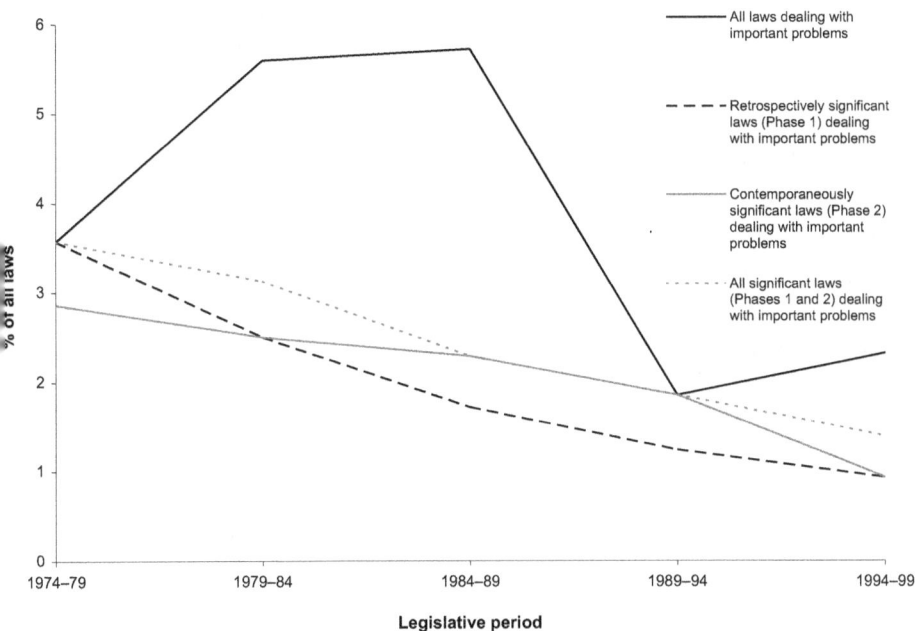

Fig. 5.3   Percentage of all laws addressing important problems, 1974–99

Source: Author's analysis of legislative output, news coverage in *El Nacional,* and public opinion data from about one hundred surveys conducted by various firms.

The decline in policy addressing important issues is particularly stark in light of the enormous challenges facing Venezuela in the 1990s. Problems like inflation, unemployment, and crime placed real pressure on the parties in government to respond to citizens' concerns, but they "had no answer for the people; there was no response to their problems" (Interview 67). In the face of these mounting problems, policy responsiveness took a turn for the worse, producing a widening gap between calls for action and the parties' response.

Instead of addressing economic and social concerns, the parties restructured government. As responsiveness to tangible problems like inflation and crime declined, parties in Congress shifted their focus to issues concerning decentralization and reorganization. From 1974 to 1984, only about 1 percent of all laws and 2 percent of important laws dealt with government restructuring, but in the decade preceding collapse, 7 percent of legislative output and 14 percent of significant lawmaking was dedicated to such reorganizations. Producing policy was clearly possible in the 1990s. But rather than developing solutions for serious and immediate issues, the parties focused on matters that served little direct purpose in resolving the terrible crisis conditions that constituted reality for most people.[10] A former COPEI president captured the problem with this dynamic: "The people just want answers to their problems. That is what matters most to the people. . . . We should have focused on resolving those [economic] problems first and then worked on other [organizational changes] later" (Interview 44). But the parties produced little policy dealing with important problems, and responsiveness decayed.

Party Responsiveness Outside the Legislature?

Of course, my approach to assessing responsiveness by analyzing legislation does not consider policies enacted unilaterally by the executive, such as the neoliberal policies that Pérez and his technocrats implemented without party support at the outset of his second term. Parts of this agenda, like reducing or eliminating subsidies and price controls and restructuring the tariff system, are not reflected in legislative output. But although Pérez embraced market reforms, he convinced neither party elites nor the Venezuelan people that the policies would work, and there was widespread resentment about the neoliberal measures among the public and members of Pérez's own party (Corrales 2002; various interviews).

People's rejection of the reforms was most evident in the 1989 Caracazo and was also manifested in the findings of numerous surveys, which at best showed only modest support and mostly indicated outright opposition to neoliberalism (Corrales 2002, 55). Pérez was well aware of the unpopularity of the reforms, but he proceeded with his agenda, albeit in a slightly scaled-back form. Perhaps the people could have forgiven Pérez for his policy reversal and for the painful austerity had he been successful. But the policies were largely ineffective. There was a brief reprieve from inflation from 1990 to 1993, but even then it remained higher than in the 1970s and early 1980s, and prices escalated again in 1994.[11] Furthermore, wages continued the downward trend they had maintained since the 1980s. More than half the population languished in poverty, and informality continued to increase.

---

10. Also, as I explore in chapter 7, the reorganizing that preoccupied legislative output in the 1990s had the unintended consequence of undermining clientelist linkage.

11. It is interesting to note that crime, the third most important problem identified by citizens during the Pérez/Velásquez term, also increased. It has been forcefully argued that rising crime rates are an endemic problem associated with the implementation of neoliberal policy reforms (Portes and Hoffman 2003).

Although the reforms had some macroeconomic success, the benefits did not reach ordinary people. So while Pérez may have envisioned his program as an economic solution, the people did not see his actions as responsiveness but rather as contradicting the policies and outcomes they desired.

Furthermore, even if we consider the executive's neoliberal reforms as denoting some sort of responsiveness, it was a response outside the parties. Pérez's own AD, which controlled the legislature, had essentially no role in developing the reform package, and while portions of COPEI supported the policies, the party as a whole was divided over the issue and likewise played no formal role in their development or implementation (Interviews 36, 39, 55, 58). Within AD, Pérez's policies were supported by some in the younger generation. But the old guard that controlled the party apparatus opposed the policies and resented Pérez for excluding them from his decision making. They used the party to impede his efforts whenever possible, while not offering any alternatives (Interviews 38, 42, 48, 49, 54, 56, 58, 62). Congress, the parties' main venue for policy influence, was not supportive of Pérez's policies and instead delayed the reforms. Most of the measures were enacted without legislative backing, and when Congress did appear to enact neoliberal laws, they tended to be pale reflections of what the administration was already doing without legislative support (Naím 1993; G. Torres 2000). Where he was able to reform, Pérez acted unilaterally as president, with no party collaboration. Therefore, even if the neoliberal agenda could be viewed as responsiveness to national problems despite citizens' objections to it, the reforms were not enacted or even supported by the party organizations, accentuating the fact that these efforts did not offer party-based policy linkage.[12]

While the executive branch made some unilateral efforts to respond to important issues, albeit through highly unpopular measures, the response provided by the party organizations was incomplete and insufficient. As a former president observed, "[AD and COPEI] forgot that they were *social* democratic and *social* Christian. . . . There were many studies conducted [about economic and social problems], but the results stayed in notebooks. The parties did not act on the problems [of the people]" (Interview 38; emphasis by interviewee). While opposing Pérez's reforms and obstructing his agenda, AD failed to promote alternative solutions to the country's

12. Caldera also resorted to neoliberalism in the late 1990s. The same logic that discounts Pérez's actions as providing party-based policy linkage applies to Caldera's effort, because neoliberalism remained unpopular, making the reforms a perverse form of responsiveness. Also like Pérez, Caldera was a man without a party, although Caldera worked in concert, rather than at odds, with the parties in the legislature, allowing his agenda to be more effectively captured in the legislative responsiveness measures.

problems. A past AD secretary general criticized his party's handling of the economic situation: "The response to the economic crisis was a great error by the party. At first, the party did not offer an opinion about the crisis, and then when the party did offer its opinion, the party confronted the government, but the president always wins [in such confrontations]. CAP [Pérez] informed us of what he was doing with the policies, and we talked about it. But it was purely discourse without action. The party did nothing" (Interview 51). The parties made few attempts to address the crisis, leaving the country floundering. They were aware of people's concerns, but they did not step up efforts to address them. In fact, legislative activity in critical policy areas actually declined. Although policy may not have entirely resolved the crisis, if people had observed the parties working on their behalf, they may have been more willing to extend them grace. Instead, frustration with unresponsiveness grew.

Citizen Assessments of Responsiveness

Survey data unmistakably indicate that Venezuelans recognized this decay of policy responsiveness and were increasingly upset by the parties' inaction. A 1993 survey asked Venezuelans three questions concerning the parties' responsiveness, and most respondents did not think that government listened to or addressed their concerns (table 5.2). The 1993 data are troubling, particularly when compared to similar questions asked at the party system's height. In 1973, 73 percent of respondents thought that elections made government pay attention to the people, and in 1983, about 66 percent agreed with this statement.[13] But by 1993, only 22 percent felt elections promoted accountability, a 44-point drop. Also in 1983, 46 percent of those surveyed agreed that elected officials paid attention to people after elections, but ten years later, less than 15 percent thought members of Congress paid the people at least some attention once elected.

Venezuelans also felt that the parties ignored the country's problems. Surveys conducted by Consultores 21 in the decade preceding the system's collapse asked people whether they thought that the parties were working to resolve the nation's concerns, paralleling the legislative responsiveness analysis above.[14] Fig. 5.4 displays the annual percentage of respondents who

13. Source: Baloyra 1973, Batoba 1983.
14. Consultores 21 surveys are national urban samples. Each survey has a sample size near 1,500. The question was worded, "¿Cuánto cree que están trabajando los partidos políticos para resolver los principales problemas del país: están trabajando mucho, algo, poco o nada?"

Table 5.2 Citizen evaluations of responsiveness, 1993

Survey question	Response	N	%
How much attention do members of Congress pay to people once elected?	Much	40	2.1
	Some	224	12.0
	A little	604	32.4
	None	998	53.5
	Total	1866	100.0
Do you think elections make government pay more attention to the people?	Yes	409	22.3
	No	1428	77.7
	Total	1837	100.0
Does government listen to the people?	Much	69	3.6
	Some	290	15.2
	A little	487	25.6
	Not at all	1059	55.6
	Total	1905	100.0

Source: Author's calculations based on data from the Universidad Simón Bolívar's Banco de Datos Poblacionales and José Vicente Carrasquero.

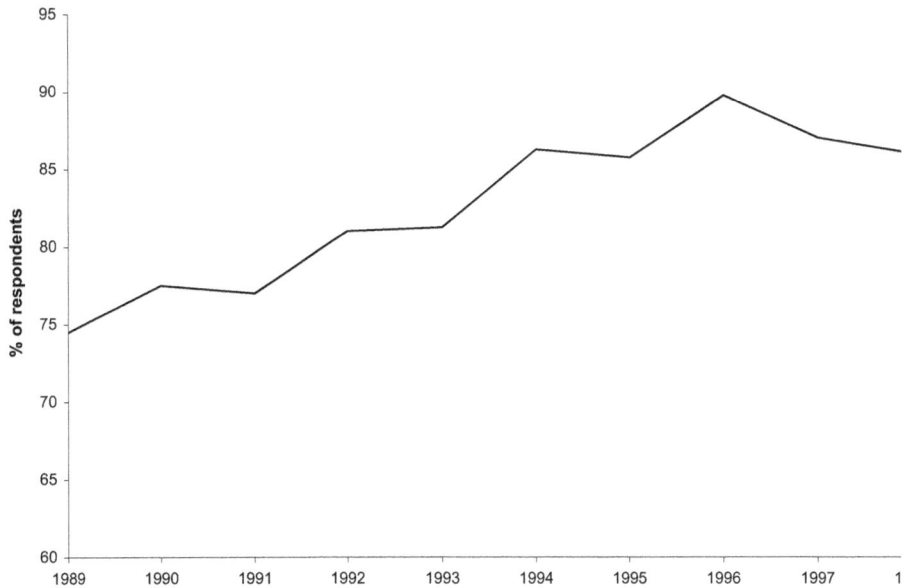

Fig. 5.4 Survey respondents who did not think parties worked to solve Venezuela's problems

Source: Survey data from Consultores 21.

answered that the parties were working very little or not at all to accomplish this. In 1989, about 75 percent thought the parties were doing very little or nothing, marking a significant increase over 1983, when 56 percent negatively evaluated politicians' efforts to address national concerns. Moreover, frustration with failed responsiveness increased steadily throughout the 1990s, deepening to such an extent that by the time of collapse, dissatisfaction with the parties' performance was nearly unanimous. This displeasure, with policy activity generally and with the parties specifically, mirrors the absence of responsiveness observed in the legislative activity analysis. Thus, by the end of the period, the parties were doing very little to confront the country's problems, and frustrated Venezuelans repudiated the parties for neglecting their concerns.

CONSTRAINTS HINDERING POLICY RESPONSIVENESS

In the face of increased pressures from the escalating crisis, policy responsiveness by the parties in power deteriorated during the late 1980s and 1990s. Why did the parties neglect programmatic answers to the crisis even as discontent swelled? The answer lies in the nature of the crisis and the limits on adaptation imposed by a conflict between international constraints and the parties' ideological traditions and established policy patterns.

In part, the crisis itself, which involved the exhaustion of the old development model, undermined the viability of existing policy patterns. Throughout the 1980s, there were signs of economic deterioration. On 8 February 1983, which came to be known as Viernes Negro (Black Friday), the bolívar was devalued from its long-standing exchange rate of 4.3 Bs. to the U.S. dollar, and over the next fifteen years, the nonpreferential exchange rate fell to about 34 Bs. to the dollar. Following initial devaluation, Venezuela entered an extended period of decline characterized by stagnation, heavy foreign debt burdens, and declining oil revenues (Coppedge 1994a; Karl 1997). While some moderate growth occurred in the mid- to late 1980s, inflation and unemployment increased simultaneously (Gómez Calcaño and López Maya 1990). This economic decay heightened pressures on the parties to correct the deteriorating quality of life and other pressing economic and social issues. But at the same time, rising debt obligations and declining revenue placed fiscal limitations on the state, making it difficult to find solutions to ever more complicated problems. Additionally, between 1983 and 1986, the price of oil dropped from $29 to $13.5 per barrel and remained low through the

1990s (OPEC 2003), seriously destabilizing the country's financial situation. Old political strategies based on "sowing the petroleum" were no longer adequate and certainly could not be employed to extract the country from the crisis. Fiscal constraints removed easy answers from the range of options and made policy innovation both necessary and challenging, meaning that the parties in government had less capacity to address the mounting problems (Interview 59).

At the same time that crisis conditions intensified, the parties encountered considerable constraints on policy making, limiting their latitude in redressing the country's ills. As the crisis emerged and other Latin American countries began to sign IMF agreements in the first half of the 1980s, Venezuela initially maintained relative autonomy (Naím 1993), and Lusinchi was able to avoid implementing market-based reforms (Coppedge 1994a; Williamson 1990). However, with the stagnation and decline of oil prices, the downturn became a sustained crisis by the end of the 1980s. When Carlos Andrés Pérez returned to the presidency in 1989, international reserves were depleted, the fiscal deficit was significant, and foreign debt payments became almost insurmountable as they absorbed nearly 50 percent of export income, creating a balance of payments crisis (World Bank, various years). Aside from a slight reprieve in 1992 and 1993, the crisis and its negative consequences persisted over the next decade. As the crisis deepened, external factors, namely the international financial community's consensus in favor of neoliberal solutions to the debt crisis, played an increasingly salient role in domestic policy making. In this context, Pérez signed an IMF agreement, pledging himself to a "rigidly defined" neoliberal adjustment program (Gómez Calcaño 1998, 216). Then, in 1996, Caldera also succumbed to the pressures of escalating inflation and international policy directives and signed a letter of intent that obligated the country to adhere to a comprehensive reform package in exchange for new IMF and IDB loans. International financial institutions' neoliberal pressures and the IMF agreements restricted policy autonomy considerably.

Moreover, these international constraints limited policy making to options that were generally unpopular and that contradicted established policy patterns. Economic policy in Venezuela traditionally followed state-led development strategies, but as the crisis intensified, international constraints removed these customary policy devices from the parties' arsenal. Thus, available responses were largely limited to options that conflicted with the parties' ideological identities. This conflict was particularly severe for AD, which was the largest party in Congress throughout the 1990s and held considerable influence over legislative activity under the Pérez and Caldera governments. But even COPEI's traditional Christian democratic ideology was threatened by policies advocating removal of the state from the business of public welfare provision. Market reforms violated the ideological positions of the statist parties and required them to conform to conditions imposed by the same international institutions the parties had once vilified. This conflict with their ideals posed problems for party leaders who viewed such reforms as embarrassing and as having the potential to weaken the party and alienate supporters (Corrales 2002, 102; Interviews 45, 47, 48, 50). While this conflict led the executive to succumb to neoliberalism, it caused the parties themselves to be largely unresponsive, only occasionally becoming reluctant neoliberals.

If the theory concerning the interplay between crisis and constraint is correct, the constellations of economic challenges and international pressures that conflicted with parties' ideological identities should have produced specific predictable patterns of party (un)responsiveness. In particular, as the crisis materialized in the mid-1980s, domestic decision makers remained largely insulated from international constraints as stockpiled reserves cushioned the economy's fall. In this environment, party leaders' primary motivation was to shield their organizations from difficult or risky decisions, as they hoped to endure the crisis. We would therefore expect to see some policy responses that were consistent with established strategies and ideologies, but no dramatic or potentially risky innovations. However, as both the crisis and international constraints deepened in the 1990s, constricting the parties' range of options, I anticipate the onset of programmatic indecision and paralysis and, therefore, limited policy responses to pressing problems. The following sections trace how these expectations played out from the beginning of the crisis under Lusinchi through the last days of the party system under Caldera.

Staying the Course Under Lusinchi

In the mid to late-1980s, as the economy began decaying, Venezuela remained relatively free from international constraints, allowing the parties to maintain traditional oil-based development, albeit in a scaled-back form. As one COPEI leader reflected, "There was an economic crisis, but because there was still money, [the parties] just kept on doing what we had always done" (Interview 46). For instance, efforts to combat the rising cost of living focused on alleviating the effects of inflation through programs like transportation bonuses and worker dining privileges and by centrally controlling prices, rather than combating inflation itself (Kelly 2005). As external constraints remained limited, Lusinchi and an AD-led Congress did not take innovative steps to address the situation but instead stayed true to the party's statist legacy and acted within established policy-making patterns, as they sought to endure, but not actively resolve, the crisis.

Furthermore, as demonstrated above in figs. 5.2 and 5.3, although *overall* legislative output addressing serious problems remained relatively high under Lusinchi, *significant* policy activity in these areas decayed steadily throughout the 1980s. Instead of confronting economic challenges with creative policies, Lusinchi and AD relied on stockpiled international reserves to insulate themselves from the gathering storm and avoid controversial decisions (Interviews 11, 30, 58). AD operated "within the existing administrative framework of large public works projects and social programs that Venezuela had always had. [The party employed] the same programs and approaches as always. . . . There were no changes in direction; [the party leadership] failed to introduce changes" (Interview 56). This strategy of minor adjustments rather than significant policy actions may have been adequate to weather an ordinary downturn, but it could not counter the increasingly monumental issues of the time.

The history of oil windfalls created by petroleum boom and bust cycles provided incentives to implement only minor policy adjustments and wait out the crisis. During good times, the country's oil wealth insulated political leaders from having to make difficult decisions and enabled the accommodation of a variety of competing constituencies (Karl 1997; Kelley 1986; Myers 1986). When faced with economic downturns, instead of raising revenue through taxation, the parties in government typically turned to foreign borrowing, muddling through until the next boom (Interviews 58, 80; Karl 1997). In interviews, party leaders of various stripes acknowledged the influence of this oil mindset in undermining their incentives to innovate and head off the crisis before it escalated. An AD policy advisor explained the dynamic most vividly: "Petroleum was like a relaxant, softening the stress and exigency of the situation. There was the idea that [AD] would just wait a while and then continue down the same path" (Interview 14). Rather than make hard choices, the parties hoped that oil prices would rebound and rejuvenate the economy (Interviews 15, 54). As long as Venezuela was shielded from international influence, the parties were able to introduce slight policy modifications that helped alleviate the negative effects of the crisis on ordinary citizens, but they did not engage in significant innovations.

Contradictory Constraints and
Party Immobility Under Pérez and Caldera

However, as the cushion of international reserves disappeared and the depth of the crisis became apparent in the late 1980s, opportunities for heterodox solutions closed. Now the parties had to confront the challenges presented by the crisis within the severe constraints imposed by international financial institutions.

By the late 1980s, the parties faced contradictory incentives. Their statist legacies encouraged party leaders to stay the course of oil-led development and preserve domestic constituencies. But as the economy deteriorated, international pressures for market reforms intensified. "The parties found themselves trapped between two major movements: one was the so-called neoliberal movement, and the other was the movement promoting state-led growth. [But] the parties offered nothing, neither one" (Interview 14).

AD's behavior clearly illustrates how the confluence of these contradictory pressures greatly constrained maneuverability, creating uncertainty and inaction. Initially, AD kept its distance from Pérez's neoliberal agenda but guardedly allowed him latitude to enact reform, even though his policies contradicted party ideology and policy tradition. However, after AD lost considerable ground in the December 1989 regional elections, traditionalists (*ortodoxos*) began to gain the upper hand in the party power struggle, and from that point forward, AD became a de facto congressional opposition to Pérez (Corrales 2002, 122–24; various interviews). But disoriented by conflicting constraints and lacking visionary leadership, AD offered no alternative strategy for confronting the crisis (Interviews 42, 48, 49, 50, 51, 56). Although the party sponsored two separate efforts at ideological renewal in the 1990s, each was motivated by one of the competing policy movements, and they produced contradictory results. One effort, led by Carlos Canache Mata, an AD party operative and CEN member, essentially recommended staying the party's traditional course of action (AD 1993). The second, led by Andrés Stambouli, an academic consultant who had been recruited by Luis Alfaro Ucero to lead AD's ideological foundation, proposed a moderated neoliberal strategy (AD 1994; FRL 1997). However, the documents produced under each effort made little impact, as the party remained frozen and unresponsive (Interviews 47, 50, 56). Ultimately, AD opposed Pérez's neoliberal strategy and allowed him to be forced from office before his term ended, but the orthodox faction controlling the party did not offer an alternative approach to address escalating problems.

By the time new national elections were held in December 1993, AD had demonstrated thorough incompetence in dealing with the crisis, and the electoral result was abysmal. The party nominated former Caracas mayor Claudio Fermín for the presidency. Fermín, who had affiliated with the party's pro-Pérez wing and developed wide personal appeal as mayor, was given little campaign support from the party and won only 24 percent of the vote (Interviews 45, 48, 49, 50, 56). AD congressional candidates fared only slightly better, winning 55 seats in the Chamber of Deputies (27 percent) and 16 in the Senate (32 percent). COPEI also struggled in the 1993 elections and subsequently controlled only 26 percent of seats in the Chamber and 28 percent in the Senate. Together, the two major parties clung to a slim majority in both chambers, giving them one more chance at legislative responsiveness. It would prove to be their last.

In the final term before collapse in 1998, the parties faced continued demands that they confront the deepening crisis, even as international financial institutions sustained pressure for market reforms. Entangled in these constraints, the parties provided little legislative responsiveness. No laws addressing the three most important problems—cost of living, crime, and unemployment—were passed in the first two years of the legislative term. As the parties saw their hold on power slipping away, they began sacrificing their ideological commitments for access to clientelist resources. So in the last three years of Caldera's term, AD supported his neoliberal shift in exchange for access to the state (Interviews 41, 45, 47, 82).[15] The party succumbed to external pressures and to the organization's exigent financial circumstances, abandoning its statist ideals (Interviews 37, 47, 48, 49, 50, 56). Even when AD finally accepted the international neoliberal consensus and helped Caldera enact his reforms in the late 1990s, policy responsiveness remained limited, and the few attempts that were made proved widely unpopular. International constraints that contradicted domestic policy patterns undermined the parties' capacity to address the crisis. As a result, the final years before the system's collapse saw policy paralysis and decay rather than the innovation that was desperately needed.

In the 1980s, AD controlled the legislature and maintained its legacy of state-led development. Without strong international constraints, the boom-bust cycle of the oil economy, together with the party's statist legacy, encouraged a wait-and-see attitude about the crisis, resulting in minor policy adjustments but few significant steps toward resolving the country's

15. See chapter 7 for more details on the AD-Caldera alliance.

problems. When Pérez took office in 1989, the economy had deteriorated to a point where external pressures demanded neoliberal reform, but AD's legacy provided a countervailing motivation that drove the party to remain true to its developmentalist tradition. As a result, the party became a de facto opposition without offering any alternative policy response. Policy stagnated, and the crisis continued to fester. By the time Caldera took office in 1994, AD's capacity to address policy concerns had been largely discredited, and the parties in the legislature continued to face the same conflicting constraints as they had under the Pérez government. In the face of contradictory international and domestic pressures, legislative responsiveness further deteriorated despite the crisis. The parties certainly could not point to their record of achieving policy responsiveness as a basis for attracting votes, and this form of programmatic linkage decayed.

LACK OF VIABLE MEANINGFUL ALTERNATIVES

Thus, parties in government failed to address pressing concerns and experienced programmatic weakening. But of the two major parties, only AD controlled the legislature (and the executive) in the late 1980s and 1990s, and only AD was directly implicated by the failure to provide effective solutions to the mounting crisis. Policy responsiveness was not successful, but programmatic linkage could have been achieved if other system parties had provided ideological options distinct from AD's failed governance.

The opportunity for offering a viable and meaningful alternative to the status quo came via COPEI. As AD's primary competitor in the 2.5-party system, COPEI typically provided center-right opposition to AD and was the only other traditional party with a reasonable chance of controlling government. Also, because AD and COPEI were the system's two major parties and the failure of both was a defining element of collapse, the survival of one of them as a major player could have saved the system, whereas their joint decay put the entire system at risk. As long as AD and COPEI continued to furnish meaningful and viable options, programmatic linkage could be sustained at the system level, even if one party failed to provide policy responsiveness. But if the two parties ceased to provide programmatic alternatives, voters would be left without viable choices, threatening linkage at the system level. I argue that this is precisely what occurred. The disappearance of ideological differences between the two parties, created by interparty collusion, eliminated meaningful alternatives, and thereby undermined the programmatic appeal of the entire system.

While smaller parties, such as MAS and La Causa R (LCR), may have provided alternatives to AD, they were not major components of the system and were not generally considered viable governing parties on the national stage. Because they did not hold the same pivotal positions in the system as AD and COPEI, their ability to fill the system-level gap in programmatic linkage was limited. Furthermore, MAS, the most significant of the non-major parties, was an important part of the coalition that brought Caldera to power and supported his policies. As a result of collaborating in the failed Caldera government, MAS also sacrificed its capacity to offer an alternative to the status quo. But declining support for smaller parties, while unfortunate for the parties themselves, did not pose the same sort of threat to the system as the deterioration of AD and COPEI. Given the centrality of these two major parties in shaping the traditional system, I focus most of my discussion concerning the fading of viable meaningful alternatives on the interactions between these two parties.

Ideological Convergence

In part, COPEI's programmatic discrediting may have stemmed from voters' inability to distinguish the party from its founder, Caldera. The feud between Caldera and COPEI developed in the late 1980s when the party ran Eduardo Fernández, a former Caldera protégé, as its 1988 presidential candidate. Fernández had captured the party machinery and won the nomination over Caldera, provoking the former president's ire as he distanced himself from the party and refused to campaign for Fernández (Interviews 39, 58). Other leaders contributed to the feud by pushing Caldera to the party's periphery (Interviews 39, 66, 73). When he finally abandoned COPEI and ran as an independent in 1993, he actively undermined the party. Both the fact and the context of Caldera's departure weakened COPEI's appeal (Interview 62; Morgan 2007).

Furthermore, while this rift lured COPEI voters away from the party, some could not fathom a Caldera candidacy separate from COPEI and continued to see their vote for Caldera as a vote for his former party (Interviews 37, 39). As one COPEI leader explained, "Many people never realized that Caldera had left COPEI. His presidency really hurt the party because it was full of mistakes and those errors were associated with COPEI" (Interview 39). For the many voters who did not grasp the split between Caldera and his old party, COPEI's efforts to distance itself from him only reinforced perceptions of infighting and ineffectiveness (Interviews 46, 79). It is possible, then, that COPEI was partly discredited by the failure of the Caldera government, even though the party organization held no responsibility for or influence in the government's policy-making efforts.[16]

But the conflict and confusion surrounding Caldera's separation from COPEI is an incomplete explanation of the party's loss of programmatic credibility. More significantly, Venezuelans increasingly failed to discern any meaningful distinction between COPEI and AD. As policy responsiveness failed, voters could not find a programmatic alternative to the status quo. Instead of meaningful options, people saw similar policy stances and collusion between the parties. This lack of differentiation, which was created by governing agreements between the parties, resulted in the joint discrediting of AD and COPEI and the deterioration of programmatic linkage in the system as a whole.

Historically, the party system had offered some meaningful ideological options, but in the 1990s, these distinctions evaporated. Public opinion polls conducted in 1973, 1983, and 1998 provide snapshots of how Venezuelans' perceptions of the ideological space in the party system changed over time.[17] Each survey asked respondents to place themselves and the major parties or their presidential candidates on a left-right scale. In 1973, respondents perceived significant ideological differences in the offerings of AD and COPEI. When asked to identify the ideological location of each party's presidential candidate, Venezuelans recognized meaningful differences. They placed adeco Carlos Andrés Pérez significantly to the left of copeyano Lorenzo Fernández on a three-point ideology scale, with Pérez receiving an average placement of 2.29 and Fernández being located at 2.53.[18] In 1983, this structure remained intact, and respondents continued to locate AD significantly to the left of COPEI. AD received exactly the same placement in 1983 as its presidential candidate had ten years earlier; COPEI's position was also consistent over time, with a mean placement of 2.54.[19] Thus, in the 1970s and 1980s, the ideological locations of the two parties were statistically and substantively different, with the gap between them representing about 12 percent of the scale. But by 1998, people no longer saw any differences in the ideological placements of the two parties. Respondents located

16. Several ministers in Caldera's government, such as Hilarión Cardozo and Julio Sosa, had strong ties to COPEI, but they served in the cabinet as independents or members of Convergencia, not COPEI representatives.

17. Sources: Baloyra 1973, Batoba 1983, and RedPol98.

18. Two left candidates, José Vicente Rangel and Jesús Paz Galarraga, were placed at 1.25, significantly left of Pérez.

19. MAS, the primary left party at this time, was placed to the left of AD at 1.39.

both at exactly 6.5 on a scale ranging from 1 (left) to 10 (right). "In the end, AD and COPEI were exactly the same" (Interview 35).

The 1973 and 1998 surveys also asked respondents to identify their own ideological placement and partisan affiliation. There were notable ideological differences between AD and COPEI supporters in 1973, with adecos situating themselves significantly to the left of copeyanos. However, these differences had evaporated by 1998. To examine changes in partisans' ideological self-placement over time, I created standardized ideology scales ranging from 0 to 1 for 1973 and 1998. While there was no statistically significant change in copeyanos' position between 1973 and 1998, adecos shifted significantly to the right over this twenty-five-year period. In 1973, adecos averaged a score of 0.63 on the 0-to-1 ideology scale, but by 1998 they had shifted right, to an average position of 0.76. At the time of the system's collapse, neither the parties nor their supporters were ideologically distinguishable from each other.

The disappearance of distinctions between the two parties can be traced in large part to the increasing conservatism of AD. In the late 1990s, the party abandoned its ideological identity in exchange for clientelist resources from the Caldera government and thus sacrificed its credibility as a party of the center-left. In reality, both parties' ideologies seemed to fluctuate somewhat during the 1990s. But COPEI only vacillated marginally within the right part of the spectrum, between Christian democracy and neoliberalism, whereas the prevailing rightward shift of AD raised serious questions about the party's commitment to its center-left legacy. COPEI, under the leadership of Eduardo Fernández, embraced market reforms and supported Pérez's general policy direction in the early 1990s (Interviews 30, 49, 59, 89). The party's neoliberal tilt continued with the nomination of its 1993 presidential candidate, Oswaldo Álvarez Paz, who advocated pro-market reforms in the campaign (Interviews 55, 79). But after its poor showing in the 1993 elections, COPEI abandoned the neoliberal turn that had occurred under Fernández and Álvarez Paz. Instead power returned to former President Luis Herrera, a member of the party's more populist wing, who restored COPEI to its Christian democratic roots. In practice, COPEI did not change its ideological orientation significantly in the 1980s and 1990s, but simply made modifications to its general center-right orientation as power shifted between party factions (Coppedge 1999).

In AD, change was clearly afoot in the 1990s. In the first part of the decade, Pérez's reforms and the presidential candidacy of the pro-market Claudio Fermín created the public perception that the party was breaking with its statist legacy (Interviews 47, 48, 50, 52, 53). Although the party organization itself opposed Pérez's policies and failed to provide financial or logistical support to what it considered to be Fermín's doomed candidacy, the public words and actions of these highly recognizable leaders created the perception that the party was moving right (Interviews 45, 48, 49, 50). By the late 1990s, this perception became reality. Luis Alfaro Ucero's orthodox faction, which had been staunchly statist, controlled the party apparatus during the Caldera government and acquiesced to neoliberal reforms in exchange for resources for the AD machine (Interviews 47, 48, 56, 59). As a result of the ascendancy of pragmatism over ideology, the party's policy agenda drifted right (Interview 52). By 1998, an AD president had implemented market reforms, an AD presidential candidate had campaigned on a neoliberal platform, and the party organization and its top leadership had supported the neoliberal reform program of an old adversary. Voters were not misguided in sensing that AD had abdicated its position as a center-left party (Interviews 50, 52, 56).

When asked directly, few Venezuelans responded that the parties provided them with meaningful choices in the 1990s. They did not think opposing parties would pursue distinct policies. According to a 1993 survey conducted by IVAD, 70 percent of respondents believed that AD and COPEI were basically the same, with only very small differences, unmistakably indicating that the traditional party system did not provide meaningful options.

Interparty Agreements Obscure Ideological Distinctions

External pressures from international financial institutions constrained policy options, pushing all the parties in a neoliberal direction regardless of their ideological legacy. But these international factors alone cannot explain why AD opposed neoliberal policies when advocated by a member of its own party and then provided support for similar policies when put forward by an old opponent, nor can they account for the complete lack of differentiation between the parties by the late 1990s. To understand this convergence, we must look to institutional patterns that pushed parties into alliances, which, when combined with the crisis and international constraints, eventually caused all the traditional parties to accept a rightist policy orientation. These alliances eroded ideological distance between parties and undermined the system's programmatic structure. As the theory anticipates, interparty agreements produced the mutual discrediting of all the major parties, extending programmatic deterioration to the system level.

Two major features of the Venezuelan system created strong incentives for party leaders to form interparty alliances: historical patterns of pact making and intraparty fragmentation. Since the democratic transition, when the parties signed the Pact of Punto Fijo, interparty agreements had been a staple of Venezuelan politics. Pacts were often used to build consensus and were an especially common strategy during crisis (Borges Arcila 1996; Kada 2003; Karl 1997). For example, major efforts to forge interparty agreements were made in the fragile transition period and after the 1983 Black Friday devaluation (Lyne 2008, 113; Navarro 1995). Using interparty agreements as a mechanism for building consensus and stabilizing politics in times of uncertainty became a touchstone to which traditional elites returned in the crisis years of the 1990s. The parties made several attempts to create formal pacts, including the 1990 Pact for Reform and the 1992 Acuerdo Nacional (de los Ángeles Fernández 2001; Navarro 1995). Even as the parties began to crumble, their leaders continued to pursue pact making as a strategy for sustaining the system. For instance, AD leader Luis Alfaro Ucero sought to construct a consensus in support of democracy that would have backed a national unity candidate for the presidency in 1998 (Interviews 14, 48, 49). While these attempts to return to pacted governance did not achieve the same success as earlier pacts in constructing a *formal* consensus to support the parties and party-dominated democracy (de los Ángeles Fernández 2001), they do suggest a pattern of alliance building that persisted through the 1990s and continued to play a pivotal role in structuring politics via more informal channels.

Despite the short-lived attempts to create formal pacts in the 1990s, informal agreements nevertheless dominated politics in the decade leading up to collapse. "There were groups of identification between AD and COPEI. Adecos and copeyanos who supported [neoliberal] policy in some ways had stronger ties to each other than to those sectors of their own parties who opposed the policies and vice versa" (Interview 55). Pérez received more support for his neoliberal project from sectors of COPEI than from his own party (Interviews 39, 59). COPEI Secretary General Eduardo Fernández, presidential candidate Oswaldo Álvarez Paz, and their allies worked closely with the Pérez administration (Interviews 25, 30, 46, 55, 89), and many of the technical experts who populated Pérez's cabinet had stronger ties to COPEI than to AD (Interviews 2, 39, 42, 55, 56, 62).

Old guard leaders, who opposed the reforms, also reached across party lines, eventually producing the Caldera-Alfaro alliance that monopolized politics in the mid- to late 1990s (Interviews 14, 39, 45, 62, 66). The alliance between AD and longtime rival Caldera obscured any semblance of pro-grammatic structure left in the system. Many people had voted for Caldera precisely because they wanted to be rid of AD, and watching Caldera collaborate with AD violated their intent. The heterodox platform that Caldera initially advocated in 1994 and 1995 did not contradict AD's traditional interventionist stance, but the alliance became extremely problematic when Caldera made his pro-market turn in early 1996. In contrast to AD's militant opposition to Pérez's neoliberal project, the party continued supporting Caldera after this programmatic shift, abandoning its position on the center-left. Alfaro claimed that AD's decision to continue backing Caldera was altruistic—AD was protecting the democratic regime in the face of serious threats, and solidarity in the face of crisis superseded programmatic preferences (Interview 48). The more realistic rationale was that AD obtained much-needed access to power and resources for clientelism in exchange for supporting Caldera (Interviews 48, 49, 56). Regardless of the motivation, the alliance distanced AD from its ideological roots, discredited the party, and eliminated programmatic options from the system.

At the same time, interparty alliances were the norm in Congress. Coalitions shifted often in the last legislative term before the system collapsed; virtually all parties of any import were in alliance with one another at some point and were therefore implicated in failed governance. Initially, AD and COPEI formed an agreement to divide up legislative leadership positions, and together with LCR, they opposed Caldera's early efforts to legislate via decree (Crisp 2000, 180; Koeneke 1998). But by mid-1994, AD withdrew from this alliance and instead backed a pro-Caldera coalition that included Convergencia and MAS. Then, in February 1996, even as MAS party leaders remained important actors in Caldera's cabinet, the MAS congressional delegation withdrew from its coalition with AD and Convergencia and instead joined COPEI and LCR to control Congress as the Triple Alliance. These three parties remained in power into 1997 as part of the Tetra Alliance, which also included Patria Para Todos (PPT) after the division of LCR produced this party (*El Nacional* 1997b). But by the end of 1997, COPEI distanced itself from this group and returned to an agreement with AD. Thus, in the final year before collapse, the two major parties once again controlled legislative power (Koeneke 1998). By the end of the term, the parties that united to pass the September 1998 enabling law, which gave Caldera decree authority, included AD, COPEI, MAS, and Convergencia (*El Nacional* 1998). These alliance patterns created the perception that the parties were not ideologically distinct and implicated them all in failed responsiveness. As a result, every party in the traditional system was caught up in the programmatic deterioration of the 1990s.

Factionalism also pushed elites to form interparty alliances. The internal struggle for power that characterized Venezuelan parties has been well documented (Coppedge 1994a). Under the pressure of economic and social crisis in the 1990s, intraparty tensions increased as party leaders competed over shrinking resource pools and as policy decisions had more profound implications. Rather than addressing the crisis, "the parties were occupied with internal wars and competitions" (Interview 80). The extreme factionalism during the 1990s is evident in the internal dynamics of both AD and COPEI. Opponents of Pérez within his own party contributed to his early departure from office and subsequent criminal prosecution (Interviews 42, 45, 48, 49, 53). Following AD's poor performance in the 1993 elections, the dominant Alfaro-led faction purged the party, forcing out thousands of adecos (Interviews 26, 41, 45, 53, 73). Ironically, Alfaro himself was expelled before the 1998 elections, as his popularity waned and a competing group gained the upper hand. Conflict within COPEI was even more intense. The discord between Fernández and Caldera produced a traumatic rift when Caldera broke from COPEI and formed his own party (Interviews 32, 37, 44, 73, 79).

These divisions produced incentives for competing leaders to look to other parties for allies who might help them gain an edge. Also because of the ideological diversity that proliferated within the ranks of AD and COPEI in the late 1980s and 1990s, elites could sometimes find common ground with members of the opposing party more easily than with their own co-partisans. This was clearly the case for Pérez, who counted on the support of COPEI's Fernández, and for Caldera in the alliances he forged with MAS and AD (Interviews 41, 44, 45, 49).

In addition to generating incentives for interparty alliances, party divisions also caused confusion regarding the ideological positions and programmatic intentions of the parties themselves. Lack of internal consensus obscured efforts to make programmatic appeals, because voters were unsure where the party was truly located along the ideological spectrum. Moreover, voters could not be certain about which of the competing factions, with their distinct visions of society, would control the party apparatus and determine policy. Factionalism weakened distinctions between parties by sending mixed signals to confused voters about the party's programmatic goals.

Thus, internal divisions created uncertainty about the parties' true positions and motivated interparty agreements that undermined the programmatic structure of the system. The Venezuelan legacy of pacted governance also encouraged party elites to forge alliances in the face of crisis, as they hoped to promote the stability that pacts had achieved in the past. But as these agreements proliferated, AD and COPEI, as well as MAS, aligned with each other for part of the decade and thereby created the perception that none of the system parties could provide a meaningful alternative to the status quo. In the end, the lack of distinctiveness between AD and COPEI became so acute that the two parties withdrew their support from their 1998 presidential nominees and backed a single candidate, former copeyano Henrique Salas Römer. This move carried the conflation of the two parties to its logical conclusion, expressing electorally what most Venezuelans readily recognized as a complete lack of programmatic distinction between AD and COPEI.

At the height of the party system, Venezuelans had identified programmatic differences between the two major parties. However, by the 1990s, the space between the parties closed. Historical patterns of pact making and internal party squabbles created incentives for cross-party alliances and obscured the parties' positions. As a result, voters no longer saw the major system parties as providing meaningful programmatic choices.

FAILURE OF PROGRAMMATIC LINKAGE AND PARTY SYSTEM COLLAPSE

In the decade leading up to the collapse of the Venezuelan party system, the parties faced mounting pressures to respond to an economic crisis that stemmed from the exhaustion of the country's oil-led development model. But rather than stepping up responsiveness, parties' legislative activity was increasingly unrelated to citizens' problems. The economic crisis stressed the system, requiring action, but international constraints demanded policies that contradicted the parties' statist inclinations. In this context, the parties in power faced two potentially hazardous options. They could stay the course, deciding that change posed a greater risk than waiting out the crisis. Or they could attempt to adapt to meet the new demands, estimating that the possible benefits of change outweighed the danger. During the late 1980s and early 1990s, the incentives created by AD's ideological legacy and the underlying expectation that an inevitable oil boom would bail them out of the crisis encouraged the traditional elites to stay the course rather than push for significant policy innovation. However, as the crisis intensified, the constraints imposed by international financial institutions escalated, further limiting the parties' options. It was not simply the presence of an economic crisis that caused deteriorating policy responsiveness. Rather, the particular policy demands stemming from the crisis, together with the constraints generated by the international context, placed pressure on the parties in government to engage in policy making that contradicted their ideological legacies, severely restricting the system's latitude in accommodating demands.

Lack of valence responsiveness drove many Venezuelans to seek alternatives to the status quo, but they found no viable options within the traditional system. Throughout the 1990s, interparty agreements implicated all the traditional parties in programmatic failure. Where there had once been clear distinctions between AD and COPEI, Venezuelans no longer perceived any ideological differences. People did not experience responsiveness from the parties in power, nor were they presented with options for alternative leadership within the system. The entire traditional party system, therefore, ceased to offer programmatic linkage to much of the population, and voters could no longer reject the status quo while still supporting the system.

6

SOCIAL TRANSFORMATION AND
FAILING GROUP INCORPORATION

[The traditional party system] excluded millions of Venezuelans [who experienced] lack of opportunity, poverty, and misery. This exclusion today constitutes the primary conflict of Venezuelan society.

—Former MAS president, *interview with author, November 2003*

The previous chapter traced how programmatic representation in the Venezuelan system decayed significantly beginning in the late 1980s. As the parties neglected policy responsiveness and ideological differences vanished, the system needed sound interest incorporation to help preserve linkage. However, this chapter demonstrates that incorporation also decayed in the 1990s. The parties' traditional base, built around the class cleavage, shrank and gave way to previously excluded sectors whose interests and structures challenged those of entrenched groups. As Venezuela endured economic crisis and attempts at neoliberal reform, society transformed dramatically, and the structure of the major class-based cleavage underwent fundamental change. Historically salient groups, like the working class, declined, while typically marginalized groups, like the informal sector, grew.[1] These changes produced the complete restructuring of the dominant cleavage away from the worker-owner divide and toward a cleavage based on differences between the formal and informal sectors. This chapter outlines the major changes in the politically salient cleavage in Venezuelan society, details the threat

1. The informal sector is composed of people "not incorporated into fully commodified, legally regulated working relations, but [who survive] at their margin in a wide variety of subsistence and semi-clandestine economic activities" (Portes and Hoffman 2003, 43).

that the restructuring of this divide posed to the entire party system, and addresses how established organizational patterns and entrenched interests seriously constrained the parties' response to the social transformation.

SOCIAL TRANSFORMATION AND RESTRUCTURING OF THE SALIENT CLEAVAGE

By the late 1980s, Venezuela faced a severe economic crisis. International reserves practically disappeared, inflation mounted, and oil prices failed to recover from their precipitous decline in the middle of the decade. But the parties did not provide an answer to this crisis and neglected programmatic linkage. Typically, relying on close ties to historically influential sectors had been a successful strategy to help carry the parties through the tough times. However, the crisis produced a drastic social transformation that threatened the cleavage structure upon which the system's interest-based linkages had been built, demanding reorientation of incorporation.

Interest incorporation in the old Venezuelan party system was based on the traditional class cleavage. Historically, the most influential groups were those that reflected interests pertaining to their members' positions in the production cycle, namely workers, capital owners, peasants, and middle-class managers. As a whole, the system successfully incorporated the major concerns of the functional groups reflecting the distinct facets of this cleavage, with each group finding representation in the system. In essence, the entire party system was configured to integrate the main interests that composed Venezuelan class structure.

Together, these interests encapsulated a substantial portion of the population at the party system's height in the 1970s and early 1980s. However, the poor, the unemployed, and the informal sector—essentially those without a stable place in the production cycle—did not find incorporating linkage. Because the system was structured to accommodate the traditional class cleavage, it could not easily integrate excluded interests whose very existence called into question the viability of dominant economic and social patterns. But throughout the party system's heyday, the marginalized were few in number and politically insignificant. Their exclusion, therefore, posed no threat to linkage.

However, dramatic changes reconfigured Venezuelan society in the 1990s. These changes did not simply affect the relative size of the groups representing the traditional class cleavage, which were already integrated into the party system. Rather, they constituted a major transformation in the structure of the dominant cleavage. Because this change reconfigured society, such that previously excluded groups grew in size and political relevance, this not only weakened individual parties but threatened the entire structure of incorporation in the system.

In large part, this restructuring was brought on by two major, interrelated economic processes that profoundly reshaped Venezuelan society in the late 1980s and 1990s: (1) economic crisis resulting from the exhaustion of the import-substitution industrialization (ISI) development model based on oil rents and (2) the neoliberal reforms designed to resolve certain aspects of this crisis. All of Latin America suffered under the inflation, debt burdens, and balance of payments crises associated with the end of ISI and then endured escalating unemployment, poverty, and informality brought on by neoliberal adjustments. But "in Venezuela, the contrast between the prosperity and state interventionism of the 1970s and the recession and neoliberalism that subsequently characterized the nation was perhaps more marked than anywhere else on the continent" (Ellner 1996, 89).

These processes had a profound impact on Venezuelan social structure, fragmenting the popular sector between those with stable formal employment and those without work or with uncertain prospects in the informal sector (Portes and Hoffman 2003; K. Roberts 2002b). The inflationary pressures of the crisis caused wages to lag behind prices, increased impoverishment, and exacerbated inequality (K. Roberts 2002b, 6). Then, the neoliberal reform efforts under Pérez's El Gran Viraje and Caldera's Agenda Venezuela led to deindustrialization, reduced the size of the public sector, and undermined the traditional working class (Buxton 1999a; K. Roberts 2003b). Outsourcing, privatizations in major sectors, including telecommunications, ports, steel and airlines, and efforts to shrink the state weakened organized labor and reduced the portion of the workforce located in the public sector (Ellner 2003, 167; K. Roberts 2002b). Structural adjustment policies, which liberalized trade and interest rates, heightened competition from imports and undermined domestic industries in textiles, apparel, vehicle parts, and many small and medium-sized enterprises (Lander 1996, 59). But business owners did not bear the brunt of these adjustment policies; rather, they passed the burden on to their workers, reducing labor costs through the elimination of jobs, labor flexibilization, and the cutting of real wages (Iranzo 1994; Lander 1996). These changes created a "dualization" of the labor market in which a few elite workers in internationally competitive firms retained stable jobs in the formal sector, while many others succumbed to low-skill, low-wage work or fell into informality (Valecillos 1992). Inequality increased and living conditions deteriorated even as social spending declined (Lander 1996; K. Roberts 2002b, 2003b).

Together, these adjustments produced a shift away from agriculture and industry—the parties' traditional bases of support—and toward services (K. Roberts 2003b). Meanwhile, groups typically excluded from incorporating linkages grew, as many workers fell out of the formal sector and into informality and unemployment, weakening class-based organizations and profoundly restructuring society (Ellner 2003; Levitsky 2007; K. Roberts 1998). Table 6.1 tells the story of the dramatic social transformation that occurred between the party system's apex and its decay in the 1990s. Historically incorporated groups, including organized labor, peasants, and the public sector, experienced significant erosion between the system's heyday in the 1980s, when the traditional class cleavage structured society, and its collapse in 1998, when old class divides were no longer salient. At the same time, groups neglected by traditional incorporation strategies, like informal and unemployed workers, expanded.

With the exception of professional and managerial workers, the percentage of the workforce in each of the groups reflecting the traditional cleavage decreased significantly. Two of the parties' most loyal and successfully incorporated sectors—peasants and labor—underwent dramatic decline. The percentage of the workforce in unions and in the agricultural sector both fell by at least 50 percent between the zenith of the party system in the early 1980s and its collapse in the late 1990s. The public sector also shrank considerably as a result of privatizations, outsourcing, and other neoliberal reforms (Ellner 2003). Furthermore, although professionals did not lose workforce share, they nevertheless lost income as their wages decayed throughout the 1990s, weakening their economic and political capacities (Sáinz 2005).[2]

As the parties' traditional constituencies contracted, groups excluded from party-led incorporation expanded. The proportion of unemployed Venezuelans, who were not integrated into the party system through mechanisms like unions and professional associations, nearly doubled between the system's height and its collapse in 1998. The marginalized informal sector grew from 34 percent in 1980 to nearly half the workforce at the time of collapse.[3]

2. Of the incorporated groups, middle-class professionals had the most tenuous ties to the traditional parties and were among those who became increasingly disenchanted with the old system (Salamanca 1995).

3. The OCEI and INE sources used here classified the informal sector as follows: a self-employed person in a nonprofessional job; an owner, employee, or unpaid family help in a business of less than five; or a domestic worker (Ortega 2003, 13).

Table 6.1 Social transformation between the early 1980s and the late 1990s

	% of total labor force	
	Early 1980s	Late 1990s
Traditionally incorporated groups		
Union members[a]	40	15
Agricultural sector[b]	16	8
Public sector[c]	22	16
Professional and managerial workers[d]	14	14
Traditionally unincorporated groups		
Informal sector[c]	34	49
Unemployed[c]	6	11

Note: Columns do not total 100 because categories are not mutually exclusive. For example, many public sector workers are also union members.

[a] Data for the early 1980s and 1995 from ILO. The estimate for the 1980s is conservative; some sources place unionization as high as 45 percent (Díaz 2000).
[b] 1980s data for 1984 from ILO; 1990s data for 1997 from ILO.
[c] 1980s data for 1980 from OCEI; 1990s data for 1998 from Instituto Nacional de Estadística.
[d] 1980s data for 1983 from ILO; 1990s data for 1995 from ILO.

Informality at the end of the 1990s was even higher than during the pre-oil boom era, suggesting that Venezuela was undergoing more foundational economic and social changes than those produced by normal oil cycles. Also, because informal workers support more dependents on average than formal sector workers, it is likely that an even larger proportion of the population was reliant on income from the informal economy than these workforce figures suggest.

Putting Venezuela in regional context helps highlight the drastic nature of these changes. In 1990, Venezuelan informality was near the Latin American average of 41 percent, but by 1999 its informal economy was substantially larger than the regional norm. While on average informality across the region increased by 5 points to 46 percent, Venezuelan informality increased by 10 points—from 42 percent in 1990 to 52 percent in 1999 (Sáinz 2005, 71). The entire region experienced social change in the 1990s, but the shift in Venezuela was more dramatic than in many other countries. In fact, among all developing countries for which data were available, Venezuela, along with Bolivia and Kenya, experienced the largest increases in informality over the course of the 1990s (ILO 2001).

Another feature of Venezuela's social transformation was mounting poverty. The percentage of households below the poverty line more than doubled between 1982 and 1997. In 1982, 26 percent of households were in poverty (CISOR 1982). By 1997, this number had risen to 61 percent of households and nearly 70 percent of individuals, while 37 percent of people lived in extreme poverty (CISOR 1997). Like informality, poverty increased more rapidly in Venezuela than in any other country in the region (Buxton 2003, 123). At the same time, the once large and vibrant middle class withered away, constituting only about 10 percent of the population by the end of the 1990s, after a decade filled with job losses and salary cuts (Hellinger 2003, 38). A significant concentration of income occurred as all but the wealthiest quintile of Venezuelans lost relative income shares between the early 1980s and the late 1990s (K. Roberts 2003b, 60). Increasingly, Venezuelans faced the instability of unemployment or informal subsistence and lacked the security associated with work in sectors protected by party-affiliated unions, professional associations, or peasant organizations. People fell into informality and poverty and encountered financial instability, while they also lost access to mechanisms of incorporation for voicing these concerns in the political system.

The parties' traditional constituencies constituted over 60 percent of the economically active population in the early 1980s, but by the time the system collapsed, this proportion had reversed, with the informal sector and unemployed together totaling about 60 percent. By the end of the 1990s, a substantial majority of Venezuelans operated outside the formal economy and were, consequently, not represented through conventional interest incorporation. This dramatic social transformation reconfigured the dominant cleavage, moving it away from traditional class divisions and toward a conflict between formal and informal sectors, which required considerable restructuring of incorporation strategies. Moreover, the speed and depth of this shift, which occurred more rapidly and provoked more profound change than similar processes in other developing countries, demanded immediate adaptation to reach the burgeoning nonformal sectors and thereby incorporate a significant portion of society.

By the 1990s, then, society had changed markedly. The social configuration upon which the party system's incorporation strategies had been built declined in relevance, as the traditional class cleavage lost salience and was reformulated around the formal-informal divide. By the end of the 1990s, competing sides of the old cleavage—formal sector workers and employers—found that they shared many interests. Together, they coordinated national work stoppages and attempted to force Hugo Chávez from office. As differences between workers and owners lost salience, the popular sector was divided between the organized working class, which continued to affiliate with the traditional political elite, and the informal and unemployed, who tended to support Chávez. As the traditional class divide deteriorated, the salient distinction became the instability of informal work versus relative stability in the formal sector. This new cleavage, rather than reflecting divisions based on one's position in the production cycle, was built on stark differences between the comparatively privileged, who found a steady source of income in the formal economy, and the growing masses, who remained outside established patterns of production and lacked economic certainty.

As the informal sector grew and the cleavage structure transformed, the entire party system faced serious challenges to its patterns of incorporation. With the new formal-informal cleavage, the system only incorporated one side of the social divide. All the old parties had built linkage by incorporating traditional class interests, and the patterns of interactions between parties emphasized their relative prowess in incorporating different groups competing around this cleavage. However, incorporation based on old class interests specifically excluded the burgeoning informal sector.

As detailed in chapter 3, substantial shifts in the structure of salient cleavages destabilize incorporating linkages across the entire system. Parties in a system work together to reflect different facets of politically relevant social divides. So when the structure of divisions shifts, the whole system and its component parties are pressured to adapt and reorganize around the new patterns of societal interests. The Venezuelan transformation from a worker-owner to a formal-informal divide constitutes this sort of fundamental change in cleavage structure, which threatened to undermine incorporating linkage throughout the system if the parties did not respond.

In the face of this challenge, the party system had two options for sustaining incorporating ties with a significant portion of the population. The parties could reverse the social change and resurrect the relevance of the traditional class cleavage that had informed all of their incorporation efforts, or they could adapt and reach out to the increasingly salient interests that corresponded with the informal side of the newly structured divide. However, the parties did not successfully implement or even actively pursue either option, relying instead on a narrowing support base rooted in the old cleavage structure. Arresting and reversing the social transformation, while attractive to party leaders, was beyond their reach, and organizational constraints limited their capacity to adapt and integrate emergent interests.

INFORMALITY: A PROBLEM THE PARTIES COULD NOT SOLVE

As the parties encountered dramatic social changes that challenged the logic of their incorporating linkages, one strategy for responding to this threat would have been to extend policies and services that mitigated the growth of informality and unemployment and helped people find stable formal sector work. Such an approach would have reversed the transformation and reinvigorated the relevance of traditional linkage mechanisms, limiting the pressure on parties to achieve the dramatic organizational adaptations required if the informal sector was to be successfully incorporated. In interviews, many traditional party leaders explained that their organizations saw informality and unemployment as problems that could be solved or at least temporarily endured (Interviews 14, 39, 44, 47, 50, 56). A former AD party president said that the party "considered the informal sector to be the result of inadequate social policy" (Interview 47). A pivotal COPEI leader remarked that the party recognized the growth of informality but perceived it as an economic problem that could be remedied "through job creation [that would] eliminate and thereby incorporate the informal sector" (Interview 39). Some leaders suggested that informality might have been counteracted through traditional social programs or through the sorts of employment policies and job creation tactics promoted by the parties in the 1970s. Others were more sanguine about the threat posed by the drastic social changes. These leaders held the attitude that escalating informality and unemployment were expressions of temporary problems, which would eventually abate when economic normalcy (read, oil prosperity) resumed and allowed the social structure to return to its ordinary equilibrium. A prominent member of AD's CEN explained that party leadership viewed informality as the temporary result of inadequate economic policy, a problem that would resolve itself or dissipate over time as the economy improved (Interview 56).

However, the economic processes driving the social transformation were profound and plagued countries across the entire region. They went beyond ordinary ebbs and flows in oil prosperity and instead constituted a major shift instigated by the exhaustion of ISI. The parties' efforts in the 1980s to make ordinary policy adjustments and thereby mitigate the seemingly inevitable march toward higher informality and unemployment were entirely unsuccessful. As we observed in chapter 5, the parties managed to formulate some small policy responses to pressing economic and social problems under

Lusinchi, but these efforts did not slow the deterioration of opportunities for stable work. Unemployment nearly doubled over the 1980s, reaching 10 percent by 1989, and informality increased by eight points to almost 40 percent between 1979 and 1989. Although party leaders advocated standard social policies to counteract the cleavage transformation, these minor modifications clearly did not have the capacity to arrest the change.

As the crisis intensified in the late 1980s and early 1990s, the parties' policy response decayed. The responsiveness analysis in chapter 5 revealed that in the 1990s there was very little policy activity designed to counteract informality, unemployment, and "the immense creation of the poor" (Interview 30). Despite party leaders' rhetorical emphasis on informality as a problem to be solved, they acknowledged that their organizations did not enact policies targeting the issue (Interviews 9, 14, 39, 44, 48, 50). On the contrary, some laws the parties passed in Congress supported the executive's privatization efforts and changed labor policies in ways that undermined employment in the formal sector and hastened the growth of informality and unemployment. Instead of combating informality, party leaders abdicated their responsibility and looked to the executive to be the driving force in counteracting increases in informality and unemployment. This sentiment was stated most clearly by a former president of AD: "Addressing the issue of the informal sector should have been done by the [executive]. The party could not do anything about it because those are policies of the state" (Interview 50). Thus, the parties did not enact policies that combated the shifts in social structure or that created more formal sector jobs.

While in theory some efforts to reverse the social change could have been advanced by the executive, in reality Venezuelan presidents, like the parties, faced considerable constraints imposed by the international push toward neoliberalism, which limited their ability to resolve the lack of stable employment. In the face of these external pressures, both Pérez and Caldera implemented pro-market reforms like privatization, the elimination of public projects, and trade liberalization. These policies were designed to halt the debt crisis, but they also exacerbated and accelerated social changes, forcing more workers into the informal sector and threatening the parties' incorporation strategies. The reforms were largely outside the parties' control, as the policies were compelled by international financial institutions and implemented with little party consultation or influence (Corrales 2002; Naím 1993). Certainly, neither the executive nor the parties provided relief from the tide of social change, as neoliberalism only heightened the transformation.

Moreover, rather than trying to provide policies that would help informal workers, much government interaction with them was aimed at control and regulation. Local governments often implemented ordinances to limit the locations, hours, and tactics of informal workers, undermining their capacity to make a living. In 1996, *El Nacional* reported on a typical effort to control the informal sector in the Libertador municipality of Caracas. The AD- and COPEI-controlled municipal council passed an ordinance regulating locations where informal workers could operate and limiting who could run "small businesses." Two organizations representing informal sector interests—Coordinadora de Trabajos del Comercio Informal and Federación Latinoamérica de Trabajadores del Comercio Informal—objected to the ordinance as harmful to informal workers' ability to make a living and as placing unconstitutional limits on their rights. But the organizations were not consulted about the ordinance and were not even aware of its passage until after it was approved, leaving them to object fruitlessly after the fact (C. Delgado 1996). At the national level, conflict also simmered between government and the informal sector. For example, the tax administration (SENIAT) sought to force informal workers to pay taxes, even though they were generally excluded from the benefits that taxes funded. On the whole, limits on policy flexibility and pressure to embrace neoliberalism heightened the conflict, pitting the state against the informally employed and unemployed while also hastening the growth of these sectors. Rather than helping people exit these precarious situations, the parties were immobile in the face of dramatic social changes that undermined the very logic of their incorporation strategies.

ORGANIZATIONAL CONSTRAINTS ON NEW INCORPORATION

In the face of escalating informality and unemployment, which the parties were unable to combat or alleviate with government policy, their organizations encountered the considerable challenge of integrating the rapidly growing ranks of people living outside the formal economy. Superficially, it might seem obvious that the parties would have been motivated to pursue the burgeoning nonformal sectors as a new base of support. However, strong constraints imposed by the nature of the party organizations themselves limited their capacity to adapt their incorporation strategies and embrace interests reflecting the informal side of the newly structured societal divide.

These constraints created incentives for the entire party system to remain committed to established supporters and restricted its latitude to incorporate new interests.[4]

Two major organizational constraints pushed the parties to maintain their established incorporation trajectory, such that their strategies remained centered on the traditional class cleavage. First, given the diffuse structure of the burgeoning informal sector, its interests were not easily accommodated alongside hierarchically organized, traditional class-based interests, particularly in the Venezuelan context of highly routinized incorporation strategies (Buxton 1999a; Crisp 1998a; Levitsky 2007). To incorporate the new interests, the parties needed to organize them in ways that fit these entrenched incorporation patterns or reconfigure established organizational structures. But the disorganized and diverse nature of the informal sector created considerable obstacles to organizing and unifying its scattered interests, and highly institutionalized incorporation patterns could not reasonably respond to the rapid and fundamental changes in society (Ellner 2003; K. Roberts 2002b). Second, the interests of the informal sector ran counter to those of already integrated groups, limiting the parties' capacity to maintain ties to established interests while also reaching out to new ones (Diamond 1999; García-Guadilla 2003; Piattoni 2001b). The restructuring of the dominant cleavage thus presented serious threats to incorporation, and these two constraints ultimately led to stagnation, not adaptation.

New Interests Do Not Align with Established Incorporation Strategies

Traditional incorporation in Venezuela followed highly entrenched, hierarchically structured patterns (Coppedge 1994a; Navarro 1995). The parties and major class-based interests emerged at the same time, shared leaders, and developed similar organizational configurations, which facilitated the parties' ability to incorporate traditional interests (Levine 1998; Urbaneja 1992). The parties and established functional interests, including labor, peasants, business elites, and professionals, maintained nationally comprehensive, vertical organizations. The parties' Leninist-style structures were centrally controlled by a small set of powerful leaders (*el cogollo*), and sectoral interests were captured through peak organizations, which included the labor confederation CTV, the peasant federation FCV, the business organization

---

4. As I will discuss in chapter 7, the parties instead relied increasingly on conditional exchanges to win support from the growing portions of the population excluded from traditional patterns of incorporation.

FEDECAMARAS, and several national associations representing specific white-collar professions. These parallel organizational patterns, in which both the parties and major functional groups were structured vertically, eased party penetration and incorporation of societal interests through corporatist integration mechanisms (Buxton 1999a; Coppedge 1994b).

However, the rapidly growing informal sector did not fit the prevailing logic of hierarchically structured incorporating linkages. The informal sector "was not organized in any systematic way" (Interview 56). Neither grassroots nor elite-driven efforts provided structure to emergent interests; certainly nothing developed that reflected hierarchical patterns similar to those characterizing the formal sector groups (Interview 65). Instead, informal sector interests were fragmented and heterogeneous, making collective action difficult (García-Guadilla 2003, 193; K. Roberts 2002b). As society changed, existing vertical conduits for incorporation could not easily be retasked with integrating disparate, horizontally patterned informal interests. Established peak associations could not articulate the concerns of "large groups of citizens who were either unorganized or affiliated with a myriad of decentralized, community-based organizations" (K. Roberts 2003b, 62). Venezuelan institutions of incorporation had been effectively designed to channel the specific hierarchically structured interests that dominated society under the traditional model of oil-led development (Crisp 1998a, 35–36). But as this model deteriorated and society shifted in fundamental ways, old institutions were rendered obsolete because their strategies did not correspond with the new interests' organizational logic.

Because the informal sector's decentralized structure did not fit dominant patterns of incorporation, integrating their interests demanded herculean adaptation efforts by the traditional parties and their affiliated organizations. However, the highly institutionalized structures of the parties and peak associations severely limited their "organizational capacity to adapt" and accommodate interests that had a divergent configuration (Levitsky 2007, 222). In light of these limits on adaptation, the most viable strategy for integrating the informal sector involved investing considerable energy and resources to organize their disparate interests and encapsulate them in vertically structured collectives that fit existing incorporation patterns. But pinpointing areas of commonality in the diverse sector and developing an organization around these mutual goals required rethinking established strategies (Interview 14). And the prospective benefits that a party might accrue by shifting its focus toward the informal sector could only be reaped after sustained and costly exertion. Given these risks and the uncertainty of success, organizing and integrating the informal sector was not an appealing avenue for party entrepreneurship (Interviews 39, 43). Furthermore, because some party leaders calculated that increased informality was transitory and thought that the customary class cleavage would quickly return to its old equilibrium once oil prices inevitably rebounded, they were especially wary of risky efforts to incorporate a group that was likely to lose relevance as soon as the economy recovered. Although this perception would prove to be mistaken, it was, nevertheless, a widely held view among party leaders. The clear reality of a heterogeneous, disorganized informal sector and the prevalent perception that the social changes were only a brief departure from the usual structure of society generated strong, and seemingly logical, incentives for the parties to maintain established incorporation strategies rather than reach out to new groups.

Competing Concerns of Traditional and Emerging Interests

The second major organizational constraint limiting innovative incorporation pertains to the conflicting interests of the informal sector and traditionally integrated formal sector groups. The divergent goals and interests of these groups are well documented in recent literature on the ramifications of the debt crisis and neoliberalism (Levitsky 2007; Portes and Hoffman 2003; K. Roberts 2002b; Weyland 1996). In Venezuela, formal and informal workers were at odds over policies aimed at directing benefits toward the traditional working class, like minimum wage increases and other employment-based benefits, which did little to aid those in the informal sector. Social policy reforms of the 1990s, including changes in labor, social security, pension, and health care legislation, focused on minimizing damage to formal workers rather than addressing the needs of the informal sector. Meanwhile, general social programs that benefited the poor regardless of employment status, like price subsidies and public services, were the first to be cut, even while traditionally incorporated groups held on to their benefits (Myers 2004, 159).

Unions tried to insulate organized labor from the reforms by guarding traditional, employment-based benefits. However, informal workers who did not benefit from union-advocated policies lacked solidarity with organized labor's demands and often did not participate in strikes designed to protect the privileged few in the formal sector (García-Guadilla 2003). Instead, excluded urban sectors were critical in instigating the more spontaneous forms of protest that erupted as neoliberal reforms chiseled away at the little state assistance that informal sector workers received (K. Roberts 2003b). The 1989 Caracazo evidences the conflicting interests and strategies of the two groups. The days-long protest against neoliberalism in general and against cutting the transportation subsidy in particular began in Caracas and spread throughout urban centers across the country. The demonstrations were instigated by the urban poor, who saw the elimination of the subsidy as eroding one of their few state benefits and undercutting their ability to eke out a living. As the cities exploded, the parties and their union allies were completely surprised by the frustration manifested in protests they had not planned and could not diffuse (Buxton 1999a; Ellner 1993, 89). In fact, as many as 5,000 protests occurred in the three years following Pérez's neoliberal reforms, and most were *not* channeled through organized labor (Ellner 1995, 149).

As the informal sector grew and as unionized workers and middle-class professionals constituted a relatively advantaged but shrinking segment of society, the formal-informal divide became more discordant. In terms of group-based material benefits as well as policy positions, the informal sector did not gain from and instead frequently opposed formal sector goals. Because of these conflicting interests, satisfying formal and informal workers simultaneously did not seem viable, particularly as resources deteriorated and policy latitude declined. As a result, party leaders were faced with a trade-off. They could either continue down the familiar path of appealing to conventional class interests, or they could strike out on a new course, attempting to build a base among the growing informal sector while risking alienation of their committed formal sector base. Parties were thus forced to choose between their shrinking base of loyal supporters and the growing, but disorganized and heterogeneous, sectors excluded from incorporation.

In light of the conflict between entrenched, hierarchical incorporation patterns and the decentralized informal sector, the parties estimated that the costs associated with alienating committed supporters and expending resources to build a new base were too high. Abandoning historically stable foundations for an uncertain base in informality seemed shortsighted and foolhardy (Interview 41). Given the unstructured and heterogeneous character of the informal sector, the parties did not want to risk undermining their traditional formal sector constituencies. Therefore, instead of advocating the competing concerns of those excluded from existing incorporation strategies, the parties and their allies in traditionally incorporated groups neglected the burgeoning informal sector. Instead, the parties relied more heavily on their established but shrinking constituencies in the formal part of the economy.

The social transformation of escalating informality and unemployment undermined the traditional class cleavage around which the parties had built their incorporating linkages. With the change, their established strategies enabled them to capture less than 40 percent of the population, and the party system was faced with the challenge of integrating the majority of Venezuelans who were now outside the scope of traditional incorporation. Successful responses to this pressure could have involved the incorporation of informal sector interests by existing parties, the emergence of new system-sustaining parties that reflected the changed cleavage structure, or the integration of informal workers into the ranks of established party-affiliated organizations like the CTV. However, because of the severe constraints on adaptation outlined above, individual parties, allied organizations, and the system as a whole failed to integrate emergent interests.

Neglect by Individual Parties

The great majority of traditional party leaders with whom I discussed the party system's response to escalating informality readily acknowledged that their parties did little to integrate the informal sector. Even after considerable probing, all but one of the former AD, COPEI, and MAS leaders I interviewed were unable to recall anything the parties had done to integrate the informal sector beyond encouraging the government to implement basic safety-net social policies, which they advocated primarily to protect their traditional constituencies, not the informal sector. A former AD CEN member explained that the party's leadership never discussed issues surrounding the growth of the informal sector, because the party thought it owned popular affection and therefore "did not try to include new people or new groups" (Interview 49). Another CEN member clarified that while AD realized that the informal sector was growing, "there was no tactic to incorporate them; we never tried to organize or include them" (Interview 56). Many AD leaders agreed that the party was completely unprepared for the social transformation and lacked the capacity to incorporate excluded interests (Interviews 14, 28, 48, 54). They lamented that as new sectors emerged and grew, their interests could not be channeled by the parties and therefore never found political expression in the system (Interviews 14, 54). The situation in COPEI was largely the same. One copeyano justified the lack of integration by stating that "the informal sector exists; it happens. There was a bit of an attitude in the parties that this sort of thing happens, but it will pass. There was really a sense of business-as-usual in the parties" (Interview 39). A former COPEI president suggested that while some local leaders tried to capture informal sector support, "this was done by individual leaders, not really by the party as an organization" (Interview 43). Overall, both parties "lacked the capacity to integrate [excluded] groups" (Interview 37).

Interviewee after interviewee admitted that the parties did not make even fleeting attempts to organize or incorporate the informal sector. Even though the parties had originally built their now entrenched constituencies among peasants and labor by organizing and mobilizing them, carrying out similar efforts to build new support in the informal sector seemed too difficult or risky. In fact, when asked about efforts to organize rapidly growing yet excluded sectors, several party leaders scoffed at the idea, as though the suggestion was preposterous. Only one AD leader pointed to some efforts to reach out to emerging social groups. However, his discussion emphasized strategies to tap into the emerging neighborhood movement, which was most prominent in middle- and upper-class areas (García-Guadilla 2003), and he acknowledged that the party organization showed little interest in supporting these efforts. Furthermore, much neighborhood outreach aimed to integrate newly autonomous municipal governments into the party structure and infiltrate the neighborhood associations, not to represent excluded groups (Interview 51; AD documents; Levine 1998; Salamanca 1995). In essence, the popular sector was left "without an effective voice" (Lander 1996, 67).

Organizationally, neither AD nor COPEI nor MAS adapted to accommodate the new social reality. Although the parties responded to new, direct elections of mayors and municipal councils by restructuring to accommodate municipal affairs at the highest levels of their organizations and thereby endeavored to retain control over local governments (AD 1996; COPEI 1991; MAS 1994), none of the parties made organizational changes to accommodate the informal sector. Unlike unions, peasants, and professionals, the informal sector lacked any representation in the party organizations. Just as interviews with former party leaders suggested, extensive searches through newspapers revealed essentially no party attempts to integrate informal workers into party structures, even at lower levels or in less formalized ways. Small, typically clientelist appeals, such as make-work jobs, were offered to the poor and to informal workers by individual local leaders promoting their personal candidacies, but these sectors were not integrated into the organizations (Interviews 43, 44, 51; Myers 2004). Some small communitarian organizations, like Centro al Servicio de la Acción Popular and Ferias de Consumo Popular, began to develop activities in poor areas and sought resolution for basic problems like food and job scarcity, but the parties did not tap into or support these efforts (Salamanca 1995).

During their founding era, the parties had cultivated successful incorporation strategies by mobilizing and organizing peasants and labor (Levine 1973; Myers 2004; various interviews). However, as the social structure changed forty years later, these same parties did very little to build new bases of support, abdicating the opportunity and responsibility presented by the informal sector (Urbaneja 1992). Even party leaders who had played key roles in early organizing efforts seemed to view the disorder and potentially temporary character of the informal sector as debilitating impediments, preventing the parties from drawing this group into their constituency. They "failed to recognize, much less make a place for, the new interests, groups, and capabilities being created in the society at large" (Levine 1998, 195).

Even new parties, which emerged in the 1990s and did not pose a foundational threat to the traditional conception of Venezuelan party democracy, failed to develop constituencies that reflected changing societal divisions. These parties offered opportunities for system-maintaining change that could have expanded incorporation to new groups, but they did not fulfill this promise. Caldera's new party, Convergencia, was a personalistic vehicle that never developed any appeal beyond his persona. La Causa R was perhaps the most promising and truly new emerging party, but its strongest support came from traditional, albeit radicalized, blue-collar workers of heavy industry in the Guyana region, making it highly dependent on the traditional class cleavage (Hellinger 1996; López Maya 1997). Although LCR did develop some ties to Pro-Catia, a nongovernmental organization that promoted the interests of one of the poorer sectors of Caracas, the resulting support it received was largely limited to the Catia neighborhood (Salamanca 1995). The party's organized base in Caracas remained small, as it failed to build general support among the urban poor (Hellinger 1996, 126; Levine 1998; Interview 41). In interviews, current and former leaders consistently pointed to organized labor as important to LCR, but informal workers were never mentioned as central to the party's base. The new parties of the early 1990s, like their older counterparts, failed to integrate the informal sector.

Incorporation Through Targeted Policymaking?

The parties also failed to implement policies targeted to address the needs of the informal sector. Traditional programs, which provided assistance to poor Venezuelans of all stripes through subsidies, price controls, and public benefits, deteriorated in the neoliberal era as social expenditure dropped below 1968 levels (Lander 1996). Other social programs were targeted to help only those employed in the formal sector and did not reach the urban poor and unemployed (Interview 52). One of the central weaknesses of government policies as they pertained to informal and unemployed workers was the lack of protection provided for them under the social security system. Informal workers had no rights under the pension system, were not protected by government employment policies, and did not benefit from numerous other employment-based programs. By 1996, social security reform had made its way to the forefront of the political agenda. Pressure to reform the ailing system provided an opportunity to extend coverage beyond those employed in the formal sector. However, although the parties acknowledged that "the social security system should not only be for the formal sector as it was, but should also allow for the inclusion of the informal sector" (Interview 47), the reform effort did not include informal sector voices. Instead, President Caldera resurrected the old tool of tripartite commissions between government, business, and organized labor to develop a new framework for social security (Iranzo and Patruyo 2001). Despite the pressing need to extend coverage to informal workers, they found no place on the commission that drafted the legislation. Not surprisingly then, the Tripartite Agreement Concerning Social Security, which the commission drafted, neglected accommodations for the informal sector.

In the legislature, the proposal was modified to include allowances for informal workers to opt into the new pension system. But for all practical purposes, buying into the system was impossible for most of them, as they struggled to survive and lacked extra money to put away in a pension fund. Other congressional revisions increased protections for the highest paid formal workers without extending benefits to the poor. Simultaneous reforms to the severance system, which had been an additional source of pension income, also ignored the informal and unemployed, as did new unemployment and worker training legislation (Bottome 1997, 1998). Even contemporary analysts who supported the general direction of Caldera's neoliberal agenda criticized these reforms for neglecting to provide coverage for the informal sector.[5] While policies designed to target excluded sectors could

5. These reforms also undermined the social security and unemployment system for the parties' traditional base in the working class (Buxton 2003; Ellner 2003). Additionally, many of the reforms to the social security system were scheduled to take effect in 1999 but were never implemented, because by that time the party system had collapsed and Chávez had taken office.

have served as a means of attracting their support, the parties did not pursue this possibility and instead cut the few benefits they once had.

Conventional Corporatist Organizations Provide No New Links

Outside party organizational efforts or targeted policy making to integrate the informal sector, the parties could have relied on their traditional popular sector ally—organized labor—to help incorporate emergent interests. In practice, however, organized labor ignored the informal sector or treated it with hostility. For instance, despite the obvious fact plastered all over the news that informality was increasing, a few former AD and COPEI leaders disputed this reality. Most notable among those who rejected the evidence of informal sector growth was an influential AD labor leader, who had held a position on the party's CEN and served as president of the CTV (Interview 52). His dismissal of and antagonistic attitude toward informality mirrors a more general failing on the part of functional organizations to serve as conduits for integrating emergent sectors into the parties. In theory, the parties could have used the CTV as a mechanism to channel the growing informal sector. But as the economic pie shrank in the 1990s, conflict rather than synergy characterized the relationship between formal and informal workers.

Numerous factors complicated the possibility that organized labor might help incorporate the informal sector. Impediments to informal sector unionization included the conflicting interests of formal and informal workers, difficulty recruiting and organizing the transitory informal sector, and the short-term demand orientation of informal workers versus the longer time horizon of unions. The two groups' divergent educational and socioeconomic backgrounds also undermined popular sector solidarity. Throughout the 1990s, rather than promoting social protections that would have helped formal and informal workers alike, such as price controls and subsidized public services, the CTV deepened the rift between these sectors by advocating employment protection policies and increases in the minimum wage. These policies only exacerbated the relative tenuousness of informality by making formal sector workers more expensive to employ and more difficult to let go. Even as the informal sector grew, unions paid it little attention, in part because they considered informality a passing anomaly but also because they saw a zero-sum game in which the interests of the informal sector had

---

Chávez postponed the reforms, and eventually the Chávez-dominated legislature passed entirely different measures.

to be sacrificed for the needs of the privileged formal workers (Iranzo and Patruyo 2001). This lack of attention from traditional unions and parties persisted despite the emergence of a handful of mostly local groups endeavoring to organize informal sector workers, such as the Federación de Asociaciones de Buhoneros and individual associations that developed around specific informal markets (Tabuas 1995). These entities might have served as an organizational seed for the parties or the CTV to cultivate. But it was not until after the system collapsed that the CTV, succumbing to pressures from the ILO and competition from pro-Chávez unions, began reaching out to informal workers.

On the whole, the parties, their allies, and the system they composed made few efforts to incorporate emergent interests in the 1990s. Despite extensive social restructuring, the old parties did not incorporate the informal sector into their organizations, new system-sustaining parties stuck to conventional incorporation patterns, social programs did not target excluded sectors, and existing corporatist mediators did not reach out to integrate informal workers.

PARTY SYSTEM RELIANCE ON TRADITIONAL INTERESTS

Facing threats to incorporation from the growth of long-excluded groups, the parties could not roll back the social changes. They shunned the unorganized informal sector and avoided risky innovation that might have alienated core supporters. Instead, as established interests waned and new groups surged, the parties further retrenched within the security of the known by increasing their dependence on historical allies in the formal economy (Interviews 35, 64). Increased power of traditional class-based interests in the parties and in policy making provides further evidence of the system's failure to respond to social restructuring and reveals a continued reliance on groups that reflected the decaying traditional class cleavage.

Early in Carlos Andrés Pérez's second term, organized labor lost ground within AD as a result of his neoliberal turn, which hurt the working class. Despite the support AD's Labor Secretariat provided for Pérez's candidacy and regular meetings between the two (Sanchez 1990), Pérez was no advocate for workers, and through 1990, labor floundered. AD's Buró Sindical vacillated between the traditionalist *ortodoxa* faction of the party and the pro-Pérez *renovadora* faction, overall lending more support to the latter group early in his term. Although labor provided some resistance, it was not central in galvanizing opposition to neoliberalism.

However, by mid-1991, labor increasingly aligned with the orthodox faction against Pérez. Initially, these were alliances of convenience based on shared goals (Carrillo 1991), but over the course of the 1990s, the coalition between labor and the ortodoxos solidified. Eventually, this faction, led by Luis Alfaro Ucero, gained control of the party. Labor's role in the dominant anti-Pérez alliance cemented its political influence in AD throughout the rest of the decade, and it became a major strategic ally for Alfaro. Although some members of the party opposed the Buró Sindical's close ties to the ortodoxos, labor movement influence did not weaken. Even as the size of the working class decreased and unions' incorporating capacity deteriorated, labor's power only increased within AD.

The process surrounding the 1998 campaign speaks clearly to union influence and the party leadership's dependence on labor in the last years before the system collapsed. The Buró Sindical's shaping of the campaign process began with manipulating the procedures for selecting the party's presidential nominee. Nearly two years before the December 1998 presidential elections, the labor section of the party, led by Labor Secretary César Gil, began to direct the course of the internal campaign for the party's nomination. On behalf of the Buró Sindical, Gil proposed and the CEN adopted a postponement of intraparty discussion about the campaign, which prohibited campaigning by potential nominees (Escalante 1997). Instead, party activity was supposed to focus on disseminating the party's program. This move gave free rein to those who controlled AD's organization to consolidate power and directly benefited Alfaro, who dominated the party machinery from his position as secretary general.

However, by late 1997, uncertainty about AD's presidential candidate began to undermine the party's electoral prospects. At this point, the Buró Sindical modified its earlier proposal, suggesting that AD choose a consensus candidate, a plan purportedly aimed at avoiding internal acrimony and allowing the party to begin mounting its campaign (Colomine 1997b; El Nacional 1997d). This proposal to select the candidate based on the acclamation of AD leadership violated 1993 revisions to the party statutes that required the party base to select the presidential nominee. As CEN members pointed out at the time in the press and subsequently in interviews, the strategy of allowing only party leaders to select the candidate excluded any sectors of the base not incorporated in the upper echelons of the party organization (Leal Perdomo 1997a; El Nacional 1997c; various interviews). Despite these pitfalls, the unionists' idea gained momentum in late 1997 as an increasing number of party leaders gave it their support. By early

1998, other major functional groups—including professionals, educators, and women, as well as adeco governors—followed the labor movement's lead in backing centralized selection of the party nominee (Y. Delgado 1998; Escalante 1998).[6] This shift toward general support for the idea of a consensus candidate gives some credence to the notion that, as Gil gloated in an interview, "the labor movement *does* always win [in AD]" (Colomine 1997d; emphasis mine). Moreover, it paved the way for the CDN (Comité Directivo Nacional) to reform party statutes and circumvent the requirement that the presidential candidate be selected through a direct primary, thus enabling Alfaro's nomination.

The clear intent in seeking to choose the party's nominee through consensus was to benefit Alfaro, who was the Labor Bureau's ally. The labor movement's support for Alfaro and its increasingly open backing of his nomination played a central role in delivering the candidacy into his hands. Despite the lack of support for Alfaro among the population at large—as evidenced in numerous surveys—the party leadership aligned with their traditional supporters in the union movement and other functional groups, manipulating party rules and appointing him as their nominee. Even after being nominated, Alfaro had little electoral appeal, with popular support generally lingering below 10 percent throughout the campaign. Nevertheless, party backing of the labor movement's candidate only waned immediately preceding the elections. In the end, the party leadership recognized what many had long prognosticated: Alfaro's candidacy could attract very few votes. But it was not until just weeks before the election that the labor movement lost its ability to control party decision making, and at the prompting of regional leaders, the party withdrew its support from Alfaro and backed the candidacy of former copeyano Henrique Salas Römer.

Thus, at a moment when AD needed to show a fresh face and new vision, the influence of labor led to the selection of the tedious and elderly Alfaro, one of the party's most entrenched leaders and a man whom many saw as old-fashioned and corrupt. From outside the party, this decision made little sense. However, Alfaro had strong allies among leaders of unions and other functional organizations, which facilitated his ability to win the nomination and further indebted this powerful adeco to organized labor (Interviews 41, 42, 52). Labor was perceived as a critical element in any strategy to unite

6. AD governors' support of this labor-led proposal speaks to the spread of power bases from the central party organization to regional leaders. The governors' support for Alfaro helped him secure the nomination, but more importantly, their abandonment of him right before the December presidential elections contributed to his ungraceful removal as the party's candidate.

the party and thereby achieve electoral success (Colomine 1997a). And the relationship of mutual dependence between Alfaro and union leaders gave labor considerable clout as the party neared its nadir. What the party failed to appreciate was that uniting traditional interests within the party was no longer a sufficient strategy for winning national elections because the social changes that the country had undergone in the 1990s weakened the pull of established functional groups and shifted a substantial majority of the population outside the bounds of conventional group-based appeals.

All the old parties continued to rely on traditional corporatist linkage structures rather than reaching out to unincorporated interests. Throughout the late 1990s, the parties emphasized the importance of maintaining dominance in labor unions and professional associations, even though they represented an ever-shrinking portion of the population. For instance, a 1997 document issued by AD's CEN highlighted the party's success in the internal elections of unions, professional associations, and student organizations as a major accomplishment for the organization (Leal Perdomo 1997b), and until the party system's collapse, AD controlled unions in key sectors, including petroleum, iron, construction, and transportation (Colomine 1997d).

In COPEI, the professional wing, which was traditionally the most influential in the party, continued to play an important role (Interviews 21, 58). And although functional groups in COPEI were not as decisive as labor in AD, these traditional interests were on the winning side in the internal debate surrounding COPEI's 1998 presidential nominee because they were part of the coalition that supported independent Irene Saéz. Besides the labor movement, which was not typically a stronghold for COPEI, the traditional functional groups, including the party's professional and agrarian wings, backed the pro-Saéz faction led by former President Luis Herrera Campíns (Pulgarín 1997b).[7] This faction, like the pro-Alfaro labor-backed faction in AD, dominated COPEI in the last years before the system's collapse. Moreover, as in AD, traditionally incorporated interests remained powerful in COPEI and shaped the party in its final moments in the spotlight.

The system of interest mediation in Venezuela had become so entrenched that even as the social landscape changed dramatically, the parties intensified their ties to historical allies in an effort to survive. As one former adeco leader acknowledged, "The interests the parties were representing were the interests of unions and of business. But we [in the old parties] stopped

7. COPEI labor was divided, failing to provide definitive support to any faction (*El Nacional* 1997a; Pulgarín 1997a).

representing the interests of the people" (Interview 42). The parties deepened their dependence on shrinking formal sector interests. Because they were reluctant to invest in organizing a diffuse and heterogeneous informal sector whose structure conflicted with their hierarchical, entrenched incorporation patterns and whose interests were at odds with those of their established supporters, the parties did not embrace emerging interests. As a result, the informal sector lacked interest-based linkage, and the scope of incorporation narrowed significantly.

EMERGING GROUPS REJECT THE PARTY SYSTEM

Throughout the 1990s, those excluded from incorporation experienced deteriorating conditions even as their numbers increased. The gap between formal and informal sector earnings widened over the course of the decade, and the negative ramifications of economic adjustments in this regard were more severe for informal workers. While wages for all Venezuelans underwent a sustained decay, the incomes of the informally employed were significantly lower than those of the shrinking proportion of workers now in the formal sector (Márquez and Portela 1991). By 1997, the average hourly wage in the formal sector was 49 percent greater than that in the informal sector. Even after controlling for education, formal sector workers earned significantly more than informal workers (Orlando 2001). Moreover, the poverty rate in the informal sector was four times greater than in the formal sector (Orlando and Pollack 2000; Riutort 1999). During the decade leading up to collapse, the percentage of informal workers who did not make enough money to afford the basic food basket increased to nearly 40, while less than 20 percent of formal sector workers experienced such extreme poverty. Thus, although conditions for all Venezuelans deteriorated in the 1990s, the rapidly growing ranks of unemployed and informal workers bore the brunt of the crisis. The traditional parties did almost nothing to alleviate the suffering of these excluded groups, nor did they attempt to integrate their interests into the system through existing or new organizational channels. Instead, the parties continued to cater to and rely on their traditional base even as it eroded in size and influence.

The unincorporated groups responded to these worsening conditions and lack of inclusion as one might expect, turning their backs on the traditional party system. Although people from all walks of life abandoned the system in the 1990s, the flight was much more pronounced among those who lacked interest incorporation, especially the poor and unemployed. In nationwide public opinion surveys conducted by DATOS, Venezuelans were occasionally asked about their employment status as well as their partisan ties and their views of political parties. These data enable us to assess support for the traditional party system, comparing the rate of decay across incorporated versus excluded groups. Partisan sympathies evaporated much more quickly among unincorporated sectors of society. Between 1982, at the party system's height, and 1996, near its collapse, support for AD and COPEI declined by 65 percent among typically excluded groups, specifically the unemployed and self-employed.[8] On the other hand, although government employees, with their strong incorporating ties, also withdrew support from the traditional parties, the level of exodus among public sector workers was much lower, at only 47 percent during the same time period. The rate at which excluded groups abandoned the traditional parties was considerably higher than the pace of departure among incorporated sectors. The difference in the rates of partisan decay between these two groups is statistically and substantively significant. By 1996, the proportion of public employees committed to the traditional party system was nearly twice as large as the proportion among self-employed or unemployed workers.[9]

Other survey data provide further confirmation of low system support among those excluded from incorporation. As discussed earlier in the chapter, the Venezuelan social security system did not cover informal sector workers, making a respondent's lack of public social protection a good proxy for informality. A 1991 DATOS survey demonstrates that party membership rates were significantly higher among Venezuelans covered by social security than those who were not provided basic social protection by the state.[10] This stands in contrast to survey findings in the 1980s, when party militancy rates for those covered and not covered by the social security system were not statistically distinguishable. Additionally, in a 1996 survey, respondents answered questions about the functioning of several political and social institutions, including political parties. Parties were by far the least supported institution, with 77 percent of the sample assessing their performance as inadequate. Here again we observe a divide between the rich and poor, as approval of party performance was significantly higher

8. Tapping informal sector employment in surveys conducted during this time period is necessarily crude. Other research demonstrates that the great majority of informal sector workers in Venezuela are self-employed, while very few formal sector workers are self-employed (Orlando 2001). So I use self-employment as a proxy for informality.

9. Significance level of $p < .01$.

10. Significance level of $p < .05$.

among the middle and upper classes than among the lower classes.[11] But no class divide was evident in support for other institutions, including Congress, military leaders, the media, and the Supreme Court. Only in the case of the parties did the poor have more negative perceptions than the rich. While income differences were not salient in relation to understanding many other parts of public life, the party system's failure to incorporate the poor led them to reject the parties and the system as a whole.

Groups neglected by the party system grew rapidly in the 1990s, and they responded to continued exclusion and decaying conditions by abandoning the system. Extreme social change reduced the size and influence of the party system's established base and expanded the ranks of unincorporated Venezuelans outside the formal economy. But the system neither combated the social ill of informality nor reached out to incorporate this burgeoning sector. Entrenched interests, which conflicted with the goals of new groups, and established patterns of incorporation, which could not easily accommodate the disparate and heterogeneous nature of the informal sector, created incentives for party leaders to stay the course rather than adapt. The parties continued to orient their activities and organizations around traditional interests and did not attempt to build an alliance between the formal and informal segments of the popular sector. New parties that emerged in the early 1990s likewise failed to capture the restructured social cleavage as they followed existing patterns of linkage rather than blazing new and uncertain paths to build support. Even social policy reforms failed to extend protections to the informal sector. Meanwhile, the parties' traditionally incorporated allies declined in size and significance, making them dependent on a shrinking support base.

The decay of incorporation, once a centerpiece of the party system's linkage profile, together with the decline of programmatic representation analyzed in the previous chapter, completely exposed the system. Consequently, it came to rely increasingly on decaying clientelist networks. In the next chapter, I explore how clientelist demands grew and resources fell short by the late 1990s, undermining the last vestige of linkage.

---

11. Significance level of $p < .05$.

7

RESOURCE SHORTAGES AND CLIENTELIST EXCESSES

The serious downfall [of the party system] was that the parties substituted their ideological message for a clientelist one. . . . They turned to offering privileges, scholarships, jobs, and other benefits. They ceased being ideological political parties and became simply sources of clientelism. This determined the crisis of the political parties.

—**Former COPEI secretary general,** *interview with author, November 2003*

Clientelist exchanges were used to provide political support. There came a time when the resources were not sufficient, and the party could not satisfy the demands. But the people thought the money just stayed at the top in the hands of the politicians.

—**Former AD CEN member,** *interview with author, July 2006*

Venezuela's traditional parties long utilized conditional exchanges as a means of providing linkage, especially among poor and excluded sectors of society. A former AD secretary general explained his party's strategy: "To attract voters, [AD] had its local groups. Each community might have several neighborhood groups of maybe fifty families. For example, leaders of these community groups would go to the local party leader and say, 'We are having problems with water service.' Then the party leader would go to Hidrocapital and tell them about the problem so it could be fixed. This would make the people think, 'Oh, the party leader is good because he fixed our problem; we should vote for AD so that they keep on fixing our problems.' This type of exchange led people to vote for the party" (Interview 51). The parties even trained their members to offer conditional benefits to their friends and neighbors. A COPEI publication, *The activist: A copeyano in service to his community,* was circulated among party members, encouraging them to help achieve concrete benefits for their communities in the name of the party. Using a step-by-step process, the publication taught party activists how to act as local clientelist mediators. To attract new party supporters, they were told to identify their neighbors' specific manageable problems and then make sure that the party settled these issues, overseeing their resolution personally. The provision of such material benefits to obtain political support was an important part of the party system's linkage framework.

This sort of direct exchange, in which people trade political support for excludable benefits or services, is called clientelism (Magaloni, Diaz-Cayeros, and Estévez 2007, 182) and had been commonplace in the Venezuelan system since its consolidation in the 1970s. Clientelism offered a means of linking the poor and otherwise excluded to the state, and material benefits provided additional inducements for party support from the working and middle classes. But at the height of the system, these incentives were neither the exclusive nor the clearly dominant form of linkage, as the parties also employed programmatic appeals and incorporation.

However, policy responsiveness decayed and ideological distinctions between the traditional parties disappeared, making programmatic appeals more and more irrelevant as the 1990s progressed. Likewise, incorporating linkages failed to integrate the growing number of people without stable formal sector employment. As both programmatic appeals and incorporation decayed, the parties relied increasingly on clientelism to link people to the system. However, as this chapter will explain, clientelist linkages also deteriorated, and by the late 1990s, all three types of linkage had decayed, imperiling the entire party system.

EXPLAINING THE DECAY OF CLIENTELISM

Furnishing linkage by providing material benefits in exchange for votes exposes parties to a particular set of challenges. In contrast to programmatic or incorporating linkages, clientelism emphasizes immediate, tangible benefits, rather than the purposeful pursuit of objectives with a broader or longer impact. Clients are primarily focused on obtaining the best deal they can arrange for themselves and their families. They do not possess long time horizons and are much less likely to tolerate and oftentimes much less able to endure parties that do not meet some basic need. Clientelist parties without sufficient resources to satisfy escalating demand thus face impatient and unforgiving voters, and parties that cannot deliver find themselves at risk. Such parties are, therefore, extremely susceptible to situations in which supply cannot meet demand (Lyne 2007; Piattoni 2001b; Scherlis 2008). When constraints on resources limit parties' ability to deliver, clientelist linkage decays. I have theorized that increased demand stems from social changes that expand the need for or cost of material exchanges (Lyne 2008; Magaloni, Diaz-Cayeros, and Estévez 2007; Piattoni 2001a) and from political decentralization, which multiplies the number of separate electoral contests for which repeated clientelist benefits are needed and undermines distributional efficiencies associated with centralized elections (Dávila and Delgado 2002; Luna 2007; Ryan 2004; Sabatini 2003). The supply of clientelist inputs is reduced by economic crisis (Hopkin and Mastropaolo 2001; Kitschelt and Wilkinson 2007a) and by reforms that limit partisan access to state resources (Harbers 2010; Warner 2001).

When voters demand clientelism but cannot find the linkage they seek from one party, their need for immediate, tangible benefits drives them toward other parties making similar material promises, intensifying the pressure for clientelism across the system. Because clients lack strong partisan ties and readily move from one party to another, challenges from heightened demand threaten all parties that offer such linkage. Likewise, economic crisis and reforms that rationalize the state and remove partisan influence from public benefit distribution severely constrain all parties' resources. As demand swells and resources dry up, many people who wish to trade their votes for direct material incentives are unable to make the exchange they seek. This leads to a growing throng of people who want to participate in the clientelist system but do not receive any benefits. They are, therefore, left without linkage.

As the Venezuelan party system relied more on clientelism in the mid-1990s, the parties faced challenges from escalating demands and constraints due to a shrinking and increasingly inaccessible resource pool. Poverty and uncertainty put pressure on the parties to furnish more clientelist exchanges to somehow meet the most basic needs of the desperate population. Reforms associated with political and fiscal decentralization threatened clientelism, simultaneously increasing the number of benefits the parties needed to provide in order to secure local and regional offices and decreasing the party organizations' control over decentralized resources. At the same time, economic crisis and efforts to rationalize the state and remove partisan influence from social benefit distribution restricted the parties' resources for clientelism. Ultimately, demand outstripped supply, and the traditional parties were unable to salvage linkage through raw exchange. As fewer people received politically motivated benefits and more voters lacked linkage, the entire party system was discredited. Clientelism was increasingly viewed as a corrupt arrangement that benefited a select minority, rather than a viable form of linkage available to many.

SOCIAL CHANGES CREATE MOUNTING DEMAND
FOR CLIENTELISM

Social changes that create more potential clients generate pressure on parties, particularly when they are reliant on clientelism and cannot integrate new voters through other mechanisms. Expansion of a clientelist electorate through rapid population growth or the sudden extension of suffrage creates greater demand (Lyne 2008). Moreover, when people struggle to make ends meet or fear for their physical safety or survival, they are uncertain about what the future holds and are likely to prefer immediate material exchanges over less tangible and longer-term linkage arrangements (Piattoni 2001b, 210). In other words, as people fall into poverty or grapple with doubts about the future, they will likely demand clientelist benefits, increasing pressure on the distribution system (Hale 2007; Magaloni, Diaz-Cayeros, and Estévez 2007). In Venezuela, the ranks of those seeking clientelist benefits increased dramatically in the decade leading up to party system collapse as the population grew, poverty engulfed an ever-expanding portion of the electorate, and the once-substantial middle class seemed to disappear.

Although Venezuela never experienced a sudden spike in population, the populace grew by about 2 to 3 percent annually between 1970 and 2000, more than doubling over the thirty-year period. Leaders of AD, COPEI, and MAS pointed to this growth as a source of strain on their clientelist systems as it tested state resources (Interviews 19, 37, 59, 60). Government spending and oil income per capita declined significantly and steadily beginning in 1981 and reached low points in the late 1990s (fig. 7.1). The population grew, albeit gradually, but petroleum income did not, thus straining the system of distribution based largely on oil revenues (Interview 37).

Population growth without proportional increases in state revenue suggests that unmet demands for clientelism may have increased. But if people had found representation through other avenues, a larger population would not have necessarily pressured the parties for greater material exchanges, because programmatic appeals and interest incorporation may provide linkage

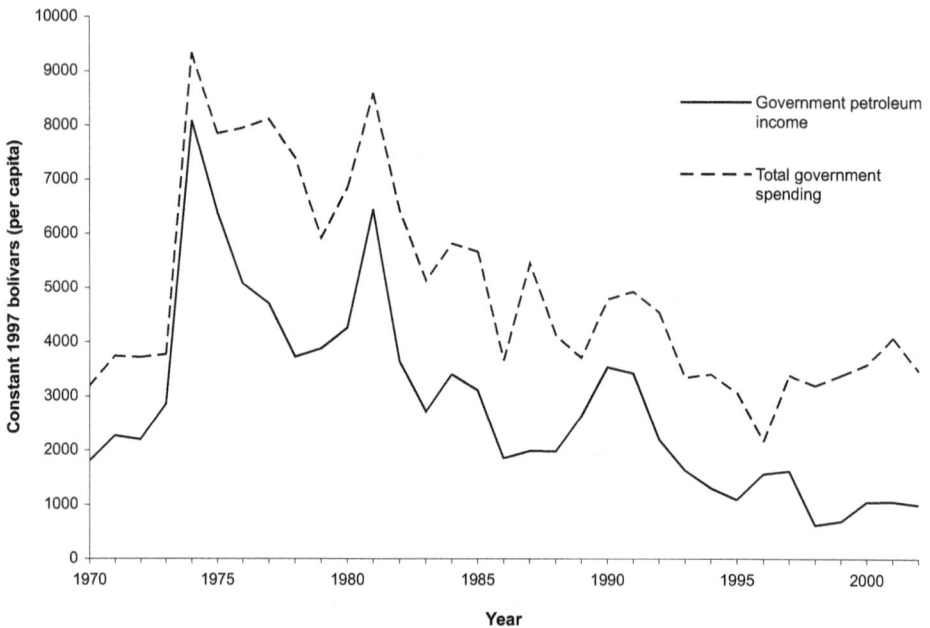

Fig. 7.1 Government spending and oil income (per capita), 1970–2002

Source: Data from Fernández (2003), based on original data from the Oficina Nacional de Presupuesto, Instituto Nacional de Estadística, and Banco Central de Venezuela.

for many without requiring significant increases in resources. However, as chapters 5 and 6 demonstrated, these strategies had deteriorated significantly by the 1990s. Clientelism was the only mechanism that remained for linking much of the growing populace. And for those who preferred less conditional forms of linkage, clientelism could only provide a poor or illegitimate substitute for the more substantive linkage they sought.

More significantly, social deterioration associated with the economic crisis of the 1990s placed substantial new pressure on the parties for clientelist exchanges. As detailed in the previous chapter, the numbers of informal and unemployed workers swelled in the 1990s, yet the parties did not accommodate their interests through incorporation. Instead, they relied on their classic tactic for dealing with unincorporated groups—purchasing support through clientelism. But as more people lost their jobs or fell into informality and the portion of the population outside the formal sector surpassed 60 percent, the parties had to find more and more material benefits to maintain linkage with the burgeoning group of unincorporated voters (Interview 48).

Furthermore, as people fell into poverty, incomes lagged behind price increases, inequities widened, and uncertainty about the future escalated.

More people were reluctant to wait for programmatic responses to their problems and instead sought immediate benefits, intensifying clientelist pressures. For many, these material demands became a last resort necessary for survival.

The share of the Venezuelan population in poverty increased steadily beginning in the early 1980s. Poverty levels were at a low point in 1982, with only about 10 percent living in critical poverty. However, by 1995, over one-third of the population was indigent and 71 percent were in poverty (CISOR, various dates). The upsurge in poverty over this period is astronomical. In 1997, over 9 million more Venezuelans were impoverished than had been in 1982. According to CEPAL estimates, no other Latin American country experienced this kind of poverty increase in the same period.[1] The poverty levels in this formerly prosperous nation surpassed the regional average, estimated at 43.5 percent in 1997, placing Venezuela in the company of countries like Peru and El Salvador (CEPAL 2008). Consequently, as more Venezuelans sought material exchanges in order to make ends meet, the parties faced an onslaught of new clientelist demands.

The once sizeable middle class, viewed as a centerpiece of the Venezuelan success story, also shrank and lost purchasing power (Interviews 8, 21, 30, 54, 64). By 1995, Venezuela's average real income was the lowest it had been since 1952 and was only half of what it had been in 1982 (Baptista 1997, 145). Fig. 7.2 presents an approximation of how the middle class fared during the 1980s and 1990s, depicting average incomes for the third and fourth quintiles in constant bolívars. The income of these middle sectors declined substantially. Average income of the fourth quintile, which includes households earning more than the bottom 60 percent and less than the top 20 percent, dropped steadily beginning in 1982. In less than fifteen years, the fourth quintile lost over two-thirds of its earning capacity. This decline in the standard of living, particularly for middle-class Venezuelans who had become accustomed to a certain quality of life, undermined faith in the parties while also escalating material demands. The impoverishment of society and the growing divide between the rich and everyone else is also evidenced in increasing income inequality. Inequality, measured using the 90–10 ratio,[2] remained relatively stable throughout the 1980s and into the early 1990s, suggesting that severe income disparities were not manifested until after the onset of economic crisis and neoliberal reforms. Yet inequality escalated

1. CEPAL (2008) estimates place the Venezuelan poverty rate at 25 percent in 1981 and 48 percent in 1997.
2. Source: UCAB Poverty Project, calculations based on OCEI's Encuesta de Hogares.

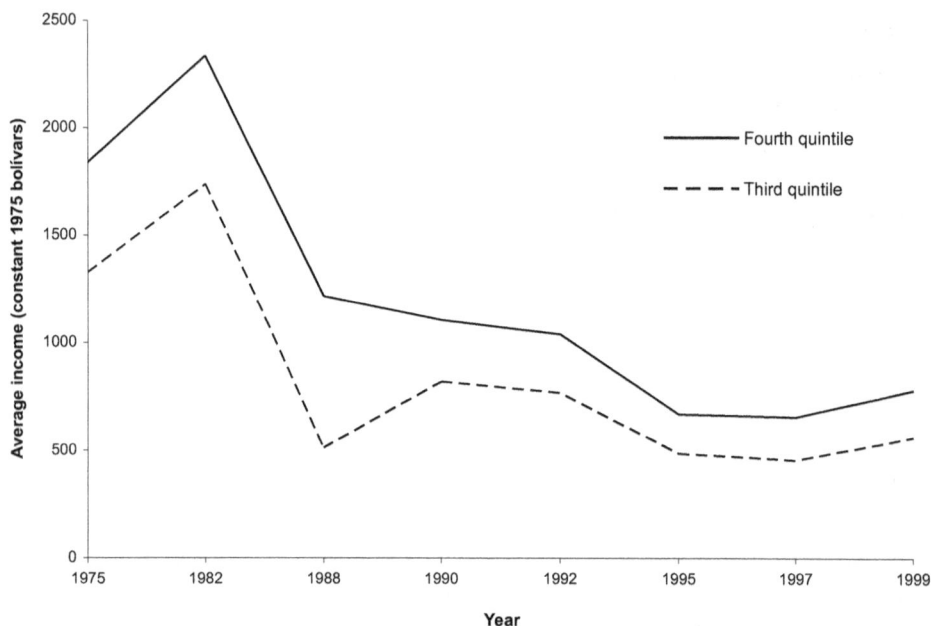

Fig. 7.2 Average income for the third and fourth quintiles, 1975–99

Source: UCAB Poverty Project calculations, based on Encuesta de Hogares, Oficina Central de Estadística e Informática (Venezuela).

markedly in the years immediately preceding the party system's collapse. In the 1980s, the top 10 percent of earners made about eight times more than the poorest Venezuelans. But by 1997, the top decile was earning almost seventeen times more than the bottom decile, stretching the gap between rich and poor to levels unmatched during the 2.5-party system. As the middle class fell into poverty, the ranks of those seeking clientelism swelled.

Population growth that outpaced petroleum income, the swift descent into poverty that afflicted many, and the attendant decimation of the middle class contributed to heightened clientelist demands. Before the economic crisis, "petroleum wealth permitted the satisfaction of everyone, [the parties] could maintain the clientelist system. . . . But the population and their demands were increasing . . . and petroleum income was not" (Interview 37, with former COPEI secretary general). Additionally, poverty frequently drove people to opt for the immediate tangible benefits provided by clientelism; more families faced hardship, and as a result their material demands escalated (Interview 38, with former president). Many politicians and party leaders pointed to middle-class impoverishment and mounting inequality as strains on the party system. In particular, the lower quality of life experienced by many formerly middle-income Venezuelans heightened their irritation with the system. Frequently, in news reports and op-ed pieces in the late 1990s, AD and COPEI leaders acknowledged that growing poverty and inequality raised clientelist demands on the party system and even threatened democracy (Canache Mata 1997; Colomine 1997c; Durán 1998). AD leader Pedro Paris Montesinos explained that "the middle class is disappearing and the exasperation and tension this awakens may produce an overflow of demands that neither the parties nor anyone in civil society will be able to contain" (quoted in Reyes Rodriguez 1997). The poverty that so suddenly assaulted Venezuela also aggravated citizens' uncertainty. As a result of desperate personal situations, many were unable to wait for substantive responses and were unwilling to forgive the parties' inability to meet their demands. But although "expectations [for clientelism] increased, the answers did not come" (Interview 49).

DEMANDS AND CONSTRAINTS GENERATED BY DECENTRALIZATION

Beyond the demands created by escalating poverty and inequality, the Venezuelan parties encountered pressures on clientelism caused by decentralization. Although decentralizing reforms are frequently implemented with the goals of improving participation, efficiency, accountability, and democracy (Diamond and Tsalik 1999; Fox 1994; Grindle 2000; Rondinelli, McCullough, and Johnson 1989), in practice they can pose serious challenges to parties and party systems, especially those reliant on clientelism (Harbers 2009; Ryan 2004; Sabatini 2003).

Political decentralization amplifies clientelist demand, as parties need more financial and organizational resources to turn out the vote more frequently (Dávila and Delgado 2002). Separate electoral contests multiply demand over the levels experienced under concurrently held elections, which allow parties to offer a single exchange for consistent party-based votes on behalf of its candidates at all levels (Grindle 2000; Luna 2004). With political decentralization, local and national politics are decoupled, promoting the autonomy of subnational elites who develop their own clientelist machines that undermine the efficiency of resource distribution (Falleti 2005; Ryan 2004). As the number of contests on the electoral calendar increases, the purchasing power of each clientelist exchange dwindles and the benefits distributed do not effectively serve the goals of the central party apparatus;

thus, more resources are required to win (Luna 2007; Sabatini 2003). On the supply side, fiscal decentralization may restrict the resource pool available to the central party and lead to inefficient allocation of dwindling funds as local elites target distribution to enhance their own power rather than benefit the party apparatus (Crook and Manor 1998; Harbers 2010).

In Venezuela, political decentralization threatened clientelism by heightening demand and undermining interdependence between different levels of the party, while subsequent fiscal decentralization weakened clientelist capacity by limiting the resources under the national parties' control. Here the Venezuelan experience contrasts with the survival of some of its neighbors, such as Argentina, where decentralization was a long-standing element of politics to which the parties were well adapted (Falleti 2005; Rumi 2005), or Costa Rica, where the parties did not have to confront the challenges of decentralization in the midst of economic crisis (Escobar-Lemmon 2001; Ryan 2004). The Venezuelan parties, on the other hand, confronted challenges from new decentralization dynamics simultaneously with the demands generated by crisis, poverty, and uncertainty, further weakening clientelist linkage capacity.[3]

Political Reform Efforts in the 1990s

In response to pressure from some segments of political society and in fulfillment of a campaign promise, President Lusinchi created the Presidential Commission for the Reform of the State (COPRE) in 1984. The commission brought together representatives from various sectors, including the parties, academia, and civil society (Kulisheck and Canache 1998), and was charged with proposing political, administrative, and judicial reforms and promoting the development of civil society (Martz 1995).

COPRE was not initially expected to have much impact, but it took on a life of its own, going far past Lusinchi's intent (Kornblith 1998a). In 1986, COPRE made its first proposals, advocating reforms to establish a more democratic and efficient state, including gubernatorial elections, decentralization, party democratization, judicial reform, and economic restructuring (COPRE 1986; Gómez Calcaño and López Maya 1990; Interview 54). Among the most significant changes stemming from these recommendations were electoral, administrative, and fiscal reforms that sought to devolve authority away from the national government and weaken the central party

---

3. See chapter 11 for more on the contrasting processes in Venezuela and Argentina.

apparatuses (de la Cruz 2004; Lalander 2004; Penfold-Becerra 1999). A 1988 law created the office of mayor and eliminated presidential control over gubernatorial appointments. Venezuelans voted to elect leaders to these local and regional offices for the first time in 1989. Also that year, Congress passed the Decentralization Law, which allowed states to request administrative control over various policy arenas, and the Municipal Regime Law, which governed municipalities' role in local service delivery (de la Cruz 2004; Escobar-Lemmon 2003). In 1993, interim president Ramón J. Velásquez issued a presidential decree creating FIDES (Fondo Intergubernamental para la Descentralización), which was to channel national resources to support state and local efforts to assume administrative competencies.[4]

The intended goal of decentralization was to restructure institutions so that representation and accountability would improve and efficiency would be enhanced. The COPRE slogan was "Democratize the democracy" (Crisp 2000, 189). Reformers viewed decentralization as a "bright promise" for strengthening "citizens' faith in the democracy as well as a means to improve the quality and coverage of public services" (de la Cruz 2004, 181–82). The hope was that legitimacy and stability could be restored by improving representation and cleaning up the vices of excessive bureaucratization, clientelism, and corruption (Buxton 1999b; Combellas 1997; de la Cruz 1992; Grindle 2000; Philip 2000).

Assessments of the reforms suggest that at least some of these goals were achieved. Decentralization opened political spaces and provided access for new groups and ideas (Kornblith 1998b; Welsch and Carrasquero 1989). The direct election of mayors and governors arguably enhanced subnational politicians' ties to voters (Lucena 2003), making them more responsive and accountable to the community (Grindle 2000; McCoy and Smith 1995, 149). Some have even argued that political decentralization "kept the moribund

4. Beyond COPRE-inspired efforts at decentralization, the legislature also passed electoral reforms in the early 1990s, which sought to foster a stronger sense of connection between voters and their representatives. The reforms changed the legislative election system from pure, closed-list proportional representation to a mixed system, first used in the 1993 elections. In the new mixed system, half the legislature was elected directly by name from single-member districts and the remaining seats were distributed using proportional representation to achieve a legislature with a composition proportional to each party's national vote share. Establishing this German-inspired mixed system did not, therefore, change the overall composition of the chamber because the number of seats granted to each party was still based on the performance of its list. The intent of the new system was to improve participation by promoting local accountability through the single-member districts, while preserving partisan ties through the list votes (Kornblith 1998b). Despite considerable reluctance from their more conservative elements, the parties ultimately supported this compromise, hoping to regain popular support without sacrificing central party control and thereby use the reform to retain their hold on power.

system alive for a decade" (de la Cruz 2004, 187; for a similar argument, see Grindle 2000 and Lander 1996).

Unfortunately for the party system, the reforms were unsuccessful in restoring its credibility. In fact, COPRE specifically attacked the traditional party apparatuses, seeking to undercut the power of the central party bosses and put an end to clientelist linkage strategies (Grindle 2000; Combellas 1997). But rather than fostering new linkage based on local programmatic appeals, decentralization enabled subnational politicians to build their own bases of support through clientelist exchange, merely proliferating demand for direct material benefits while weakening the established parties (Aragort Solórzano 2004; García-Guadilla and Pérez 2002; McCoy and Smith 1995). As a result, the reforms had profound negative consequences for the existing linkage system. On balance, neither the quality nor the quantity of ties between people and their government improved in the 1990s. Instead, the reforms increased the demand for benefits, disrupted national clientelist networks, created inefficiencies, and limited central party access to resources for distribution, thereby undermining clientelism—the one remaining form of linkage in the parties' repertoire.

The Costs of Electoral Decentralization

Political decentralization, through the establishment of separate subnational elections, multiplied the number of electoral processes, repeatedly requiring the parties to ante up resources to get out the vote. Rather than having one nationwide contest every five years, as the pattern had been in the early days of democracy, elections abounded. In the ten years preceding the system's collapse in 1998, Venezuelans went to the polls seven times, making almost twice as many trips as they had at the system's height between 1973 and 1983.[5] The additional elections were costly for the parties. The increased frequency of electoral contests required expending organizational and financial reserves if a party desired to pursue influence at all levels of government. Political strategists and party leaders considered regional and local offices to be important prizes, not only as harbingers of future national prestige but also in terms of controlling political power. Winning these contests

---

5. Venezuelans made four trips to the polls between 1973 and 1983—three national, one local. The first local elections were held in 1979. But in the decade before collapse, they voted in national elections in 1988, 1993, and 1998, and in local and regional elections in 1989, 1992, 1995, and 1998. In 1998, local, regional, and congressional contests were held concurrently, while the presidential race was decided in a separate election a month later.

was a priority to which the parties dedicated considerable effort. But constantly promoting participation in campaign rallies, cultivating partisan turnout through election day activities, and monitoring the voting process taxed party activists' commitment and drained party coffers. And for voters won over by clientelist exchanges, the parties were forced to find material benefits to offer at every election. Electoral decentralization thus stretched the parties' clientelist networks, multiplying the pressure to produce these benefits in repeated contests throughout the country at all levels.

Decentralization also led to the proliferation of local governments, which demanded additional resources from the central party organizations that sought to sustain their local presence. In 1978, Venezuela had only 188 municipalities, but by 1995 there were 330 (Lalander 2004, 149). Each required the parties to expend energy and resources in order to hold on to power and to develop local machines. In contrast to the 1970s, when controlling the national executive meant that a party also dominated state and municipal governments, introducing separate subnational elections and creating new municipalities in the 1990s meant that parties had to compete in many more races—in over 300 municipalities as well as 22 states and the federal district—if they wished to retain influence across the country.

In addition to the multiplication of electoral contests, which increased demands for clientelism, decentralization required the parties to restructure themselves in ways that presented challenges to their clientelist distribution networks. On the surface, the parties seemed to adapt to the changes brought on by decentralization (Lalander 2004, 157). They established offices to oversee and assist affiliated local and regional governments. AD, COPEI, and MAS enacted internal party reforms in the mid-1990s, responding to new institutional incentives created by the direct election of mayors and governors as well as the mixed electoral system. For instance, in an effort to select popular local personalities for the party ticket and thereby gain an edge in subnational or single-member district races, all three parties increased the involvement of their members and even nonpartisans in choosing candidates. For the 1993 contest, AD and COPEI even took the selection of their presidential nominees to the base by holding primaries.[6]

However, the organizational changes enacted by the parties to respond to electoral and administrative devolution did not address the challenges that decentralization presented to their clientelist distribution networks.

6. Motivated by a lack of resources and their defeat in 1993, as well as the increasing isolation of the party leadership, both parties reverted to centralized decision making in the selection of their 1998 presidential nominees.

Thus, the parties found themselves losing control of their only remaining linkage mechanism. As a result of electoral decentralization, local and regional politicians developed personal followings and in many cases formed their own patronage networks to support their individual candidacies. Historically, these local and regional leaders had been appointed. As a result, they lacked electoral legitimacy and were without independent power bases; instead, they relied heavily on the central party, just as the party depended on local partisans to carry out its work. The national organization and local leaders were thus interdependent. The central party funneled resources downward, and individual leaders used them to develop party support, while also winning power for themselves. However, the establishment of direct, separate elections for each level of government diluted this interdependence and weakened the party apparatus. Networks that had previously been operated by loyal partisans to serve the party apparatus were no longer designed to support only the central party. Rather, they functioned primarily to underpin the ambitions and power of individual local and regional candidates (Interview 44), who used central party resources directed to the subnational level primarily to support themselves rather than getting out the partisan vote (Interviews 39, 41; Grindle 2000; Sabatini 2003). Therefore, to win the decentralized elections, parties had to supply these local networks with clientelist inputs, but the central party apparatus received little in return. Before decentralization, local investments had yielded electoral support to the entire party in centralized elections; after decentralization, the local distribution of resources brought only limited benefits to the party organization.

As decentralization enabled subnational leaders to develop their own bases of support, they became less subservient to the party and only aligned with the central apparatus when it suited their self-interest. In time, regional leaders even exerted decisive influence in national-level party decisions. The contingent nature of the relationship between the central party organization and subnational leaders that developed with decentralization was manifested in the role of regional party leaders in the traditional parties' seemingly erratic selection of their 1998 presidential nominees. In AD, Luis Alfaro Ucero consolidated power in the 1990s from his pivotal positions as secretary of organization and then secretary general. Using his power, Alfaro was very careful to funnel clientelist resources to the regional party leaders, fostering among them a sense of loyalty to himself. When the party's Labor Bureau proposed Alfaro as a consensus candidate for the 1998 nomination, the governors were quick to lend their support to the man who had been instrumental in their own rise to power, seeing in his candidacy an opportunity for continued access to fuel for their individual clientelist machines. However, Alfaro's campaign never took off. As the December elections neared, the AD governors, who feared that Alfaro's defeat would cut them off from central government resources, led a revolt that ultimately caused the party to ditch him as their nominee. At the last minute, AD put its support behind former copeyano governor Henrique Salas Römer, whose candidacy provided the most viable alternative to Hugo Chávez. Likewise, within COPEI, the governors convinced their party to withdraw its support from the independent candidacy of Irene Saéz and cast their lot with Salas Römer as well.

The adeco governors' initial support for Alfaro was a result of the benefits he channeled toward their personal networks. In a similar way, their abandonment of him was motivated by a desire to maintain access to resources. By backing a possible winner in Salas Römer, instead of a sure loser in Alfaro, the governors hoped to earn some goodwill for their regional administrations from someone who had a more realistic chance of gaining control of government purse strings and might provide state resources to them in the future. Despite the investment that Alfaro had poured into regional leaders, when the resources seemed to be drying up, they abandoned him. COPEI governors similarly sought affiliation with a winner rather than continuing to back a loser, which would have certainly led to the loss of power and resources.

The dynamics surrounding the 1998 campaign suggest that regional leaders' support for their central party apparatus was conditional. As long as they received resources from the party, the governors were happy to support its leadership. But when party decisions undermined the governors' personal power and threatened the resources needed to feed their networks, they were unwilling to sacrifice themselves for the party. Decentralization increased the resources needed to win additional elections and to feed the emerging networks of regional leaders. However, the parties' investment in these goals did not generate the sort of unqualified support to which the parties had grown accustomed, making clientelism not only more costly but also more risky. The creation of local and regional leaderships promoted the independence of subnational politicians, who no longer relied exclusively on the apparatus and instead used central party resources for their own political benefit. Because decentralization "provided opportunities for state-level leaders to generate local bases of support that could be independent of politicians in Caracas, [it] was a major step toward dismantling a system of centralized party control and clientelism" (Grindle 2000, 38).

The Central Parties Lose Their Resource Monopolies

Further aggravating the strain on clientelism, subnational resources that had previously been employed to support national party organizations were now put to use feeding personal or regional clientelist machines. The national party lost control of local and regional patronage jobs. Instead, subnational leaders utilized these positions, along with other government resources, for their personal promotion, not in service of the party (Interview 51). The loss of party monopoly over local and regional governments and the growing pot of resources controlled by these subnational entities limited the funds available to the central party organizations.

Typically, the party controlling the presidency had used executive appointment power to name loyal partisans to the governorships of every state, which intertwined the party apparatus with subnational governments, ensured party control over decentralized resources, and made regional leaders dependent on the national party. But the Lusinchi presidency presented the last opportunity for centralized appointment of subnational leaders. With the onset of subnational elections in 1989, the national party apparatuses gradually lost control over local and regional governments, weakening the ties between different levels of their organizations and removing access to important patronage positions and subnational resources. Under Lusinchi, AD had loyal partisans in power in the governors' offices across all the states. After the first gubernatorial elections in 1989, the two traditional parties lost a little ground, winning 90 percent of the races, with AD controlling eleven governorships and COPEI seven (Penfold-Becerra 2000). But by 1995, the two parties controlled just 62 percent of the governors' offices (Lucena 2003, 261). Their monopoly over municipalities also decayed, as they won only 85 percent of mayoral races that year (Maingon 2002). The parties could no longer distribute these jobs as patronage and gradually saw their power monopoly at the subnational level wane.

Furthermore, in losing control of local and regional governments, the parties also lost access to public resources distributed via these decentralized entities. When the president controlled subnational governments, the party in power had a complete monopoly over regional resources. But with the introduction of direct elections, the parties lost access to funds controlled by opposition governments at the local and regional levels (Geddes 1994; Monaldi and Penfold 2006). Therefore, AD leaders soundly criticized President Pérez when he limited potential party resources by distributing funds to the states in equitable ways instead of privileging AD-controlled regions (Interviews 48, 53). The situation only worsened after the introduction of revenue sharing through FIDES and the passage of a 1996 law giving states control of 70 percent of their own oil revenues. As a result of these initiatives, decentralization cost the parties access to significant distributional opportunities; instead, the revenues supported autonomous local networks or opposition parties. Particularly costly to AD and COPEI was losing control of wealthy states like Bolívar, Carabobo, and Zulia, which all fell into the hands of new parties or personalist movements in the 1990s.[7] The traditional parties maintained strongholds in poorer and less developed regions, like Trujillo and Monagas, but control of these areas contributed little to the maintenance of their clientelist machines, as they did not generate resources.

The central parties also lost portions of their clientelist networks due to their enervated influence in subnational governments. Loyal partisans in subnational government positions and the local wings of the organization were essential to the parties' ability to distribute favors to their clients. As a former AD CEN member remarked, before decentralization, the use of "[gubernatorial appointments] had been an important tool for distributing and controlling power" (Interview 41). Afterward, central party control of these posts was not guaranteed: "Governors and mayors could no longer be counted on automatically . . . to deliver votes to the party's candidates at national levels [or to] distribute patronage in accordance with the direction of party leaders" (Grindle 2000, 83). Thus, the parties lost access to decentralized resources and were cut off from old distribution networks, while regional leaders were empowered. As the parties' power monopoly waned, distributing clientelist resources efficiently became more difficult.

The difficulties that political and fiscal decentralization presented to the parties' distribution networks were devastating. Each separate electoral process required new benefits and therefore increased clientelist demand. Subnational leaders developed independent bases of support, eliminating interdependence between the local, regional, and national levels of the party organizations. And the parties' inability to control decentralized resources and distribution networks undermined the availability and efficiency of benefits offered in clientelist exchange.

7. Former copeyano turned independent Henrique Salas Römer and his son controlled Carabobo from the first gubernatorial elections in 1989 through collapse in 1998. Andrés Velásquez of LCR won the governorship of Bolívar in 1989 and was reelected in 1992, although Bolívar returned to the old parties in 1995 with Jorge Carvajal representing a coalition that included AD. In Zulia, AD and COPEI lost the governorship in a special 1993 election, when MAS and Convergencia won with Lolita Aniyar de Castro. In 1995, Francisco Arias Cárdenas of LCR won in Zulia.

But decentralization was not the only factor contributing to the vaporization of funds needed to satisfy mounting clientelist demands. The parties also faced resource constraints due to the economic crisis and loss of access to the state. State resources and party-based revenues, like donations or dues, dry up during economic crisis (Hopkin and Mastropaolo 2001; Kitschelt and Wilkinson 2007a; Lyne 2008). Clientelist inputs are also likely to be undermined by reforms that reduce access to state resources for partisan-based distribution, such as professionalizing the bureaucracy or rationalizing the distribution of social funds (Hale 2007; Warner 2001). In Venezuela, economic crisis, deteriorating petroleum revenues, and associated declines in social spending decimated the pool of resources typically targeted toward clients. Furthermore, reforms designed to eliminate partisan influence over government programs exacerbated resource shortages. The parties were thus separated from their lifeblood of clientelist inputs, putting substantial stress on the system and undermining the last vestige of linkage.

Economic Crisis and Diminishing Resources

Economic deterioration complicated the parties' ability to deliver clientelist goods. Government revenue declined as oil prices plummeted in the mid-1980s and then stagnated in the 1990s. The state's nonpetroleum income also dropped precipitously between 1988 and 1990 and remained low throughout the following decade (Fernández 2003). Debt and mismanagement exhausted the country's international reserves by the late 1980s, placing considerable pressure on the state to reduce spending. Public spending per capita was cut by two-thirds between the early 1980s and the party system's 1998 collapse (see fig. 7.1). In this context, the parties were unable to keep delivering the goods people expected and consequently experienced a decline in their capacity to use clientelism to link excluded groups to the state.

The economic crisis struck the traditional party organizations at their core. By the mid-1990s, AD and COPEI were struggling to maintain their most basic operations. Both had to take financial constraints into account, scaling back their party conventions and candidate nomination processes (Nuñez 1994). COPEI closed the doors of many party offices across the country in the 1990s (Interview 84). AD, having built an enormous national headquarters in the 1980s, struggled to keep the lights on and the water running (Suárez Molero 1993). It was forced to renegotiate its debt to the utility companies, resulting in significant reductions in usage of even basic services like telephone lines (Nuñez 1993). Without adequate funds to sustain these ordinary operations, AD and COPEI were certainly hard-pressed to raise the resources they needed to satisfy mounting clientelist demands.

The parties also implemented unprecedented internal control over campaign expenditures in the 1990s, attempting to maximize the impact of diminishing resources (El Nacional 1995; Reyes Rodriguez 1998a). They exercised particular austerity in races for decentralized offices, as the central party attempted to restrain the spending of local and regional leaders, who were often forced to find their own funds (F. Torres 1995; Vinogradoff 1989). AD and COPEI closely controlled any resources coming from the central party, and candidates claimed that they lacked central party support (Interviews 42, 45). By the late 1990s, clientelism was a pivotal, if not the only, source of the parties' electoral appeal. Yet serious financial constraints made it difficult to provide material benefits.

Along with the general economic crisis and the loss of party-based funds, public sector resources for social programs also declined in the period leading up to party system collapse. The parties had relied heavily on clientelist distribution of social funds for health care and education to drum up electoral support. Loyal partisans in control of the government entities overseeing such programs had historically endeavored to make sure that the party name was associated with service delivery, engendering party support through the distribution of social benefits. But even as the parties became increasingly dependent on clientelism, the amount of money that the government apportioned to social services declined. Social spending per capita, depicted in fig. 7.3, experienced a fifteen-year pattern of decay beginning in the early 1980s, reaching its nadir in 1996 when the state spent only 624 bolívars per person—a reduction of over 75 percent from its zenith in 1981. While some Latin American countries increased social spending to combat the effects of crisis and reforms in the 1980s and 1990s, Venezuela did not (Saínz 2005, 75). Venezuelan spending per capita was right around the regional average at the beginning of the 1990s, but by 1997 most other countries in the region outpaced Venezuela in this area (Saínz 2005). With the loss of these funds, the parties' strategy of using public service distribution to generate clientelist linkages became virtually impossible. The parties lost their capacity to satisfy social demands because there was little to distribute (Interviews 39, 49, 54).

Another consequence of the crisis was the impoverishment of the middle class, which not only created demand for clientelist linkage, as discussed above, but also deprived the parties of important sources of exchange. The

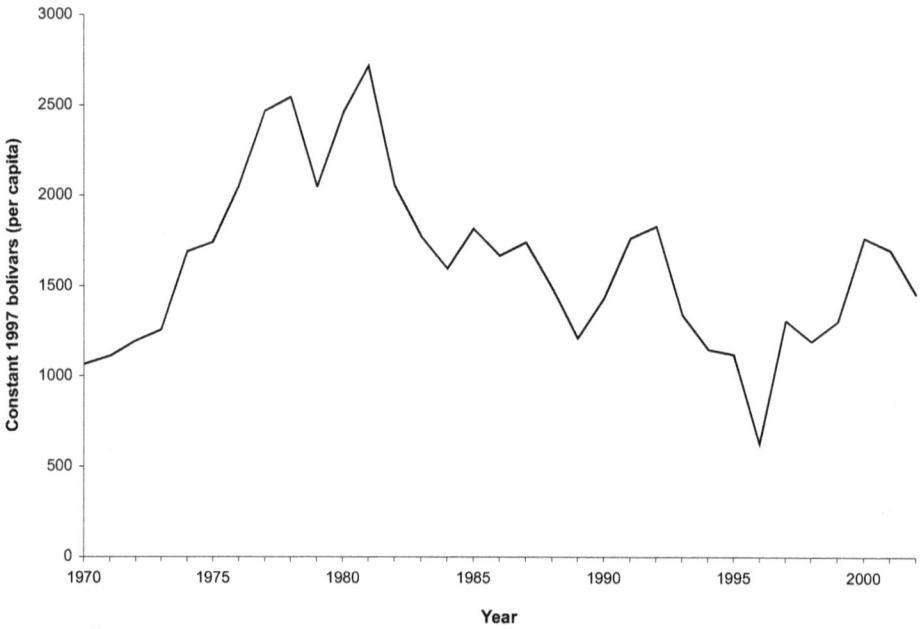

Fig. 7.3   Social spending (per capita), 1970–2002

Source: Data from Fernández (2003), based on original data from the Oficina Nacional de Presupuesto and Banco Central de Venezuela.

parties had traditionally relied on their middle-class supporters to provide professional services at the party houses for little or no cost, which fostered partisan sympathies among the beneficiaries. However, as middle-class professionals faced declining wages or lost jobs, their ability and willingness to provide free medical, legal, or educational services as part of their party's clientelist offerings dissipated. Middle-class party militants were focused on their own survival. They could not be concerned with supporting the party when their own families could barely make ends meet. Instead of helping to provide clientelist goods for their party to give to poor voters, many former professionals fell into poverty and became increasingly reliant on the party themselves (Interviews 44, 48, 50). In a variety of ways, then, the crisis limited the parties' capacity to deliver clientelist goods.

Parties' Lack of Access to Resources

The impact of the crisis was devastatingly magnified by the parties' loss of access to the few remaining resources. As a result of reform efforts as well as partisan infighting, the parties lost their traditional avenues for obtaining inputs for their machines. At the precise time when it was crucial to maintain a flow of resources to sustain clientelism, the parties were cut off. Both AD and COPEI scrambled for any scraps they could find, but without means of accessing clientelist resources, exchange-based linkage decayed.

COPEI provides the clearest case of lost access to clientelist inputs because the party did not regain control of government purse strings after Luis Herrera Campíns' unpopular administration ended in 1984. Instead, AD governed for two consecutive terms, and then Caldera abandoned his old party and governed without it. Nevertheless, COPEI made efforts to preserve its distributional capacity. Traditions of power sharing between AD and COPEI meant that the outsider was not completely excluded, so at least while an AD president was in office, COPEI retained some access to the state. But as one COPEI leader noted, "When we were in the opposition, there simply was not as much money for the party as when we were in government" (Interview 46).

To make matters worse, during the second Caldera administration, COPEI lost virtually all access to government resources when Caldera ostracized his old party, barring it from the state apparatus. However, because many voters continued to associate Caldera with COPEI, they expected the party to be able to deliver benefits. But it had no access. And even though COPEI joined alliances that controlled Congress for a few years in the second half of the 1990s, this did not yield many material benefits. Thus, the fissure between Caldera and COPEI exacerbated the party's loss of access to resources. When a party is not in government, it misses out on opportunities for clientelism. When exclusion persists for a long time—fifteen years in the case of COPEI—the party risks losing its base because it cannot meet demands. By the late 1990s, COPEI's party machinery was running on fumes.

AD's exclusion from clientelist resources took a less direct path, but the effects were just as destructive. Rather than losing access as a result of electoral defeat and a party split, as with COPEI, AD's machine suffered from reform efforts that rationalized the state and cut the party off from resources. Throughout the Lusinchi administration, the AD government was careful to channel funds to the party. Lusinchi's appointment of all the party's state-level secretaries as governors speaks strongly to this close allegiance between party and government. However, with Carlos Andrés Pérez's return to the presidency and his implementation of structural adjustment reforms, AD lost access to the resources it needed to maintain clientelism.

The neoliberal reforms that Pérez advocated at the outset of his second term rationalized the state and limited the availability of material goods for clientelist exchanges. The reforms increased transparency, making it more difficult for AD to play intermediary between the people and state benefi-cence. For instance, as part of his reform efforts, Pérez eliminated existing social programs and established new ones, with the aim of replacing politi-cally motivated distribution with economically based targeting. The programs that Pérez cast aside had traditionally been controlled by the parties, enabl-ing them to distribute services based on political goals and to claim credit for social benefit delivery. AD wanted Pérez to maintain the existing "pop-ulist programs" so that it might retain the political gains that came from being associated with the distribution of material goods (Interview 50).

But Pérez circumvented AD and established new programs that replaced party-mediated benefits with direct subsidies that excluded the parties. Not only were the new social programs widely criticized for being underfunded and for failing to stem the painful effects of adjustment, but they also re-moved the parties from the social policy equation, eliminating opportunities for clientelism. Although the depoliticization of social policy was laudable from a technocratic perspective, in terms of party survival, the reforms hurt. One pro-reform member of AD's CEN explained this dynamic well: "Pérez wanted to separate himself from the clientelist, populist model of the past. But the party, which lived off of clientelism, saw that its power could diminish with the reforms. The party resisted the reforms in order to main-tain its populist and clientelist system. So by implementing the reforms, Carlos Andrés [Pérez] chose to sacrifice his own party by weakening its access to populist social programs" (Interview 49). Technocrats constructed the new programs outside the ordinary social services structure, and experts decided who would benefit from the programs and who would not, remov-ing political calculus from the equation. AD was not involved in the design or implementation of the new policies, limiting its ability to use the pro-grams to generate partisan support. The neoliberal reforms also privatized state-owned corporations in significant sectors of the economy and cut other public sector jobs, eliminating the parties' capacity to use patronage to build support (fig. 7.4). As poverty and other social ills increased, AD was no longer associated with clientelist efforts to offset these problems, and the apparatus lost much of its ability to offer conditional material exchanges. It is worth noting that AD's inability to target social spending toward Vene-zuelans otherwise excluded from the political system stands in stark contrast to the way in which the Mexican PRI and the Argentine Peronists strategi-cally employed state resources to bring disconnected voters back into the fold (Burgess and Levitsky 2003). These parties' allies in the presidency channeled resources into politicized social funds that helped sustain the parties' clientelist coffers. But in Venezuela spending was both reduced and rationalized.

In his efforts to depoliticize economic and social policy, Pérez fought constantly with AD as he tried to go it alone. He distrusted those he called "the dinosaurs" of the party bureaucracy and failed to consider AD's interests. Instead of attempting to court the party and address its needs, Pérez manifested his independent streak and sought out the support of experts regardless of past ideology or partisanship. Oftentimes, AD leaders accused him of favoring and consulting more closely with COPEI and parties of the left than with his own party. Pérez's neglect of AD's needs provoked considerable ire from its leaders, who accused him of trying to kill the party. But after losing the battle to control AD, Pérez estimated that working with an "antiquated" party would obstruct, not facilitate, his reforms. He therefore kept AD and its leadership out of positions of power and enacted his reforms, blocking party access to the resources it needed to survive.

Pérez and the party clashed publicly over bureaucratic appointments. Only a handful of cabinet ministers were affiliated with AD, and those who were adecos tended not to have the president's ear or were considered by the party to be renegades, just like Pérez. Throughout his term, AD leaders frequently called for greater party representation in his cabinet. The party was especially frustrated by its exclusion from social ministries, which were focal points for distributing benefits with clientelist potential. Instead, anti-AD technocrats and businesspeople ran pivotal ministries like Education, Health, and Family, where many new social programs were based. The party was also forced to surrender important cabinet positions that awarded government contracts, like Transportation and Communications and Urban Development. Losing these ministries and their distributional opportunities weakened AD's ability to meet clientelist expectations. Repeatedly and publicly, AD leaders implored Pérez to place loyal adecos in key positions of the "Social Cabinet" so that "programs having to do with the government's contact with the marginalized and popular classes [would] be in the hands of men politically and ideologically identified with AD" (Brando 1990, paraphrasing AD Secretary General Humberto Celli). The party thus fought to maintain access and reap benefits associated with distributional policies but was marginalized throughout Pérez's presidency.

Almost five years of conflict between AD and Pérez produced considerable decay in the capacity of the party's clientelist machine. AD became increasingly desperate for resources. But like COPEI, it found itself outside the presidency following Caldera's 1993 election. A long history of animosity between Caldera and top adecos suggested that the resource drought might only worsen. However, after his election, Caldera was reliant on a diverse coalition of small parties that had won limited legislative seats, and given the bitter split between Caldera and COPEI, an alliance between the two was not an option. To conjure up the congressional backing he needed, Caldera was in search of pragmatic allies. At the same time, Luis Alfaro Ucero desperately needed fuel for the AD machine. Despite the acrimony of their past, the two politicians abandoned their ideological moorings and their personal distaste and struck a deal.

Although AD claimed that its cooperation with Caldera was aimed at stabilizing the regime (and for some leaders this may have indeed been the intent), the arrangement marked a valiant effort by AD to find clientelist inputs so that it might provide some benefits to an increasingly frustrated populace. In exchange for supporting Caldera in Congress, Alfaro received access to contracts and bureaucratic positions as well as other resources for his clientelist machine. Several of Alfaro's detractors have claimed that this agreement predated the election, with Alfaro's cronies supporting Caldera's campaign rather than working for the AD candidate, Claudio Fermín (Interviews 45, 47, 55). Regardless, it is quite clear that after Caldera took office, he had an arrangement with Alfaro guaranteeing government positions and contracts to well-placed adecos (Interviews 47, 48, 49, 82), which restored some of AD's access to clientelist resources.

Regrettably for AD, the Alfaro-Caldera pact primarily benefited Alfaro himself, enhancing his personal power and turning him into "the power behind the throne" (pro-Pérez adeco Hector Alonzo López, quoted in Durán López 1996). But the arrangement brought only limited benefits to the party, helping a select few. The pact revealed AD's hopeless situation, and the inadequate resources gained through this scheme did not alleviate the discrediting of the party. Public contracts could only reach a handful of fortunate businesspeople with party ties. Government jobs, while more numerous than contracts, were also constrained to a small and declining portion of the population. As the crisis intensified in the late 1990s, the overall size of the public sector shrank and reached its lowest point since before the consolidation of the 2.5-party system (fig. 7.4). The number of patronage jobs therefore declined considerably during the Caldera administration (Baptista 2005), further limiting AD's ability to build support through partisan distribution of public employment. The failure of this desperate and unlikely pact to produce support for AD was articulated by a former party president:

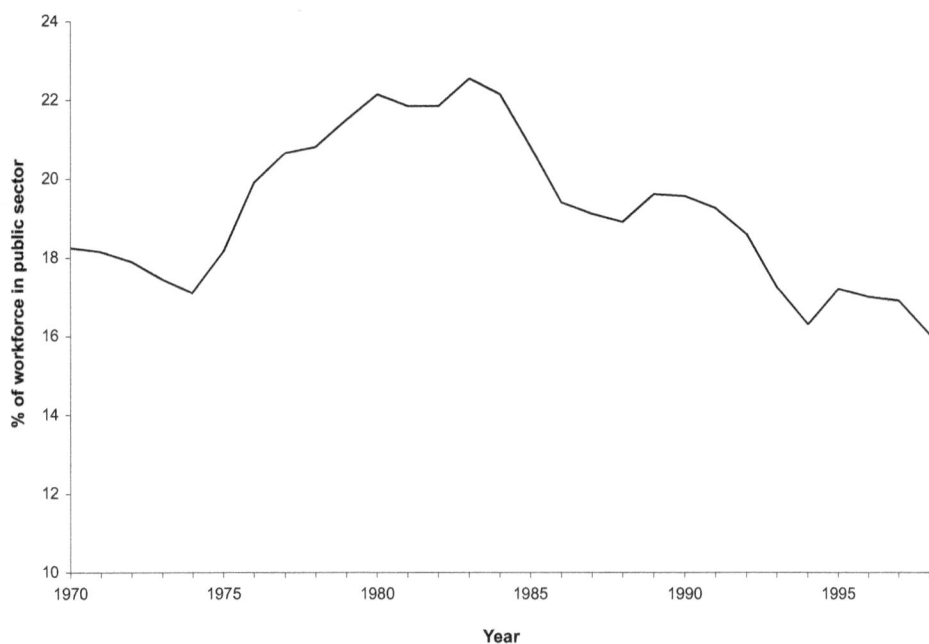

Fig. 7.4 Public sector employment, 1970–98

Source: Data from the Oficina Central de Estadística e Informática (Venezuela).

"Unfortunately the agreements between AD and Caldera served such that only a few people accrued privileges like government contracts, but it was not something that helped the party" (Interview 50). The arrangement could not overcome the resource constraints created by rationalizing reforms, so demands for clientelism escalated and linkage capacity deteriorated.

Furthermore, the Alfaro-Caldera pact turned AD into a party of government in the eyes of politically astute Venezuelans, weakening its credibility as Caldera stumbled about aimlessly for much of his term. Because AD gave top priority to obtaining material resources for clientelist exchanges and supported its longtime political nemesis, the party lost the little programmatic credibility that it had managed to maintain. The pact highlights the reckless manner in which AD endeavored to obtain even a few drops of fuel for its machine. Although the arrangement provided benefits to only a small portion of the connected and influential party faithful, AD leadership was nevertheless willing to abandon any semblance of programmatic appeal to obtain these insufficient resources. The desperation of the party and the supremacy of clientelism are brought into stark relief by these last, frantic machinations.

By the end of the 1990s, all the parties in the system faced escalating demands for direct exchanges. Social changes heightened pressures for clientelism. Decentralization also escalated demand while simultaneously challenging the hierarchical parties' capacity to dole out benefits efficiently. The economic crisis limited the parties' resources, hurting their clientelist machines. Furthermore, COPEI's loss of influence in the executive restricted its access to public funds, and state reforms rationalizing the bureaucracy and removing the parties from social benefit distribution limited AD's ability to manipulate the delivery of government benefits for partisan ends. As a result of new pressures on the system and heightened resource constraints, most Venezuelans found themselves outside party-controlled clientelist distribution networks.

As demands for direct material exchanges increased and the availability of resources to satisfy them diminished, the parties' remaining linkage form lost its allure. However, they continued to emphasize the importance of clientelism until the very end. In an interview just months before the system finally imploded, Luis Alfaro Ucero told a reporter, "Of course, the [party] machinery helps [win elections]; it is a supremely important instrument in any electoral process. *In the machinery we find the success or failure of the party*" (quoted in Reyes Rodriguez 1998b; emphasis mine). Alfaro's comment highlights the fact that the party had ceased viewing policy, ideology, or connections with society as pivotal ingredients in its electoral success. Rather, the central focus was fueling the clientelist machine to get out the partisan vote. With programmatic representation essentially absent and incorporation narrowing, only clientelism remained. But even as more people sought material benefits, economic crisis and lack of access to public resources limited the parties' ability to meet these demands. As a result, many Venezuelans no longer saw a reason to support the old parties and became disenchanted with the entire system.

Without linkage, a growing segment of the population lost tolerance for the material exchanges that had come to characterize politics. Instead of viewing clientelism as a legitimate form of linkage for building support among those excluded from programmatic or incorporating ties, people increasingly saw corruption where there had once been representation (Interviews 4, 5, 38, 67). In writing about Mexico, Shefner (2005, 244) explains why many people come to reject clientelism as corrupt: "Neoliberal policy, with its attendant reduction in resources and national spending prerogatives, undercut[s] the logic behind clientelist informal politics. In short, the pool used by the government for basic needs provisions drie[s] up, as the neoliberal mandate reduce[s] all forms of social expenditure. The urban poor, confronted with economic policies under which their political worth [is] devalued, [respond] by rejecting clientelist politics." Clientelism is palatable as long as the system satisfies demand and provides people with linkage. But when people are excluded from the exchange system and also lack linkage through other forms, clientelism turns to corruption in their minds (Hopkin and Mastropaolo 2001).

In Venezuela, the popular attitude toward corruption was "soft and tolerant" until the economic crisis became acute and linkage deteriorated (Romero 1997, 19). Without some benefit from the state—be it programmatic, interest based, or clientelist in nature—people became increasingly frustrated and attributed the parties' inability to deliver linkage to corruption. Public opinion surveys conducted from the 1970s through the 1990s asked respondents about the most important problem confronting Venezuela. Corruption did not emerge as a top issue in these surveys until the 1990s. Before 1991, consistently less than 10 percent, and typically less than 5 percent, named corruption as a serious issue. But from 1991 until 1998, there was not a single year in which fewer than 10 percent identified corruption as the most important problem; in five of those years, the percentage surpassed 15. Furthermore, Venezuelans increasingly thought that government was failing to combat this corruption. At the beginning of 1994, 54 percent of respondents in a nationwide survey agreed that President Caldera was fulfilling his campaign promise to bring an end to corruption, while only 40 percent did not think that he was meeting this obligation.[8] By 1997, when asked this same question, 87 percent of Venezuelans said that Caldera had ignored the corruption problem.

In the absence of benefits from the state, more and more people viewed clientelism as a corrupt practice that only served the interests of a select few. As a former AD CEN member explained, "There came a time when the resources were not sufficient, and the party could not satisfy demands. But the people thought the money just stayed at the top in the hands of the politicians" (Interview 49). Because the parties did not fulfill linkage expectations, frustration grew and accusations of corruption, real and imagined,

---

8. The question read, "¿Usted diría que el Presidente Caldera está cumpliendo su promesa de acabar con la corrupción?"

mounted. No one was getting what they needed—whether they sought programmatic, incorporating, or clientelist ties—and the entire system was discredited as corrupt. Meanwhile, the parties' persistent but futile efforts to sustain clientelism only drew negative attention to their dirty, rusty machines. As a result, these last frenzied attempts to find resources for clientelist distribution also contributed to programmatic disenchantment: people did not observe the traditional elites combating corruption, but rather saw the parties making use of any means necessary (corrupt or not) as they frantically tried to unearth enough clientelist resources to survive.

In essence, the party system was experiencing the ramifications of clientelism's vulnerabilities. The impoverished population was not willing or able to wait for the situation to improve. Raw need pushed many to demand immediate gratification, particularly as the uncertainty associated with the protracted crisis made waiting for the parties to provide public goods a risky prospect. However, this same crisis, together with decentralization and rationalizing state reforms, also made it difficult for the parties to deliver material benefits. Therefore, at the very time when the parties needed voters to be flexible and willing to wait out the crisis, the short time horizons of clientelism dominated people's political calculations. The parties, of course, contributed to this impatience and uncertainty by allowing other forms of linkage to deteriorate. Without programmatic alternatives or incorporation, clientelism was all that remained. As even it failed, people turned elsewhere for representation.

8

LINKAGE FAILURE AND MASS EXODUS
FROM THE PARTY SYSTEM

The previous three chapters traced the processes through which linkage furnished by the old party system decayed. The system ceased to offer meaningful programmatic appeals, growing interests in society were not incorporated, and clientelism reached fewer Venezuelans even as demand for such exchanges intensified. By 1998, the traditional system's attempts at linkage were desperate and emaciated reflections of a once strong representational profile.

In this chapter, I assess how this loss of linkage played into Venezuelans' decisions to abandon the traditional parties and reject the system they formed. According to the argument I have advanced, Venezuelans who lacked linkage should have been more disposed to reject the system and either embrace extra-system alternatives or disconnect from party politics entirely. I test this proposition through analysis of partisanship, voting decisions, and views of the parties at the pivotal moment when the old party system was replaced by a new one. The analysis reveals differences between citizens who remained true to the traditional parties and those who did not, illuminating how linkage decay promoted abandonment of the system and caused collapse.

Because one of the primary functions of a party is to represent its base, a party without supporters lacks purpose and declines. Identification with the traditional Venezuelan parties began to decay in 1989 and continued a dramatic, unabated deterioration for the next decade. At its peak in 1988, partisan identification with AD and COPEI surpassed 70 percent of Venezuelans. With MAS supporters included, almost 78 percent affiliated with a traditional party. By the time the system collapsed in 1998, however, only 25 percent of the population identified with the three parties. Electoral support for the old parties also decayed. AD and COPEI presidential candidates received over 93 percent of the vote in 1988. Five years later, their candidates attracted only 46 percent of voters. By 1998, the two giants of Venezuelan politics did not even support their own candidates, but instead backed Henrique Salas Römer of Proyecto Venezuela, who won less than 40 percent of the vote. Abstention rates nearly doubled over the 1990s, as more people withdrew from electoral politics entirely.

The 1998 elections were the critical moment in which decay became collapse. The 2.5-party system gave way to a multiparty system in 1993, and when the two major parties lost control of government after the 1998 elections, collapse was complete. To assess the role of linkage failure in prompting this exodus from the old system, I analyze public support for the traditional parties at the precise moment of collapse, using data from RedPol98, a nationwide face-to-face survey conducted in November 1998 after the legislative elections that dealt a heavy blow to AD and COPEI and before the victory of Hugo Chávez in the December presidential race.[1]

THEORIZING (LACK OF) PARTY SUPPORT UNDER CONDITIONS OF SYSTEM COLLAPSE

The model of party system collapse I have developed argues that threats to a party system's core linkage strategies, together with constraints that limit adaptation, result in linkage decay. When linkage failure is so extensive that the main system parties no longer connect a majority of voters to the state, the system collapses. Chapters 5, 6, and 7 detailed the process by which threat and constraint undermined linkage in the Venezuelan system. Here I assess whether this linkage failure prompted people to leave the old system. I expect people who did not find suitable programmatic representation, who were not connected through incorporated groups, or who sought but did not find clientelist exchanges to be the most likely to abandon the system.

We have seen how Venezuela's traditional parties failed to provide policy answers to the economic crisis that beset the country. The absence of policy responsiveness likely pushed people away from the old system, as negative perceptions of government economic performance caused dissatisfaction.

---

1. RedPol98 was designed by several Venezuelan scholars and conducted by DATOS. It was in the field from November 13 to 27.

Respondents who were displeased with economic policy making did not find programmatic linkage through policy responsiveness and were, therefore, less likely to support a system party than were those who viewed economic policy more positively.

Additionally, the major parties' convergence during the 1990s is likely to have eradicated opportunities for ideologically motivated linkage. People want to support parties with ideological positions similar to their own (Franklin and Jackson 1983; Shanks and Miller 1990). However, by the mid-1990s, the major system parties provided no viable alternative to the status quo, which was characterized by center-right ideology and repeated returns to neoliberalism (chapter 5). Even MAS provided little hope for relief, as the party had compromised itself by repeatedly collaborating with traditional elites and supporting Caldera's neoliberal policies. Frustration with the parties' indistinguishable positions likely prompted Venezuelans, especially those on the left, to look outside the system for alternatives. If respondents holding negative assessments of policy performance or lacking suitable ideological options withheld support from the traditional system, then decaying programmatic linkage contributed to exit from the old system.

I have also argued that narrowing interest incorporation prompted the growing ranks of the unincorporated to reject the system. Both AD and COPEI were hierarchical organizations in which traditional class-based interests were integrated and given privileged status (Crisp 2000; Martz 1966). But outside established functional groups, people lacked group ties to the parties. This absence of linkage became a threat in the 1990s as the formal and public sectors shrank and unemployment grew (ILO 1998). Because the parties did not reach out to the escalating population outside the formal economy (chapter 6), people not captured by the traditional class cleavage found few opportunities for incorporation. Those without such ties were much less likely to find linkage than members of integrated sectors like unions and professional associations, making the unincorporated more inclined to exit the old system.

I also expect the insufficiency of clientelism to have contributed to rejection of the party system. At their height, the parties used clientelism to attract support from those who lacked programmatic or incorporating ties. But in the 1990s, demands for clientelism increased at the same time that available resources dwindled, reducing the reach of clientelist linkage (chapter 7). I expect to find that people most reliant on clientelism, such as those without steady sources of income, abandoned the traditional parties because of shortfalls in the delivery of clientelist benefits.

Thus, people without linkage are prime candidates for rejecting the system. In the Venezuelan context, negative evaluations of policy responsiveness and left-leaning ideology suggest that a respondent could not find programmatic representation in the traditional system. People without ties to integrated groups were unlikely to connect to the system through interest incorporation. And those most dependent on clientelism were inclined to become dissatisfied with the parties' inability to meet demands.

THE ROLE OF LINKAGE FAILURE IN CAUSING SYSTEM COLLAPSE

Data and Measurement

If linkage decay caused people to leave the system, then those who withdrew support from the old parties by the 1998 election are likely to have been upset with the lack of programmatic, incorporating, and/or clientelist ties. To assess if differential access to linkage affected whether people left the system, I use RedPol98 data to contrast respondents who remained loyal to the traditional parties with those who rejected the old system. If linkage failure caused the party system exodus, we should observe weaker linkage options for those who abandoned the system than for those who continued to support the old parties.

The great majority of people who did not identify with the party system at the moment of its collapse had supported a traditional party in the not-too-distant past. Among RedPol98 respondents who did not affiliate with a traditional party and who reported having voted in the 1988 presidential election, 87 percent voted for Carlos Andrés Pérez of AD, Eduardo Fernández of COPEI, or Teodoro Petkoff of MAS in that contest. Because a significant majority of people who were independents or who supported a new party at the time of the system's collapse had voted for traditional party candidates at some point in the previous ten years, examining the differences between people outside the traditional system and party loyalists in 1998 allows me to contrast the attitudes and experiences of people who left the old system with those who did not. I apply this strategy in assessing the role of linkage decay in the exit calculus.

The analysis includes three major sets of variables to assess whether decay of each linkage type undermined support for the old parties. To judge whether programmatic decline provoked departure from the system, I include two independent variables. The first measures evaluations of economic policy in order to capture perceptions of policy responsiveness. The theory suggests that people with negative views of policy making were less likely to maintain affiliation with a traditional party.[2] Second, using ideological self-placement, I examine whether lack of affinity with the traditional parties' center-right consensus caused respondents on the left to become frustrated with the absence of ideological options and abandon the system.[3]

To identify people who were unlikely to have found interest incorporation, I distinguish between respondents who belonged to unions, professional associations, or other employment-based organizations and those without membership in these groups.[4] If narrowing incorporation weakened traditional party support, people outside historically incorporated groups should have been more inclined to leave the system than those with such ties.

I also expect people with unsatisfied clientelist demands to be likely candidates for abandoning the traditional parties. While the survey did not ask respondents whether they sought clientelist exchanges or whether such exchanges had been offered, we can still identify the sorts of people who were most likely to seek individual material benefits in return for their votes. The poor, especially those lacking regular sources of income and living in uncertainty, are likely to seek clientelism as part of their survival strategy (Auyero 2000). My analysis in chapter 7 supports the applicability of this perception in Venezuela, where poor and informal sector voters were primarily linked to the parties through clientelism, rather than programmatic appeals or incorporation. I identify likely clientelism-demanding constituencies as people without steady incomes. Using the survey instrument to capture this idea, I code potentially frustrated clients as people who were unemployed or who possessed unskilled or unstable employment.[5] If their demands went unmet, those seeking clientelism lacked linkage and almost

---

2. The survey question used is "¿Qué piensa usted de la política económica del actual gobierno? ¿Diría usted que esa política económica ha sido muy buena, buena, mala o muy mala?" Higher values indicate more negative assessments.

3. The survey question used is "En la política, la gente habla de 'izquierda' y de 'derecha.' Hablando en terminos generales, ¿Dónde se ubica usted en esta escala?" I coded the scale so that 1=derecha (right) and 10=izquierda (left).

4. The survey question used is "¿Pertenece usted a un sindicato, gremio o algún tipo de asociación o no?" 1=nonmembers.

5. Employment categories classified as potential clients include street vendors, chauffeurs, taxi drivers, etc. The reference category includes professionals with a university education, business owners, technical experts, blue- and white-collar employees under contract, retired workers who likely had pension income, and full-time students who tended to belong to more affluent upper- and middle-class families.

certainly would have looked outside the system for some form of representation or assistance.

Beyond the items measuring the effects of deteriorating linkage, I include several variables to assess and control for potential alternative explanations. Previous research has found that economic evaluations influence party support (Fiorina 1981; Kelly 2003; MacKuen, Erickson, and Stimson 1989). Additionally, other studies about Venezuela have pointed to economic crisis as a direct cause of party system collapse, arguing that crisis itself provides the most powerful explanation (Borges Arcila 1996; Hillman 1994; Molina and Pérez 1998). I include measures of economic evaluations in the analysis to assess the accuracy of this view that the deteriorating economy directly caused abandonment of the traditional parties. But I have argued that the effect of crisis on system collapse, while important, occurs indirectly via its influence on linkage and is mitigated or exacerbated by contextual constraints. This theoretical framework suggests that the influence of economic evaluations should be insignificant or small, only reflecting ordinary patterns of economic voting, rather than having the substantial impact suggested by accounts of collapse that privilege economic conditions as the main cause. To test for a direct relationship between economic deterioration and partisanship, I include retrospective idiotropic and retrospective sociotropic evaluations of the economy as independent variables.[6] These items tap the effect of economic conditions themselves, as opposed to measuring policy efforts to combat these conditions.

Finally, I control for demographic characteristics, which political socialization theories suggest generate long-standing partisan attachments (Miller and Shanks 1996). Given the fluidity of Venezuelans' party ties in the 1990s, ordinary sociological explanations may be irrelevant. Nevertheless, it is possible that the persistence of traditional party support was promoted by characteristics that encourage strong partisan commitments (Franklin and Jackson 1983). For instance, older respondents may have developed stronger ties than the young (Abramson 1975). People with fewer political or civic resources, like the uneducated or poor, may have had weaker political commitments

6. The two survey questions used are (1) "En terminos generales, ¿usted diría que la situación en el país está mejor, igual, o peor que hace un año?" and (2) "Y en estos momentos, ¿dígame si usted vive mejor, igual o peor que como vivía hace un año?" Higher values indicate negative evaluations. I do not include prospective evaluations, which measured expectations about the economic future under a new government, because my goal is to assess the impact of the ongoing economic crisis. In other work (Morgan 2007), I found that positive prospective idiotropic evaluations increased support of the new left. Including prospective evaluations produces no significant changes in the findings.

and thus been more easily swayed toward new parties. And, despite the creation of women's committees by both AD and COPEI, men have historically dominated Venezuelan politics, possibly limiting strong partisan ties among women. To consider these potential effects, I include measures of age, class, education, and sex.

Motivations for Abandoning the Traditional Party System

To assess how linkage decay affected Venezuelans' support for the traditional parties and thus contributed to party system collapse, I analyze partisanship, vote choice, and assessments about the status of the parties at the pivotal moment of collapse. In measuring partisanship, I divide respondents into four major categories: old party supporters (19 percent), new left party supporters (35 percent), new right party supporters (25 percent), and independents (21 percent).[7] I then conduct multinomial logit analysis to compare people who remained loyal to the traditional parties with those who left the party system.[8] Table 8.1 presents the results of this analysis. In terms of the key variables measuring lack of programmatic, incorporating, and clientelist linkage, we expect positive coefficients, which indicate that higher values on the independent variables, in this case measures of *lack* of linkage, increase a respondent's likelihood of identifying with the nontraditional grouping specified at the top of the column, rather than backing the old parties.[9]

The analysis supports the argument that dissatisfaction with linkage prompted exodus from the old system. Each of the independent variables included to assess the effects of linkage failure has a significant effect,

7. The survey question used is "¿Con cuál partido simpatiza usted?" The traditional party grouping included adecos (15 percent), copeyanos (3 percent), and *masistas* (1 percent). The new left included MVR, PPT, and LCR. The new right included Convergencia, Movimiento IRENE, and Proyecto Venezuela.

8. Multinomial logit is appropriate because the underlying assumption concerning the independence of irrelevant alternatives, which specifies that each category on the dependent variable is independent, is theoretically satisfied because none of the party groupings are close substitutes (Kennedy 1998, 235). Also, the results of the Hausman post-estimation test (Hausman and McFadden 1984) allow us to accept the null hypothesis that the alternatives are independent. Furthermore, multinomial probit analysis, which I conducted without imputing missing data because the Clarify program does not support probit, produced the same basic results as logit, which allows imputation.

9. Respondents who supported one of the traditional parties serve as the reference group. Due to loss of cases from missing data, I used Amelia (King et al. 2001) to impute missing values. The findings of the analysis conducted on the imputed data sets (N=1500) are not significantly different from the findings of a separate analysis conducted on the dataset that included only those cases without missing data (N=1193).

Table 8.1 Effects of linkage decay on partisanship: Multinomial logit analysis

	New left	New right	Independents
Programmatic linkage			
Negative economic policy evaluations	.38**	.22	.16
	(.13)	(.13)	(.14)
Left ideology	.33**	.11**	.19**
	(.03)	(.03)	(.04)
Interest incorporation			
Outside incorporated groups	.82**	.95**	1.37**
	(.22)	(.24)	(.26)
Clientelism			
Clientelism-demanding constituency	.50*	.16	.49*
	(.20)	(.21)	(.21)
Economic evaluations			
Negative retrospective pocketbook evaluations	.03	−.14	.19
	(.12)	(.12)	(.13)
Negative retrospective sociotropic evaluations	.19	.09	−.10
	(.16)	(.16)	(.18)
Socio-demographic controls			
Class	.19	.41**	.45**
	(.12)	(.12)	(.13)
Education	.13	.14	.20*
	(.09)	(.09)	(.10)
Age	.001	−.23**	.07
	(.06)	(.06)	(.06)
Male	.21	−.28	.03
	(.18)	(.18)	(.19)
Constant	2.54**	1.19*	.27
	(.52)	(.55)	(.60)
N (model significance)		1500 (.00)	
Log likelihood		−1454.49	
Likelihood ratio (df)		299.6 (30)	
Pseudo R^2		.09	

Note: Reference category is respondents affiliated with AD, COPEI, or MAS. Standard errors in parentheses, $*p \le .05$; $**p \le .01$. Analysis conducted using the Amelia multiple imputation program (King et al. 2001) with the Clarify package in STATA 10.

Source: Author's analysis of RedPol98, provided by Banco de Datos Poblacionales, Universidad Simón Bolívar.

undermining support for the traditional parties. The two measures of dissatisfaction with programmatic representation—negative evaluations of economic policy and left-leaning ideological positions—reduced loyalty to the traditional parties. If people did not approve of government's response to the severe economic pressures confronting the country, they were significantly more likely to support a new left party than to identify with one of the old parties. The coefficients for the new right and independents are also in the expected positive direction, with the coefficient for new right supporters nearing statistical significance. Lack of responsiveness to economic problems thus undermined the appeal of the traditional parties and enhanced support for new left alternatives.

The absence of ideological alternatives within the traditional party system also weakened it. While Venezuelans on the right side of the spectrum tended to remain loyal to AD, COPEI, or MAS, those on the left were significantly more likely to embrace an alternative outside the system. As the relative size of the ideology coefficients indicate, respondents on the left were most likely to identify with new left parties, but they were also more likely to be independent or even support the new right rather than back a traditional party.

The somewhat counterintuitive finding that new right supporters were statistically left of traditional partisans brings to light the difficulty of understanding the precise meaning of logit coefficients. To facilitate interpretation, I calculated simulated predicted probabilities, which enable us to discern the coefficients' substantive implications. I estimated the change in the probability of falling into a particular partisanship category if an otherwise average respondent were to move from minimum to maximum value on each independent variable.[10] Table 8.2 shows these changes in probabilities.

With these more substantive interpretations of the coefficients in hand, we can return to the ideology scale. Moving from right to left on the scale substantially increases the probability that a respondent will affiliate with the new left and slightly increases the chances of claiming political independence, while decreasing the chances of identifying with a traditional party or the new right. Most illuminating is the contrast between changes in the

10. This analysis was conducted using Clarify (King, Tomz, and Wittenberg 2000), with each variable set to its appropriate measure of central tendency: education, policy evaluations, ideology, and economic evaluations set to their means; class and age to their medians; and incorporation, clientelism, and sex to their modes. To estimate change in probability, each variable is alternately set to its minimum and maximum observed value to determine the probability of supporting each party grouping at these values.

Table 8.2 Effects of linkage decay on partisanship: Change in predicted probabilities

	Traditional parties	New left	New right	Independents
Programmatic linkage				
Negative policy evaluations	−.11	.13	—	—
Left ideology	−.22	.39	−.20	.02
Interest incorporation				
Outside incorporated groups	−.18	.02	.06	.10
Clientelism				
Clientelist constituency	−.04	.06	—	.04
Economic evaluations				
Pocketbook evaluations	—	—	—	—
Sociotropic evaluations	—	—	—	—
Socio-demographic controls				
Class	−.12	—	.11	.09
Education	−.08	—	—	.07
Age	.04	—	−.25	—
Male	—	—	—	—

Note: Only those effects shown to be significant in table 8.1 are reported here. Cell values represent change in the probability of belonging to the column group when moving from the minimum to the maximum on the independent variable, with all other variables set to their appropriate measures of central tendency. Analysis conducted in STATA 10 using Clarify (King et al. 2000).

— indicates lack of statistical significance.

probability of supporting an old party versus changes in the other categories. A shift from right to left decreases the probability of backing a traditional party by 0.22; the change is in the same direction but smaller for the new right. Meanwhile, moving from right to left increases the probability of affiliating with the new left by 0.39.

The predicted probabilities demonstrate that people on the left did not find a home in the traditional system, abandoning it in favor of other options, particularly new left parties. This supports the hypothesis that those on the ideological left were especially frustrated with the absence of ideological differentiation created by the rightward shift that the traditional parties experienced during the 1990s. Likewise, as discussed above, respondents frustrated with policy unresponsiveness abandoned the traditional parties and instead supported new left options. Together, the findings concerning negative perceptions of policy responsiveness and the absence of ideological options suggest that the deterioration of programmatic representation undermined support for the traditional parties.

The narrowing of incorporation and the inadequacy of clientelism also contributed to the exodus from the party system. People without union or professional association membership were significantly more likely to embrace the new left, the new right, or independence than support a traditional party. Being outside the system's work-based constituencies decreased the probability of remaining loyal to the old parties by eighteen points, but increased the probabilities of supporting the new left and the new right and of being independent (table 8.2). The growing ranks of unincorporated Venezuelans were likely to withdraw from the party system.

The analysis also suggests that potential clients, hoping for linkage through material exchanges, failed to find the benefits they sought and turned away from the traditional parties. Though the measurement of frustrated clients is crude, we nevertheless find significant effects on partisanship. Potential clients who faced economic uncertainty were significantly more likely to be independent or support the new left than to back a traditional party. The only nontraditional category unable to attract significant support from potential clients was the new right, which extended policy- and group-based appeals aimed at the upper and middle classes, rather than basic material promises for the poor. Lack of stable employment decreased the likelihood of loyalty to a traditional party by 4 points while increasing the probability of supporting a new left party by 6 points, a swing of 10 points between the two groups. The decay of clientelist networks weakened support for the party system and encouraged frustrated clients to seek alternatives.

Thus, the failure of each type of linkage had a significant impact, undermining traditional party loyalties. Decay of programmatic representation, narrowing interest incorporation, and inadequate clientelism caused people to shift their support to extra-system options that promised to provide linkage where the old system had failed.[11]

11. We observe some significant effects for class, education, and age. Supporters of the new right and independents had higher class status than traditional partisans. Independents had higher education levels, and members of the new right were younger than traditional partisans. There were no significant demographic distinctions between the old party faithful and those affiliated with the new left.

On the other hand, despite previous research demonstrating the influence of the economy on partisanship generally and other work emphasizing the centrality of economic crisis in causing party system collapse, the analysis suggests that economic evaluations did not have a direct effect on Venezuelans' decisions to exit the old system. In light of the consistent finding that economic problems have undermined support for incumbents throughout the developing world (Kelly 2006; Pacek and Radcliff 1995; Remmer 1991), this result may seem surprising. However, the absence of significant effects for economic evaluations aligns well with the theoretical framework developed in this book. I have argued that while crisis conditions pose a challenge to party systems, it is the system's (in)ability to sustain linkage in the face of these conditions that determines whether it will collapse. The findings support this expectation.

When the multinomial logit analysis of partisanship includes independent variables measuring linkage, as in table 8.1, these measures emerge as the primary factors shaping partisan loyalties. In this context, evaluations of the economy do not affect partisanship directly; the linkage variables are more powerful explanations. However, in a separate analysis that included economic evaluations but left out the linkage measures, economic perceptions had significant effects on partisanship. Negative idiotropic and sociotropic assessments pushed people away from the traditional parties, whereas positive economic evaluations encouraged loyalty to the old system. Thus, it is not that the economic crisis had no effect on the process of party system collapse. Rather, this effect occurred indirectly by creating pressure for linkage that the party system was unable to resolve. Poor economic conditions challenged the traditional parties' linkage mechanisms, and when they could not sustain partisan ties in the face of crisis, people abandoned the system. Ultimately, it was this linkage failure, produced by both crisis and constraints, not economic conditions alone, that motivated Venezuelans to leave the traditional parties.

Further analysis reinforces the significance of linkage failure for understanding Venezuelans' abandonment of the party system. To assess whether the same theoretical framework used to explain partisanship also illuminates declining electoral support for the traditional parties, I analyzed reported vote choice in the congressional elections held immediately prior to the RedPol survey, as well as intended vote in the imminent presidential elections.[12]

12. The question about the congressional elections read, "¿Por cuál lista de partido o plancha votó para las elecciones de la cámara de diputados?" The question about the presidential elections read, "¿Por cuál de estos candidatos votará usted en las próximas elecciones para presidente?"

Using the same set of independent variables and the same set of party groupings that I employed in studying partisanship, I found the results for vote choice to be strikingly consistent with my theory and with the findings concerning partisanship above.[13] Absence of programmatic linkage because of policy unresponsiveness and limited ideological differentiation significantly undermined electoral support for the traditional parties and increased the likelihood of either not voting or backing one of the emerging alternatives in both the congressional and presidential races. Respondents who lacked linkage through membership in traditionally incorporated constituencies were unlikely to vote for the old parties and instead supported new electoral options or abstained. People likely to seek clientelist benefits also withdrew electoral support from the traditional parties, at least in the presidential elections, and intended to abstain or vote for the new left. On the other hand, we continue to observe no significant effects for economic evaluations on vote choice, just as we found in the partisanship analysis above.

An additional question in the RedPol survey tapped more general assessments of the Venezuelan parties, asking respondents whether the parties could be fixed.[14] Logit analysis of this question, using the same independent variables as above, likewise reveals very similar causal patterns.[15] Together, these additional analyses of electoral support and of overall evaluations of the parties reinforce the finding that lack of linkage caused Venezuelans to reject the traditional party system. The small core of people with whom the traditional parties maintained successful linkage were much more likely to remain loyal, whereas those who were abandoned by the parties and left without programmatic, incorporating, or clientelist ties withdrew their support from the old system.

LINKAGE FAILURE AND COLLAPSE: CONCLUSIONS

This chapter illuminates why so many Venezuelans left the old parties and embraced new ones, culminating in the system's collapse in the 1998 elections. Analysis of support for the parties at this pivotal moment reveals that

13. The full results and a detailed description of this analysis are available from the author upon request.

14. The question read, "¿Cree usted que los partidos políticos venezolanos tienen arreglo o no tienen arreglo?"

15. The full results and a detailed description of this analysis are available from the author upon request.

frustration with the system's failure to link a growing portion of society was the catalyst behind collapse.

Lack of programmatic representation undermined support for the traditional parties. Economic crisis demanded a policy response, but the parties made little effort to address mounting concerns. Rather than engaging in risky policies that violated their ideological legacies, the parties opted to wait out the crisis, hoping that an upsurge in oil prices might enable them to avoid the tough trade-offs the crisis demanded. But the crisis deepened, discrediting the parties in government and driving voters to look for meaningful alternatives to the status quo. However, throughout the 1990s, AD and COPEI became increasingly interchangeable. Pérez's support for neoliberalism during the last adeco presidency marked a rightward shift by the historically social democratic party, and important factions within COPEI supported the reforms. Then, by the late 1990s, the old guards of both AD and COPEI, embodied in Luis Alfaro Ucero and the now independent Caldera, also succumbed to pressures to accept neoliberalism, pushing the remaining interventionist factions of the elite rightward and eradicating ideological options from the system. Patterns of interparty agreements and the need for political allies prompted leaders to cross party lines and align with former opponents in competing organizations. These coalitions, which included AD, COPEI, MAS, Convergencia, and even LCR, blurred distinctions between parties and created the perception that the system offered no meaningful alternatives. Voters, particularly those on the left, became discontented with this center-right consensus. The loss of ideological differentiation had a profound effect, as people on the right were approximately five times more likely to remain loyal to the old parties than those on the left.

Incorporation also proved inadequate. People connected to the parties through membership in effectively incorporated functional groups, like professional associations and unions, were much more likely to continue supporting the system than those unrepresented by the traditional class cleavage. Over the course of the 1990s, the proportion of people incorporated through functional groups declined considerably. But because their hierarchically structured organizations favored entrenched interests over new groups with competing concerns, the parties failed to integrate emerging sectors. By the mid-1990s, most people did not find linkage through incorporation, making them more inclined to leave the traditional parties.

Finally, in light of increased demands for clientelism and a shrinking pool of resources available to the parties for material exchanges, potential clients were increasingly unlikely to receive the benefits they sought from the traditional parties and turned to other possibilities. The dramatic social change that created greater levels of poverty and uncertainty and the introduction of separate subnational elections heightened demand for clientelist inputs. At the same time, economic crisis and reforms that constrained resource access limited the funds available to the parties for satisfying these growing demands. Because clientelist benefits could not satiate pressure for material exchange, many frustrated clients abandoned the traditional parties.

Together, then, challenges to the parties' core linkage strategies and constraints on appropriate adaptation produced the deterioration of all three forms of linkage in the system. Loss of linkage weakened Venezuelans' commitment to the traditional parties and caused them to abandon the system. In the final part of the book, I show how these same patterns played out in other cases of collapse and explore how other threatened party systems managed to survive.

PART 3

PARTY SYSTEM COLLAPSE AND SURVIVAL IN
COMPARATIVE PERSPECTIVE

9

A COMPARATIVE APPROACH TO ANALYZING
PARTY SYSTEM COLLAPSE

Venezuela serves as an empirically poignant and theoretically powerful case of collapse. But party system collapse is not a distinctively Venezuelan phenomenon. As demonstrated in chapter 2, other established party systems have suffered similar fates. Italy's party system collapsed in the early 1990s amid economic crisis and social change. The long-standing alliance between the Christian Democrats and the Socialists was discredited, the Communists lost relevance, and the old party system gave way to a combination of regional and personalist parties. In Colombia, as the Liberals and Conservatives faced mounting violence, unprecedented economic decline, and institutional reforms requiring considerable adaptation, the parties decayed and became increasingly irrelevant actors. Bolivia's old system lost its grip on power as much of the population languished in poverty and ethnic divisions became politicized, making way for Evo Morales's ascendance to the presidency in 2005. At the same time, other party systems have also faced serious challenges but managed to survive. In this third part of the book, I assess the generalizability of the theory of collapse elaborated in chapter 3 by examining a broader set of cases of collapse and survival. The cross-national analysis provides an opportunity to extend the argument beyond the Venezuelan case while also ruling out potential alternative explanations.

In the rest of this chapter, I identify the cases for cross-national analysis and detail how these comparisons facilitate a rigorous test of the theory and exclude other hypotheses. I begin by examining the four collapse cases—Bolivia, Colombia, Italy, and Venezuela—to identify areas of difference between them, which enables me to rule out these differences as rival explanations of collapse. I then select negative cases for analysis, with the goal of assessing whether the theory also accounts for the divergent outcome of system survival. I pair each instance of collapse with a party system that shared many common features and faced the threat of collapse yet managed to survive. I conclude this chapter by discussing the process of structured, focused comparison that I employ to assess the theory consistently in each case.

In chapters 10 and 11, I carry out the cross-national analysis. Chapter 10 broadens the test, showing how the Italian, Colombian, and Bolivian party systems followed the theorized process of collapse detailed in the Venezuelan case. Each faced similar challenges to their linkage profiles, while specific contextual factors limited all the systems' ability to respond to these threats. Thus, the four cases align with the theoretical model of core threats to linkage in a context of adaptation-impeding constraints, which resulted in the failure of all forms of linkage and system collapse. Even as these party systems failed, other comparable systems faced similar obstacles and nevertheless endured. To assess how survival is possible, chapter 11 analyzes important moments of crisis in the paired comparisons of system survival in Argentina, Belgium, India, and Uruguay. I demonstrate that collapse was possible in these cases, but in each instance, at least one form of linkage was sustained, enabling the system to survive. Linkage endured either because it was not fundamentally challenged across all types or because contextual constraints did not limit adaptation. Examining instances of survival in this way clarifies the significance of each component of the causal process delineated in chapter 3.

COMPARING INSTANCES OF COLLAPSE TO ELIMINATE POTENTIAL ALTERNATIVE EXPLANATIONS

To explore the extent to which my theory accounts for each occurrence of collapse, chapter 10 analyzes the three other collapses of established party systems in Europe and Latin America between 1975 and 2005: those of Bolivia (2005), Colombia (1998–2002), and Italy (1992–94). The four collapse cases vary on a range of institutional and party system factors, and features that differ across cases are unlikely explanations of the shared outcome of collapse. Therefore, this most-different systems element of the research design enables me to introduce variation across cases of collapse on a range of variables, which represent potential alternative explanations, and thus rule them out (Przeworski and Teune 1970). Here I discuss how the four cases differ with regard to institutional features, like electoral rules and presidentialism versus parliamentarism, and party system effects, like number of parties and institutionalization, suggesting that these are not necessary conditions for collapse.

Theories emphasizing the importance of electoral rules for understanding party systems suggest that certain electoral institutions are incompatible with particular party system structures (Cox 1997; Duverger 1954). Specifically, changes away from proportional representation (PR) and toward single-member districts (SMD) might marginalize some smaller parties and could even put the system at risk. The cases of Venezuela, Bolivia, and perhaps Italy, which all moved away from pure PR around the time of party system collapse, might seem to align with this argument, but the Colombian experience directly contradicts the idea that party system collapse is caused by changes in electoral rules that encourage fewer parties.

Historically, Venezuela elected its national legislature with closed-list PR, but it switched to a mixed PR and SMD system for the 1993 legislative elections. Similarly, Bolivia moved from PR to a mixed system for the 1996 elections. Italian electoral law also changed to a mixed system from open-list PR, although not until 1994, when collapse had been under way for two years and was already nearly complete (D'Alimonte and Bartolini 1997). But the extent to which the new mixed systems squeezed the party systems toward bipolarity was limited because the overall composition of the legislature was still determined by the PR party vote; thus, the new electoral systems did not affect the translation of votes into seats (Gilbert 1995; Salazar Elena 2004). Despite this caveat and the indeterminate timing in the Italian case, these three cases might lead one to believe that the mixed system somehow undermined the parties and challenged system structure.

However, Colombia clearly contradicts this pattern. Colombian electoral laws historically employed a personalistic form of PR in which multiple competing lists ran under the same party label. In 1991, constitutional reforms *lowered* entry barriers and created a single national constituency for the Senate rather than multiple regional-level constituencies (Gutiérrez Sanín 2007). These changes opened the electoral process up to *more* competitors, rather than constraining it further, as could have occurred in the three other countries with the move from PR to mixed systems. The Colombian experience is at odds with the other collapse cases, suggesting that specific electoral rules do not themselves threaten party system survival in a consistent way. Party systems with different electoral institutions that underwent diverse types of change all experienced collapse.[1]

Comparing the four collapse cases also reveals that both presidential and parliamentary forms of government have experienced collapse, eliminating presidentialism as a possible causal variable. In his classic work, Linz (1990) argued that parliamentary systems are more stable and more effective for representation than presidential ones. However, of the four cases of collapse, only two were purely presidential—Colombia and Venezuela. Italy had a parliamentary system, and Bolivia had a parliamentarized version of presidentialism in which the legislature typically selected the president from among the top vote getters in the popular election (Mayorga 2005). This diversity suggests that presidentialism does not inherently imperil party systems, as systems under other forms of government are also vulnerable to collapse.

Furthermore, the four failed party systems differed considerably in their structure. Venezuela had a 2.5-party system, and the Colombian system was dominated by two parties. Italy and Bolivia stood at the other end of the spectrum with multiparty systems. In Italy, the communist left was pitted against three to five other parties, and in Bolivia competition revolved around three main parties and a handful of smaller ones.[2] Party discipline also varied across the four party systems. For instance, Venezuela's nearly perfect discipline in the legislature contrasts with the Colombian parties' extreme fractionalization.

Additionally, the four systems possessed different levels of institutionalization. Some scholars have suggested that institutionalization promotes stability and governance (Dix 1992; Mainwaring and Scully 1995a; Sánchez 2008), while others have argued that too much or too little institutionalization weakens party systems (Dietz and Myers 2007). Given the significance of institutionalization in existing arguments about party system stability, it is particularly relevant that the cases of collapse analyzed here provide variation across the entire spectrum of the variable. The Venezuelan system possessed high levels of institutionalization (Dietz and Myers 2007;

1. The theory I posit considers how other institutional reforms—namely political decentralization, which in some countries was concurrent with the shift away from PR—challenged clientelist linkage. The data for Venezuela in chapter 7, as well as the evidence for Italy, Bolivia, and Colombia in chapter 10, support the importance of decentralization in undermining linkage, but not the significance of changes in national-level electoral rules.

2. The average effective number of parties in the legislature's lower house during each country's pre-collapse era was 2.4 for Colombia (1978–94); 3.2 for Venezuela (1973–88); 4.8 for Bolivia (1985–2002); and 4.1 for Italy (1976–92).

Kornblith and Levine 1995), whereas Bolivia stood at the other end of the continuum with an amorphous and unstable system (Mainwaring and Scully 1995a). The Colombian and Italian systems had moderate levels of institutionalization. Boudon (2000) argues that institutionalization was only modest in Colombia, below Venezuelan levels, and that it was particularly weak in the areas of party organization and discipline. The Italian system also qualified as moderately institutionalized, without volatility but with low programmatic clarity (Farneti 1983). Neither high, nor moderate, nor low levels of institutionalization assured stability, as systems at all levels of institutionalization collapsed.

Thus, these cases of collapse manifested different party system characteristics and operated in distinct institutional contexts. Comparing the cases enables me to focus the analysis on factors and patterns that were similar across all four, rather than being distracted by competing explanations that are only relevant in some of them.

CONTRASTING INSTANCES OF SURVIVAL

In addition to extending my analysis to the three other instances of collapse, I examine cases in which party systems have been surprisingly resilient. By contrasting the processes of linkage failure that led to collapse in some countries against those systems that maintained linkage and survived, I assess whether my theory distinguishes between instances of system failure and success. Here I outline how I selected instances of survival for analysis. I identified relevant cases and created paired comparisons, matching each collapse case to a similar system that endured despite some comparable challenges. Based on this process, the negative cases I selected for analysis are Argentina in the 1990s and early 2000s, Belgium in the 1970s, Uruguay in the late 1990s and early 2000s, and India in the 1980s.[3]

Identifying Relevant Negative Cases

In selecting negative cases, or non-collapses, I had two major considerations. First, I included only relevant cases so as to avoid overrepresentation

3. With the survival cases, just as with the collapses, it is crucial to identify a specific time period for analysis. For example, Bolivia has not always constituted an instance of collapse; rather the analytical focus must be on 2005, when its system failed. The same logic is true for instances of survival. We should focus on critical moments when the system was particularly

of survival cases and reap the greatest benefit from the contrast between positive and negative observations. Typically, scholars recommend including negative cases that closely resemble positive ones, especially on hypothesized causal factors (Ragin 2000; Skocpol 1984). Mahoney and Goertz extend this recommendation, specifying that the most relevant cases are those that share at least one independent variable hypothesized to influence the outcome of interest, which in this case is system collapse. When choosing non-events, they advise that scholars should only consider cases "where the outcome of interest is *possible* . . . [while] cases that are *impossible* should be relegated to a set of uninformative and hence irrelevant observations" (2004, 653; emphasis in original).[4]

I implemented this guideline for negative case selection by only considering instances of survival that had positive values on more than one of the independent variables in the theoretical model of collapse. As specified in chapter 3, these central causal factors are the *challenges* posed by crisis, social transformation, and political decentralization, as well as the *constraints* imposed by contextual factors, specifically international policy guidelines that contradict party legacies, interparty agreements, organizational patterns limiting new group incorporation, and reforms preventing party access to clientelist resources. Table 9.1 displays the values of these factors in the four selected negative cases. As the table makes clear, I also designed the array of cases such that each independent variable was present in at least one negative case.

I intentionally chose cases in which collapse seemed possible or even likely but was nevertheless averted—in other words, these are surprising instances of survival. Near misses pose a particular challenge to theory, as the account of the causal process must be able to parse out the differences that resulted in divergent outcomes despite similar circumstances. Explaining how these at-risk systems survived moments of crisis allows me to test the importance of each hypothesized component of the collapse process.

---

vulnerable. So, when selecting negative cases for analysis, I specify both the country and a particular time period during which the system was at risk for collapse.

4. Goertz and Mahoney (2004) also specify that cases should be considered irrelevant if they possess a characteristic that is widely known from previous research to make the outcome of interest impossible. I considered this recommendation when selecting negative cases. But existing research on collapse is sufficiently underdeveloped, so identifying factors that make collapse impossible is not feasible and excluding cases based on consensus in the literature is not possible.

Table 9.1 Theorized independent variables present in selected cases of party system survival

	Argentina, 1990s	Belgium, 1970s	Uruguay, 1990s	India, 1980s
Crisis conditions	Economic crisis	No	Economic crisis	No
International policy constraints[a]	IMF agreements	No	IMF agreements	IMF loans, but considerable autonomy
Interparty agreements[b]	No	Christian Democrats always in coalition	Colorados and Blancos, but not FA	No
Social transformation[c]	Deindustrialization; deunionization; informalization	Regional and ethnolinguistic divides activated	Deindustrialization; deunionization; informalization	Ethnic cleavages activated
Organizational constraints on new interest incorporation[d]	Historical union ties; conflicting interests	Constraints that slowed, but did not prevent, new cleavage incorporation	No	Single-party incorporation not viable amid ethnic conflict
Electoral decentralization[e]	No	Autonomous regional governments created	Separation of local and national elections	Local elections implemented, but not until 1993
Reforms limiting party resource control[f]	Decentralized parties and partisan state spending assured access	40 percent of government funds regionalized, but public funds for parties increased	Subnational share of public spending up more than 50 percent	Regional variation, but extensive fiscal decentralization

Note: Gray shading indicates absence of factor; white equals presence.

[a] International agreement or intergovernmental organizations strongly limited policy latitude.

[b] All the major pro-system parties participated in ideologically diffuse coalitions, pacts, or formal agreements at some point during the crisis.

[c] Politically salient social cleavage(s) changed in either structure or type.

[d] Newly salient interests conflicted with the goals of entrenched groups and/or did not fit established patterns of interest articulation.

[e] New or newly separated elections were established for subnational offices such as governor or mayor.

[f] State reforms like rationalization or decentralization cut parties off from resources they had manipulated for political ends. Data for Belgium from Heisler (1977); for Uruguay from Panizza (2004); for India from Crook and Manor (1998).

Creating Paired Comparisons

My second guiding principle in selecting instances of survival was motivated by the logic of Przeworski and Teune's (1970) most-similar systems design, in which cases are chosen based on similarities on relevant variables (also see Ragin 1986). I selected each negative case to pair with one positive case of collapse, matching them on variables with potential theoretical importance: party system features, linkage profiles, and threats to representation. By matching cases on party system features like institutionalization and system structure, I am able to rule out these variables as singularly sufficient causes of collapse. By pairing cases that shared similar linkage profiles and challenges, yet experienced divergent outcomes, I emphasize the significance of the hypothesized combinations of factors and causal pathways for understanding collapse. I matched Argentina to Venezuela, Belgium to Italy, Uruguay to Colombia, and India to Bolivia. I discuss the similarities between these cases here, while chapter 11 explores why they reached divergent outcomes.

I paired Argentina's party system survival with Venezuela's collapse because they possessed similar party system features and linkage profiles and faced many of the same challenges in the 1990s. In terms of party system features, both were institutionalized 2.5-party systems, with two major parties and several smaller ones. The two main parties in Argentina, the Justicialist or Peronist Party (PJ) and the Radicals (UCR), shared many similarities with Venezuela's AD and COPEI, respectively. All four were supported by multiclass coalitions and by the 1980s had moderate ideologies. The PJ and AD had populist traditions and maintained particular appeal among the working class, while UCR and COPEI had more conservative roots that attracted stronger support from the middle and upper classes. The linkage profiles of the Venezuelan and Argentine systems also paralleled each other, utilizing some programmatic appeals but relying especially on incorporation and clientelism. Finally, Argentina and Venezuela encountered many of the same obstacles to linkage. Argentina was embroiled in an economic crisis even more severe than Venezuela's, suffered under broad neoliberal reforms during the 1990s, and experienced significant social change via informalization of the economy.

Belgian party system survival provides an effective counterexample to Italian collapse. Both advanced democracies possessed moderately institutionalized multiparty systems with three to four parties.[5] Belgium and Italy

5. Using Mainwaring and Scully's (1995a) criteria and operationalizations, the two systems fell into the institutionalized category with low volatility, strong ties to society, moderate levels of

each had large Christian democratic parties as well as significant parties in the social democratic family and smaller parties of the right. Their linkage profiles were also similar. While each system offered some ideological options to voters, the demands of coalition government frequently diluted these distinctions, and in both countries the Christian democratic party was a major player in almost every postwar governing coalition (Gilbert 1995; Hooghe 1991). So there were some programmatic appeals, but in neither case were they the only forms of linkage, as both systems incorporated class and religious cleavages and utilized clientelist exchanges. The Italian and Belgian systems also faced similar threats from extensive decentralization processes and social transformations that weakened the class cleavage and heightened the salience of other social divides.

I pair Uruguay's survival with Colombia's collapse because of similarities in the systems' institutionalization and structure as well as commonalities in linkage patterns and obstacles to linkage maintenance. Mainwaring and Scully (1995a) classified both systems as institutionalized, with Uruguay scoring 11.5 on their 12-point scale, and Colombia scoring 10.5.[6] Additionally, the two were among only a handful of countries in Latin America where the earliest cadre-style parties remained important players into the late twentieth century. Despite all the parties being highly factionalized, Uruguay's Colorados and Blancos and Colombia's Liberals and Conservatives dominated their respective systems for over one hundred years (Morgenstern 2001). Their linkage strategies were likewise parallel, with clientelism being their chief means of attracting support (Luna 2008; Martz 1997).[7] Colombia and Uruguay also encountered parallel challenges to linkage. Both struggled to sustain clientelism in the face of social transformation and political decentralization that heightened demand, and economic crisis and state reforms that limited resources.

Finally, I identified India as the most suitable relevant case of non-collapse to pair with Bolivia. Unlike other Latin American cases, India matched Bolivia on important party system features, linkage profiles, and threats challenging

---

legitimacy, and fairly effective party organizations. Using data from the *European Journal of Political Research*, I calculated the effective number of parties for each legislature. In the period analyzed here, the 1960s and 1970s, the Belgian legislature had three to four effective parties. Before its collapse, Italy also had three to four effective parties.

6. Boudon's (2000) recent recalculation places Colombia at a 9, marginally within the institutionalized category.

7. But as I will discuss further below, the emergence of the center-left Frente Amplio in Uruguay provided an ideological alternative in the system, infusing it with programmatic appeals that the Colombian system did not have.

the systems.[8] India (1970s) and Bolivia (1980s–1990s) were both inchoate multiparty systems in which parties tended to coalesce around two major coalitions, making their system dynamics similar (Chhibber 1999; Mayorga 2005).[9] In terms of linkage, both systems relied on clientelism augmented with programmatic appeals and incorporation (Salazar Elena 2004; Van Cott 2000; Wilkinson 2007). The major challenges confronted by the two systems were also similar. Each experienced major social changes during the period of threat, which heightened the salience of ethnic divides and also spurred demand for clientelism, and decentralization processes posed potential adaptation challenges for clientelist networks.

STRUCTURED, FOCUSED COMPARISONS

In the cross-national analysis, I employed structured, focused comparisons (George 1979). Based on the theory reviewed in fig. 9.1, I asked "a set of standardized, general questions of each case" (George and Bennett 2005, 69). For each step in the theorized causal process, I ask whether a case possessed the hypothesized explanatory factor. These questions are outlined in table 9.2, with separate entries for the causal process theorized to produce decay in each linkage type. If the theory provides an accurate explanation of why some party systems survive and others fail, all cases of collapse will affirmatively answer each relevant question in the table, while cases of survival will answer at least one negatively.

For each instance of collapse or survival, I begin by identifying the types of linkage employed in the system to build support. Based on the answer to

8. When choosing a comparison case for Bolivia, I was particularly concerned with finding a less developed, non-transitioning democracy that possessed an inchoate multiparty system in which the parties coalesced around two blocks. I also prioritized finding a country that faced the challenge of increasingly salient ethnic diversity. I considered Ecuador because of its ethnic diversity and inchoate party system, but the authoritarian interlude with the 2000 coup that toppled President Mahuad led me to reject Ecuador as a suitable match. Other countries in Central America were also excluded because of the transitional nature of their democracies and ongoing patterns of civil conflict into the 1990s. Because no Latin American country met the criteria outlined, I turned to Asia, where I found that the Indian experience paralleled the Bolivian case on these important facets and in other ways.

9. Bolivia scored 5.0 on the 12-point institutionalization scale (Mainwaring and Scully 1995a, 17). Following the same criteria, I calculated institutionalization in India as falling between 5.0 and 6.0. India scores poorly on stability (volatility is 30–40 percent), earning it a 1.0 on this criterion. It also scores low on ties to organized interests measured by party age, again receiving a 1.0, with most Indian parties founded after 1950. Indian party organizations are widely known for being weak (Krishna 2007), so the country scores a 1.0 or 1.5 in that regard. Finally, party legitimacy in India is moderate, resulting in a score of 2.0 or 2.5.

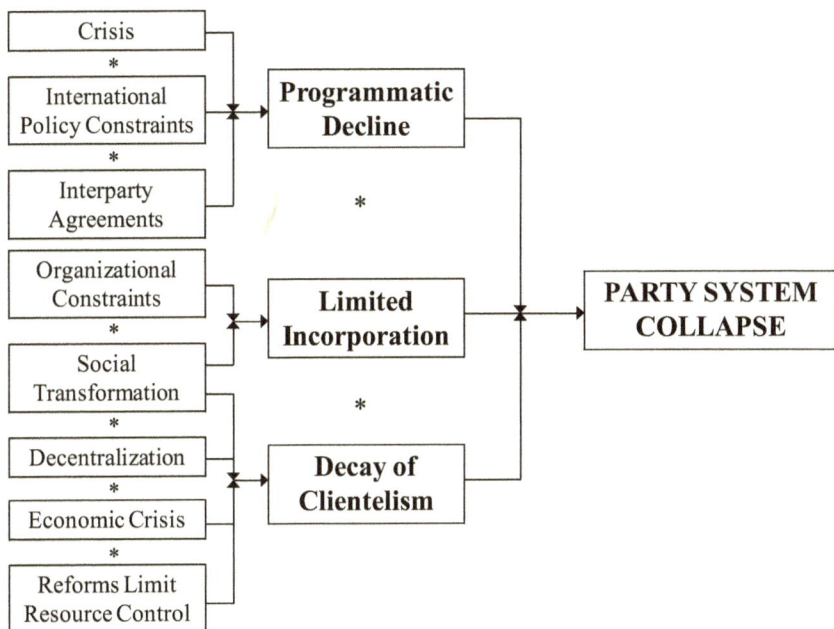

Fig. 9.1 Full model of party system collapse

Note: * stands for the logical AND. Factors in bold are part of the core theoretical model; factors in standard font are part of the secondary model. Joint arrows indicate a conjunction of necessary causes. Notation follows Goertz and Mahoney (2005).

this question, I explore, in turn, the causal path hypothesized to produce the decay of each relevant linkage type. If a system used programmatic appeals, I ask whether a crisis stemming from the shortcomings of the established policy model demanded a response. I also explore whether the presence of international commitments or pressures that conflicted with parties' legacies reduced capacity for appropriate programmatic adaptation and eliminated certain policy options. Then, to assess the extent to which policy unresponsiveness infected all the parties across the system, I ask whether ideological options were blurred by interparty agreements.

If interest incorporation was an important linkage mechanism, I examine whether relevant social divides experienced transformation either in the structure of the primary cleavage or in the type of salient divisions. I also examine organizational constraints on incorporating these new interests. Were they easily integrated through existing avenues of incorporation? Did new groups' concerns conflict with those of established interests?

Table 9.2   Questions asked of cases in conducting structured, focused comparisons

Asked of all cases:

- What types of linkage were significant parts of the system's representational profile?

If programmatic linkages were significant:

- Did the party system encounter a crisis of its policy model?
- Did international pressures constrain policy and conflict with parties' legacies?
- Did interparty agreements undermine potential alternatives to the status quo?
- Did policy responsiveness decay and ideological options disappear?

If interest incorporation was significant:

- Did salient cleavages transform in structure or in type?
- Did the new social structure challenge routinized incorporation patterns?
- Did new interests challenge the concerns of entrenched groups?
- Did interest incorporation narrow?

If clientelist exchanges were significant:

- Did social transformation increase demand for clientelism?
- Were separate subnational elections established?
- Did crisis conditions limit resource supply?
- Did political reforms reduce parties' access to resources?
- Did clientelism decay?

If the party system offered clientelist exchanges as a significant linkage strategy, I ask whether social transformation and the establishment of separate subnational elections resulted in more pressure for clientelism. With reference to resource availability, I examine whether crisis conditions restricted supply and whether political reforms constrained access to politicized funds for clientelism. Finally, for each linkage strategy employed in the traditional party system, I ask whether the parties' capacity to attract support via that strategy decayed in the period leading up to the system's collapse.

Exploring this series of questions enables me to systematically test the ability of the theory of linkage failure to explain why some party systems collapsed while others managed to survive. It is to this structured comparative analysis that I now turn.

10

BANKRUPT REPRESENTATION IN ITALY, COLOMBIA, AND BOLIVIA

When there is no longer any ideological or group foundation to the [party-voter] relationship, it is purely a market exchange, so if clientelist networks cannot meet demand, they are susceptible to failure.

—Paraphrased translation of Andrés Dávila Ladrón de Guevara and Natalia Delgado Varela, "La metamorfosis del sistema político colombiano"

The theory outlined in chapter 3 as well as the analysis of Venezuela suggests that linkage failure causes party system collapse. When a system faces threats to its core linkage strategies and contextual constraints limit its ability to adapt in order to respond to such challenges, linkage deteriorates and the system collapses. This was the causal process that produced collapse in Venezuela.

In this chapter, I explore whether the same process played out in the three other collapse cases. I assess whether the Italian, Colombian, and Bolivian party systems encountered similar challenges to their core linkage strategies and examine whether common constraints impeded adaptation, undermining linkage and producing collapse. I sketch each collapse, detail the system's linkage profile, and trace the process that led to system failure. At the end of the chapter, I highlight the common patterns of threats to linkage and constraints on adaptation experienced in all four cases.

ITALY: THE END OF IDEOLOGY, FRUSTRATIONS WITH CLIENTELISM, AND BREAKDOWN

From the postwar era through the 1980s, the centrist Christian Democratic party (DC) dominated Italian politics. Although cabinets were unstable, the DC was the core party in every governing coalition from 1947 to 1992 (Daniels 1999; Waters 1994). Within Italy's multiparty system, the DC exercised influence as the locus of power among potential governing parties, which included the Socialists (PSI), the Social Democrats (PSDI), the Liberals (PLI), and the Republicans (PRI) (D'Alimonte and Bartolini 1997; Gilbert 1995). Outside these core governing parties stood the Italian Communist Party (PCI), the permanent opposition that consistently received about a third of the vote but was excluded from governing even though it was allowed access to positions in the state bureaucracy and had some influence in policy making (Colazingari and Rose-Ackerman 1998; LaPalombara 1987).[1] The stagnant configuration of DC- and PSI-led governments with communist opposition characterized the Italian system through the 1960s, 1970s, and 1980s.

But by the mid-1990s, support for the DC and PSI had almost evaporated, and the PCI had splintered. Historically, these parties had typically won about 80 percent of the seats in the Chamber of Deputies. After the 1994 election, these major traditional parties were left with less than a third of the seats and the party system fractured, meeting the definition of collapse.[2] In their place emerged the coalition Polo delle Libertà, which brought together media baron Silvio Berlusconi's Fuerza Italia, the regional autonomy party Lega Nord (LN), the Alleanza Nazionale (AN) of former fascist and conservative forces, and several smaller parties. This coalition controlled over 50 percent of seats, giving Berlusconi the prime ministership. Here I show how the hypothesized challenges and constraints produced linkage failure and led to the Italian collapse.

Linkage in the Italian *Partitocrazia*, 1970s and 1980s

The traditional Italian party system had a mixed linkage profile, which relied heavily on clientelism but also employed programmatic appeals and interest incorporation. Programmatic representation was largely based on ideological

---

1. Small neofascist parties were also excluded from governing.
2. PSI held 2 percent of seats; PPI (Partito Popolare Italiano; formerly the DC), 5 percent; PDS (formerly the PCI), 17 percent; and Refounded Communists, 6 percent.

differences between the centrist catchall DC and the leftist PCI. The PSI, initially a center-left party, offered little in terms of ideological distinction from the DC, as they both moved toward the center in the 1970s and 1980s (Gilbert 1995). Thus, the primary ideological divide centered around the communist issue (Carter 1998). The exclusion of the PCI from governance created a blockage in the system, prohibiting meaningful ideological alternation in government. But as long as communism remained a credible threat, the communist-anticommunist divide offered some programmatic options to voters (de Micheli 1997; Waters 1994). In terms of policy responsiveness, the Italian parliament generated more legislative output than many other European countries (Kreppel 1997). However, by the 1980s, a perception prevailed that Parliament was unable to produce substantive legislation dealing with important issues (Furlong 1990; Kreppel 1997, 328–29).[3] Instead, most laws were insignificant *leggine* (small laws) that tended to be clientelistic (della Sala 1993). Some policy responsiveness occurred, but the ideological difference between the Communists and their detractors was the primary programmatic appeal.

The party system also incorporated the major class and religious cleavages that had traditionally shaped Italian society. Interest integration under the old party system was a mix of corporatism and pluralism. Although incorporation was weak and fragmented, major cleavages were represented, with the parties advocating for salient societal interests (Golden 1986; Shefter 1994). In terms of the class cleavage, the DC was pro-business, while the PCI was worker focused. The peak business association, Confindustria, channeled and represented business interests, and Coldiretti (National Confederation of Farmers) represented farmers, with both organizations closely tied to the DC and able to mobilize votes for the party (Waters 1994). Unions were important instruments for party appeals. The parties had considerable influence in their respective labor confederations—the Christian democratic CISL (Italian Confederation of Free Trade Unions), the left-leaning CGIL (General Confederation of Italian Labor), in which Communists and Socialists competed, and the Socialist-dominated UIL (Union of Italian Labor) (Golden 1986; LaPalombara 1987). Additionally, the DC's ties to the Catholic Church and its interest association Catholic Action captured the religious side of the religious-secular cleavage, while the secular side was represented by the PCI (Barnes 1974; Knutsen 2004). Aside from providing guaranteed channels for transmitting these major groups' interests to the

3. Legislative productivity declined almost monotonically in the postwar era until the early 1990s (Kreppel 1997).

state, the parties also offered group-based clientelism by extending material benefits to their members (LaPalombara 1987; Waters 1994).

The most important component of the Italian party system's linkage profile was clientelism (Gilbert 1995; Leonardi 1980; Rhodes 1997). Even policy, in the form of *leggine* that served microsectional concerns (Di Palma 1977), and interest incorporation, in the form of group-membership networks, enhanced clientelist tactics (della Sala 1997). The DC used clientelism to hold its diverse coalition together (Tarrow 1977; Waters 1994), and other parties likewise resorted frequently to this strategy to build support. The dominant DC and the PSI shared resources with each other and with their smaller coalition partners (Gilbert 1995). By the end of the 1980s, even the Communists participated in this resource sharing, receiving about 25 percent of available clientelist goods in exchange for providing legitimate opposition (Colazingari and Rose-Ackerman 1998; Panebianco 1988a; Pizzorno 1992). The parties exploited central government expenditures—particularly public works projects, which were comparatively large—to attract support (Golden and Picci 2008). Public sector employees were attracted by patronage, business owners by incentives and contracts, the urban poor through petty clientelism, and so on (Allum and Allum 2008; Chubb 1981; Waters 1994). In summary, at its height the Italian system provided diverse linkage options, including ideological choices and incorporation of major societal interests, with clientelism serving as a major mechanism for attracting support.

Italian Party System Breakdown

Given the three-pronged linkage profile of the Italian party system, exploring the process leading to its collapse requires analysis of the failure of each linkage type. The Italian system's collapse is in large part a tale of increasing reliance on clientelist exchanges as ideological distinctions disappeared and social structure changed. This dependence on clientelism became increasingly unsustainable in light of mounting demand and resource constraints, leading to the failure of the last vestige of linkage and thus party system collapse. I analyze the challenges and constraints that resulted in the failure of each linkage type in turn.

Programmatic Decline

Throughout most of the postwar period, the Italian economy was lauded as exemplary. Annual growth rates over 5 percent were not anomalous in the 1960s and 1970s, and declining poverty pointed to Italian success (LaPalombara 1987). During these good times, the parties' limited substantive policy making kept pace with the country's needs, and appeals to communist and anticommunist ideology distinguished between those in government and opposition.

However, in the 1980s, a significant economic crisis undermined the Italian party system's ability to maintain programmatic appeals. With burgeoning budget deficits, the country developed one of the highest debt-to-GDP ratios among OECD members. Public debt escalated past 100 percent of GDP, and interest payments became the largest area of public expenditure by the 1990s (della Sala 1997). Unemployment increased steadily, reaching 12 percent by the mid-1990s (OECD, various years), and the Italian lira collapsed in September 1992, confirming Italy's status as "the sick man of Europe" (Gilbert 1995, 133).

Amid decaying economic conditions, people demanded a response. But the status quo of old policy tools, slow policy making, and limited substantive legislation could not address the mounting problems (Gilbert 1995; Kreppel 1997). And as the situation deteriorated, party leaders found their policy latitude constrained by the process of monetary union, set in motion by the 1990 Delors Report and specified further under the 1991 Maastricht Treaty on European Union (Bohrer and Tan 2000; ECB 2008). The Maastricht convergence criteria stipulated that countries wishing to enter monetary union had to attain public deficits below 3 percent of GDP, public debt levels at 60 percent of GDP, central bank independence, and inflation rates within 1.5 percentage points of the three most stable EMU countries (della Sala 1997, 20–21). Given the treaty demands, old patterns of dealing with economic pressures were no longer viable in highly indebted Italy, where achieving the convergence criteria required austerity. The old tactic of expanding the public sector to lower unemployment was not compatible with Maastricht goals, and oft-used strategies of manipulating monetary policy and inflation rates were not viable (Gilbert 1995; Rotte 1998; Sandholtz 1993). Instead, Italian governments in the early 1990s felt compelled to raise taxes and cut spending even as people cried for an answer to the deepening recession (della Sala 1997; Kondonassis and Malliaris 1994). Despite mounting frustration, the Maastricht criteria constrained government's programmatic response, and the governing parties could not adjust policy to combat pressing issues.

Programmatic decay reached the system level, as essentially all of Italy's "pro-system" parties governed jointly during this period and together contributed to the deterioration in responsiveness. Rather than just one or two parties being discredited, the governing coalition included five parties: DC, PSI, PSDI, PRI, and PLI. Thus, all the parties of significance, with the exception of the "anti-system" Communists, were responsible for the policy inactivity. As responsiveness failed, Italians were increasingly dissatisfied, and because the pro-system parties governed together, none were insulated from growing discontent (Colazingari and Rose-Ackerman 1998; Fabbrini 2000; Morlino 1996). The five governing parties "proved themselves no longer capable of providing enough policy responsiveness," harming the programmatic linkage capacity of the party system as a whole (Pasquino 1997, 46). The complicity of all the pro-system parties in the failure of policy to respond to pressing demands thus undermined programmatic representation throughout most of the Italian party system.

The Communists escaped some of this programmatic discrediting, but the PCI was never a viable party of government, which weakened its credibility as a meaningful alternative to the status quo that could be expected to deliver a response (Gilbert 1995; Hopkin and Mastropaolo 2001; Kertzer 1996).[4] Nevertheless, deteriorating responsiveness would not have spelled the complete failure of programmatic linkage if the parties could have continued to draw on anticommunist rhetoric. Although the long-standing agreement among the pro-system parties, which excluded the PCI, made ideological differences between governing parties irrelevant (Daniels 1999), the communist-anticommunist divide remained a point of ideological distinction (Carter 1998). But with the fall of the Berlin Wall and the end of the communist threat in Europe, fear of communism no longer served as a motivation to vote for the DC or its coalition partners. The governing parties lost their primary ideological appeal of anticommunism (Morlino 1996; Waters 1994), and the Communists lost their moorings (Eubank, Gangopadahay, and Weinberg 1997). Italians, particularly the northern middle class, ceased to support the unresponsive and now ideologically indistinguishable parties of the old system (Daniels 1999; Gilbert 1995).

The end of communism also led to the demise of the PCI, the only remaining programmatic alternative in the system. The PCI struggled with its identity in a post-Soviet world (Kertzer 1996), and the party divided. The soft-liners, who won control of the old PCI apparatus, renamed it the Democratic Party of the Left (PDS) to strengthen its moderate left appeal and shore up its democratic credentials. The hard-liners broke away from the

---

4. Following the historic compromise, the PCI also provided behind-the-scenes support to the government, which may have undermined its programmatic independence.

PDS and established the Refounded Communists (RC). The collapse of communism and this internal dispute left both remnants weakened and unable to regain former electoral successes (Daniels 1999). With the decay of communism, the governing coalition and the Communists lost any remaining distinctiveness, and voters saw no viable alternatives to the status quo.

The pattern of programmatic linkage decay in Italy closely follows the theoretical model of challenge and constraint. Crisis demanded a response, but conflicting international constraints and parties' ideological and policy-making legacies limited policy latitude and undermined programmatic responsiveness. Interparty agreements and decaying ideological distinctiveness eliminated meaningful alternatives and produced programmatic decay across the entire system.

Limited Interest Incorporation

At the same time, significant changes in the kind of salient cleavages threatened interest incorporation, while the parties' organizational structures limited their capacity to accommodate increasingly significant regional divides. The traditional framework for incorporation rested on two cleavages: religious-secular and worker-owner. Throughout the 1970s and 1980s, two changes weakened the salience of these cleavages. Secularization undermined the importance of Catholicism, and deindustrialization and high unemployment limited unions' strength and appeal. In their place, regional divisions between north and south became increasingly relevant.

Secularization debilitated the Christian Democrats' incorporating capacity. Despite the fact that most Italians still identified themselves as Catholics, by the 1980s fewer than 30 percent reported attending church weekly, down from close to 70 percent in the 1950s (Leonardi and Wertman 1989, 177). The end of communism's atheist threat accelerated the demise of Italy's religious cleavage (Levite and Tarrow 1983). A Europe-wide analysis of religion and partisanship found that Italy experienced one of the most dramatic decays in the correlation between religious and political identities between the 1970s and 1990s (Knutsen 2004), as many non-practicing Catholics shifted their allegiance away from the DC toward non-confessional parties (Morlino 1996). The religious-secular cleavage lost political relevance, and the party system was increasingly unable to capture support through religious organizations or appeals to religious identity and values.

At the same time, deindustrialization and mounting unemployment weakened the traditional class cleavage and undermined the utility of unions and other work-based organizations for effectively incorporating broad swaths of society (Daniels 1999; LaPalombara 1987). Both agriculture and industry shrank in the 1980s, while the service sector grew, accounting for 60 percent of the workforce by 1992, when the system began to collapse (World Bank, various years). Given weak union influence in the service sector, overall unionization declined (Santi 1988). From a peak of 49 percent, unionization rates dropped below 35 percent by the end of the 1990s, with most of the losses occurring in the late 1980s and early 1990s, immediately preceding the party system's collapse (Baccaro, Carrieri, and Damiano 2002). Also weakening the organized working class, unemployment nearly doubled over the course of the 1980s, reaching 12 percent (World Bank, various years), and the size of the public sector, a union stronghold, declined (LaPalombara 1987). Moreover, as the economy deteriorated, the parties and Confindustria forced Italy's workers to accept a collective bargaining agreement in which they sacrificed many of the gains that had been made over the past twenty years; most notably, wage indexation was abolished. The abandonment of workers' interests in this agreement suggests a general weakening of organized labor. The proliferation of autonomous unions without party ties further undermined the incorporating role of the three major union confederations in the late 1980s (Baccaro, Carrieri, and Damiano 2002). Deindustrialization and the major confederations' decline weakened party capacity to integrate significant swaths of society through traditional union-based strategies.

As religious and class cleavages faded, regional divisions emerged in their place (Daniels 1999; Morlino 1996). This newly salient cleavage pitted the more developed north against the more clientelistic and mafia-ridden south (Gilbert 1995). The parties' organizational structures made them ill equipped to incorporate the increasingly relevant regional divide. Specifically, the old parties lacked significant regional organizations. Within the DC, for example, power was centralized in the national party, and although there was considerable local autonomy, the most important locus of decentralized power was below the regional level. The DC had regional entities, but unlike the national, provincial, and communal levels, these regional branches were not part of the original structure established in the early postwar period. Instead, they were set up in the 1970s and were never imbued with many formal or informal powers (Leonardi and Wertman 1989). The Communist Party organization similarly placed little emphasis on the regional level of the party; rather, the central party apparatus and the local section were the most significant loci of power (Hellman 1988). Because of the relative unimportance of their regional organizations, the parties were poorly prepared to accommodate increasingly influential regional interests and calls for autonomy. Furthermore, regional demands often took on the antagonistic tone of a zero-sum game in which satisfying the demands of one region meant sacrificing those of another. For parties attempting to win broad influence at the national level, regionally oriented appeals provided little opportunity for netting a gain across the entire country, alienating more people than they attracted.

Social transformation away from religious and class cleavages and toward regional divisions posed a serious challenge to the party system's maintenance of group incorporation. The parties' organizational structures made it particularly difficult to accommodate emerging regional concerns, and their interest-integrating capacities narrowed to such a point that most Italians no longer saw their group identities or interests incorporated in the system.

Decay of Clientelism

With the deterioration of programmatic appeals and incorporation, the Italian parties became heavily reliant on clientelism to furnish linkage (Gilbert 1995; Hopkin and Mastropaolo 2001), and the need for resources grew as more and more people were only attracted to the parties for the material benefits they offered (Waters 1994). But clientelism also came under stress in the late 1980s and early 1990s. The costs of providing clientelist linkage escalated, even as resources available to the parties for such exchanges diminished markedly. Increased costs stemmed from social changes and electoral decentralization, while state reforms and economic crisis shrank resources, producing clientelist shortages and mounting frustrations.

Social changes increased clientelist demand. Along with development and deindustrialization came an increase in the size and wealth of the Italian middle class (LaPalombara 1987), and petty clientelism became increasingly ineffective for attracting support from this growing group. Rather, the payoffs needed to win middle-class support, such as public works contracts or subsidies, were more expensive than traditional clientelist exchanges (Chubb 1981; Piattoni 2001a). Increasing unemployment also heightened pressure for clientelism as the unemployed sought patronage jobs in the public sector (Rotte 1998). But the public sector shrank in the early 1990s, further frustrating those demanding patronage employment.[5]

5. Public sector employment dropped from 22.5 percent of the workforce in 1990 to 16.3 percent in 1995 (ILO 2009).

Italy also implemented electoral decentralization in the early 1990s, which generated demand for clientelism while simultaneously reducing the gains that these exchanges brought to the central party. For the first time, in June 1993, Italians directly elected their own mayors (Gilbert 1995). The local elections occurred separately from national elections, which were held in 1992 and 1994. This new electoral process compelled the parties to provide additional material benefits to attract votes in repeated elections, requiring them to ante up three times in only three years to win support at the local and national levels.[6] With separate electoral processes, resources expended in local races did not necessarily accrue benefits to the central party apparatuses. The decentralized elections, as well as the introduction of the mixed system for legislative elections, heightened the power of local politicians in relation to the party organization. As local leaders grew in stature, they had reduced incentives to use the resources they received to serve the party as well as their personal machines. The parties increasingly found themselves expending resources to win elections, yet receiving few benefits for their organizations in return (Hopkin and Mastropaolo 2001).

Other reforms undermined the availability of resources that the parties needed to meet the increasing pressures for material exchanges. The reform that struck most directly at the heart of the parties' resource stream was the 1993 referendum that eliminated public financing for political parties. With the passage of the new campaign finance law, individual candidates could apply for campaign expenditure reimbursement, but the party *organizations* could receive no public funds. This strengthened the power of individual politicians and weakened the parties. For the highly indebted traditional parties, the loss of this major revenue source was like a death knell for their clientelist networks (Rhodes 1997).

Additionally, state-rationalizing reforms stemming from efforts to meet the Maastricht criteria in the context of economic crisis limited the access points for rent seeking and made public resources less available for political ends (della Sala 1997). Privatizations designed to alleviate budget deficits and trim an overextended state apparatus reduced patronage jobs in the public sector and eliminated parties' ability to distribute state-owned industry funds as clientelist benefits (Chubb 1981; della Sala 1997; ILO 2009; Leonardi 1980). Efforts to reduce fiscal deficits and rein in inflation also led to cuts in public spending and welfare state retrenchment, shrinking funds for clientelism (Bohrer and Tan 2000; Carter 1998). Moreover, the economic

6. These three elections were in addition to the June 1991 and April 1993 referendums in which the parties also campaigned for their favored positions.

crisis itself limited clientelist resources (Gilbert 1995; Hopkin and Mastropaolo 2001).

In addition to the economic downturn and state reforms, which constricted both public and private resources, the parties faced an organizational context that exacerbated the demands for clientelism and stretched already scarce resources. By the early 1980s, as the hegemony of the DC declined, large multiparty coalitions became necessary for the pro-system parties to retain control of government. In fact, for much of the 1980s, the Socialist Bettino Craxi—rather than a Christian Democrat—led this coalition as prime minister. During this period, the Socialists shifted to the center and sought more clientelist resources for their supporters, mimicking the catchall DC (Hopkin and Mastropaolo 2001). The Socialists challenged the DC's control of the state apparatus, and "the great share out" of 1986 saw the PSI win control of hundreds of politically important jobs in the state bureaucracy (Gilbert 1995, 12). Smaller parties in the coalition and even the PCI received funds for their machines, stretching shrinking resources further (Colazingari and Rose-Ackerman 1998; Leonardi 1980).

These patterns of increased demand, stemming from social change and decentralization, as well as a constricting resource base caused by economic crisis and lost access, brought the parties to the point of desperation. All the traditional parties were running annual deficits and were deep in debt. By the time the system collapsed in 1994, the Christian Democrats, Socialists, and PDS (formerly the Communists) together owed almost 150 billion lira and were essentially bankrupt (Rhodes 1997).

To supplement their incomes and attempt to satisfy growing demand, the parties increasingly turned to illegal sources of funds in the form of bribes, kickbacks, and Mafia payments. But as their grasp on power weakened, the parties were no longer able to stave off investigations and even trials concerning these illicit activities, as they had in the past (Carter 1998; Waters 1994). When the Tangentopoli (Bribesville) scandal broke in 1992 and eventually produced Craxi's resignation, as well as an investigation into longtime DC leader Giulio Andreotti's Mafia association, it exposed crumbling clientelist networks. As scrutiny of the parties' finances intensified under the judiciary's Operation Mani Pulite (Clean Hands), the parties were no longer able to feed their clientelist machines with illegal sources of revenue, further weakening their capacity to reach citizens through clientelism (Gilbert 1995; Rhodes 1997).

These investigations did not suddenly reveal corruption and clientelism—Italians had known about these tactics for many years (Rhodes 1997; Waters

1994). But corruption had been tolerated because it brought many advantages. As these advantages dissipated, people grew frustrated (Carter 1998; Hopkin and Mastropaolo 2001). With the revelations of Tangentopoli, Italy's clientelist networks were no longer tolerable because the scandal revealed what many Italians had come to suspect: clientelism was not a mechanism of inclusion but rather "excluded the majority of citizens, the smaller sized firms and a large number of interest groups" (Waters 1994, 174). As clientelism reached a shrinking segment of the electorate, this shift in perspective spurred mounting condemnation of the entire party system.

Comparative Portrait of Collapse
Despite differences in party system structure and political institutions, the Italian party system collapse occurred in much the same way as the process in Venezuela. The party systems faced crisis, social transformation, and political reforms in a context of specific constraints that impeded necessary adaptation. As a result, all three types of linkage failed, and both systems collapsed. In Italy, economic crisis challenged the party system to address policy demands, but the contradictions between entrenched policy patterns and the constraints of the Maastricht criteria made ramping up responsiveness almost impossible. Coalition governments as well as the collapse of communism removed meaningful ideological options from the system, undermining the programmatic appeals of all the parties. Social changes attendant with secularization and deindustrialization weakened the importance of old religious and class cleavages and enabled the emergence of regionalism as a politically salient divide. This cleavage challenged the parties' organizational structures and contradicted their desire to exercise power at the national level, limiting their capacity to address regional concerns. In this context, the parties' clientelist networks faced increased demand resulting from social change and political decentralization, while economic crisis and reforms that restricted partisan access to the state shrank the funds available for distribution. Clientelism failed to benefit the majority of Italian citizens, and people abandoned the party system amid a blaze of accusations, which left only wisps of smoke where the Italian parties had once been.

COLOMBIA: CRUMBLING CLIENTELISM AND PARTY SYSTEM DISINTEGRATION

Throughout the twentieth century, two major parties, the Liberals and the Conservatives, dominated Colombian politics. After periods of violent conflict between them and unsuccessful efforts to entrench single-party dominance by both, the parties agreed that joint rule was perhaps the only viable path to peaceful governance. The 1958 National Front (NF) agreement established a system of mutual guarantees and installed a limited democracy in which control of the presidency alternated. Cabinet offices, legislative seats, judicial posts, governorships, and mayoralties were divided equally between the parties, and passing legislation required a two-thirds majority. Reforms to the Constitution in 1968 eliminated some of the NF constraints within the legislative branch, but alternation in the executive remained in place until 1974, when the first competitive presidential elections were held (Hartlyn 1988). Even after the end of the NF restrictions on competition, the two parties remained the dominant legal political actors in Colombia for more than twenty years, and the remnants of coalition rule were not lifted until the 1991 Constitution (Hartlyn and Dugas 1999).

However, by the 1990s, conflict had escalated between the state, paramilitary organizations, guerrillas, and drug cartels. And as their clientelist networks fell apart, the parties began to decay. The Liberals and Conservatives, which had historically dominated the legislature, often winning 80 to 90 percent of the seats, were replaced by atomistic forces in 2002, marking the collapse of the Colombian system. With collapse, the two traditional parties controlled less than 50 percent of the seats in both houses of the legislature, and the number of parties in the system exploded from about 2.5 to more than six (Boudon 2000; Gutiérrez Sanín 2007). In the analysis that follows, I outline the Colombian system's traditional linkage profile and then analyze how linkage came under pressure and why the parties were unable to sustain ties between society and the state, producing collapse.

Linkage in Colombia's Two-Party System, 1974–1998

Colombia's return to open elections in 1974 marked the end of many National Front restrictions and the beginning of true interparty competition. After the NF, programmatic appeals and interest incorporation did not attract many voters to the traditional parties. Old reservoirs of partisan affect had begun to decay with the onset of the NF in the 1950s, and ideological differences dissipated over years of shared governance. Colombian civil society had always been weak and offered little in the way of linkage (Archer 1995; Kline 2004). Instead, clientelist exchanges dominated the system's linkage profile (Bejarano and Pizarro 2005; Schmidt 1980).

Before the NF, partisan differences between the Liberals and Conservatives were intense and often escalated into violence, but the power-sharing agreement muted partisan strife. To achieve peaceful coexistence, the parties emphasized their commonalities, producing ideological convergence (Gutiérrez Sanín 2007). The agreements limited interparty differences and instead encouraged conflict within the parties as factions competed for status and access to clientelist resources (Archer 1995; Boudon 2000). By the end of the NF period, there were essentially no programmatic distinctions between the two parties, and factions across parties were sometimes closer ideologically than were factions in the same party (Archer 1995; Hartlyn 1988; Kline 1988). The parties also offered little in the way of policy responsiveness. They were unable to address important national issues (Martz 1997) and failed to meet one key programmatic promise: peace. Rather, policy making was particularistic (Escobar 2002), with 78 percent of legislation consisting of pork-barrel laws that treated local or regional issues while only 22 percent addressed national concerns (Pizarro Leongómez 2006, 92).

Interest incorporation also held an insignificant place in the Colombian linkage profile. The system did not reflect major cleavages in society, and both parties were heterogeneous in terms of socioeconomic and regional support (Archer 1995; Hartlyn 1988). Divisions along the religious cleavage, with Conservatives advocating for the Church, had disappeared by the end of the NF. During the era of partisan violence, autonomous civic associations were destroyed, and the National Front subsequently squelched associational life outside the parties (Hartlyn 1988). Although the parties maintained minor connections to unions, peasant groups, and producer associations, and unaffiliated groups emerged over time, neither the Conservatives nor the Liberals aggregated collective interests in a meaningful way (Bejarano and Pizarro 2005; Hartlyn 1988; Kline 2004). Instead, the parties divided class-based organizations along party lines to limit mobilization (Hartlyn 1988). Colombia had no peak producer association speaking for business, and there was no pattern of consultation with the private sector (Hartlyn 1988; Kline 2004).[7] Workers' representation was even more disparate, enervated by internal divisions, with separate union federations for each party as well as several smaller organizations. In the 1980s, the two party-affiliated unions, CTC (Liberals) and UTC (Conservatives), represented only 34 percent of union memberships, and overall unionization rates were low (Kline 2004). The parties endeavored to integrate peasants through the Juntas de Acción Comunal (JAC) and later through the peasant

7. The two associations representing the largest business interests in Colombia were ANDI (Asociación Nacional de Industriales) and FEDECAFE (Federación Nacional de Cafeteros de Colombia). But these groups did not have formal ties to the parties (Kline 2004).

association ANUC (Asociación Nacional de Usuarios Campesinos), but these groups operated either as clients of the parties or independently from them, and the peasant groups declined with urbanization. Where significant interest associations existed, their influence often occurred outside the party system (Kline 2004; Rettberg 2005).

Programmatic appeals and interest incorporation did not attract many Colombians to the Liberal and Conservative parties. Rather, the parties maintained linkage almost exclusively through conditional clientelist exchanges (Boudon 2000; Schmidt 1980). "It was the underlying patron-client relationship . . . that provided the basis for the parties" (Martz 1997, 68). Most political disputes and legislation centered on resources, not policy (Hartlyn 1988; Pizarro Leongómez 2006), and internal party factions competed among themselves for benefits to distribute. Individual candidates established personal fiefdoms using clientelist resources, diluting the meaning of the party labels (Boudon 2000; Crisp and Ingall 2002). New parties that endeavored to enter the party system in the 1980s and 1990s were also co-opted into clientelist linkage patterns, sacrificing programmatic clarity for clientelist resources (Boudon 2001; Dix 1987; Escobar 2002). Clientelist exchanges were the centerpiece of Colombian party politics.

Colombian Party System Disintegration

Given the preeminence of clientelism in the Colombian system, exploring linkage failure and its role in precipitating the system's collapse requires a focus on clientelist decay. In the post-NF period, programmatic appeals and interest incorporation were not significant components of the system's strategy. Therefore, exploring their deterioration is not central to understanding the system's failure, and my discussion of Colombia's collapse centers instead on the deterioration of clientelism. However, before examining clientelism, I briefly demonstrate that even in Colombia, where programmatic appeals and interest incorporation were not important, the same general processes of economic crisis, social transformation, and contextual constraints reduced the linkage capacity of these strategies even further.

The NF and interparty collaboration after the end of the formal power-sharing agreement obliterated ideological distinctions between Liberals and Conservatives, and policy responsiveness was poor for some time. However, in the 1990s, as violence spiraled out of control and low and negative growth rates exacerbated the sense of crisis, demand for solutions escalated (Archer 1995; Dugas 2003). Lack of responsiveness became a matter of life and death, but rather than elected leaders taking control, guerrilla groups seemed to be gaining the upper hand, controlling 40 percent of Colombian territory by the late 1990s (Boudon 2000). Additionally, despite mounting economic pressures, policy activity in this arena remained stagnant, and limited efforts to respond to the crisis failed (Chernick 1998; Martz 1997; Moreno 2005). International policy constraints also restricted the parties' policy latitude, as pressures from the United States on counternarcotics and counterterrorism often contradicted the concerns of domestic constituencies (Bejarano and Pizarro 2005; Gutiérrez Sanín 2007). Thus, escalating violence and economic decline heightened pressure for programmatic answers, while international demands limited responsiveness. Furthermore, the legacy of the NF, collaboration in government, and lack of distinction between the two parties made it difficult for Colombians to assign blame for this policy immobility, so frustrations with unresponsiveness undermined programmatic linkage across the entire system.

Limited interest incorporation in Colombia also narrowed further during the 1990s. The economic downturn and resulting neoliberal policies enervated already weak unions and damaged the coffee sector (Gutiérrez Sanín 2007; Kline 2004). Violence and the drug economy transformed society and accelerated urbanization, and in the 1990s, more than 1.2 million out of 40 million Colombians were forcibly displaced from their homes by the violence (Isacson 2002, 1). This displacement broke up the rural associations that had linked peasants to the parties, damaging one of their few group-based ties (Gutiérrez Sanín 2007, 407–8). The social transformation completely decimated the little interest incorporation that had existed in the Colombian system.

Decay of Clientelism

The Colombian party system was, therefore, heavily dependent on conditional exchanges to build support. However, in the face of increased demand and resource constraints, the parties were unable to sustain even this form of linkage. Social changes and political reforms heightened demands for clientelism, while the escalating security crisis, economic downturn, and state-rationalizing reform efforts limited the resources available to meet these rising costs.

Social changes, in the form of geographical displacement and destruction of collective identities, weakened collective clientelist networks and increased the number of clients seeking benefits, outpacing the parties' capacity to meet demand (Boudon 2000). From the end of the NF through the early 1990s, clientelism featured politicians using state resources to feed networks based on community ties and sectoral interests (Dávila and Delgado 2002; Schmidt 1980). However, the negative effects of the drug trade and violence produced extreme dislocation. An estimated 2 million people were internally displaced between 1985 and 2000, giving Colombia the world's largest internally displaced population (Arboleda and Correa 2003, 831; CODHES, various dates). These processes uprooted communities and destroyed local networks (Arboleda and Correa 2003). Meanwhile, economic crisis undermined sectoral collectivities (Dugas 2003). With the erosion of communal and sectoral ties, parties could not achieve efficient distribution through existing networks (Gutiérrez Sanín 2007). The drug economy spurred "greater demands for material rewards . . . because there [were] increasing numbers of poor and marginal Colombians living without the 'protection' of a traditional *patron*" (Kline 1988, 37). The number of clients demanding benefits increased exponentially during the 1990s, and the expense of extending material appeals to individual Colombians far surpassed the costs of satisfying old networks (Dávila and Delgado 2002; Gutiérrez Sanín 2007). Linkage based on generalized vote buying became prohibitively expensive (Escobar 2002; Gutiérrez Sanín 2007).

Political reforms, namely the establishment of separate subnational elections for mayors and governors and the elimination of party-printed ballots, also strained clientelist linkage. These changes aggravated competition for funds and created uncertainty about their effectiveness, increasing cost and waste. Historically, the president appointed mayors and governors, promoting interdependence between different levels of government and generating loyalty between local and departmental officials and national party leaders. But a 1986 constitutional amendment established direct mayoral elections, held for the first time in 1988, and the 1991 Constitution instituted gubernatorial elections, removing centralized control over these offices (Chernick 1998; Escobar-Lemmon 2006; Martz 1997).

Creating separate elections for these positions escalated demand for clientelism and broke the pyramidal structure of the clientelist system (Archer 1995; Dávila and Delgado 2002). Under the old appointment process, a system of agreements between politicians at different levels of government allowed a party or faction to engage in a single clientelist exchange and gain access to office at all levels (Gutiérrez Sanín 2007). But with separate, direct elections, the effects of one clientelist exchange could not be multiplied to produce both national and subnational power. Voters now demanded clientelist benefits for every ballot they cast for mayor, governor, legislature, president, and so on, escalating demand for clientelist inputs (Dávila and Delgado 2002). Also, as clientelist networks no longer spanned the local, departmental, and national levels, it became every candidate for him- or herself (Dávila and Delgado 2002). Neither party nor factional ties could hold coalitions together, as politicians became electoral entrepreneurs seeking resources to fuel their personal networks and win their own elections (Boudon 2000). As more leaders sought to develop their own client base, it became increasingly difficult to satisfy demand (Gutiérrez Sanín 2007, 275).

The elimination of party-printed ballots in the 1991 Constitution also exacerbated demand for clientelism by making it more difficult for politicians and parties to effectively target and monitor clientelism. Under the 1886 Constitution, the Colombian state did not provide ballots. Instead, parties and factions distributed their own—a valuable tactic in monitoring clientelist exchanges (Medina and Stokes 2007). Partisan ballots gave politicians considerable control over voting, helping to guarantee that when clients went to the polls, they cast their ballots for the party or faction that had sponsored their votes (Escobar 2002). The 1991 Constitution eliminated these *papeletas* (little paper ballots) and replaced them with a government-issued ballot, or *tarjetón electoral* (large electoral card), that contained all candidate names (Martz 1997). Without party-controlled ballots, patrons were less certain about the effectiveness of clientelist benefits, causing them to hedge their bets and spread out benefits to more clients to ensure victory (Dávila and Delgado 2002). As a result, politicians wasted more funds on voters who "robbed [them] by accepting the money and then voting for another candidate" (Escobar 2002, 37). The tarjetón increased the costs of vote buying and required more benefits to achieve the same outcome as before, intensifying the need for clientelist resources.

Even as social transformations and political reforms heightened demand, crisis conditions limited the resources available for clientelism, and other reforms reduced party access to state funds. In particular, violence and economic recession reduced clientelist resources available to the parties. The costs of fighting an internal war soared in the 1990s, as the boom in the drug trade expanded the magnitude of the conflict (Dugas 2003). Coca cultivation exploded, more than quintupling over the course of the 1990s (U.S. Department of State, various dates; U.S. General Accounting Office 2003). The scope of the conflict was so great that half a million people died violently between 1980 and 2000, and the homicide rate in the 1990s was higher than that of all other Latin American countries except El Salvador (Institute of Legal Medicine and Forensic Sciences, cited in Bejarano and Pizarro 2005, 248). The homicide rate more than doubled between 1980 and the mid-1990s, reaching almost 80 per 100,000 people (Policía Nacional de Colombia, various dates). The resources expended in counterinsurgency and counternarcotics efforts reduced the funds available for clientelism (Bejarano and Pizarro 2005; Garfield and Arboleda 2003).

Furthermore, "in the second half of the 1990s, as the armed conflict and violence were dramatically increasing, economic growth slowed down, and toward the end of the decade there was a serious recession" (Garfield and Arboleda 2003, 45). By the late 1990s, Colombia faced its most dire economic situation since the 1930s. Although when compared with the economic troubles of its neighbors the crisis might be viewed as moderate, in the Colombian context it stood out as exceptionally severe. Negative growth rates, expanding fiscal deficits, and a growing debt burden challenged the parties' ability to obtain the resources they needed for clientelism. Moreover, the standard neoliberal response to economic crisis, which was implemented in Colombia by Conservative party president Andrés Pastrana (1998–2002), reduced the flow of resources (Pizarro Leongómez 2006). Austere economic policies exacerbated resource constraints and undermined clientelist linkage (Boudon 2000).

In addition to the resource constraints generated by these crises, political reforms cut off the central party apparatuses' access to resources, weakening the parties and strengthening individual candidates. The introduction of direct elections for mayors and governors eliminated patronage opportunities. As long as these offices were filled by presidential appointees, they had provided opportunities for party leaders to reward loyal followers with influential patronage jobs. But "the popular election of mayors weakened the party faction leader; now he no longer had 60 mayors that he could appoint at his whim, rather he had to fight for votes in 125 municipalities in order to obtain victories for loyal mayors" (regional party leader, quoted in Gutiérrez Sanín 2007, 259).

Replacing appointees with directly elected leaders also eliminated party control over local and departmental funds, which became especially problematic as fiscal decentralization advanced. The 1991 Constitution expanded the proportion of the national budget allocated to departments and municipalities (Escobar-Lemmon 2003), committing more than 40 percent to subnational government transfers (Martz 1997, 296). Although the national government retained considerable authority over the specific policy areas and programs where this money was spent, the devolution of resources in a context in which parties could not install loyal partisans as subnational executives severely constrained the capacity of the central party apparatuses to politically manipulate these funds. Instead, autonomous individual candidates used decentralized resources for their personal networks. This state restructuring contradicted the hierarchical logic of clientelist exchanges and limited the efficacy of distributed resources (Gutiérrez Sanín 2007). Over the 1990s, the parties' role in providing clientelism decayed, and electoral "microenterprises" replaced them (Gutiérrez Sanín 2007, 258; Pizarro Leongómez 2006).

The 1991 Constitution also significantly reduced the funds that could be easily channeled toward clientelism by eliminating individual legislators' control over *auxilios parliamentarios*, or pork-barrel funds. Before 1991, the Colombian budget process guaranteed national and departmental legislators pots of money purportedly to use in support of development projects in their districts. In reality, "politicians created hundreds of fictitious foundations and corporations countrywide to which they diverted most of the pork-barrel funds"; these were used to provide direct cash exchanges to support the politicians' clientelist networks (Escobar 2002, 34). The 1991 Constitution eliminated the auxilios, undercutting easy access to state funds for clientelism (Dávila and Delgado 2002; Gutiérrez Sanín 2007). In response, politicians tried to disguise auxilios within legislation, trading their support of the executive's legislation for clientelist resources, a method that was much more constraining and proved inadequate (Archer and Shugart 1997; Escobar 2002).

In a last effort to salvage linkage, some party factions sought out private, illegal funds furnished mostly by drug money (Escobar 2002). Despite ongoing suspicions about the use of drug money to finance campaigns, it was not until the parties were already considerably weakened that a series of scandals erupted in the mid-1990s, exposing the role of such funds in sustaining the parties (Gutiérrez Sanín 2007). In the second round of his successful 1994 presidential campaign, Ernesto Samper accepted unprecedented funding from illegal sources, namely the Cali Cartel, channeling these funds toward vote buying (Gutiérrez Sanín 2007, 380–83). Like the Italian Mani Pulite, Colombia's Proceso 8000 brought numerous politicians to trial for receiving drug money, although Samper himself retained amnesty and avoided prosecution. These revelations made it much more difficult for politicians to fund clientelism with illegal donations (Dávila and Delgado 2002). The resource constraints imposed on the parties, therefore, caused them to rely increasingly on illegal sources even as they were no longer powerful enough to limit damaging publicity and prosecution. As scandals mounted and drug barons turned their support to local politicians rather than funding the central parties and presidential campaigns, this last source of funding dried up (Gutiérrez Sanín 2007). The taint of corruption contaminated the entire party system as fewer voters received benefits from clientelism and instead saw a corrupt system designed to prosper only a handful of elites.

Comparative Portrait of Collapse

In Colombia, the exhaustion of clientelism occurred in a context in which both programmatic representation and interest incorporation were weak. Like Venezuela and Italy, where the failure of other linkage forms accompanied clientelist decay, the Colombian parties' inability to sustain adequate clientelist linkage led to system collapse. In Colombia, as in the other two cases, the pattern of linkage failure follows the theoretical model. Significant social changes and electoral decentralization increased demand for material exchanges, while crisis conditions and resource-constraining reforms limited funds for clientelism. In Colombia, the growth of the drug economy, escalating violence, and urbanization created significant dislocation, removing people from traditional networks and causing them to seek exchanges directly from the parties. Establishment of separate subnational elections increased competition among politicians to find resources for their machines, and parties lost control of the distribution process. At the same time, fiscal decentralization and other reforms siphoned resources away from the central party apparatuses. As costs for fighting the internal war escalated and the economy deteriorated, there were simply not enough resources to satiate exploding demand for material benefits. As clientelism failed, the Colombian system lost its only vestige of linkage and collapsed.

BOLIVIA: POLICY CONVERGENCE, ETHNIC MOBILIZATION, STRAINED CLIENTELISM, AND COLLAPSE

When Bolivia returned to democracy in 1982, a moderate multiparty system emerged and was dominated by three sets of parties (Conaghan and Malloy 1994; Malloy and Gamarra 1988; Mayorga 2005). These were the party of the Revolution, MNR (Movimiento Nacionalista Revolucionario); the personalist party of military man Hugo Banzer, ADN (Acción Democrática Nacionalista); and left parties like MIR (Movimiento de la Izquierda Revolucionaria) and PCB (Partido Comunista de Bolivia). A left coalition, UDP (Unión Democrática y Popular), won the presidency immediately following the democratic transition (Gamarra and Malloy 1995).

But soon after the transition, the region-wide debt crisis hit. Inflation soared, reaching annualized rates of over 20,000 percent in some months of 1985; fiscal deficits surpassed 75 percent of GDP; and debt service routinely exceeded 30 percent of exports (ECLAC 1987; Malloy 1991, 38). The disparate UDP, led by President Hernán Siles (1982–85, MNRI), made repeated failed attempts to deal with the crisis, initiating and halting at least six different stabilization packages. These failed attempts only intensified the crisis and delegitimized the governing left coalition (Conaghan and Malloy 1994, 108). In 1985, early elections turned the presidency over to founding MNR leader and former President Victor Paz Estenssoro (1985–89). Paz Estenssoro, with the support of Banzer's ADN, swiftly enacted an austere stabilization program to deal with inflation and fiscal deficits (Conaghan and Malloy 1994; Malloy 1991). The severity of the crisis under the UDP and the initial success of Paz Estenssoro's neoliberal agenda resulted in the decline of the left and the emergence of a pro-market consensus among elites. By the mid-1980s, all the major parties ascribed to the same basic neoliberal policies (Birnir and Van Cott 2007; Van Cott 2003; Whitehead 2001).

But as neoliberalism's long-term ramifications, including unemployment, poverty, and negative growth, manifested in the 1990s, the parties did not abandon economic orthodoxy (Domingo 2001; Mayorga 2005). As a result of these policies, major social disruptions plagued Bolivian society. Labor and peasant movements weakened and were supplanted by groups excluded from traditional patterns of incorporation, such as informal sector workers, *cocaleros* (coca growers), and indigenous identity organizations (Barr 2005; Mayorga 2005; Van Cott 2003; Yashar 1999). Clientelist demand escalated, but resources could not keep pace (Gill 2000; Gray-Molina 2001; Mayorga 2005, 2006; Van Cott 2005). By 2002, the traditional parties barely held a majority of seats in the legislature, and 2005 marked the system's collapse, as the traditional parties lost control of the legislature and the moderate multiparty system transformed into one with only two major parties. After the 2005 elections, MAS (Movimiento al Socialismo), the party of President Evo Morales, held 55 percent of the seats in the Chamber of Deputies, and PODEMOS (Poder Democrático y Social), a right-wing coalition spawned partly from the old parties, controlled 33 percent.

Linkage in Bolivia's Neoliberal-Era Party System, 1985–2005

The Bolivian party system employed a multifaceted linkage strategy that amassed considerable support through clientelist exchanges but also integrated salient social cleavages and provided effective, albeit ideologically constrained, policy responsiveness on some significant national issues (Gamarra and Malloy 1995). The system initially offered ideological options, with parties ranging from the leftist UDP coalition to the centrist MNR to ADN on the right (Conaghan and Malloy 1994; Domingo 2001). However, after Siles's dismal administration, the left deteriorated and lost its ideological footing (Domingo 2001; Gamarra and Malloy 1995; Van Cott 2003). When Paz Estenssoro's neoliberal policies relieved hyperinflation (Whitehead 2001), the parties, including the old left, converged around a neoliberal consensus (Mayorga 2005, 2006). So no matter which party they voted for, Bolivians received the same basic policy prescriptions (Conaghan and Malloy 1994; Salazar Elena 2004). Programmatic representation was not furnished primarily via meaningful ideological options.

However, the parties did offer substantive policy answers to some of the country's most significant problems, resolving the untenable situation of extreme hyperinflation and heavy debt burdens (Conaghan and Malloy 1994). Addressing the economic crisis lent programmatic legitimacy to the party system (Mayorga 2006). Over time, the parties neglected other escalating issues, particularly social problems created by neoliberalism, but in the late 1980s and early 1990s, they responded successfully to at least some serious policy challenges (Barr 2005; Whitehead 2001).

The party system also integrated interests representing the class cleavage, which was politically salient at the outset of the neoliberal era. In Bolivia's corporatist system of interest integration, the peak business organization, CEPB (Confederación de Empresarios Privados de Bolivia), was particularly influential (Mayorga 2005). Worker concerns were also integrated via the central union, COB (Confederación Obrera Boliviana) (Barr 2005; Conaghan and Malloy 1994; Mayorga 2005). Labor and peasant interests found a voice through their affiliation with and organizational ties to parties of the left and MNR. The rural population held a strong allegiance to the party as a result of its agrarian reform policies (Conaghan and Malloy 1994; Domingo 2001), and there was a formal power-sharing agreement between MNR and the COB, which gave the union unique access (Barr 2005). Although the left deteriorated following the return to democracy and MNR's popular ties weakened when Paz Estenssoro repressed labor opposition to his neoliberal policies, worker interests nevertheless continued to find some opportunity for linkage, largely through group-based material benefits. And through the 1990s, the system still dimly reflected the worker-owner cleavage that had polarized society since the 1952 Revolution (Gamarra and Malloy 1995). In this system of incorporation, indigenous concerns were largely absorbed under the general heading of peasant interests, which were represented through MNR and labor unions (Van Cott 2005). During the 1980s, the conflation of ethnic concerns with integrated class interests successfully downplayed indigenous identities and facilitated the system's capacity to absorb most of society through a single salient class cleavage (Salazar Elena 2004; Whitehead 2001).

The parties also used clientelism to maintain linkage (Gamarra and Malloy 1995; Malloy 1991), and in the neoliberal era, they became increasingly reliant on clientelism to hold the system together (Domingo 2001). Clientelism helped the parties maintain ties with the popular sector and the portions of the indigenous population not captured by the class cleavage (Barr 2005; Van Cott 2000). Over time, clientelism also became the centerpiece of governing coalitions (Salazar Elena 2004). Even new parties, like UCS (Unidad Cívica Solidaridad) and CONDEPA (Conciencia de la Patria), sought access to state resources for clientelism and were quickly co-opted through coalition politics (Barr 2005; Gamarra and Malloy 1995). Clientelism was an important means of linking society to the state, and together with policy responsiveness and incorporation, it rounded out the party system's linkage portfolio. Because the Bolivian party system employed programmatic appeals, incorporation, and clientelism, analyzing its collapse requires exploring the deterioration of each.

Bolivian Party System Collapse

Programmatic Decline
Following the disastrous UDP administration (1982–85), Paz Estenssoro's stabilization package, Nueva Política Económica (NPE), brought hyperinflation under control, reduced debt, and increased exports (Mayorga 2006). Subsequent governing coalitions led by different parties maintained similar policies. The economic crisis and uniform neoliberal response undermined ideological differentiation, as the parties governed together in an array of market-oriented coalitions. But some policy responsiveness remained, as the parties addressed the core elements of the crisis (Mayorga 2006). However, as inflation receded and other issues came to the fore, the parties made few

steps to resolve these new problems, and policy responsiveness, like ideological differentiation, evaporated.

By the late 1990s, a different kind of crisis, stemming from the long-term shortcomings of neoliberalism, threatened Bolivia (Salazar Elena 2004). Hyperinflation was no longer a problem, but "deep economic stagnation and deterioration of living conditions" demanded a response (Mayorga 2006, 157). Throughout the 1990s, economic growth was unimpressive, and by 1999 real growth deteriorated to less than half a percent and then stagnated around 2 percent in the early 2000s (Mayorga 2006; World Bank, various dates). GDP per capita declined between 1980 and 2000, entrenching Bolivian incomes as the lowest in South America (Barr 2005; Whitehead 2001). As a result, many Bolivians resorted to subsistence tactics, and over 65 percent of workers fell into the informal sector (Barr 2005; Mayorga 2006). Despite the macroeconomic achievements of neoliberalism, "vast numbers of ordinary citizens . . . believe[d] that the reform process [had] closed off, rather than opened up, their opportunities for self-improvement" (Whitehead 2001, 14). This new crisis was a catalyst for discontent, and the party system's failure to address persistent poverty, inequality, and lack of growth eroded its programmatic credibility (Barr 2005; Domingo 2001).

International constraints limited the parties' capacity to provide a policy response. The IMF and World Bank exerted considerable pressure on Bolivia to stay the neoliberal course (Salazar Elena 2004). However, their orthodox policy prescriptions provided no response to rampant social problems like unemployment and informality, and by the late 1990s, these inadequacies were undeniable, as over 60 percent of Bolivians lived in poverty (Van Cott 2003, 769). As conditions deteriorated, President Banzer (1997–2001), once a pro-market advocate, attempted to reverse the reforms. But international opposition prevented him from following through, highlighting the parties' inability to move beyond neoliberalism and respond to the crisis (Mayorga 2005).

International influences also restricted Bolivian drug policy to coca eradication, which exacerbated the escalating crisis. Throughout the neoliberal era, coca provided an informal economic safety net, boosting rural incomes and generating employment (Alvarez 1995; Conaghan and Malloy 1994, 198). Drug-related exports provided influxes of foreign exchange (Malloy and Gamarra 1988), with the value of cocaine exports estimated to be twice that of legal products (Conaghan and Malloy 1994). Many workers lost jobs in the public and formal sectors, especially miners terminated when the state mining company COMIBOL (Corporación Minera de Bolivia) closed, and they turned to the informal sector to survive (Van Cott 2005). A large segment of this sector resorted to growing coca (Alvarez 1995; Conaghan and Malloy 1994). Conservatively, 10 percent of the workforce supported itself through the drug industry in the 1990s (Alvarez 1995; Williams 1999). Coca eradication was, therefore, unpopular. But U.S. pressure to heighten eradication efforts was strong and dominated bilateral relations (Alvarez 1995; Salazar Elena 2004). Given Bolivia's dependence on aid, U.S. influence was profound, limiting economic policy options and closing off the safety valve of the coca economy (Malloy and Gamarra 1988). As eradication efforts intensified, destroying close to 90 percent of the coca crop in the late 1990s, frustration swelled (Van Cott 2003, 2005).

Furthermore, interparty agreements limited the possibilities for alternatives to these increasingly unpopular economic and drug policies. The institutional strictures of Bolivia's "parliamentarized presidentialism" (Mayorga 2005, 159) pushed the parties into a series of pacts, which eventually resulted in numerous parties of the status quo and no real opposition. Under the Bolivian Constitution, if no presidential candidate won a majority in the popular election, Congress selected the victor. Until Evo Morales, no Bolivian president won office outright, requiring multiparty congressional coalitions to determine a winner. This presidential selection process necessitated coalition building. Beginning in 1985, when Paz Estenssoro developed the Pact for Democracy, which included his own MNR and Banzer's right-wing ADN, coalitions with different constituent parties routinely crossed old ideological boundaries (Mayorga 2005). Between 1985 and 2005, governments were typically supported by two of the three major parties—MNR, MIR, and ADN—and the alliances were very pragmatic (Van Cott 2003). These pacts were formed without regard for the parties' original ideologies, and no significant policy differences distinguished one coalition from another. After the Pact for Democracy, a different configuration supported President Jaime Paz Zamorra (1989–93, MIR), with the formerly leftist MIR crossing the ideological spectrum and embracing the rightist ADN. When Banzer was selected president in 1997, his grand coalition consisted of ADN, MIR, CONDEPA, UCS, and NFR (Nueva Fuerza Republicana) (Mayorga 2006). And by the time Sánchez de Lozada was selected as president for the second time in 2002, his personal share of the vote was so low, at only 22 percent, that he had to put together a coalition with archrival Paz Zamorra's MIR to bar Evo Morales from office (Barr 2005). By the late 1990s, all the traditional parties, as well as CONDEPA, NFR, and UCS, had joined governing coalitions with one another at some point. Even former left and populist parties supported floundering neoliberal policies.

Bolivia's parliamentarized presidentialism pushed the parties to govern together. By 2002, none could credibly offer an alternative to neoliberalism because each had been complicit in maintaining the status quo. The Bolivian parties' efforts to reach consensus "resembled the efforts made by Venezuelan party leaders. . . . But just as Venezuelan *partidocracia* ended up isolated from popular opinion and vulnerable to exclusion by the Chavista movement, it appears Bolivia's . . . political class [had] reason to fear the same fate" (Whitehead 2001, 16). While the coalitions temporarily eased governability, they also eliminated programmatic alternatives.

In summary, then, as the theory expects, programmatic linkage in Bolivia decayed as a result of escalating crisis in the context of international policy constraints and interparty agreements. Although neoliberalism resolved the problem of hyperinflation, it created and then neglected other issues that reached crisis levels in the 1990s. International pressures limited the parties' ability to address these issues, and responsiveness decayed. At the same time, interparty agreements pushed once disparate parties toward common positions and eliminated ideological alternatives, causing programmatic linkage decay across the entire system.

Limited Interest Incorporation

The incorporation of major societal concerns also deteriorated markedly in the 1990s. The traditional class cleavage lost salience and was replaced by ethnic and regional divides. However, the traditional party organizations were ill equipped to absorb the emerging interests.

Since the 1952 Revolution, the Bolivian party system, particularly MNR, had structured interest incorporation around the class cleavage, integrating functional groups representing business, organized labor, and peasants (Barr 2005). The parties endeavored to depoliticize the cultural aspects of ethnic identity and incorporate the indigenous population based on socioeconomic status—typically as peasants (Yashar 1999). Ethnicity in Bolivia had always been highly correlated with life chances, enabling the parties to utilize class as a rough approximation for ethnicity. While many indigenous Bolivians did not feel represented through this system, class-based incorporation nevertheless captured enough people to lend it credibility.

However, as the debt crisis and neoliberalism undermined worker and peasant interests, the class cleavage decayed, and ethnic identities increased in salience. The crisis and neoliberal response crippled organized labor (Gill 2000; Mayorga 2005). The peak union COB first opposed the failed leftist government and then made a stand against Paz Estenssoro's neoliberal policies (Mayorga 2005). But the government squashed its former ally, jailing labor leaders and undercutting one of the major pillars of the corporatist system (Conaghan and Malloy 1994). Jobs in the formal and public sectors were cut drastically—more than 50,000 formal sector jobs disappeared during Paz Estenssoro's administration alone (Conaghan and Malloy 1994, 186).

Historically, peasant organizations were a major means of incorporating the indigenous population, as most Bolivian Indians were concentrated in rural areas. But economic crisis, structural adjustment, and coca eradication caused severe dislocations in the mining and agricultural economies, producing substantial urbanization that resulted in more than half the indigenous population residing in cities by 2001 (Van Cott 2000, 2003). This migration process weakened peasant organizations and disconnected many urban migrants from traditional group-based linkage. These urban migrants served as an easily mobilized base for indigenous social movements that ran counter to class-based patterns of incorporation (Van Cott 2000). Furthermore, the benefits of MNR's agrarian reform during the Revolution had long since faded, weakening the party's sway over the indigenous people who remained in rural areas (Birnir and Van Cott 2007; Domingo 2001). These shifts made incorporating indigenous Bolivians into the party system through their class status as peasants an increasingly untenable strategy.

Bolivians who lost their formal sector jobs as a result of economic displacement or who moved to urban areas as a result of agricultural dislocation were either unemployed or resorted to basic subsistence tactics (Barr 2005). By the late 1990s, about 65 percent of Bolivians eked out a living in the informal sector (Mayorga 2005).[8] In the informal economy, drug-related activity grew, with an estimated 350,000 employed in coca production and processing (Conaghan and Malloy 1994; Machicado 1992). Highland peasants and former miners, who had been displaced by closure of the state tin company, turned to coca to replace lost incomes (Mayorga 2005; Van Cott 2003). However, as coca eradication intensified under Banzer, this safety net was also threatened (Conaghan and Malloy 1994; Gill 2000; Van Cott 2005). Eventually, these former miners and peasants became a locus of cocalero and indigenous organizing (Van Cott 2003).

Because fewer indigenous Bolivians were part of the formal economy and many migrated to the cities, they no longer found their interests voiced through traditional functional organizations (Mayorga 2005; Van Cott 2000). Divisions between the shrinking formal sector and the growing informal

8. In the 1970s and 1980s before neoliberalism, the informal sector employed about half the workforce, suggesting that the informal sector increased by 15 percentage points in the neoliberal era (Casanovas 1986; Dora Medina 1986).

sector weakened popular sector solidarity and diminished the salience of class-based appeals (Conaghan and Malloy 1994). Unions and peasant associations were no longer adequate for integrating the indigenous population into the system (Salazar Elena 2004; Yashar 1999).

As the traditional class divide decayed, Bolivia experienced rapid growth in autonomous organizing. Neighborhood associations, informal workers' unions, indigenous groups, and cocaleros surfaced to form a fragmented civil society without connections to the party system (Barr 2005). Among these emergent groups, the "indigenous movements surged as crucial articulators of popular dissatisfaction" (Van Cott 2003, 753). Ethnicity replaced class as the major politically relevant divide in Bolivian society, pitting the impoverished, dark-skinned majority concentrated in the highlands and the outer rings of cities against the wealthy, lighter-skinned minority in lowland enclaves (Van Cott 2000, 769). Instead of ethnic issues being encapsulated within the traditional class cleavage, economic and social struggles became identity conflicts (Mayorga 2006). State reform had unintentionally politicized new cleavages and mobilized new social actors who challenged the party system's mechanisms of interest representation (Yashar 1999, 101). Indigenous leaders developed autonomous parties and interest associations in an effort to force the state to address demands being ignored by the party system (Van Cott 2000, 169). Indigenous and cocalero demonstrations swept the entire country in the late 1990s and early 2000s, overwhelming the Bolivian government and highlighting the party system's ongoing failure to accommodate their interests (Whitehead 2001).

It was imperative for the party system to accommodate politicized indigenous identities, with which more than 60 percent of Bolivians identified (Van Cott 2005). However, it "failed to integrate sufficiently the diverse social and ethnic-cultural identities" (Mayorga 2005, 158). The parties were unable to accommodate burgeoning ethnic demands, as they conflicted with the parties' nationalist perspectives and contradicted the class-based patterns of interest incorporation that they employed (Domingo 2001). Because the party organizations had built interest incorporation around the hierarchical patterns of the traditional class cleavage, the diffuse new grassroots forms of pluralist mobilization were not compatible with the parties' entrenched strategies. As a result, the traditional parties failed to reflect the increasingly salient ethnic identities that had come to replace old patterns of class-based incorporation. At their founding, it seemed that CONDEPA and UCS might provide an outlet for new interests, as they capitalized on the ethnic cleavage and attracted poor indigenous and mestizo voters without threatening the major parties. But as these new parties joined the old in governing coalitions and resorted to clientelism, they also lost their appeal among excluded Bolivians, and the system remained unable to incorporate ethnic demands (Barr 2005; Mayorga 2006).

As the integrating capacities of class-based interest associations diminished, old patterns of incorporation became unviable. Emerging instead was a more pluralist system based on new cleavages that had been unintentionally politicized by neoliberalism's destruction of the formal economy. However, these new cleavages and the proliferation of grassroots organizations could not be easily accommodated within the parties' hierarchically structured organizational patterns, in which incorporation strategies relied on articulating class interests. As a result, incorporation deteriorated (Barr 2005; Yashar 1999).

Decay of Clientelism

Clientelism faced strains of its own in the decade leading up to the system's collapse. Social changes and electoral reforms heightened demand for material exchanges while economic crisis and fiscal decentralization limited the resources available to the parties. By the early 2000s, the parties could not sustain sufficient clientelist payouts, and the system collapsed.

Demand for clientelism escalated as the social ramifications of the economic crisis and the neoliberal response emerged over the 1990s. Neoliberalism was painful, particularly for low-income sectors hurt by job cuts, reductions in government expenditures, and declines in the real minimum wage (Conaghan and Malloy 1994, 186–87). Growth stagnated, leaving nearly 65 percent of the population in poverty (World Bank, various dates). Unemployment persistently plagued about 20 percent of the workforce throughout the 1990s (Conaghan and Malloy 1994; Mayorga 2005).[9] As these issues went unresolved, a growing portion of the population relied on petty clientelist benefits to survive, heightening demand for material exchanges (Van Cott 2000).

Social dislocations also multiplied the pressures on the clientelist system. Similar to the Colombian experience of displacement, which resulted from internal conflict, in Bolivia structural adjustments like the mine closings and coca eradication also caused severe dislocations (Mayorga 2005; Van Cott 2003). Former miners migrated to coca-growing regions and peasants

---

9. Before neoliberalism in the early 1980s, unemployment was typically at or below 10 percent (INE 2008).

relocated to urban outskirts, driving numerous Bolivians out of traditional community networks (Birnir and Van Cott 2007; Van Cott 2005). In their new contexts, people became atomized and were less likely to benefit from functional or community-based clientelism (Barr 2005; Yashar 1999). Instead, they pressured the parties for individual benefits, heightening the number of demands on the system (Birnir and Van Cott 2007, 106; Conaghan and Malloy 1994). The same dislocation processes also reduced the geographical isolation of potential clients (Van Cott 2000), removing people from a context of scarcity where the only sources of clientelism were the major parties, and relocating them to environments where multiple patrons sought to purchase their support. As the parties competed for votes, the costs of successfully attracting support based on clientelism mushroomed (Birnir and Van Cott 2007; Domingo 2001).

Electoral reforms also amplified demands for clientelism, as new voters and electoral processes pressured the system. Although suffrage was extended to illiterates during the Revolution, many Bolivians remained excluded from political participation into the 1990s through isolation and race-based hierarchies (Van Cott 2000). In 1992, only 53 percent of men and 35 percent of women in rural Bolivia were registered to vote. At the extreme, only 19 percent of lowland Indians possessed voter identification cards in 1997 (Ticona, Rojas, and Albó 1995; Van Cott 2005). To rectify this situation, Bolivia's autonomous National Electoral Court (CNE) sponsored an intensive voter registration campaign concentrated in rural areas from the mid-1990s through 2002 (Mayorga 2005; Van Cott 2005).[10] In the fourteen months leading up to April 2002 alone, the CNE registered over 1.1 million voters (Van Cott 2005, 87). Overall enfranchisement expanded from 1.88 million voters at the time of the democratic transition to over 4 million in 2002, increasing registration rates to 80 percent in urban areas and 60 percent in rural ones (Mayorga 2005, 163–64). This flood of typically poor and disconnected new voters who were likely to seek exchange-based linkage seriously strained the parties' efforts to sustain clientelism.

Other electoral changes also increased pressures on the clientelist system. Like the three other cases of collapse, Bolivia experienced an extensive process of decentralization beginning with the 1994 Law of Popular Participation (LPP). As in Italy, Venezuela, and Colombia, this process included fiscal decentralization as well as the establishment of directly elected local governments and executives. In Bolivia, the reforms were so profound that

10. The CNE was established in 1991. Upon its initiation, it pursued an aggressive registration campaign to promote the transparency and legitimacy of the electoral process.

one scholar has called it the "most ambitious decentralization program in the hemisphere" (Barr 2005, 82).[11] These reforms increased demand for and reduced the supply of clientelist resources.

The LPP created local governments where none had previously existed and established popular elections, first held in 1995, to select local officials, including mayors (Barr 2005; Grindle 2000). These reforms increased the number of electoral processes for which clientelist exchanges were necessary while also multiplying the number of candidates seeking resources to fuel their personal networks. Separate local and national elections made it difficult for parties to control resources through pyramidal clientelist exchanges between levels of government, which could have conserved resources by providing a single benefit to buy support for all the party's nominees. Instead, individual candidates made direct appeals, heightening the resource strain.

Decentralization also reduced the resources available for partisan distribution. The LPP, as well as the Administrative Decentralization Law passed in 1994, increased the guaranteed fiscal transfers that local and regional governments received from the national government (O'Neill 2003). Between 1994 and 1999, the proportion of tax revenue being transferred to municipalities doubled from less than 10 to 20 percent (Mayorga 2005, 169; Van Cott 2000).[12] The reforms also decentralized the overall structure of public investment. In 1994, 75 percent of public spending was targeted to national-level programs; by 1997, 75 percent occurred at local and departmental levels (Gray-Molina 2001, 70). As local governments were granted autonomy over the use of these devolved resources, the parties quickly lost control of the funds and were unable to efficiently put them toward political ends (Barr 2005; Gray-Molina 2001). Moreover, participatory planning and budgeting processes strengthened the oversight capabilities of local grassroots organizations and weakened the parties' ability to channel local resources for partisan ends (Gray-Molina 2001). In fact, one of the stated goals of decentralization was to undermine the patronage system (Van Cott 2000, 170). The traditional parties never had strong local organizations, and they operated in a hierarchical fashion (Gamarra and Malloy 1995; Mayorga 2005).

11. As in the other cases of collapse, decentralizing reforms were implemented under international and domestic pressures in an effort to bring government closer to the people and thereby enhance legitimacy (Grindle 2000). Unfortunately, in all four cases, the reforms only undermined the party systems' last remaining vestige of linkage.

12. Before the 1994 reforms, only 61 municipalities had ever received transfers from the central government. Decentralization created 187 new municipalities, with all 311 receiving fiscal transfers (Gray-Molina 2001, 66).

Thus, shifting resources to the local level limited the extent to which the centralized parties could exploit them (Gray-Molina 2001).

Economic constraints also limited the resources available for distribution. When Paz Estenssoro first implemented his NPE, he protected clientelist resources from cuts and established a social emergency fund to provide temporary patronage jobs in an effort to secure support from his ally, the ADN, and dissident sectors of his own MNR (Conaghan and Malloy 1994; Gamarra and Malloy 1995). Therefore, initial public sector cuts were limited (Malloy 1991). Yet subsequent restructuring dried up clientelist resources (Birnir and Van Cott 2007; Mayorga 2005, 172). As Mayorga notes, "Key state institutions—the Central Bank, the Office of the Controller General, the National Electoral Court, and the former state-owned enterprises—were taken out of the spoils system" (2005, 172). Together, neoliberal restructuring, fiscal decentralization, and sustained economic deterioration limited funds for clientelism at the same time that social changes and electoral reforms heightened demand, causing decay of this last type of linkage.

Comparative Portrait of Collapse

Party system collapse in Bolivia followed the expected pattern of linkage failure also experienced in the other collapse cases. In Bolivia, economic stagnation, accompanied by extremely high rates of unemployment and poverty, challenged the parties to provide a programmatic response. But external pressures constrained policy to a narrow range of options, while internally, coalition governments, which included all the major parties in succession, eliminated ideological alternatives and led to the discrediting of all the parties. Programmatic representation disintegrated. At the same time, the significance of the traditional class cleavage waned, and ethnic identities increased in salience. The traditional parties were structured to emphasize class-based incorporation and depoliticize ethnicity, making the collective integration of these polarizing identities difficult, if not impossible. As a result, the parties' capacity to integrate important groups contracted. Finally, mounting poverty, unemployment, and social dislocation increased demand for clientelism, as did the influx of new voters enfranchised by the CNE and the establishment of directly elected local governments. As the parties lost control of local governments and politicians, fiscal decentralization reduced their access to funds for clientelism. The economic downturn of the late 1990s and early 2000s and reforms to rationalize the state further constricted resources, and clientelism decayed. Without adequate programmatic appeals, interest incorporation, and clientelist linkages, the system collapsed.

The theory of party system collapse developed here asserts that linkage decay, caused by core challenges and constraints, leads to collapse. Table 10.1 summarizes the key independent variables for each collapse case. The far left column displays the specific challenges hypothesized to jeopardize each of the three linkage mechanisms as well as the constraints expected to restrict the party system response to these challenges. If the relevant challenges and constraints are present, then the associated form of linkage is expected to decay. When all components of a party system's linkage profile deteriorate, the system collapses. All four cases of collapse experienced the anticipated pattern, and every linkage type that had once been present in these systems' portfolios deteriorated and produced collapse. As discussed above and reiterated in the table here, challenges to core elements of linkage threatened the maintenance of representation, while contextual constraints curbed adaptation, damaging linkage and resulting in system failure.

Where programmatic linkage once existed in Venezuela, Italy, Bolivia, and, to a much lesser extent, Colombia, crisis conditions stemming from exhausted policy models demanded a response. However, international constraints undermined responsiveness by restricting policy to options that contradicted ideological and policy-making legacies. Meanwhile, differences between parties evaporated as a result of interparty agreements that minimized programmatic distinctions between viable system parties and eliminated meaningful alternatives to the status quo.

Where major societal interests had been reflected in the Venezuelan, Italian, and Bolivian systems, social transformations challenged the parties' incorporating mechanisms. In Venezuela, the class cleavage was restructured around a formal-informal divide, while Italy and Bolivia experienced the decaying significance of class-based interests as new kinds of identities grew in salience. These new cleavage patterns contradicted existing incorporation strategies and entrenched interests were threatened, limiting the parties' ability to reach out to new groups. As a result, incorporation narrowed.

In all four cases, growing demands and inadequate resources produced the decay of clientelism. Social changes and various political reforms proliferated demand for clientelism. In particular, the creation of separate, subnational elections in all four cases multiplied the need for clientelist inputs to purchase votes in repeated electoral contests, while also undermining the hierarchical logic of clientelist distribution and eliminating the central

Table 10.1 Theorized independent variables present in cases of party system collapse

	Venezuela, 1998	Italy, 1994	Colombia, 2002	Bolivia, 2005
Crisis conditions	Economic crisis	Economic crisis	Economic crisis; violence	Economic crisis
International policy constraints[a]	IMF agreements	Maastricht criteria; fall of communism	U.S. drug policy; neoliberal pressure	IMF agreements; U.S. drug policy
Interparty agreements[b]	Patterns of shifting alliances implicated all old parties	*Pentapartito* coalitions included all pro-system parties	National Front followed by interparty cooperation	Each party entered pro-neoliberal governing coalitions in 1990s
Social transformation[c]	Deindustrialization; deunionization; informalization	Secularization; deindustrialization; regional divide activated	Urbanization; internal migration; informal/illegal economy	Displacement; informalization; ethnic divide activated
Organizational constraints on new interest incorporation[d]	Strong union ties and set organizational patterns at odds with informal sector	Parties lacked regional presence; power centralized in national organizations	NA[g]	Ethnic identity conflicted with set patterns of national, class-based incorporation
Electoral decentralization[e]	Introduction of separate state and local elections	Introduction of separate local elections	Introduction of separate state and local elections	Creation of new local governments with separate elections
Reforms limit party resource control[f]	Loss of control over oil revenue; lost partisan control of state	Public funding for party organizations eliminated; cuts in public employment; privatizations	Neoliberal rationalization; 40 percent of national budget transferred to subnational level	Doubled subnational transfers; state reform reduces resources available to parties

Note: Gray shading indicates absence of factor; white equals presence. See each country section for details and sources.

[a] International agreement or intergovernmental organizations notably limited policy latitude.

[b] All the major pro-system parties participated in ideologically diffuse coalitions, pacts, or formal agreements at some point during the crisis.

[c] Politically salient social cleavage(s) changed in either structure or type.

[d] Newly salient interests conflicted with the goals of entrenched groups and/or did not fit established patterns of interest articulation.

[e] New or newly separated elections were established for subnational offices such as governor or mayor.

[f] State reforms like rationalization or decentralization cut parties off from resources they had manipulated for political ends.

[g] Group-based incorporation was never a linkage strategy employed by the traditional parties in Colombia (Archer 1995; Kline 2004). Because this variable pertains only to the process producing the decay of interest incorporation, it is not relevant for the Colombian case. However, the social transformation variable has ramifications for clientelism and is therefore still relevant.

parties' access to patronage resources. At the same time, crisis conditions reduced resources for clientelism, and political reforms promoting fiscal decentralization and apolitical, market-based distribution limited the resources available to the parties for partisan manipulation. Escalating demand and shrinking resources stressed clientelist networks. As fewer people benefited from clientelism, those excluded from exchange-based relations saw corruption, not linkage. With the deterioration of clientelism, the last vestige of linkage, all four systems collapsed.

Ultimately, these party systems encountered serious challenges to their core linkage strategies, while constraints restricted appropriate adaptation, producing linkage decay and system collapse. In the next chapter, I explore how comparable party systems facing some similar challenges managed to maintain at least one form of linkage and survive.

11

SURVIVAL TACTICS IN ARGENTINA, BELGIUM, URUGUAY, AND INDIA

Having shown how the processes of collapse in Italy, Colombia, and Bolivia closely followed the Venezuelan pattern, in this chapter I compare each collapse with its paired instance of survival. I explore how a party system similar to each case of collapse in system structure, institutionalization, and linkage profile managed to survive despite facing some comparable obstacles. As detailed in chapter 9, I matched cases based on these party system features and on shared values on key independent variables, resulting in four paired comparisons: Venezuela versus Argentina, Italy versus Belgium, Colombia versus Uruguay, and Bolivia versus India.

Here I assess the challenges and limitations present in each instance of survival, comparing them to those faced by the paired collapse case. I show how the surviving system sustained at least one form of linkage, either because linkage did not encounter a foundational threat or because specific contextual constraints were absent. If all linkage deteriorates, the system collapses, but if one linkage strategy is maintained, the system survives.

ARGENTINE ENDURANCE VERSUS VENEZUELAN COLLAPSE: MAINTAINING LINKAGE DURING CRISIS

Following Argentina's return to democracy in 1983, the party system took on a form similar to that of Venezuela. Both were institutionalized 2.5-party systems dominated by one catchall party on the center-left and another on the center-right (Mainwaring and Scully 1995a; Szusterman 2007). The systems also employed similar, mixed linkage strategies. Interest incorpo-ration based on the traditional class cleavage was important in both (Levit-sky 2003a; McGuire 1995), and they used clientelism to attract support from excluded groups (Brusco, Nazareno, and Stokes 2004; Levitsky 2001a). The Argentine system, like the Venezuelan, also offered some program-matic appeals, as differences between the Radicals (UCR) and Peronists (PJ) provided choices at the polls (Luna and Zechmeister 2005).

Furthermore, Argentina faced challenges similar to those that threatened Venezuela. Economic crisis and social transformation jeopardized linkage in both systems during the 1990s. In Argentina, the crisis and neoliberal adjustment were among the most relentless in Latin America. Inflation sur-passed 3,000 percent, and growth rates and the balance of payments were commonly negative during the crisis (Burgess and Levitsky 2003). Argen-tine neoliberalism has been characterized as the most severe in the region (Gwartney, Lawson, and Block 1996). Peronist president Carlos Menem (1989–99) slashed regulations, subsidies, and tariff barriers, privatized almost all state enterprises, and cut hundreds of thousands of federal jobs (Burgess and Levitsky 2003, 890; Murillo 2001). The crisis provoked signif-icant social transformations similar to those in Venezuela, including the loss of formal and public sector jobs and increased poverty and informality.

However, in a notable divergence from the Venezuelan experience, the Argentine PJ survived these threats, facilitating the adaptation of the party system rather than its collapse. Of the three linkage types in Argentina, only incorporation disintegrated in the 1990s. Despite the challenges confront-ing the system, it was able to continue offering some programmatic appeals as well as sufficient clientelist exchanges to sustain linkage and avert col-lapse. Here I examine how the Argentine system endured while its Vene-zuelan counterpart did not.

Deterioration of Group-Based Incorporation

As in Venezuela, Argentine incorporation suffered serious setbacks in the 1990s. Traditionally, the system had reflected the politically salient class cleavage (McGuire 1995), with worker interests encapsulated by the PJ and business and professional interests represented by the Radicals (Collier and Collier 1991; Gibson 1996). Peronist ties to organized labor were strong. Unions provided the party with financial and organizational resources through the extended authoritarian period and democratic transition (Levit-sky 2003a). But during the 1980s and 1990s, the class divide decayed, as economic crisis and neoliberalism provoked deindustrialization, deunionization, and informalization. "The passage of thousands of workers from factory work to informal and precarious jobs [was] the most significant economic phenomenon" of the 1990s (Cieza and Beyreuther 1996, cited in Auyero 2000, 31). By 1999, unionization had declined nearly 50 percent since the 1980s (*Latin American Weekly Report* 2000). Unemployment soared to over 20 percent by 1995, and many poor and unskilled Argentines joined the ranks of the structurally unemployed (Auyero 2000; Stokes 2001, 47). In Buenos Aires, households living in poverty increased from 11.5 percent in 1980 to 25.8 percent in 1995 (Golbert 1996). The Argentine parties, like their counterparts in Venezuela, saw their traditional bases erode as the middle class was impoverished, unions lost influence, and workers fell into unemployment and informality. The class cleavage was restructured around the formal-informal divide.

Both the Argentine and Venezuelan party systems faced considerable obstacles to incorporating these emerging social groups. The goals of unemployed and informal workers often ran counter to the interests articulated by those in the formal economy. And although organized labor lost ground within the PJ throughout the 1990s, which provided the party some maneuvering room, like the Venezuelan parties, it did not incorporate these new subordinate sectors (Levitsky 2003a). Not only did the concerns of these new groups contradict the goals of labor, but organizing and representing the disparate and heterogeneous interests of the poor, unemployed, and informal sector challenged the party systems' customary incorporation mechanisms (Burgess and Levitsky 2003; K. Roberts 1998). Moreover, the impoverished and unemployed often preferred tangible, individual benefits, which they relied on to survive (Auyero 2000). As the worker-owner divide lost salience, the party system was unable to organize and channel concerns of the informal side of the new class cleavage.[1] The parties instead relied on clientelist exchanges to foster popular sector support (Auyero 2000; Levitsky 2007). Thus, as in Venezuela, social transformation increased the size and significance of unincorporated sectors whose interests contradicted those of established groups and whose (lack of) structure ran counter to existing mechanisms for incorporation through peak unions and business

1. This is not to say that the parties did not establish other mechanisms for linking to emerging groups. They used clientelism to draw support from informal workers and the urban poor (Levitsky 2003a), although the parties did not provide them with group-based incorporation. Following the debt crisis and the 2001 economic crisis, some efforts to reach out to these groups, such as the Jefes y Jefas program for the unemployed, were made, but not until after the threat to the party system had passed.

associations. This core challenge to linkage in a constrained organizational context resulted in significant narrowing of incorporation in both systems.

Persistence of Programmatic Representation

Unlike the Venezuelan experience, however, the Argentine party system sustained other forms of linkage as incorporation failed. Programmatic representation was never the most significant linkage strategy in Argentina, but the system did offer some programmatic appeals. Although Argentina faced an economic crisis and international policy constraints that were arguably more severe than those in the Venezuelan case, different party structures and patterns of interparty interaction mediated these threats in Argentina and exacerbated them in Venezuela. This allowed the Argentine system to sustain some programmatic links despite these challenges, while the Venezuelan system did not.

First, the elasticity and decentralized structure of Peronism enabled Menem to enact neoliberal reforms without completely abandoning the party's historical legacy. Although some PJ activists saw Menem's pro-market policies as an abandonment of the party's roots (Auyero 2000), others accepted his nationalist rhetoric, particularly surrounding the Convertibility Law, as following the general contours of Peronism (Corrales 2002). Ultimately, the Peronists provided Menem with his primary legislative support, typically approving softened versions of his legislation that protected their clients' interests while still advancing his neoliberal agenda (Burgess and Levitsky 2003; Corrales 2002). The ideological flexibility of the PJ permitted implementation of the reforms necessitated by the domestic crisis and demanded within the international context without directly contradicting the party's historical legacy and without alienating all the party's supporters (Corrales 2002; Szusterman 2007).[2] Thus, Menem was able to provide some successful policy responses to pressing economic concerns, which did not directly violate all elements of the Peronist legacy (Stokes 2001). These policy appeals were particularly successful among upper-class voters who benefited from the neoliberal reforms (Burgess and Levitsky 2003; Levitsky 2001b). This stands in contrast to Venezuela, where international policy constraints contradicted the parties' established policy legacies, limiting programmatic latitude to unpopular policies that ran counter to

2. Unlike the PJ and both Venezuelan parties, UCR's ideological legacy coincided with international policy goals, facilitating its eventual acceptance of neoliberalism.

their traditional ideologies and strategies. Furthermore, because Argentina's provinces retained long-held control over public spending and employment in subnational governments, many local Peronists did not implement the rationalizing reforms of neoliberalism or even expanded provincial spending to counter the most painful effects of the policies (Benton 2003; Corrales 2002). While Menem adopted neoliberal policies at the national level, this local autonomy allowed states and localities to distance themselves from the policies if they proved unpopular with their constituencies, offsetting potential negative consequences that could have resulted from Menem's decision to follow international policy prescriptions for addressing the crisis (Burgess and Levitsky 2003; Levitsky 2001a).

Second, the nature of interparty interactions in Argentina helped preserve programmatic representation through maintenance of some ideological distinctions between parties. In Venezuela, the parties repeatedly engaged in pacts and governing agreements, which eased governability but sacrificed diverse representation (Coppedge 1994a; Morgan 2007). As the Venezuelan parties joined openly pragmatic coalitions in the 1990s, they converged ideologically; voters saw no distinctions between them and lost patience with the lack of meaningful policy alternatives. In Argentina, however, agreements between the major parties were generally absent from interparty relations. Quite to the contrary, animosity and distrust long characterized the relationship between the Radicals and Peronists, making collaboration unlikely (Corrales 2002). Although Peronist president Menem and Radical president Fernando de la Rúa (1999–2001) made efforts to build bipartisan support for their policies, in neither case were they successful in convincing opponents to join long-standing, grand coalitions (Chen 2004; Corrales 2002, 58).[3] In de la Rúa's case, failure to win PJ support led to rapid economic decay and his resignation in late 2001 (Chen 2004). But even amid this extreme governability crisis, the parties refused to collaborate in constructing any sort of agreement. Critics might suggest that this

3. One apparent exception was the 1993 Pacto de Olivos between Menem and Raúl Alfonsín (UCR), which enabled the passage of a constitutional reform and allowed Menem to seek immediate reelection. However, several features of this arrangement suggest that it was not indicative of long-standing patterns of interparty agreements. First, the pact constituted a temporary détente in a prolonged conflict between two political *leaders*; it did not mark an ongoing accord between *parties*. Second, the pact was an expression of Alfonsín cutting his losses in the conflict with Menem. In this way, it was, in practice, an outcome of conflict, not cooperation (Carrizo 1997, 393–94). Third, the scope of the agreement was narrow and pertained only to the issues surrounding the constitutional reform. It did not constitute a wide-ranging agreement, nor did it entail policy cooperation on economic or social issues (Cheresky 1996, 1998). Thus, the pact did not obscure the parties' policy positions and was not part of a pattern of interparty agreements.

lack of cooperation undermined stability. However, by acting independently, the parties ensured that Argentine voters would continue to have some meaningful alternatives at the polls into the early 2000s.

Some identifiable differences between the two major parties persisted throughout the crisis period. UCR opposed Menem's policies, initially adopting an anti-reform stance (Corrales 2002, 68). Even as most of the parties came to accept different versions of market economics, UCR, in its alliance with the new center-left party FREPASO (Frente País Solidario), provided alternative programmatic offerings on non-economic issues (Levitsky 2000). When analyzing party systems' ideological structures, Mainwaring and Torcal (2006, 212–15) found differences between Radical and Peronist voters in the mid-1990s. Additionally, FREPASO offered the frustrated middle class an outlet that did not threaten the system (A. Seligson 2003). Although the ideological differences were not large, they were statistically significant, and Mainwaring and Torcal's ranking of programmatic structuring placed Argentina ahead of all other Latin American countries except Chile and Uruguay. Alternatively, they found no ideological differences between AD and COPEI, which aligns with my account of programmatic convergence between the major Venezuelan parties. Another study examining the ideological structuring of Latin American party systems found that Argentina remained one of the most programmatically differentiated party systems in the region through the late 1990s, with the parties providing meaningful alternatives to voters (Luna and Zechmeister 2005).

Despite economic crisis and international constraints that pressured programmatic linkage in Argentina, the lack of interparty agreements permitted differentiation between the Peronists and Radicals. Also, PJ's flexibility allowed Menem to enact internationally prescribed policies without completely contradicting the party's legacy. The parties in government addressed some significant issues, while voters who disliked one party's response could turn to a different option in the system.

Clientelism as a Safety Valve for Linkage Maintenance

More significant than the maintenance of programmatic appeals, the Argentine system preserved itself by continuing to deliver clientelist exchanges. The parties had always employed clientelism to appeal to the poor and marginalized. However, as the structure of society transformed and interest incorporation lost effectiveness, material exchanges replaced sectoral ties as a central base of party support (Auyero 2000; Levitsky 2001a, 2001b).

The growing number of Argentines in the informal sector who lacked basic resources turned to political networks to survive (Auyero 2000), and the parties relied more heavily on clientelism as a means for attracting support from those who were otherwise excluded (Brusco, Nazareno, and Stokes 2004; Gibson and Calvo 2000). As a result, demands for clientelism intensified in the 1990s, even as economic crisis and neoliberalism complicated accommodation of these demands.

However, in contrast to Venezuela, where clientelist networks crumbled under the weight of unmet demands, the Argentine parties were able to deliver enough material incentives to sustain this form of linkage. In large part, the absence of resource-constraining and demand-heightening reforms enabled the maintenance of clientelism. Unlike the four collapse cases, in which the establishment of separate subnational elections exacerbated competition for resources, in Argentina no comparable changes were introduced. Argentine elections had been decentralized since the nineteenth century, and with the return to democracy, this pattern resumed (Benton 2003; Willis, Garman, and Haggard 1999). In the collapse cases, the introduction of subnational elections proliferated demand and undercut resources, but the Argentine parties faced no such pressures. They were already accustomed to decentralization, and lack of reform allowed them to avoid one major source of increased demand.

Rather than facing new clientelist pressures, the Argentine parties were accustomed to this form of electoral competition, and they employed strategies that took advantage of decentralization. Their organizational structures emphasized local party affiliates and used them as building blocks for the national party. Local base units delivered clientelist benefits such as health care, food, and jobs in exchange for votes, which bolstered support for local, provincial, and national party candidates (Auyero 2000; Levitsky 2001a; Seawright 2007). Clientelist benefits in Argentina were frequently delivered on a geographical basis, rather than the functional one common in Venezuela. The shift away from union linkages toward locally based clientelism was not a major challenge for the Argentine parties, as it had been for the more hierarchical clientelism of the Venezuelan parties (Benton 2003; Szusterman 2007). Therefore, while the parties in Venezuela, as well as Bolivia, Colombia, and Italy, faced new subnational elections and struggled to meet resource demands from increased local and state competition, preexisting decentralized patterns in Argentina eliminated this source of pressure on clientelism.

In fact, the Argentine parties' decentralized structures enabled them to use fiscal decentralization strategically to direct resources to the base. For the hierarchical Venezuelan parties, fiscal devolution cut them off from funds for political use. But in Argentina, Menem used it to channel resources to local PJ machines, targeting decentralized resources to PJ-controlled areas (Rumi 2005). At the same time, base units had always played important roles in organizing local, provincial, and national campaigns, and local clientelist networks benefited all levels of the party. Extensive fiscal transfers to the states, which increased during the 1990s, facilitated provincial party leaders' ability to repay loyal activists and brokers, cultivate personal support, and build a base for the party in national elections (Benton 2003, 122; Jones 1997). For instance, although public employment at the national level declined, the number of people employed by the states increased, with provincial employment surpassing national employment (Benton 2003, 122). Social service spending at the provincial level also skyrocketed, providing local party branches with "ample opportunities for patronage" (Corrales 2002, 207). Because traditional ties of mutual interdependence among national, provincial, and local leaders were not disturbed by new patterns of electoral decentralization, subnational resources continued to benefit all levels of the party electorally (Benton 2003; Willis, Garman, and Haggard 1999). So while the national share of public expenditures declined by at least 10 percentage points with decentralization, these devolved funds were channeled into subnational organizations that fostered support for the national party (López Murphy 1995; Willis, Garman, and Haggard 1999).

Specific features of the neoliberal reform process in Argentina also protected clientelist resources, rather than undercutting them as rationalizing reforms did in Venezuela. Menem employed a deliberate strategy of funding social spending over other programs, and he granted the PJ politicized access to these funds, allowing traditional Peronists to control the Ministry of Labor and Social Security's expanding budget (Corrales 2002, 205–7). This contrasts with Venezuela, where Carlos Andrés Pérez rationalized social spending and cut AD off from clientelist resources by choosing technocrats, not loyal partisans, to head his social programs.

The Argentine parties also had a structural advantage over their Venezuelan counterparts. In Argentina, party access to the state was an uncommon luxury that only emerged with redemocratization. Any access to state resources after the 1983 transition was a financial improvement for the Argentine parties. Even in the context of a shrinking state, they were better off than they had been under authoritarianism (Corrales 2002; Levitsky 2003a). The Venezuelan parties, on the other hand, had become accustomed to and dependent on state resources during the country's forty years of democracy, so fiscal austerity delivered a severe blow.

Therefore, while social transformation increased demands for clientelism and economic crisis conditions created resource constraints in both systems, only Venezuela experienced significant political reforms that simultaneously heightened demand and undercut funds available for clientelism. In Argentina, where electoral decentralization was already in place and other reforms guarded rather than siphoned off resources for distribution, the parties were able to sustain clientelism.

Absence of Institutional Constraints and System Survival

Despite intense economic crisis and dramatic social restructuring in Argentina during the 1990s and early 2000s, the party system avoided collapse. Although incorporation decayed, the system sustained other forms of linkage. In the face of economic turmoil, PJ's flexibility enabled the governing party to adopt policies in line with international parameters, while not contradicting all aspects of its historical legacy nor alienating its entire base. The interparty agreements present in each collapse case were absent from Argentina, thus preserving ideological alternatives and protecting the programmatic structuring of the party system.

Additionally, the party system in Argentina sustained clientelist exchanges. Because the Argentine parties were free from the pressures generated by electoral decentralization in the collapse cases, they did not have to worry about heightened clientelist demand from burgeoning electoral competitions. Furthermore, the preexisting autonomy of the parties' different organizational levels shielded local machines from state-shrinking reforms and enabled the use of fiscal decentralization as a mechanism for channeling resources to the base rather than draining them away. Other political reforms that restricted partisan manipulation of state resources in collapse cases, such as the rationalization of both social funds and the bureaucracy, were not enacted in Argentina, preserving clientelist resources and protecting this linkage form. In Argentina, a distinct institutional context and sustained party access to state resources facilitated the maintenance of programmatic and especially clientelist linkages, even while the system confronted the same economic and social challenges as those experienced in Venezuela. The comparison between Argentina and Venezuela emphasizes the theoretical claim that crisis conditions, international policy constraints, and social change are important but not sufficient to produce collapse. Only when these threats emerge along with electoral decentralization and in the context of specific institutional constraints does linkage completely decay and the party system fail.

BELGIAN ADJUSTMENT VERSUS ITALIAN BREAKDOWN: TRANSFORMING TO SUSTAIN INCORPORATION

Like its counterpart in Italy, the postwar Belgian party system was institutionalized with three major parties. Both systems employed mixed linkage strategies, extending programmatic appeals but also incorporating politically salient religious and class cleavages and offering clientelist exchanges (DeWachter 1987). However, in the 1970s, the Belgian party system encountered considerable challenges that threatened linkage maintenance. Economic restructuring resulted in the escalating significance of Belgium's ethnolinguistic divide, jeopardizing a national party system built on class and religion, and incorporation suffered as the parties struggled to adapt to this new social structure. But lack of economic crisis and few international policy constraints enabled the system to sustain programmatic and clientelist linkage and survive as the system adjusted to the newly activated cleavages.

New Cleavage Activation Threatens Incorporation

Throughout the 1970s, the political relevance of the religious-secular and worker-owner divides declined in Belgium (Pilet 2005). Instead, ethnolinguistic and regional cleavages swiftly became salient (Frognier 1978). This dramatic social transformation challenged the system's patterns of interest intermediation. As in Italy, the Belgian postwar party system effectively integrated religious and class cleavages (Lipset and Rokkan 1967; Urwin 1970). The Christian Democratic Party (CVP-PSC) reflected the concerns of the religious, the Socialist Belgian Workers' Party (BSP-PSB) encapsulated worker interests, and the Liberal Party (PVV-PLP) represented anti-clerical views (DeWachter 1987; Noiret 1994; Urwin 1970).

However, the structure of the Belgian economy changed in the 1960s. The once prosperous French Walloon region stagnated, while historically poorer, more rural Flanders underwent rapid growth and industrialization. Flanders's population and economy surpassed the historically more developed Wallonia, while the Walloon economy contracted (DeWachter

1987; Heisler 1974; Urwin 1970). With this shift, class and ethnolinguistic cleavages no longer coincided but rather conflicted. Flanders was not simply the poor, Catholic periphery, but experienced economic development, which changed class and religious identities in the region. At the same time, Walloons began to fear economic discrimination, becoming more protective of their regional interests (DeWinter 2006; Heisler 1974). Ethnolinguistic issues were increasingly distinct from religious and class divides, and competition between the regions escalated (Hooghe 1991; Rudolph 1977). But even with the emergence of the ethnolinguistic cleavage, class and, to a lesser extent, religious cleavages remained significant. As society became more segmented, incorporation required continued accommodation of old concerns as well as efforts to address new ones (Heisler 1974; Urwin 1970).

Just as the activation of regionalism challenged the Italian parties in the 1990s, Belgium's increasingly salient regional and ethnolinguistic divides threatened the system's incorporating capacity. In fact, the extent of social transformation and the associated challenge to incorporation was greater in 1970s Belgium than in 1990s Italy. Moreover, the Belgian parties were even more reliant on incorporation than their Italian counterparts, making threats to this linkage form more problematic for the maintenance of linkage overall (DeWachter 1987, 311; Hooghe 1991).

Gradual Accommodation of the Ethnolinguistic Divide

However, in dealing with this threat to linkage maintenance, the Belgian system possessed several advantages over the Italian, enabling the Belgians to avert collapse while the Italians did not. In part, different party organizational structures allowed Belgian adaptation. The Italian parties lacked regional presence, so as regional issues became significant, they were ill equipped to respond (Hellman 1988; Leonardi and Wertman 1989). In Belgium, on the other hand, the parties' regionalized structures facilitated accommodation of increasingly salient regional/ethnolinguistic divides.

Initially, the Belgian parties tried to maintain the existing system structure and integrate these new cleavages through their regional organizations (Heisler 1974). The parties granted considerable autonomy to their regional wings, allowing local and regional party leaders to control candidate selection and seat distribution (DeWachter 1987; Urwin 1970). The parties also integrated the regional and ethnolinguistic divides within their central party organs (Frognier 1978). The Christian Democrats always had two ethnolinguistic wings with two co-equal party presidents—one Walloon, one Flemish (Deschouwer 1994). The Socialists established regional constituencies for national party leaders and then provided regional leaders with seats on the national party Bureau. Only the Liberals, the smallest of the three parties, originally lacked significant regional or ethnolinguistic structures (Deschouwer 1994). But by 1968, even they were allowing their regional wings to operate virtually independently (Urwin 1970).

Eventually, the extent of ethnoregional conflict made it impossible to house both sides of the cleavage within national party organizations, no matter how much autonomy they granted to regional wings. But the parties' regionalization eventually allowed them to divide along ethnolinguistic lines and create six regional parties that mirrored the original three national ones. The parties' geographical splits accommodated the ethnolinguistic cleavage without undermining the traditional parties' survival and allowed continued representation of class and religious interests (Smith 1979). Although these divisions were not painless and occurred after extended attempts to maintain national parties, they were facilitated by regionalized structures and acknowledgement of ethnolinguistic interests in the parties (Deschouwer 1994). Furthermore, the linguistic component of the divide, while undermining unity, made clear exactly how the parties would split, encouraging cooperation and limiting ongoing contestation over the boundaries of the new "traditional" parties (Pilet 2005).

The division of the three traditional parties transformed the system from moderate pluralism to a more extended multiparty system, as the effective number of legislative parties jumped from about three in the 1960s to more than six by the 1980s. But because the parties were gradually able to reflect the new cleavage by successively dividing along ethnolinguistic lines (CVP-PSC in 1968, Socialists in 1972, Liberals in 1978) (Deschouwer 1994), they averted the complete and simultaneous collapse of their organizations, and the new regionally based traditional parties retained control of the legislature, preventing system collapse.[4] The party system essentially divided into two regional subsystems that mimicked the old national system (DeWinter 2006). Patterns of interparty interactions in the divided system did not deviate significantly from those of the unified system, as governing coalitions since the divide have been symmetrical. That is to say, if a Walloon party is

4. As discussed in chapter 2, the division, unification, or renaming of existing parties does not constitute the disappearance of those entities, but rather their reconstitution. The major Belgian parties remained intact after their divisions, meaning that the Belgian system transformed but did not collapse.

included in a coalition, then so is its Flemish counterpart, and vice versa (Deschouwer 1994). The party divisions, therefore, facilitated the incorporation of ethnolinguistic interests without sacrificing the traditional parties or the system they formed.

Maintenance of Programmatic and Clientelist Appeals

The adaption needed to integrate Belgium's ethnolinguistic cleavage took more than a decade, despite a felicitous organizational context. During this period, the party system was vulnerable, as incorporation temporarily narrowed until all the parties split and the system reflected ethnolinguistic interests. Fortunately, incorporation was not the system's only linkage mechanism, and in the 1970s, when the system was susceptible, other linkage forms remained intact.

Crisis did not challenge programmatic representation in the 1970s. As the salience of ethnolinguistic divisions increased, Belgium experienced relative prosperity and stability (Heisler 1974). The absence of crisis facilitated policy responsiveness that was adequate to maintain programmatic linkage. Belgium's stagnant governing coalitions were similar to the invariable coalition structures of Italian politics—the Christian Democrats in both countries were almost always in government. But without crisis and accompanying international policy constraints in Belgium, these coalitions did not completely undermine programmatic linkage as they did in Italy (DeWachter 1987; Hooghe 1991). Limited alternation in government and patterns of repeated Christian democratic coalitions weakened ideological distinctions between the Belgian parties. But the system did not confront an especially challenging policy environment in the 1970s, making it possible to sustain policy responsiveness, which compensated for coalitions that limited ideological options. Belgian maintenance of programmatic representation contrasts with Italian decay in the 1990s, where economic crisis demanded a response but international constraints and interparty agreements limited both responsiveness and ideological alternatives.

Lack of economic crisis also enabled the preservation of clientelism in Belgium. Although demand for clientelism increased in the 1970s, resources remained adequate to satisfy this demand. Pressures for clientelism stemmed from social transformation and political decentralization. As in Italy a decade later, social change associated with economic development and a growing middle class contributed to escalating costs for successful clientelist exchanges in Belgium. Additionally, in an effort to address ethnolinguistic and regional issues, the parties implemented decentralizing reforms, including the creation of autonomous, elected regional governments (Swenden, Brans, and DeWinter 2006). As a result, the number of elections in the 1970s almost doubled in comparison to the 1960s, exerting financial pressures on the parties (DeWachter 1987). The reforms also shifted funds to the regions, with 40 percent of central government expenditure being regionalized by 1976, somewhat limiting the parties' ability to manipulate these funds (Brzinski 1999; Heisler 1977). However, because the economy remained stable, the parties were able to sustain adequate inputs and satisfy growing demand. In fact, government funding for the parties increased in the 1970s and 1980s (DeWachter 1987). And in 1971, at the height of ethnolinguistic stresses on the system, the parties secured increased resources for their apparatuses by establishing state funding of their parliamentary delegations (Deschouwer 1994). Unlike Italy, then, Belgium did not encounter clientelist shortages resulting from economic crisis or reforms that constrained resource access. Instead, the parties were able to expand their resource pool, protecting clientelism and filling the linkage gap.

Thus, the Belgian system maintained linkage through programmatic and clientelist ties even as incorporation was seriously threatened. A party organizational context that did not inhibit accommodation of increasingly salient ethnolinguistic divisions also enabled the system to respond appropriately, albeit slowly, to dramatic social change. The absence of economic crisis in this adjustment period protected programmatic linkage from significant challenges and, together with sustained and expanding partisan access to the state, facilitated resource provision for clientelist appeals. Therefore, despite facing some similar challenges as Italy—namely, new cleavage activation, stagnant coalition governments, and increasing strains on clientelism from decentralizing reforms—Belgium's party system sustained linkage and transformed in such a way that enabled it to survive.

URUGUAYAN ADAPTATION VERSUS COLOMBIAN STAGNATION: SURVIVAL DESPITE CLIENTELIST DECAY

In Uruguay and Colombia, two parties monopolized moderately institutionalized party systems for more than a century. Colombia's Liberals and Conservatives and Uruguay's Colorados and Blancos[5] survived by building

---

5. National party adherents are called Blancos.

multiclass support based on clientelist exchanges (Lanzaro 2007; Luna 2008). Uruguayan parties and their fractions established themselves in every locality throughout the country via *clubes políticos*, where voters interacted directly with candidates and received partisan benefits (Luna 2008). At its peak, clientelism "touched almost every family in the country in some way," with approximately one out of every four Uruguayans receiving some kind of service or payment from the parties (McDonald and Ruhl 1989, 102).

In both countries, incorporation and programmatic appeals were not historically significant. In Uruguay, neither religious nor class cleavages were politicized. The primary distinction was that the Colorados were stronger in and around Montevideo, while the Blancos drew more support from rural areas (González 1995; Moreira 2000). But even this slight difference waned as Uruguay industrialized and urbanized. The parties possessed no clear ideological identities. Voters typically located both at the center-right, and there were no statistically significant differences in the ideological self-placement of their supporters (González 1995; Lanzaro 2007, 22; Mainwaring and Torcal 2006, 212). Furthermore, like Colombia, electoral incentives led to considerable fractionalism in Uruguay's parties (Morgenstern 2001). Fractionalization allowed different groups in the same party to espouse conflicting policy goals, obscuring any ideological appeal (Blake 1998; González 1995). Fractionalization also inhibited policy making, limiting substantive responses to social problems (McDonald and Ruhl 1989). Thus, programmatic appeals and incorporation were never important tactics employed by the Colorados and Blancos.

As in Colombia, clientelism instead dominated the traditional Uruguayan parties' linkage profile, and both party systems faced similar challenges to clientelist linkage. Social transformation and electoral decentralization escalated demand for clientelism, while crisis conditions and rationalizing reforms removed much-needed resources from party control.

But a significant factor distinguished Uruguay from Colombia. The Colombian left operated outside the electoral arena, opting instead for militant opposition and providing no alternative to the traditional parties at the polls. The Uruguayan left, on the other hand, pursued the electoral route. Even before Uruguay's authoritarian period (1973–85), the left had forayed into electoral politics. To contest the 1971 elections, disparate groups on the left and center-left formed Frente Amplio (FA), a coalition that included Communists, Socialists, Christian Democrats, and splinters from the Colorados and Blancos. The FA won 18 percent of the vote in these last elections before the 1973 coup (Moreira 2000; Piñeiro and Yaffé 2004). The left, like the Colorados and Blancos, was excluded and repressed under authoritarianism, but the military government did not fundamentally alter the country's political structures (Luna 2008). So with the return to democracy, FA reemerged as the third party in the system and made gains throughout the democratic period, eventually winning the presidency in 2004.

As Frente Amplio grew in significance, the Uruguayan system expanded its linkage portfolio to options not available in Colombia. FA encapsulated working-class interests, which had never been incorporated by the two traditional parties, and integrated other emerging subordinate sectors (Lanzaro 2007; Luna 2007; Moreira 2000). FA also provided an ideological alternative to the vaguely center-right Colorados and Blancos (González 1995, 158; Mainwaring and Torcal 2006). As FA's center-left orientation crystallized in the democratic era, it supplied a clear, but not extreme, statist alternative to the more pro-market status quo espoused by the two traditional parties (Alcántara Sáez and Luna 2004; Lanzaro 2007). FA introduced ideological differentiation and interest incorporation into the Uruguayan system, where Colombia had neither. As clientelism in Uruguay became increasingly unsustainable in the 1990s, these additional components of linkage sustained the party system, whereas in Colombia clientelist decay spelled system collapse.

Decaying Clientelism

The most significant threat to the Uruguayan system's survival in the 1990s came from clientelist decay. Social changes and electoral decentralization increased demand, while political reform and fiscal crisis limited resources, heightening pressures on clientelism. As in other Latin American countries, the economic crisis of the 1980s and subsequent neoliberal reforms produced social adjustment in Uruguay. Although state reforms were not as profound as in some of its neighbors, Uruguayan social structure nevertheless changed in ways that escalated demand for clientelism. Unemployment grew through the 1990s, reaching 18 percent by 2003 (INE 2005). Poverty afflicted almost a third of the population by 2002, and union membership declined by 50 percent over the 1990s (Luna 2007, 14). The pressure for clientelism grew as the traditional parties tried to combat this malaise with patronage (Luna 2008).

The 1996 constitutional reforms also created new challenges for Uruguay's clientelist networks. The separation of local and national elections heightened demand and hindered the efficiency of clientelism, exacerbating resource strain (Luna 2004, 2008). Before the reforms, local and national elections were held concurrently, and the prohibition on split-ticket voting constrained people to cast one vote for offices at all levels (Espíndola 2001). This system enabled patrons to offer a single clientelist exchange and obtain a vote in all races (McDonald and Ruhl 1989). With separate elections, voters demanded additional benefits each time they returned to the polls. Local leaders were reluctant to use resources for national-level races at the risk of not having a sufficient supply for their own elections. As one party leader explained, local leaders "reserved their political machine for local elections" (quoted in Luna 2007, 16). The separation of elections undermined the pyramidal structure of clientelist networks, eliminating interdependence between local and national leaders. As a result, the parties saw control over resources slip away and fall into the hands of individual local leaders who did not employ them to the central party's benefit (Luna 2004, 2007).[6]

In a context of declining party/fraction control over local officials, fiscal decentralization limited the clientelist resources available to their networks. The funds transferred from central to subnational governments increased by 50 percent over the 1990s (Escobar-Lemmon 2001; IMF 2004; Panizza 2004). And as national leaders lost local influence following the 1996 reforms, they were unable to direct these decentralized resources toward efficient clientelist distribution that benefited entire hierarchical networks. Additionally, as FA gained hold of major local governments, like Montevideo, the traditional parties lost access to important resources they had previously used to win support (Lanzaro 2007; Luna 2007).

The economic crisis that struck Uruguay in 2002 further restricted the funds available for clientelism beyond the cuts introduced in the 1990s (Lanzaro 2007; McDonald and Ruhl 1989). The crisis, "which mirrored that of neighboring Argentina in terms of its economic scope and social effects," limited the parties' ability to feed their clientelist machines (Luna 2007, 14–15). Embroiled in arguably the worst economic and fiscal crisis to ever confront the country, the parties lost resources, and their ability to offer selective incentives deteriorated (Altman and Castiglioni 2006; Lanzaro

6. Another 1996 reform increased demand for clientelism by ending the double simultaneous vote (DSV) to select the Senate. Under DSV, national elections served simultaneously as party primaries and presidential and legislative elections, and voters were required to cast a single vote that linked candidates for president and the lower and upper houses (Altman and Castiglioni 2006; Morgenstern 2001). When the Senate elections were de-linked from DSV, competition between party fractions increased, also escalating clientelist demand (Luna 2007).

2007; Luna 2007). Moreover, efforts to modernize and rationalize the state in response to the crisis further restricted opportunities for partisan manipulation of state resources (Luna 2004). As the model of clientelist decay predicts, social change and electoral decentralization escalated demand for clientelism in Uruguay, while at the same time economic crisis, as well as fiscal decentralization and rationalization, enervated the parties' capacity to deliver. These dynamics produced the decay of clientelism in Uruguay in much the same way that they did in Colombia (Lanzaro 2004).

Emergence of a Programmatic Alternative

However, unlike Colombia, Uruguay was not dependent on only one linkage form. As clientelism became unsustainable, the Uruguayan system also offered programmatic and group-based appeals via FA. Although programmatic linkage and incorporation faced some challenges in the late 1990s and early 2000s, the Uruguayan system was able to sustain these linkage strategies as clientelism dwindled (Lanzaro 2007; Luna 2004).

Uruguay suffered economic crisis, as the country saw GDP per capita decline each year from 1999 through 2002 and experienced negative balance of payments and unemployment that reached 18 percent (ECLAC 2009; INE 2005). But the party system maintained programmatic linkage despite this challenge by offering ideological options at the polls. Although the Blancos and Colorados failed to provide a successful policy response to the economic crisis and extensive interparty agreements between the two led to their joint discrediting, their deliberate exclusion of FA from these agreements preserved programmatic options in the system. Because FA did not participate in these agreements, the system followed a logic of traditional parties versus left opposition. Therefore, FA continued to provide an alternative to the cautious neoliberalism advocated by the Colorados and Blancos (Alcántara Sáez and Luna 2004; Luna 2004). Even though the two traditional parties did not offer much by way of policy responsiveness, the presence of FA ensured that voters could reject the status quo and still remain within the system (González 1995; Luna 2008).[7] This alternative, which provided a distinct ideological vision and remained untarnished by failed governance, enabled Uruguay to avoid the decline experienced in the collapsed

---

7. The role of FA is quite distinct from that of MAS in Venezuela. MAS, the most significant left party, was complicit in governing agreements with AD and COPEI and even joined in supporting neoliberalism under Caldera. MAS did not provide a meaningful, or viable, alternative to the Venezuelan status quo, as did FA in Uruguay.

systems, in which crisis, international constraints, and interparty agreements combined to delegitimize programmatic representation across the entire system (Gónzalez 1999).

Broad Incorporation

Frente Amplio was also able to integrate important societal interests not articulated by the two catchall parties. Since its establishment, FA had received strong support from the intellectual left and subordinate sectors that benefited from ISI, like labor and pensioners (Luna 2007), integrating one side of the class cleavage. But as ISI came to an end and crisis set in, neoliberalism undermined working-class interests. Even Uruguay, where neoliberalism was more measured than in other countries, experienced deunionization and informalization (Lanzaro 2007; Luna 2008). But almost 40 percent of the electorate remained either beneficiaries of state assistance or state employees, offsetting the political effects of some of these changes (Luna 2007). FA was thus able to continue drawing support from its traditional formal sector base, which lost some ground but was not decimated.

Furthermore, the fractionalized nature of Uruguayan parties, which allowed competing interests to coexist in a single party, facilitated FA's ability to reach out to the growing informal sector while maintaining support from traditional popular sector groups. FA formed as a coalition unified primarily by the goal of providing a left alternative to the Colorados and Blancos. But by the early 2000s, its fractions included traditional left parties like the Socialists and Communists as well as newer groups like Asamblea Uruguay and Movimiento de Participación Popular (Piñeiro and Yaffé 2004). While the old left appealed to established working-class interests, other fractions in FA reached out to new constituencies such as unemployed and informal sector workers and the disenchanted middle and upper classes (Luna 2007). Typically, the group-based goals of formal and informal workers are difficult to harmonize, but fractionalization facilitated diversity in FA, which permitted these different groups to exist within the same party. Organized labor could cast votes for traditional left parties, and emerging popular sectors could align with newer movements built on their concerns. Yet because these votes aggregated to support FA overall, the popular sector's strength was not divided by competition but was loosely unified. FA therefore sustained support from its historical constituencies and also courted other sectors, helping it shore up support as its traditional base began to decline (Lanzaro 2007; Luna 2007).

In Uruguay, less dramatic social transformation and an institutional structure that facilitated accommodation of diverse interests enabled the parties,
specifically FA, to provide interest incorporation reflecting both new and old
elements of the class cleavage. Unlike Venezuela and Argentina, where more
structured party organizations built around traditional class interests had
difficulty linking the burgeoning informal sector except through individual
clientelist exchanges, in Uruguay fractionalization facilitated the integration
of potentially competing formal and informal sectors in a single left party.

Competition Facilitates Adaptation and Survival

In the late 1990s and early 2000s, Uruguay and Colombia faced serious
challenges to the maintenance of their primary linkage strategy—clientelism. Both countries saw crisis conditions, social change, the introduction of
separate subnational elections, fiscal decentralization, and other rationalizing reforms create a situation in which available resources could no longer
satisfy clientelist demand.[8] However, in Uruguay, "FA's growth helped to
contain popular discontent while it also enhanced the level of interest aggregation in society and the significance of programmatic linkages for party
competition" (Luna 2007, 11). FA exclusion from governing pacts provided
an alternative within the system that was not programmatically discredited.
Additionally, fractionalization enabled FA to appeal to potentially contradictory interests among the subordinate classes, successfully uniting union
members, pensioners, informal workers, and the rural poor. The presence
of a meaningful opposition to the Colorados and Blancos contributed to
"maintaining the integrity of the party system and its aggregational capacity" (Lanzaro 2007, 131). The failure of clientelism in Uruguay, therefore,
was offset by the presence of a programmatic alternative and the maintenance of interest incorporation, allowing the system to survive.

INDIAN SURVIVAL VERSUS BOLIVIAN DECLINE:
CLIENTELIST DELIVERY PRESERVES LINKAGE

From the time of Indian independence in 1947 through the 1960s, the
Indian National Congress (INC) party dominated politics, typically winning

---

8. In fact, the crisis conditions in Uruguay were more severe than in Colombia, as Uruguay
experienced lower growth and higher inflation. Only on employment did Colombia perform
slightly worse than Uruguay (ECLAC 2009).

an outright majority in parliament, holding the prime ministry, and control-ling government (Kothari 1964; Morris-Jones 1978). Despite Indian society's diversity, the party was able to encapsulate a wide range of interests, prima-rily through distribution of state patronage (Chhibber 1999; Manor 1988; Park 1975). Additionally, INC leader and India's first prime minister Jawa-harlal Nehru emphasized a national secular identity for the party, seeking to promote a unified Indian society as opposed to one divided along sectoral, regional, religious (communal), caste, or other lines (Das Gupta 1988; Manor 1988). Emphasizing a national secular character over specific identities helped depoliticize potentially divisive identity politics, at least at the national level.[9] This incorporation strategy used by the INC integrated those who identified with the national secular appeals of the party, although it often ex-cluded those who prioritized narrower ethnic, caste, or religious distinctions. As long as the party was able to depoliticize contradictory ethnic interests and focus on integrating the national side of a cleavage that pitted secular unity against subgroup identity, this strategy facilitated incorporation. The party also offered some programmatic appeals, particularly to urban voters (Brass 1994; Chandra 2004, 215; Manor 1988; Wilkinson 2007). Similar to the Bolivian system, then, the Congress-dominated party system of the 1950s and 1960s employed a mixed linkage strategy that relied heavily, but not exclusively, on clientelist exchanges (Maheshwari 1976). Moreover, de-spite considerable diversity, ethnic cleavages were depoliticized in both post-independence India and in post-authoritarian Bolivia, as national secular appeals in India and class-based appeals in Bolivia helped minimize poten-tial ethnic cleavages.

However, in the 1970s and 1980s, the Congress party, under the leader-ship of Indira Gandhi and her son Rajiv Gandhi, faced increased competi-tion and eventually lost its position as the dominant party in the system (Brass 1984; Manor 1988). During the 1977 elections that followed on the heels of a two-year general state of emergency imposed by Mrs. Gandhi, Congress faced an opposing coalition, which ran as the Janata Party. This loose coalition, which incorporated elements of the noncommunist left, the center, and the right, as well as Congress defectors, united in their opposi-tion to Congress and pulled off a victory (Brass 1994; Manor 1988). Al-though Janata disintegrated into its component parts within a few years, Congress was no longer the only relevant player in the system (Narain

9. Identity-based appeals built around different ethnic groups were often used at the sub-national level, especially in contexts where one group predominated, but in national-level politics the party tried to downplay ethnic identities.

1979). By the late 1980s, the system had evolved further, such that INC and components of the old Janata coalition, most notably Janata Dal (JD) and the Bharatiya Janata Party (BJP), together with smaller and regional parties, formed a moderate multiparty system with three to four major coalitions (Brass 1994). Despite these significant changes, the Congress party did not collapse and remained an important actor. The survival of India's Congress party and the gradual adaptation of the system it once monopolized into a multiparty system stands in contrast to Bolivia's party system collapse, in which the parties that had dominated politics disintegrated. Unlike the major Bolivian parties, Congress was able to weather the growing political salience of ethnic cleavages as well as decentralization.

Politicization of Ethnic Cleavages Challenges Incorporation

During this period of turmoil and party system change from the late 1970s through the 1980s, increasingly salient communal and caste divides posed a significant threat to the Indian party system (Manor 1988). Similar to post-transition Bolivia, ethnic cleavages were not highly salient in the national politics of post-independence India, despite the presence of diverse cultural identities (Kothari 1964; Malik and Vajpeyi 1989; Manor 1988). Caste, religious, and tribal considerations were often significant in shaping subnational politics, particularly in areas where single ethnic groups were highly concentrated. But at the national and even provincial levels, the Congress party minimized ethnic divides and promoted a secular, non-caste-based polity built around national identity (D. Vajpeyi, personal communication, 17 September 2010; Varshney 2000). The INC played a balancing act, using ethnic-based representation to attract support at state and district levels while the party's national strategy relied on limiting the political significance of these identities. However, in the 1970s and 1980s, ethnic tensions mounted, and communal and caste divides grew in salience (Das Gupta 1988; Varshney 2000). As India experienced the activation of identity politics, it became increasingly difficult for Congress to build support around a unified secular identity, even at the national level. Conflicts among caste, communal, and regional groups proliferated in the 1980s, escalating well above 1960s levels (Manor 1988, 89). As ethnic politics were manifested, India experienced a steady rise in communal violence. Clashes between Hindus and Muslims more than doubled between 1975 and 1983, resulting in thousands of deaths (Das Gupta 1988; Malik and Vajpeyi 1989, 318; Manor 1988). The increase in parliamentary seats won by caste-based parties, from less than 5 percent in 1980 to more than 25 percent in 1989, evidences how the growing salience of caste identities reached the national political stage (ECI, various dates; Varshney 2000).

Because the Congress party (at least at the national level) had traditionally promoted a single Indian identity and secular values, the increasing significance of caste and communal cleavages challenged its strategy of incorporating those who identified with its national unity appeals while excluding subgroup identities (Chhibber 1999; Manor 1988). Just as the Bolivian parties subsumed ethnicity within class-based organizations, INC had endeavored to minimize ethnic identities within a national secular paradigm. In both contexts, the activation of ethnic divides challenged the logic of these strategies. Therefore, as conflict between Hindus and Muslims and Hindus and Sikhs escalated in India and increasingly pervaded national politics, identity-based parties emerged to challenge Congress's dominance. Many people no longer saw their interests captured in a single party that wanted to downplay communal identities and unify all three major groups under the banner of Indian nationalism (Malik and Vajpeyi 1989). Thus, instead of Congress supremacy in the 1980s, the party system experienced the growth of Hindu chauvinist parties, such as the BJP, as well as smaller, more regional parties appealing to Sikhs and Muslims (Kapur 2000; Manor 1988; Sen 1993). Caste tensions also exploded, limiting the feasibility of accommodating these competing groups within Congress, and intermediate castes, which were not captured in the INC, increasingly supported opposition parties (Kohli 1988). Congress made some efforts to counter these losses. For instance, in an attempt to offset the growth of the BJP, Congress moved to the right and even exhibited some signs of embracing Hindu chauvinism—a far cry from its tradition as a catchall secular party—but the BJP broadened its appeal and continued to grow (Kapur 2000; Malik and Vajpeyi 1989; Manor 1988). As the political relevance of ethnic issues spread beyond local politics and infiltrated national dialogue, Congress could not easily smooth over these divides and sustain a national secular position, which did not resonate with many voters. Old tactics, like nominating co-ethnic candidates to represent constituencies with a high concentration of a specific group, were no longer adequate. These issues ultimately altered the structure of the Indian party system. Congress surrendered its position as the only major party, and others grew in importance as they capitalized on these newly politicized cleavages (Sisson and Majmundar 1991, 111–12).

In India, as in Bolivia, the politicization of ethnic cleavages endangered the dominant pattern of integration. The traditional Bolivian parties focused on class divides, and the INC, which dominated the post-independence Indian system, emphasized national secular unity. Both strategies were designed to downplay potentially flammable ethnic tensions. So as this cleavage increased in salience and intensity, neither could accommodate ethnic interests using established strategies. In fact, in both cases, the activation of ethnic identities threatened the very foundations of the major parties.

Sustaining Clientelist Resources to Meet Demand

This significant threat to Congress's efforts at national secular integration produced a transformation of the party system. But in India the core party that monopolized the old system structure remained a major actor, preventing the system's collapse. In fact, after the Janata victory in 1977, Indira Gandhi returned as head of a Congress-controlled government in 1980, and after her death, her son Rajiv Gandhi led the party to victory in the 1984 elections, governing until 1989. Thus, the Congress party endured as a major player in the new system. Although it has seen its dominance wane and it faces many electoral competitors in a multiparty system (Sridharan 2010), the survival of this pivotal party facilitated the adaptation and transformation of the Indian party system. The growing salience of ethnic cleavages undermined Congress's national integration strategy, but it sustained other linkage forms, which enabled the party system to evolve and avoid collapse (Brass 1984).

Pivotal to the survival of INC and the Indian system was the maintenance of a steady stream of clientelist exchanges. Clientelism had been a central linkage strategy since independence, and although this linkage faced some stresses in the 1980s as the party system transformed, resources kept up with demand (Wilkinson 2007). In particular, heightened social tensions created strains on clientelism (Manor 1988, 72; Wilkinson 2007). To smooth over communal- and caste-based conflicts, Congress needed to provide clientelist benefits to ever-widening swaths of society, including the poor, the landless, Muslims, and scheduled castes, in order to keep them among its ranks (Brass 1984; Das Gupta 1988).

Political reforms also had the potential to place pressure on the clientelist system by decentralizing resources and power. In the 1980s, India continued a process of devolution that had been an important feature of politics since the development of the federal system under the British. Fiscal decentralization increased the amount of resources in the hands of state and local governments (Crook and Manor 1998). But the national party apparatuses retained considerable control of decentralized resources by exercising, through the prime minister's office, nearly exclusive influence over the president's nomination of state governors (Brass 1994). Furthermore, if the national parties lost ground to opponents at one subnational level, the central government could use its power to circumvent unfriendly officials and allocate resources directly to supporters at other levels (Brass 1988; Crook and Manor 1998). For instance, in an effort to skirt rival networks at the subnational level, Congress created Centrally Sponsored Schemes that channeled resources directly to pivotal segments of the electorate (Wilkinson 2007, 116). In essence, many so-called decentralization efforts were attempts to control lower levels of government and manage clientelist distribution (Brass 1994, 141). In fact, controlling important subnational governments facilitated continued access to clientelist resources, even when the party was out of power at the national level (E. Sridharan, personal communication, 28 September 2010). Ongoing decentralization of resources, therefore, created some stress on clientelist linkage mechanisms, but did not compromise the adequacy of clientelism because the national party enacted decentralization in ways that guarded its control of these resources.

In terms of decentralizing power through subnational elections, the founding Constitution had allowed for the possibility of local elections, but it left implementation up to state governments.[10] However, state officials reluctant to surrender power to local authorities had not established local elections following independence, and with a few exceptions, like Karnataka, voters did not select local leaders (Crook and Manor 1998). But as regional opposition parties began to gain the upper hand in state governments during the 1990s and increasingly controlled local development funds, the Congress party endeavored to circumvent state officials from opposing parties and to empower loyal local leaders through legislation requiring direct elections for local authorities, called *panchayati raj* (Nayak, Saxena, and Farrington 2002; Wilkinson 2007). After a circuitous process, the Congress-led government passed the 73rd amendment to the Constitution, which took effect in 1993 and required implementation of direct elections to the *panchayat* within a year (Singh 1994). However, as we have observed in other instances of political decentralization, subnational elections did not have the effect of increasing national party influence, which was the

10. State assemblies, although not governors, have been continuously elected since Indian independence. Thus, here the subnational unit relevant to new efforts at political decentralization is at the local level (*panchayat*) (A. Krishna, personal communication, 16 September 2010).

Congress party's intent. Instead, the central party gradually lost control over the panchayat and their resources (Wilkinson 2007).

But unlike Bolivia and the other collapse cases, in which electoral decentralization occurred simultaneously with social turmoil, economic crisis, and state-rationalizing reforms, in India the timing of subnational election implementation limited their debilitating impact. By the time local elections began to be held in 1993, threats from social change had subsided, because the system had adapted to reflect diverse ethnic identities by shifting toward a multiparty system that included ethnic-based parties. Additionally, economic crisis was not a serious issue in India during the 1980s and early 1990s. IMF influence on policy was minimal and domestic actors retained autonomy (Chaudhry, Kelkar, and Yadav 2004), such that spending on many programs exploited for clientelist ends actually increased (Chandra 2004; Krishna 2007). So while the maintenance of clientelism may have been challenged by increased demand stemming from political decentralization, the timing of the reforms, which occurred absent other significant threats to clientelism, limited the danger for overall linkage maintenance.

The lack of economic or fiscal crisis in India was particularly important for maintaining clientelism. Although social conflict increased clientelist demand, fiscal decentralization eroded the parties' resource monopoly in the 1980s, and political decentralization escalated resource pressures in the early 1990s, the Indian party system did not encounter significant budgetary limitations at the same time (Wilkinson 2007).[11] The economy expanded, with growth averaging 6 percent over the 1980s and 1990s (World Bank, various dates). Central government spending generally increased over the same period, and state government expenditures remained steady (Pattnaik et al. 2005). Investment in rural development schemes, a major source of clientelism, increased sevenfold between 1980 and 1995 (Krishna 2007, 150), and public employment also grew (Chandra 2004, 117). These overall budget expansions mitigated the effects of decentralization and social turmoil on clientelist distribution (Pattnaik et al. 2005). Even as the party system faced other threats, economic stability and fiscal latitude enabled the parties to increase the stream of government resources directed toward clientelism and thereby accommodate growing demand.

As in Bolivia, then, the Indian party system encountered the activation of ethnic divides, which threatened party strategies built on minimizing these

11. India did not experience a serious crisis in the 1980s or 1990s and, in fact, saw stable economic growth (Panagariya 2004).

identities. In both countries, the dominant parties could not accommodate the concerns of competing interests. But unlike Bolivia, the Indian system sustained other linkage forms. The lack of economic crisis and the expansion, rather than contraction, of public goods available for partisan manipulation allowed the Indian system to protect resources for clientelism. Moreover, the timing of local election implementation mitigated the ramifications that electoral decentralization might have had for linkage maintenance. The steady flow of resources, as well as some programmatic appeals, enabled the Indian party system to sustain linkage and survive.

COMPARATIVE EVIDENCE ON THE CENTRALITY OF LINKAGE FAILURE

As expected based on the theoretical model introduced in chapter 3, in all four instances of collapse, threats to each element of the system's linkage profile and constraints on adaptation prevented the parties from providing adequate linkage between society and the state, which caused the failure of the system. Alternatively, the paired instances of survival, which had similar party system features and linkage strategies as well as some comparable challenges, maintained at least one form of linkage and avoided collapse. The Argentine party system preserved some programmatic appeals and protected crucial clientelist exchanges. In Belgium, the party system faced serious threats to incorporation, which ultimately forced the existing parties to split along ethnolinguistic lines. But as the agonizing divisions occurred, the system sustained programmatic and clientelist appeals. In Uruguay, old clientelist strategies became untenable, but a left alternative to the discredited status quo and incorporation of popular sectors enabled the system to avoid collapse. Finally, the Indian system faced considerable threats from the violent activation of ethnic cleavages but averted collapse by expanding resources for clientelism.

Programmatic Decline

Tracing processes of programmatic linkage failure versus maintenance reveals patterns consistent with the theory. In every instance of programmatic decline, the party system faced an economic crisis. Venezuela and Bolivia encountered severe economic emergencies, and Italy and Colombia suffered historically significant recessions in the years preceding their collapses.

Other crisis-generating conditions were also present in some cases, with Bolivia facing social unrest and Colombia battling escalating violence. But in all four cases, economic crisis stemming from the exhaustion of established development strategies challenged the parties to provide a programmatic response, highlighting the significance of this variable.

In each case of programmatic decay, the parties also operated within important constraints on their capacity to respond successfully to the crisis. International pressures limited the parties' options to paths that were unpopular or that contradicted their ideological legacies and traditional policy patterns. The Bolivian parties were restricted by their dependence on the IMF and the United States, placing alternatives to neoliberalism and coca eradication out of reach. In Italy, the Maastricht criteria limited the parties' latitude, removing standard policy tools like deficit spending from their arsenal. The Venezuelan parties encountered international pressures toward neoliberalism despite strong statist legacies. And in Colombia, an international neoliberal consensus limited responses to the economic crisis, and U.S. anti-narcotics policies complicated the task of addressing domestic security problems.

Additionally, in every collapse case, interparty agreements undermined programmatic distinctions between major parties, eliminating the system's ability to offer viable, meaningful alternatives to the discredited status quo. Venezuela had a long tradition of interparty cooperation that began with the democratic transition and remained a mainstay of government through the 1990s, when the parties entered into a series of governing agreements with one another. These agreements blurred the distinctions between them and removed options for voters. In Italy, the parties' efforts to rule without the anti-system elements of the left and right produced governing coalitions throughout the postwar era that generally included the same cast of characters and never excluded the Christian Democrats. The Colombian National Front agreement and subsequent patterns of collaboration had the same effect, explicitly constraining electoral choices and removing ideological competition from the party system. In Bolivia, parliamentarized presidentialism created strong incentives for the parties to form coalition governments throughout the 1980s and 1990s. By the early 2000s, these coalitions had included (and damaged) every major party at some point, implicating all of them in the failed neoliberal consensus. In each case, these interparty accords resulted in the joint discrediting of the major parties and the elimination of meaningful ideological options from the party system. To find an alternative to the status quo of unresponsiveness, voters had to look outside the system.

By contrast, although Argentina faced an economic crisis arguably more severe than any of those experienced in the cases of collapse, the major parties never engaged in significant collaboration. The absence of such agreements enabled voters to find an alternative within the existing system. Likewise, Uruguay encountered a fiscal crisis in the early 2000s, but the interparty agreements there only included the Colorados and Blancos, leaving Frente Amplio unscathed and able to present a clear ideological option distinct from the center-right status quo of the two traditional parties. In these contexts, frustration with lack of performance was channeled within the system rather than directed outside it. Alternatively, the Belgian parties repeatedly resorted to coalition governments, which almost always included the Christian Democrats, following the Italian pattern. However, because Belgium did not face economic crisis or international constraints in the 1970s, the parties were able to furnish policy responses adequate for ordinary times. The lack of alternation in government did not threaten the system because the status quo was acceptable. Together, economic crisis and constraints imposed by interparty agreements and international policy limitations make programmatic representation untenable. Yet if any of these factors is absent, as in Argentina, Uruguay, and Belgium, the system is able to preserve programmatic linkage.

Narrowing Incorporation

The comparative analysis reveals important patterns concerning the narrowing of incorporation. The same basic process undermined interest incorporation in the three instances of collapse where the parties employed this form of linkage—Venezuela, Italy, and Bolivia—and in the two cases of survival where incorporation deteriorated—Argentina and India. All five experienced dramatic social transformations in either the structure or the type of salient social cleavage. These transformations in the cleavage structure generated new kinds of conflict, as interests that were historically excluded and identities that were traditionally downplayed became increasingly significant and threatened incorporation.

In each instance, these social changes also challenged existing organizational patterns. Strategies traditionally used to encapsulate the worker-owner divide, for example, proved ineffective for representing the competing interests of formal and informal sectors. In Venezuela and Argentina, the party systems' incorporation strategies had been built around the worker-owner cleavage, relying on unions, business associations, and the like to integrate major interests. However, with the processes of economic opening, deindustrialization, and informalization, the salience of the traditional class cleavage waned, and society was restructured around the formal-informal divide. The parties found it difficult to incorporate the growing ranks of unemployed and informal workers through old hierarchical corporatist mechanisms, particularly given the often competing goals of the formal and informal segments of the popular sector. Similarly, party systems with incorporation patterns built on class divides or national identity could not easily encapsulate newly activated ethnic and regional cleavages. When regional and ethnic cleavages supplanted traditional class cleavages in Bolivia and Italy and obliterated nationalist unity in India, the traditional parties' established organizational structures were ill equipped to channel these new kinds of conflict.

In all the cases in which societal change activated new cleavages (Italy, Bolivia, India) or restructured existing ones (Venezuela, Argentina) in ways that contradicted entrenched organizational patterns, incorporation narrowed and left out wide swaths of society. When established organizational structures conflicted with the patterns of new interests or when entrenched and emergent groups held conflicting goals, the system was unable to accommodate new interests and incorporation deteriorated. In Belgium, where the parties' regionalized structures facilitated gradual accommodation of increasingly salient ethnolinguistic divides, incorporation narrowed temporarily as the parties adapted, and the system had to be sustained by programmatic and clientelist linkage until incorporation could recover.

Clientelist Decay

Important patterns also emerged concerning the deterioration of clientelism in the four cases of collapse—Venezuela, Italy, Colombia, and Bolivia—and in Uruguay, a case of survival in which clientelism decayed. In each case, social changes heightened clientelist demand, while economic crisis limited the parties' capacity to expand supply. Additionally, in all five cases, significant political reforms increased competition for resources and constrained party access to resources for political ends. The reforms that undermined clientelism were similar in all five cases. Each country established separate subnational elections in the years leading up to party system collapse. Separate electoral contests increased the need for clientelist resources, as new exchanges were demanded for each return to the polls, and created competition for resources at the local and/or state level, where there had not been competition before. Political decentralization also removed subnational offices from central party control, eliminating an important source of patronage and undermining party influence over clientelist resource distribution at the subnational level. Quite contrary to most of the reformers' intent, the new subnational elections escalated demand for clientelism and, in the cases of collapse, threatened the only remaining form of linkage.

At the same time, other reforms limited parties' ability to manipulate state resources to fund clientelism. A resource-constraining reform common in the cases of clientelist decay was fiscal decentralization, which, when preceded by new political decentralization that weakened traditionally centralized party organizations, removed resources from the parties' control. In all five instances of clientelist decay, the central party apparatuses lost access to resources that were devolved away from the central government and toward subnational levels, which the parties no longer monopolized. State-rationalizing reforms—such as the shrinking of the state bureaucracy in Venezuela, Uruguay, and Bolivia, the removal of partisan considerations from social fund distribution in Venezuela, changes in campaign funding laws in Italy, and the elimination of pork-barrel earmarks in Colombia—also limited the parties' access to resources for clientelism across all five cases.

Together, these reforms exacerbated the pressures that social change and economic crisis placed on the parties' clientelist networks, producing the deterioration of clientelism. In countries like Argentina, where subnational elections were not new and parties retained access to state funds, or Belgium and India, where economic stability enabled the expansion of clientelist resources despite decentralization, clientelism remained intact as a significant form of linkage. But in Venezuela, Italy, Colombia, Bolivia, and Uruguay, where economic crisis, social transformation, political decentralization, and resource-limiting reforms were simultaneously present, clientelism reached fewer voters. This created frustration with a system that was increasingly perceived as corruptly benefitting only a select few rather than providing material exchanges for many.

Explaining Collapse, Attaining Survival

The cross-national analysis of both collapse and non-collapse cases provides considerable leverage in answering the question of why some party systems collapse while similar systems facing some comparable challenges survive. The four paired comparisons isolate the role and significance of each component of the theoretical model. This allows me to show how core challenges and specific constraints on adaptation produce the decay of each type of linkage and to demonstrate that when all linkage types decay, collapse results. The comparisons across the four cases of collapse make clear that the causal process detailed for Venezuela parallels the experiences of other countries that also suffered party system failure. Four diverse party systems in distinct contexts underwent highly analogous processes, which underscores the significance of linkage failure in producing collapse. The instances of survival suggest that absent either substantial challenges to all the core elements of a system's linkage profile or specific constraints on adaptation, a party system may sustain linkage and survive.

These findings emphasize the significance of both challenges and constraints in understanding why some party systems fail and others survive. Arguments focused on structural challenges, like economic crisis, only account for why a party system comes under stress, but cannot explain the response to this pressure. Alternatively, theories that privilege particular institutional configurations do not consider the kinds of challenges that might provoke a need for the adaptive efforts that such theories seek to explain. Only when we consider the specific constellations of core challenges to linkage and key constraints on adaptation can we fully explain linkage failure and party system collapse.

12

INSIGHTS INTO COLLAPSE AND ITS CONSEQUENCES

[Under Chávez] there has been a broadening of participation to new sectors of society. Before, many people were marginalized, but we have incorporated them into politics.

—**Member of MVR Comando Táctico Nacional,** *interview with author, December 2003*

Party system collapse is a rare but important phenomenon. Collapse creates profound shock waves that disturb the very foundations of political order. The failure of well-established party systems in Italy and Venezuela in the 1990s and the subsequent breakdown of party politics in Colombia and Bolivia were monumental events that marked significant turning points for each country. But while considerable scholarship has explored the deterioration of individual parties or changes in party systems, few efforts have been made to understand why decay aggregates to topple entire party systems. To explain this most extreme form of party system transformation, I theorized that collapse is caused by a party system's inability to fulfill its fundamental task of providing linkage between people and their government. Then, moving back the causal chain, I built an explanation of system-level linkage failure. I argued that such failure occurs when a system's core linkage strategies are threatened within a context that limits its ability to confront these challenges. An extensive body of empirical evidence elaborated throughout the book delivered consistent support for this theory.

This concluding chapter underscores the book's major findings concerning the processes of linkage failure and party system collapse. Through this review, I highlight how the book advances the literatures on representation and linkage, party adaptation, and party system structure and change. I also draw attention to some of the central empirical insights concerning

Venezuela and the seven other cases of collapse and survival analyzed here. Finally, to emphasize the real-world importance of understanding party system collapse, I detail the consequences of collapse for representation and for democracy and offer some suggestions for facilitating adaptation and avoiding collapse.

CHALLENGES, CONSTRAINTS, LINKAGE DECAY, AND TOTAL SYSTEM FAILURE

Explaining Linkage Failure and Collapse

My argument has focused on linkage provision as the central task of party systems. I hypothesized that when a system fails to connect with a majority of voters, it will collapse. Linkage may be achieved through three major strategies: programmatic representation, group-based interest incorporation, and clientelist exchanges. I argued that when systems lose the ability to attract support through all of these mechanisms, linkage fails and the party system collapses. Indeed, we observed how the loss of linkage capacity produced system failure in Venezuela, Italy, Colombia, and Bolivia, whereas the ability to sustain some form of linkage facilitated survival of the Argentine, Belgian, Uruguayan, and Indian systems.

These findings reiterate the importance of linkage delivery for party and party system survival, building on the growing literature that views parties through this analytical lens (Barr 2009; Kitschelt et al. 2010; Lawson 1980). The analysis here suggests that identifying party systems' linkage profiles is critical to understanding an array of important political dynamics. When we understand the linkage profile, we obtain substantive insight into the ways that parties connect people to the state. We are also able to recognize the avenues that are available for citizens to speak into the political process, thereby identifying opportunities for voice and influence that are feasible within the existing system, as well as those the system excludes, which therefore only occur outside conventional patterns of linkage. Perhaps most important, knowledge of a system's linkage portfolio illuminates vital information about party and system durability and the nature and quality of democracy. And because different linkage mechanisms are susceptible to different challenges and constraints, awareness of the strategies that a party or system employs draws our attention to the places from which the most fundamental threats are likely to originate.

Linkage maintenance is thus crucial for party systems, and understanding linkage profiles offers important theoretical and empirical insights. But my argument does not end with the claim that linkage failure causes collapse. I also theorized about the factors that undermine linkage. I made the case that linkage deteriorates when party systems are confronted with challenges that jeopardize their core strategies at the same time that their ability to deal with these threats is constrained. I then specified the exact constellations of threats and constraints hypothesized to cause deterioration in the effectiveness of each of the three possible linkage strategies. In the case of programmatic representation, I theorized that crisis conditions pose challenges to maintenance of policy-based appeals, demanding innovative responses to pressing problems. When crisis occurs in a context where international constraints require governing parties to pursue policy solutions that conflict with their ideological legacies, policy responsiveness decays. If all the parties are implicated in this failed responsiveness through interparty agreements, then programmatic representation deteriorates across the entire system. Interest incorporation is threatened by transformations in the structure or kind of salient social cleavages. When emergent groups' concerns or structures do not align easily with those of entrenched interests, party organizational constraints make it difficult and costly to accommodate new groups, resulting in the narrowing of incorporation. Finally, clientelism decays under the challenge of meeting increased demand if resources are simultaneously limited. Increased demand stems from social changes and political decentralization, while economic crisis and reforms that limit partisan access to resources undermine parties' ability to satisfy this demand. In each case, the theory suggests that we will observe decay when structural changes jeopardize a linkage strategy and institutional or international constraints limit appropriate adaptation.

The empirical evidence from Venezuela and from the comparative cases decidedly supports these propositions. In all four collapse cases, programmatic linkage decayed when the parties experienced crisis conditions, which stemmed from the exhaustion of established policy models, in contexts where international constraints limited policy options to those that conflicted with governing parties' ideological legacies, while patterns of interparty cooperation removed meaningful alternatives from the party system. Alternatively, the four cases of party system survival each sustained programmatic representation because at least one of these three conditions—crisis, international constraints, or interparty agreements—was absent.

I noted the deterioration of incorporation in five cases—the two survival cases of Argentina and India and the three collapse cases of Venezuela, Italy, and Bolivia. Across all of them, we observed how transformations in the structure or kind of salient social cleavage created incredible pressures on all the system parties to accommodate new kinds of interests. Because the demands and organizational structures of these new groups contradicted the parties' entrenched patterns of incorporation, adapting to reach out to emerging interests was costly and risky, and incorporation narrowed. However, in the counterexample of Uruguay, societal restructuring around newly salient group interests did not pose the same threat to incorporation because the parties' fractionalized organizations facilitated accommodation of potentially competing established and emergent interests.

Finally, we saw that where clientelism deteriorated in the four collapse cases as well as Uruguay, social changes heightened demand while economic crisis shrank the supply of resources. Furthermore, in all five cases, clientelist demand increased when the establishment of separate subnational elections proliferated the number of electoral contests and, therefore, also multiplied the inducements needed to entice people to return repeatedly to the polls and vote for traditional party candidates. This created competition for resources across the levels of government, where there had previously been centralized control and (enforced) cooperation. Simultaneously, other reforms that rationalized the state and limited partisan manipulation of resources closed off clientelist resource flows. In the face of escalating demand and dwindling resources, clientelism reached a rapidly shrinking number of voters. On the other hand, in cases of successfully sustained clientelism, economic stability (India and Belgium) or sustained partisan access to state resources (Argentina) allowed the parties to maintain or augment benefit flows in order to meet demand. Thus, analyzing cases of both collapse and survival underscores the importance of each element in the causal process that produces linkage decay, thereby emphasizing the significance of both structural challenges and institutional constraints for understanding the dynamics of party system change and collapse.

Theoretical Insights

These findings suggest several implications for our understanding of party and party system change. First, the analysis here accentuates the importance of adaptation for party and system survival. Previous studies on party or party system change have often pointed to (un)successful adaptation efforts as crucial in shaping party and system outcomes (e.g., Levitsky 2001b; Panebianco 1988b). This book lends support to this perspective by showing how massive failures to respond to new demands (breakdowns in adaptive capacity) undermined linkage and caused collapse in Venezuela, Italy, Colombia, and Bolivia.

Second, more than simply reiterating the necessity of adaptation, the analysis sheds light on the reasons why change may be required and clarifies why appropriate modifications may or may not be possible. Much of the existing literature on party and system change emphasizes either structural changes that demand a response or institutional constraints that impede necessary adaptations. This book has demonstrated the utility of a synthesized approach that draws from both of these literatures to consider the kinds of structural changes likely to threaten different linkage strategies as well as the sorts of constraints liable to impose limitations on suitable responses to these challenges. This theoretical perspective provides leverage in understanding when adaptation is necessary, what kind of adjustments are needed, and why parties and systems are likely to succeed or fail in achieving the changes crucial to their survival. By combining insights from the literatures on structural challenges and institutional constraints, I have developed a comprehensive theory of collapse that effectively elucidates common patterns of party system failure across very diverse contexts. My work thus builds on previous scholarship (e.g., J. Aldrich 1995; Coppedge 2001; Kitschelt 1994) that highlights the importance of uniting structural and institutional explanations of party and party system change, by demonstrating how threats from structural changes and incentives/constraints generated by the institutional context are together necessary for party systems to experience complete linkage failure and collapse.

Third, in specifying the precise challenges and constraints that combine to undermine each linkage strategy, the book has heightened our awareness of each tactic's vulnerabilities. Thus, the analysis not only helps us understand why party systems collapse but also offers insight into the details of the linkage decay process. By theorizing and then empirically demonstrating the vulnerabilities of each linkage mechanism, the book underscores the idea that parties and party systems are susceptible to different sets of structural challenges and institutional constraints depending on their linkage portfolios. In delineating the exact constellations of challenges and constraints that undermine each linkage strategy, the book also contributes to literatures that examine how parties and party systems are shaped by specific structural and institutional factors, such as economic crisis, social cleavages, party organizations, international institutions, and political reforms like decentralization and market-based rationalizations. For each of these independent variables, which previous scholarship suggests may play a role in influencing party or party system change, I detailed the challenge it posed to linkage maintenance or the constraint it imposed on adaptation. In this way, the analysis shed light on exactly how these factors create pressure for change or shape a party system's capacity to adapt.

Fourth, parsing out the weaknesses of each linkage strategy adds nuance to the typical view that programmatic representation is normatively superior to other forms of linkage. All linkage mechanisms have the potential to deteriorate when confronted with the perfect storm of challenges and constraints. So while policy-based appeals may enhance opportunities for meaningful representation in a democratic system, even this linkage strategy is not immune to deterioration in the face of crisis when the system also faces limitations on adaptation created by international constraints and interparty agreements.

Fifth, the book emphasizes the value of viewing party systems' linkage strategies as having three possible components. While party systems may rely almost exclusively on one linkage mechanism (as in the case of the Colombian parties' dependence on clientelism), most party systems employ multiple strategies for connecting people to the state. Often such diversity facilitates adaptation and system survival. When one linkage tactic deteriorates but other mechanisms remain in place—a process we observed in Argentina, Belgium, Uruguay, and India—parties are able to shore up support through other strategies and thereby survive. Additionally, by identifying three possible linkage tactics, the book moves beyond the common programmatic versus clientelistic dichotomy. I am not the first to suggest the importance of linkage achieved by sectoral appeals to major groups in society (see Kitschelt and Wilkinson 2007a, as well as Collier 1995; K. Roberts 2002a; Schmitter and Lehmbruch 1979). But interest incorporation often does not receive the same systematic treatment given to clientelism and especially programmatic representation. This book has illuminated how interest incorporation is analytically distinct from the other two linkage strategies and highlighted its importance for parties as they try to capture and sustain support. While there may be some empirical overlap between the various linkage strategies, such as policies directed to core constituencies and loyal supporters or material benefits that help certain sectors of the population, some strategies for pursuing incorporation cannot be captured neatly in the programmatic-clientelist dichotomy. For instance, reserved places in party apparatuses for certain sectors of society, like trade unions or business associations, and special access to party or government decision-making processes for major interests are ways that parties may build linkage around group identities and organizations, which are not captured by our typical understandings of programmatic representation or clientelism. Furthermore, by adding the dimension of interest incorporation to our view of linkage portfolios and to our analysis of linkage decay, the book builds on the work of Lipset and Rokkan (1967) in exploring how important societal transformations cause either significant adaptations or major restructuring in party systems because they create demands for new kinds of interest incorporation.

Sixth, the book enhances our understanding of individual cases of collapse by placing them in a common theoretical framework and tracing the key steps in the causal process that led to their demise. The most important contribution along these lines pertains to our understanding of Venezuelan politics. I have spelled out in considerable detail how programmatic representation, interest incorporation, and clientelism deteriorated, thus causing Venezuelan collapse. Applying my theory of bankrupt representation to Venezuela underscores the utility of the approach I have developed and illuminates important empirical nuances in the dynamics of Venezuelan politics before and after collapse. In similar, albeit less detailed, ways, the analysis also highlights the central causal process that produced collapse in Italy, Colombia, and Bolivia.

The final contribution that I wish to highlight here pertains to the conceptualization of party system collapse and the level of analysis that is necessary for understanding this phenomenon. Collapse is a system-level event that involves both the decay of the major parties *and* the transformation of the party system. (And collapse has profound ramifications for other system-level outcomes, such as democracy and representation, which I detail below.) Therefore, theories of collapse must be able to explain not only the deterioration of individual parties but also the aggregation of this failure to the system level. In the theoretical exposition and empirical analysis presented in this book, I have elucidated the process through which linkage failure contaminates entire party systems and leads to their demise. For each type of linkage, I have shown not only why individual parties might find it difficult to sustain this strategy but also why the system as a whole experiences decay in the utility of the tactic. Programmatic representation evaporates across the party system when people reject the policy status quo and interparty agreements obscure distinctions between government and opposition, removing programmatic alternatives from the party system and requiring voters to look outside the system for credible policy options or meaningful ideological choices. Loss of interest incorporation threatens the entire system only when the very logic of the dominant social cleavage is fundamentally transformed in structure or in type, undermining the incorporating capacity of not just one party but all the parties in the system because none successfully reflects the new cleavage patterns. Finally, clientelist decay infects the party system as a whole when no party has enough resources to meet demand. As dissatisfied clients move from one party to the next, this only increases the pressure on each party's shrinking pool of benefits for distribution. If system-level deterioration occurs across all components of a party system's linkage portfolio, then linkage is entirely bankrupt and the system collapses. By detailing how entire party systems lose linkage capacity, the theory of collapse developed in this book appropriately treats it as a system-level phenomenon and provides important insights not only into the shortcomings of individual parties but also into the dynamics that undermine entire party systems.

POST-COLLAPSE POLITICS: TRAGEDY OR OPPORTUNITY?

Thus far, I have detailed the origins of linkage decay and demonstrated how system-level linkage failure causes party system collapse. But what is left behind after collapse? What (or who) fills the void? What challenges do democracies face following party system failure? With party system collapse in Venezuela, Italy, Colombia, and Bolivia, politics changed in overt and subtle ways. In Venezuela, one of Latin America's oldest democracies, voters elected former coup plotter Hugo Chávez, and two of the region's most developed parties withered away. With the Italian collapse, the once dominant DC was replaced by a right-wing coalition (Polo delle Libertà) that included a media baron, a regional autonomy party, and neo-fascists. In Colombia, elite bargaining gave way to aggressive leadership by right-wing independent Álvaro Uribe. In Bolivia, collapse brought Evo Morales, a *cocalero* and Bolivia's first indigenous president, to power, giving representation to a long-excluded sector of the population.

Party system collapse clearly has the potential to transform political processes and patterns. This final portion of the book emphasizes not just the theoretical significance of explaining collapse, but reiterates the real-world importance of understanding this phenomenon by spelling out its dramatic consequences, both positive and negative. I consider what takes the place of failed party systems and demonstrate that the successors to collapsed systems rose to power by promising linkage where their predecessors failed. I also explore some of the features of post-collapse systems, highlighting patterns in how successor systems shape the quality and stability of democracy in their respective countries.

How Failed Party Systems Shape Their Successors

When a party system collapses, something new takes its place. Citizens turn to new parties or to electoral movements developed around individual leaders. In all four cases of collapse, successful heirs to the failed party systems initially offered linkage in the precise areas where the old system had not responded to demands. These new actors made programmatic appeals by offering ideological alternatives and pledging to resolve important problems that the old parties had not sufficiently addressed. They also extended promises to neglected groups that reflected newly politicized cleavages. Eventually, some new actors also turned to clientelism, but as political outsiders, most lacked the resources to credibly offer clientelist benefits during their initial rise to power.

New Parties Offer Policy Answers and
Ideological Options
In each of the four collapsed party systems, the old parties ceased to provide policy responses to important national problems, even as crisis conditions intensified the need for action. The heirs to the failed systems won support by pledging to tackle these very issues. In Venezuela, the traditional parties did not respond to the country's most pressing concerns in the 1990s, including cost of living, unemployment, crime, and corruption. In fact, as the crisis escalated, relevant policy efforts declined. As responsiveness floundered, Chávez, the primary beneficiary of the old parties' shortcomings, promised to address the issues seemingly abandoned by the traditional parties (Interviews 30, 44, 52, 77). A former AD president explained, "Over time the party system lost its vigilance in resolving people's problems. . . . This opened the door for Chávez to say that he was going to do what the parties were no longer doing—resolving people's problems" (Interview 51). In the 1998 campaign, he railed against corruption (Interview 46). His military background lent credibility to his assurances that he would address escalating crime (Interview 3). And he promised to confront the economic crisis, especially poverty and unemployment (Interviews 2, 21, 27); these commitments resonated with Chávez's supporters, who were

significantly more optimistic about their economic possibilities under his leadership than under the old parties (Morgan 2007).

Once in office, President Chávez and his supporters in the legislature took steps to fulfill people's expectations. Extending my analysis of legislative responsiveness to the Chávez era, I examined the amount and significance of legislation dealing with important problems passed during Chávez's first six years as president. About 12.5 percent of all legislation passed between 1999 and 2004 dealt with cost of living, unemployment, crime, or corruption, which represents a fourfold increase over the proportion of legislation dealing with the most important problems during the last two administrations of the old party system. Significant legislation addressing these issues also experienced a fourfold increase in the post-collapse era.[1] Much of the policy activity in these first years can be attributed to Chávez's efforts to restructure Venezuela's legislative framework, and his detractors and some legal scholars have suggested that this legislation was poorly written and ineffective. Regardless of these criticisms, however, Chávez clearly attracted support based on promises to address the country's problems, and upon taking office, he made attempts to follow through on these pledges.

The successful heirs to the failed party systems in Italy, Colombia, and Bolivia also came to power promising to address problems unresolved by their predecessors. In Italy, the most serious issues included (organized) crime, corruption, and recession (Bohrer and Tan 2000; Carter 1998; Gilbert 1995). The new parties of the Polo delle Libertà, which controlled the Italian Parliament after the 1994 elections, pledged to resolve these very concerns. The Lega Nord (LN), for instance, had a strong anticorruption appeal, based on small government rhetoric and party leaders' perceived asceticism (Daniels 1999; Gilbert 1995), and the neo-fascist Alleanza Nazionale (AN) maintained a strict anti-crime stance. Forza Italia, the largest new party, promised a second "Italian miracle" (Sznajder 1995), and the business successes of its founder, Silvio Berlusconi, lent credibility to this appeal.

In Colombia, the most important issues preceding collapse were violence, guerrillas, and unemployment (M. Seligson 2001), concerns unresolved by the Liberals and Conservatives. But former Liberal turned independent Álvaro Uribe campaigned as a hard-liner who advocated restoring order and confronting the guerrillas. As Dugas notes, "More than anything, Uribe's platform was notable for its unyielding stance on the issue of public security" (2003, 1127).

1. Based on analysis of survey data and legislation. For details, see chapter 5 and appendixes B and C.

Finally, in the year before the Bolivian system's 2005 collapse, survey respondents identified poverty, corruption, unemployment, and natural gas concessions as the country's most pressing problems (LAPOP 2004a). Evo Morales built a following by leading strikes protesting the government's gas policy and other issues, and he promised to increase income from gas and exert state control. He also positioned MAS as the voice of the oppressed (Singer 2007), and MAS voters were optimistic about the economy under a potential Morales government (Seligson et al. 2006, 94).

Successors to the failed systems also offered ideological alternatives to the decaying parties' consensus, allowing ideological distinctions to reemerge. In Venezuela, Chávez's Movimiento Quinta República (MVR) was ideologically left of AD, COPEI, Convergencia, and even MAS, which had all cooperated in governance at different points throughout the 1990s.[2] The movement of AD toward the right and the discrediting of MAS opened up space on the left, which Chávez stepped in to fill. Chávez's primary opponent in the 1998 elections, Henrique Salas Römer of Proyecto Venezuela, was the center-right option. Venezuelans considered these ideological positions when voting in 1998. Of those who placed themselves on the right side of the ideological spectrum, 69 percent voted for right candidates, while 76 percent of those on the left voted for Chávez (Molina 2002).

Ideological distinctions also reemerged in Italy, Colombia, and Bolivia. After the Italian collapse in 1994, Polo delle Libertà occupied the center-right, while the left was represented by the Progressive Alliance, which later became the Ulivo (Olive Tree) coalition (Carter 1998; Gilbert 1995). In Bolivia, Evo Morales's MAS became the main left party, embracing voters abandoned by the traditional parties' abdication of the left. On the right, a haphazard coalition formed under the banner of PODEMOS. In the 2005 election, MAS voters were significantly left of both PODEMOS and traditional party supporters (Seligson et al. 2006, 95). In Colombia, where ideological distinctions had been long subsumed by the National Front, Álvaro Uribe staked out a place on the right, advocating tough anti-violence and pro-neoliberal positions (Dugas 2003). Some left options also emerged. Polo Democrático attained a respectable second place in the 2006 presidential contest, providing electoral options on the part of the spectrum historically dominated by anti-system guerrillas (Rodríguez-Raga 2007; Ulloa and Carbó 2003). In each case, collapse opened up ideological options.

2. Source: RedPol98.

New Parties Reach Out to Neglected Groups

Furthermore, in Venezuela, Italy, and Bolivia—the three collapse cases in which incorporation had once been important but had deteriorated—the heirs to the failed parties structured themselves so as to reach out to newly salient interests that the old systems had disregarded.[3] In Venezuela during the 1990s, major social transformations undermined the traditional class cleavage and restructured it around the formal-informal divide. But the old system only integrated formal sector groups, neglecting the informal side of the cleavage and excluding large sectors of the population. Chávez and MVR catered to the informal sector and urban poor abandoned by the traditional parties. As Chávez said in a 1998 interview, "We must combat the root of social problems, hunger, unemployment, [and] abandoned children" (quoted in Blanco Muñoz 1998, 626–27). These sorts of appeals to the poor and marginalized constituted a central part of his campaign (Canache 2007, 41). In interviews, many MVR party leaders acknowledged how the old parties' inability to integrate these groups gave Chávez an opening by providing a critical support base. One MVR leader explained, "The [traditional] parties favored the interests of the oligarchy and excluded the population, but we made a promise to the people; we are obliged to serve their interests" (Interview 20).

Those who were previously excluded—like the poor, the informal sector, and the indigenous—formed the base for Chávez's rise to power. In the 1990s, the poor consistently held more positive views of Chávez than the wealthy (Canache 2002). Survey data suggest that poor Venezuelans were significantly more likely to express intent to vote for Chávez, while the wealthy were more inclined to support other options (Molina 2002). And although Chávez was elected in 1998 with the backing of various sectors, he captured the votes of the poor and lower-middle sectors by the widest margins (Hellinger 2003; López Maya 2003; K. Roberts 2003b). When Chávez faced serious challenges from an April 2002 coup attempt and then a general strike in late 2002 and early 2003, the poor provided a critical reservoir of support (Canache 2007). Informal sector workers protested the coup and subverted the strike's effort to shut down the economy (Interviews 2, 77).

Once in power, Chávez implemented programs designed to maintain support among the poor. His Misiones provided benefits such as job training, literacy classes, and affordable foodstuffs (Penfold-Becerra 2007) and

---

3. As discussed in chapter 10, the Colombian system did not use incorporation as an important linkage strategy.

reached groups that the old parties had excluded (Interview 15). Chávez also capitalized on racially based exclusion by appealing to dark-skinned Venezuelans, who were impoverished at much higher rates than their light-skinned neighbors (Hellinger 2003). The 1999 Constitution, written by Chávez's allies, reserved seats for the indigenous in the National Assembly. Indigenous leaders blamed the traditional parties for mistreating, neglecting, and taking advantage of the indigenous population and credited Chávez with making tangible, albeit small, steps to promote indigenous interests (Interviews 29, 33). Thus, Chávez used the traditional parties' neglect of these groups to his advantage, as "MVR encompass[ed] a majority of the excluded classes" (Interview 29). Meanwhile, the remnants of AD and COPEI and the new right parties spoke for the traditionally incorporated sectors. Together, the chavistas and the anti-chavistas attracted support based on the major new social divide.

In much the same way, the successors to the failed party systems in Italy and Bolivia rose to power with the backing of groups that had been ignored by the old parties. Both countries experienced the politicization of new cleavages in the decade preceding collapse. In Italy, deindustrialization and secularization weakened the worker-owner and religious-secular cleavages, which had formed the foundation for old incorporation patterns (Daniels 1999; Leonardi and Wertman 1989; Morlino 1996). Instead, regional issues took on increasing importance (Gilbert 1995). In Bolivia, economic crisis and neoliberalism produced poverty and informality, eviscerating the class divide that the system had historically incorporated (Barr 2005; Conaghan and Malloy 1994; Mayorga 2005). As class divisions lost relevance, the ethnic cleavage became increasingly divisive and significant (Mayorga 2006; Van Cott 2003).

In both Italy and Bolivia, these unincorporated groups formed a base for successor parties' ascent to power. In Italy, regional demands were particularly significant in the north, where people disdained the south (Gilbert 1995). The LN, a major coalition partner in the first government after collapse, capitalized on these frustrations. LN built a following based on calls for increased autonomy, devolution, and federalism. Its presence in the governing coalition provided an answer to the increasingly salient north-south divide (Sznajder 1995, 95–96). In Bolivia, the indigenous sought representation after decades in which the traditional parties minimized ethnic identities and emphasized class interests. Several indigenous-based parties took advantage of this opening, including ASP (Asamblea por la Soberanía de los Pueblos), MIP (Movimiento Indígena Pachakuti), and MAS (Van Cott

2005). MAS was the most significant beneficiary of the old parties' failure to accommodate ethnic cleavages. Its leader, Evo Morales, was of mixed Aymara and Quechua origin and rose to prominence as the head of the cocalero movement, which protested U.S.-prescribed eradication policies (Singer 2007). Morales came to power by attracting substantial indigenous support, calling for protection of their cultural heritage and identity and demanding an economic model that benefited them, not just the white elite (Van Cott 2005).

Thus, where the traditional parties had neglected linkage, opportunities opened up for new parties or leaders to seize upon these gaps and build support by promising to fill them, using programmatic representation and interest incorporation. Chávez, Berlusconi, Uribe, and Morales each pledged to address the issues their predecessors had abandoned and extended promises to groups excluded under the old system. Understanding the linkage failures of collapsing systems reveals the sorts of strategies likely to be employed successfully by emerging leaders in their initial ascent to power. It is not a coincidence that Chávez came to power on promises to jumpstart the economy, confront corruption, and listen to the excluded. Rather, these were the exact areas where the traditional party system had fallen short, providing an opening that Chávez successfully exploited. The failings of old systems molded the linkage strategies of their successors.

Clientelism was the only linkage form not common in the initial appeals of successful challengers to the failed systems. Over time, clientelism became important in some of the new systems' linkage profiles. In Venezuela, for instance, clientelist distribution of oil income through differential access to various social programs like the Misiones has become a mainstay of the chavista strategy (Penfold-Becerra 2007). Likewise, in the new Italian party system, vote buying has resurfaced as a significant avenue for drumming up political support, especially in the south (Allum and Allum 2008; Heller and Mershon 2005). But in no case was clientelism central in the successor system's strategy for winning office in the first place. In fact, during their initial ascent to power, the new parties typically spoke out against their predecessors' clientelist practices. The lack of clientelist appeals at the point of transition between old and new systems is likely due to the fact that new parties lacked the ability to make credible clientelist commitments (Warner 2001) and to the discrediting of clientelism as corrupt (Hawkins 2010). Most new parties do not have the resources required to offer clientelist exchanges before elections, so their capacity to fulfill clientelist promises is contingent on the uncertain prospect that they will win and thereby gain access to resources needed to follow through (Warner 2001, 124). Therefore, parties' initial ascents were built largely on programmatic pledges to resolve pressing problems, new ideological options, and reaching out to excluded groups.

Successor Party Systems and Their Relationship to Democracy

The nature of linkage is only one of several characteristics likely to change as a party system collapses. Although the successor systems to the four collapse cases differed in important ways, they had several common features. These shared characteristics suggest that both the process that produces party system failure and the collapse itself pose specific, identifiable risks and opportunities. Here I detail some of the parallels across the four successor systems, including personalism, deinstitutionalization, instability, and conflict, and I discuss the challenges that these shared features imply for post-collapse democracy.

In each of the four collapse cases, the traditional party systems were not replaced by institutionalized parties or even established civil society organizations. Rather, in all four, the most successful heir to the collapsed system was an individual political leader who constructed a personal following that propelled him to power: Venezuela's Hugo Chávez, Italy's Silvio Berlusconi, Colombia's Álvaro Uribe, and Bolivia's Evo Morales. Although their individual characteristics varied, each of these leaders developed a strategy based at least in part on his own persona.

In Venezuela, Chávez did not invest in developing a party organization (Hawkins 2003; Mejias Sarabia and Tarazón Rodriguez 2000). In fact, he has utilized various party vehicles since his first election in 1998 and has now completely replaced MVR with a new party, PSUV (Partido Socialista Unido de Venezuela). Efforts to develop either party as an entity separate from Chávez have been negligible. Even the primary alternatives to Chávez rely largely on individual leaders. As one major opposition politician reflected, "Many [of the new party] organizations are born around a single person instead of around ideas and programs" (Interview 68).

Similarly, Italy, Colombia, and Bolivia manifest patterns of reliance on personal image and charisma. The Italian prime minister after collapse, Berlusconi, was a media baron, one of the nation's wealthiest businessmen, and owner of a top Italian soccer club (Diani 1996). He established Forza Italia, which translates to "Go Italy!," as his personal electoral vehicle (Sznajder 1995). He used his own fortune to establish party clubs, much like soccer fan clubs, throughout the country and, once in office, seemed unable to separate his business persona and interests from his political duties (Gilbert 1995). Likewise, in Colombia, Álvaro Uribe wielded personalist power (Posada-Carbó 2006). Uribe resisted developing a party organization, opting instead to use an electoral vehicle in support of his candidacy and cobbling together ad hoc congressional coalitions in support of his policies (Dugas 2003). Evo Morales in Bolivia has also relied on his charisma, albeit to a lesser extent than his counterparts. He has the backing of major new social movements, including the cocaleros and the indigenous, but these groups are more fluid and less institutionalized than old bases built on traditional class interests. And MAS, Morales's party, was originally just a label abandoned by a failed traditional left party that allowed him to adopt its name in order to stage his campaigns (Van Cott 2005).

Associated with these actors' personalism was a deinstitutionalization process in which party organizations lost significance. Developing party organizations takes time, energy, and resources, whereas bases built on individuals are easily constructed (and destructed). When the old parties failed, individual leaders who lacked firm organizational underpinnings stepped in. As a result, party organizations were mostly irrelevant in the immediate post-collapse eras. In Venezuela, for example, since the old parties failed over a decade ago, neither the chavistas nor their opponents have developed anything that resembles an institutionalized party structure.

Weak party organizations and personalism pose challenges to democracy after collapse. Without party organizations to check leaders, the risk of excessive power concentrated in one person is amplified. Politics is easily subjected to a leader's whims, allowing erratic changes in policy or in the rules of the game. This uncertainty may provoke turmoil and undermine governability. The absence of strong parties in the legislature also means that the executive is unlikely to encounter constructive and substantive dialogue and may resort to unilateral action. When one individual amasses considerable power, opportunities for accountability narrow. Power concentration is particularly risky when the person who holds that power is an outsider with ambivalent or even hostile views of the political system or of the democratic regime—common characteristics of the successors to collapse (Mainwaring and Zoco 2007).

In none of the collapse cases did the system fail under pressure from well-organized or institutionalized competitors. Instead, it collapsed because of its decaying linkage capacity. Although successful heirs took advantage of the old systems' failures, it was not the presence of strong, established alternatives that caused these problems. Therefore, as old systems disintegrated, they left a power vacuum in which various nascent players competed to gain a foothold, creating uncertainty and instability.

By definition, volatility during collapse was high in all four cases because the traditional parties lost considerable vote share to other actors as part of the collapse process. But even after collapse was complete, volatility remained high. Using seat allocation data and the Pedersen index (1983), I calculated volatility in the composition of the lower house of the legislature between the collapse election and the first election after collapse in Venezuela, Italy, Colombia, and Bolivia.[4] In all four countries, volatility was quite high, well above regional averages of 8 in 1980s Western Europe and 20 in 1990s Latin America (Gallagher, Laver, and Mair 1995, 233; Roberts and Wibbels 1999, 577). In Venezuela, volatility between the 1998 collapse and the 2000 legislative elections was over 35, a marked increase above the average of about 20 during the two decades preceding collapse. In Italy, volatility between collapse in 1994 and the 1996 parliamentary elections was over 30, a significant departure from average volatility below 10 during the height of the old system (Pedersen 1983). In Colombia, volatility surpassed 50 between 2002 and 2006—almost five times its levels in the 1980s and 1990s (Roberts and Wibbels 1999). Even Bolivia, where volatility was comparatively high at about 27 during the 1980s and 1990s, saw an increase to a score of 35 between the 2005 collapse and the 2009 elections (CNE 2010; Roberts and Wibbels 1999).

The instability common after collapse poses challenges to democracy. These fluctuations create uncertainty for voters and parties, making political calculations difficult and ordinary strategies irrelevant (Moser 2001). As parties come and go, voters must learn anew what each stands for, and they face ambiguity about how new groups will perform (Hinich and Munger 1994; Mainwaring and Torcal 2006). Changing party identities, organizational structures, and ideologies require voters to adjust constantly (Roberts and Wibbels 1999). Additionally, when parties do not run for reelection, holding them accountable is nearly impossible. Without the structure provided by a stable party system, politics may devolve into chaos, weakening governability and accountability. It is also easier for new actors and outsiders to enter the system when volatility is high. But while volatility presents opportunities for access and may expand representational options, it may just as easily open the door to potential opponents of the regime.

4. The legislative volatility index is calculated by adding together the absolute values of the change in seat shares won by each party from one election to the next, and then dividing by two. The index ranges from 0 to 100 and corresponds to the net change in seat shares.

Escalation of conflict also accompanied collapse in each case. As linkage failed, the parties' ability to channel contestation deteriorated, and more contentious forms of politics proliferated. Successors to the old systems challenged as corrupt established norms of negotiation and compromise, which were typical of the interparty agreements in all four pre-collapse systems. As these new actors assumed power, old patterns of compromise gave way to conflict and contention. Of the four cases of collapse, Venezuela and Bolivia are the strongest examples of this. Both experienced dramatic escalations in conflict as their party systems deteriorated, and contention remained elevated after collapse. At the Venezuelan system's height from the 1970s through the mid-1980s, parties effectively channeled conflicting views of state and society. Likewise, Bolivia in the late 1980s and early 1990s was regarded as an exemplar of good governance and constructive participation (McNeish 2006). However, as the parties lost capacity to channel diverse interests, conflict intensified in early 1990s Venezuela and late 1990s Bolivia, with extra-institutional contestation reaching its most severe point in the years immediately *following* collapse.

With the failure of the Venezuelan party system, conflict reached unprecedented levels. In interviews, many elites noted that a major difference since the failure of the old parties was the considerable elevation in contentious politics. A major opposition politician characterized the post-collapse polity as a "permanent state of instability" (Interview 67), and an MVR leader agreed that the country had faced "high political conflict for the past five years [since Chávez took power]" (Interview 34). The constant political turmoil in Venezuela since 1998 supports this perception of instability and conflict (Smilde 2004). Repeated clashes between chavistas and antichavistas over the rules of the game, including election procedures, executive powers, and even the Constitution itself, speak strongly to the conflictual environment. Much of this turmoil came to a head during the April 2002 coup that briefly removed Chávez and provoked extended public demonstrations supporting and opposing the coup. Then, in late 2002 and early 2003, a general strike or work stoppage mounted by the opposition shut down ordinary public life for several months.

Fig. 12.1 depicts the elevated tumult of Venezuelan politics following the party system's collapse. The figure displays the number of protests counted by the human rights organization Provea in its annual reports, as well as the number of news items about protests in the major Caracas daily *El Nacional*, archived in the El Bravo Pueblo database at the Universidad Central de Venezuela (López Maya and Lander 2005). Both sources show significant

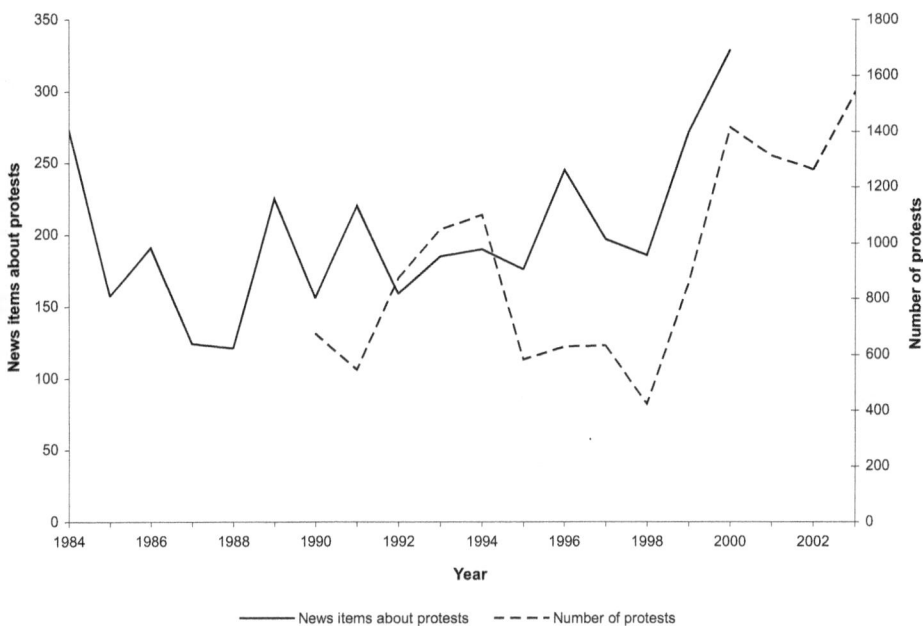

Fig. 12.1   Protests in Venezuela, 1984–2003

Note: Each year corresponds to October of the preceding year through September of the year indicated.

Source: Protests from Provea's *Situación de los derechos*. News items from El Bravo Pueblo database. Both reported in López Maya and Lander (2005).

increases in protest levels in 1999 and 2000, and the news data suggest that protest activity remained high through 2003. The number of demonstrations and news reports reached levels 50 percent higher than the average during the pre-collapse period. Analysis of the kinds of protest during the post-collapse era also points to an escalation in the intensity of conflict, as nonconventional forms of protest increased. In 1999, 63 percent of protests were confrontational and 21 percent turned violent, whereas only 15 percent fit conventional patterns. This level of nonconventional activism contrasts with the decade spanning 1984 to 1993, when conventional demonstrations constituted nearly half of all protests (López Maya and Lander 2005, 96).

The Bolivian experience followed a similar pattern. The 1980s and early 1990s were a relatively peaceful period in Bolivia. But by the late 1990s, protests, demonstrations, and road blockades were common strategies. And with the presidential victory of Evo Morales, the cocalero who spearheaded many protests, the level of conflict remained high, overwhelming ordinary political processes (McNeish 2006). National public opinion surveys conducted in Bolivia in 2004 and 2006, the years before and after the party system's failure, indicate that protest participation increased after collapse. The percentage of Bolivians who reported participating in a protest in the past year increased from 21 percent in the 2004 survey to 28 percent in the 2006 survey (LAPOP 2004a, 2006). Even though politics in Bolivia were already overheated before collapse, the level of turmoil did not subside but continued to escalate. As in Venezuela, Bolivian conflict involved contestation over basic rules of the game. Perhaps the most intense struggle focused on efforts to write a new constitution, with both government and opposition resorting to marches and protests to display their strength and pressure the other side (Madrid 2007). Regional polarization also escalated, and MAS supporters even set fire to the opposition governor's palace in Cochabamba, forcing the prefect to flee (Madrid 2007, 21). At this writing, confrontational politics show no sign of abating in Bolivia.

Although Venezuela and Bolivia are the most poignant instances of intense conflict accompanying party system collapse, Italy and Colombia exhibited similar, albeit less extreme, patterns of conflict escalation. Italy experienced a surge in protest in 1994 as the party system collapsed midway through that year. A database of protest events developed using the national news section of the major Italian daily *La Repubblica* demonstrates that the number of protests reached an all-time high in 1994 (Forno 2003). Furthermore, the scope and intensity of protests increased after collapse, as unconventional, anti-system demonstrations, like the LN's secessionist revolts, multiplied (Diani 1996; Forno 2003). The uprisings and their targets were also much more likely to extend beyond the local context to the regional or national level after collapse (Forno 2003, 6–11).

In Colombia, conflict was already quite common before the party system collapsed in 2002. But clashes between the government and leftist guerrillas opposing the system reached an all-time high under Álvaro Uribe (Avilés 2006; Farrell 2007). Of course, this sort of armed conflict between government and guerrillas was a natural outgrowth of Uribe following through on his promise to squash the guerrillas militarily. Perhaps protest activity is more comparable to the conflictual politics experienced in the other collapse cases. Traditionally, this type of contentious politics was limited in Colombia (Hochstetler and Palma 2009), with few strikes or protests being reported (Banks 2010). Though media coverage of protests remained limited, albeit with a slight uptick in the late 1990s and early 2000s, by 2004 demonstrations had increased (Almeida 2007, 124), and 19 percent of survey respondents reported participating in protests—a rate almost as high as that of Bolivia after collapse (LAPOP 2004b).[5] The Banks Conflict index (2010), which includes a variety of political conflict activities, such as protests, strikes, riots, and guerrilla warfare, also reached its highest level for Colombia in 2004, just two years after collapse. In fact, the index shows a general pattern of increased conflict over the 1990s and through the first half of the 2000s.

Thus, heightened conflict accompanies party system collapse. As established parties lose linkage capacity, the system cannot channel competing views constructively, and conflict spills outside institutionalized processes and into the streets. Furthermore, as the country transitions from the old to the new, traditional modes of politics become obsolete, and new actors challenge established conciliatory patterns. In this uncertain context, competing groups battle for the upper hand, and rules that had previously been a matter of consensus are subjected to discussion. When disputes extend to the rules themselves, conflict overwhelms typical boundaries as groups compete for survival. Party system collapse, therefore, exposes democracy to intense conflict over the fundamentals of politics. Extreme conflict levels, especially the sort observed in Venezuela and Bolivia, pose a real challenge to democracy. Although new voices are being heard in the post-collapse polity, the cacophony of competition that accompanies collapse threatens to overwhelm the democratic system if new patterns of contestation cannot be established in order to conduct competition in productive, rather than destructive, ways.

POST-COLLAPSE LESSONS

Party system collapse completely restructures not only the party system but also numerous other political patterns and processes. On the one hand, collapse opens opportunities for representation. Successful emerging actors address pressing issues that the old system neglected, giving people hope for future substantive improvements. Ideological options broaden in the post-collapse period, and voters are able to choose between alternative policy visions at the polls. Whereas the old parties excluded emergent interests aligned along newly salient cleavages, their successors appeal to these neglected interests. Therefore, while the old systems failed because of

---

5. Data on participation in protests for the pre-collapse period in Colombia were not available.

deteriorating linkage, the successful heirs to collapse capitalized on these weaknesses, building linkage where there had been none.

On the other hand, party system collapse raises the specter of tragedy by posing threats to the democratic regime. Personalistic leaders step into the power vacuum left by the old system, and without organizational constraints on individual power, horizontal accountability recedes and erratic decision making threatens stability and sound policy. If new leaders have ambiguous or antagonistic attitudes about democracy, the regime itself may be at risk. Increases in volatility that accompany collapse also pose a challenge for democracy, as uncertainty decreases voters' ability to sustain effective vertical accountability. Instability in electoral options and outcomes undermines policy consistency, limiting effective responsiveness in the long term.

Democracy is also challenged by the heightened conflict associated with decaying linkage and party system collapse. Ineffective linkage opens the door to more contentious politics as people clamor to be heard. As emerging actors struggle to redefine the rules of the game, they expand the scope of competition, increasing the level and intensity of conflict. Extreme conflict weakens governability, and protracted or violent clashes may even threaten regime survival. Therefore, although party system collapse may refresh linkage opportunities, it also exposes the democratic regime to multiple challenges, including concentration of power, limited accountability, and disintegrating governability.

Given the threats that accompany party system failure, democracy is likely better served if collapse can be avoided. Stability would be preserved and the quality of democracy enhanced if established systems could find a way to improve linkage. If a party system sustains linkage, the country avoids the threats associated with collapse while also maintaining representation. If party systems are to avoid collapse, my findings suggest several considerations that parties, government officials, and public opinion leaders should take into account. First, parties should not respond to major crises by closing ranks and working together. Commonly, when countries face challenges requiring significant policy innovation, public opinion leaders and even officeholders clamor for politicians to work together and avoid partisan conflict. However, my analysis of party system collapse shows that interparty collaboration during crisis threatens the programmatic credibility of all the participating parties. If the parties cooperate and fail to provide an adequate policy response, then voters are left with no viable alternative to the status quo, and people become frustrated with the entire system and look elsewhere for representation. Rather than entering interparty agreements during times of crisis, nongoverning parties should offer responsible opposition, thereby giving dissatisfied voters the opportunity to express frustration at the polls without jeopardizing the entire system.

Second, parties should not block entry of regime-supportive competitors. This advice may seem counterintuitive to party leaders who want to optimize their chances for winning. But the Uruguay-Colombia comparison suggests that when systems allow expansion, they accommodate unrepresented interests and improve their long-term odds of survival. Although Uruguay's Blancos and Colorados lost complete dominance much sooner than Colombia's Liberals and Conservatives, the Uruguayan parties remain significant players today, while the Colombian parties have disintegrated. Because the Colorados and Blancos did not keep Frente Amplio out of the system and FA opted for electoral politics rather than guerrilla militancy, voters found options for programmatic and incorporating linkage that the two traditional parties could not provide. When clientelism failed, other forms of linkage remained. In Colombia, on the other hand, the left operated largely outside the electoral arena, and when clientelism deteriorated, the entire system lacked linkage and collapsed. The entry of competition into the Uruguayan system enabled its adaptation and allowed the traditional parties' survival. Therefore, competition can be a good thing, for both the system and its component parties.

Finally, crisis conditions and institutional reforms do not mix. In case after case of collapse, political reforms challenged linkage maintenance by requiring the parties to adapt to new institutions at the same time that they faced other stresses from economic crisis and social change. Frequently, the reforms were motivated by a desire to increase decaying legitimacy and enhance accountability, and politicians hoped that the changes might communicate a desire to respond to public opinion and compensate for their inability to address major economic and social problems. Unfortunately, while the reforms may have pleased a small set of the population attuned to institutional complexities, they did not compensate for lack of responsiveness to basic national issues like inflation, unemployment, and crime. More gravely, the reforms created roadblocks in the parties' efforts to provide linkage, particularly weakening clientelism. Thus, while institutional reforms can often be important tools in restructuring incentives and enhancing the quality of democracy, such changes should not be implemented in the midst of crisis because they infrequently resolve the country's most pressing problems and often create more challenges for parties to overcome. If reforms are implemented under stressful conditions, they should not demand complete rationalization but should take care to preserve party access to resources in order to safeguard the system from complete linkage failure.

Party system collapse is traumatic, and although it may open opportunities for representation, it also has potentially devastating consequences for democratic stability. If a party system avoids threats to its core linkage profile or adapts in the face of major structural challenges, it is able to provide adequate ties between citizens and the state and survive. But where fundamental challenges and adverse constraints on appropriate adaptation cause the deterioration of the system's linkage strategies, the party system collapses.

In the analysis, I draw on a series of semi-structured interviews that I conducted with Venezuelan politicians during field research. I drafted the interview guide in consultation with Venezuelan political scientists. I translated it into Spanish, and then it was edited by several Venezuelans, including a political scientist and a legislative aide in the National Assembly. Then, to ensure that the intent of the questions was preserved in the translation, a professional Venezuelan translator translated it back into English. I conducted all eighty-nine interviews in Spanish without a recording device to encourage respondents to be forthright about how their own failings, as well as those of their co-partisans and other party leaders, led to the collapse of the system. The interviews generally took between 45 and 90 minutes, with the longest interview lasting over 2 hours.

I incorporated three strategies of participant selection. First, I employed a mixed tactic based on positional and reputational importance to identify individuals who were influential politicians at the time of the primary field research in 2003. The reputational sample was developed by asking every respondent to identify the political actors whom they perceived to be most influential. I used their answers to this question to create a ranking for the reputational sample. Over time, a clear set of about 15 influential political leaders emerged; I successfully interviewed 10 of them. For the positional sample, I sought to interview the president or secretary general of each party that held at least five seats in the National Assembly in 2003. For 10 political parties, I interviewed at least one of the individuals in these positions, and for 5 parties, I interviewed both the president and the secretary general.

Second, I interviewed those people who had been pivotal leaders in the traditional parties during the late 1980s and 1990s—the critical years in the collapse process—as well as other influential political leaders, advisors, and academics from the same period. I selected the formerly influential leaders based on their official positions in the parties (secretaries general, party presidents, and heads of the parties' parliamentary factions), examination of newspaper archives to identify important actors, and information gathered in the first round of interviews with contemporary influential leaders. The resulting sample captures many of the major leaders of AD, COPEI, and MAS from the fifteen years preceding the party system's collapse. I obtained participation from 48 formerly influential individuals through this process.[1]

Finally, to facilitate comparisons of the perspectives of the top echelon of party leaders to those of ordinary members of the legislature, I interviewed a random sample of 16 rank-and-file members of the 2003 Chamber of Deputies.[2] The 16 deputies interviewed as a part of this group represented AD and COPEI, as well as MVR, Proyecto Venezuela, MAS, and two very small parties.[3]

All interviewees were assured of the confidentiality of their responses, so no names or other identifying details are used in association with respondents' comments or opinions. A list of the titles and partisan affiliations (where relevant) of all the participants, as well as the code numbers used to cite the interviews in the text, is presented in table A.1.

1. There is some overlap between current and past leaders, which explains why the total number of individuals listed in this appendix exceeds eighty-nine.

2. Party leaders and legislative committee heads were excluded from the sampling frame from which this rank-and-file sample was drawn. Of the 16 legislators initially selected using the random selection procedure in STATA 7.0, 14 cooperated with my requests for an interview. One non-respondent was an ill legislator who had been replaced permanently by his *suplente*. To replace this respondent in the sample, I randomly selected an alternate, who did participate as a respondent. One MVR deputy refused to participate despite repeated requests. In addition to the 14 randomly selected rank-and-file deputies, I also interviewed two additional deputies who simply volunteered to participate when they heard about my research.

3. I cannot name the small parties that these two deputies represented because that would enable identification of the deputies, as both occupied the solitary seat held by their respective parties.

Table A.1 Interview participant records and codes

Title	Party	Type	Date	Code
Political scientist	N/A	PI	29 April 2003	1
Political scientist, advisor to LCR	N/A	PI	3 June 2003	2
Former Consejo Supremo Electoral member	N/A	PI	17 June 2003	3
Political scientist	N/A	PI	25 June 2003	4
Head of major polling firm	N/A	PI	22 May 2003	5
Head of major polling firm	N/A	PI	19 May 2003	6
Head of major polling firm	N/A	PI	5 May 2003	7
Political scientist, advisor to COPEI	N/A	PI	28 June 2003	8
Political scientist, social policy advisor	N/A	PI	1 July 2003	9
Political scientist	N/A	PI	23 July 2003	10
Editor of major news magazine	N/A	PI	20 Nov. 2003	11
Political scientist	N/A	PI	13 May 2001	12
Political scientist	N/A	PI	2 June 2006	13
Policy advisor	AD	PI	12 June 2006	14
Political scientist, social policy advisor	N/A	PI	13 June 2006	15
Political scientist	N/A	PI	13 June 2006	16
Head of major polling firm	N/A	PI	3 July 2006	17
National Assembly deputy	PV	RF	16 July 2003	18
National Assembly deputy	PV	RF	5 Aug. 2003	19
National Assembly deputy	MVR	RF	6 Aug. 2003	20
National Assembly deputy	COPEI	RF	6 Aug. 2003	21
National Assembly deputy	MVR	RF	8 Aug. 2003	22
National Assembly deputy	MVR	RF	8 Sept. 2003	23
National Assembly deputy	MVR	RF	16 Sept. 2003	24
National Assembly deputy	AD	RF	23 Sept. 2003	25
National Assembly deputy	Mi Gato	RF	30 Sept. 2003	26
National Assembly deputy	MVR	RF	1 Oct. 2003	27
National Assembly deputy	AD	RF	2 Oct. 2003	28
National Assembly deputy	CONIVE	RF	8 Oct. 2003	29
National Assembly deputy	Vamos	RF	13 Oct. 2003	30
National Assembly deputy	MVR	RF	29 Oct. 2003	31
National Assembly deputy	MAS	RF	12 Nov. 2003	32
National Assembly deputy	CONIVE	RF	16 Oct. 2003	33
National Assembly deputy	MVR	CI	6 Nov. 2003	34
Former CEN member	AD	PI	4 Nov. 2003	35
Former CEN member, cabinet official	AD	PI	18 Nov. 2003	36
Former secretary general	COPEI	PI	20 Nov. 2003	37
Former president	AD	PI	3 Dec. 2003	38
Former parliamentary fraction head	COPEI	PI	9 June 2006	39
Former CEN member	AD	PI	14 June 2006	40
Former CEN member, cabinet official	AD	PI	14 June 2006	41
Former CEN member	AD	PI	20 June 2006	42
Former party president	COPEI	PI	20 June 2006	43
Former party president	COPEI	PI	23 June 2006	44
Former presidential candidate	AD	PI	28 June 2006	45
Former parliamentary fraction head	COPEI	PI	30 June 2006	46
Former party president and secretary general	AD	PI	8 July 2006	47
Former party vice president	AD	PI	10 July 2006	48
Former CEN member	AD	PI	13 July 2006	49

Title	Party	Type	Date	Code
Former party president and secretary general	AD	PI	17 July 2006	50
Former secretary general	AD	PI	18 July 2006	51
Former head of Buró Sindical, CEN member	AD	PI	18 July 2006	52
Former CEN member, cabinet official	AD	PI	19 July 2006	53
COPRE member	N/A	PI	20 July 2006	54
Former presidential candidate	COPEI	PI	21 July 2006	55
Former CEN member	AD	PI	25 July 2006	56
Party president or secretary general	COPEI	CI	2 Oct. 2003	57
Party president or secretary general	COPEI	CI	7 Oct. 2003	58
Party president or secretary general	MAS	CI, PI	7 Oct. 2003	59
Party president or secretary general	PV	CI	22 Oct. 2003	60
Party president or secretary general	ABP	CI, PI	24 Oct. 2003	61
Major newspaper editor	N/A	CI	30 Oct. 2003	62
CEN member	AD	CI	31 Oct. 2003	63
Party president or secretary general	ABP	CI	5 Nov. 2003	64
Coordinadora Democrática[a] (CD) leader	N/A	CI	10 Nov. 2003	65
Party president or secretary general	MAS	CI, PI	12 Nov. 2003	66
Major newspaper editor	N/A	CI, PI	13 Nov. 2003	67
Head of parliamentary fraction	PJ	CI	14 Nov. 2003	68
Party president or secretary general	PPT	CI	20 Nov. 2003	69
Party president or secretary general	LCR	CI	3 Dec. 2003	70
Comando Táctico Nacional[b] member	MVR	CI	4 Dec. 2003	71
Comando Táctico Nacional[b] member	MVR	CI	5 Dec. 2003	72
National party director[c]	CONV	CI, PI	9 Dec. 2003	73
Former party president	PV	CI	11 Dec. 2003	74
Mesa de Negociación[d] member, on behalf of CD	N/A	CI	12 Dec. 2003	75
NGO leader	N/A	CI	12 Dec. 2003	76
Comando Táctico Nacional[b] member	MVR	CI	4 Aug. 2003	77
Party president or secretary general	LCR	CI, PI	22 Oct. 2003	78
Party vice president	COPEI	CI	14 June 2006	79
Party president or secretary general	PJ	CI	22 June 2006	80
CEN member	AD	CI	13 July 2006	81
Former parliamentary fraction head	LCR	PI	10 May 2001	82
Party president or secretary general	AD	CI	10 May 2001	83
Party president or secretary general	COPEI	PI	9 May 2001	84
CEN member	CONV	PI	9 May 2001	85
Party president or secretary general	PJ	CI	14 May 2001	86
National Assembly deputy	PV	CI	14 May 2001	87
CEN member	MAS	CI	15 May 2001	88
Political advisor	AD	CI	23 Sept. 2003	89

CI = Contemporary influential
PI = Past influential
RF = Rank and file
N/A = Not applicable

[a] Central organization seeking to coordinate the efforts of the anti-Chávez opposition in 2003
[b] Equivalent to AD's CEN
[c] Convergencia equivalent to party president or secretary general
[d] Group attempting to negotiate compromise between government and opposition surrounding the general strike and revocatory referendum in 2003

To identify the issues that Venezuelans considered to be the most pressing problems, I used public opinion surveys that asked them to name the
most important problem(s) facing the country. Table B.1 displays the question variations used. If a question format allowed the naming of more than
one problem, only the first problem mentioned was included in the analysis. In the case of IVAD questions that permitted naming multiple problems, the coding scheme used by the firm made it impossible to separate
the first problems that respondents mentioned from the second and third
problems they identified. In these instances, I adjusted the frequencies
so that the number of total responses equaled the number of people who
answered the question. For example, if there were 3,000 problems mentioned but only 1,000 respondents, the frequencies were reduced by two-
thirds. Despite some differences in question wording, the top problems
identified by respondents in any single year were largely consistent across
survey firms and question formats.

All the responses were grouped into the following categories: unemployment, cost of living, debt, recession, privatization, other economic issues,
bad administration/governance, crime and morality, corruption, poverty and
scarcity, health, education, housing, public works and services, transportation, pensions, other social issues, agriculture, political issues, judicial issues,
international issues, violence and protests, petroleum, other, and none.[1]
Then the frequencies for all the surveys conducted during each five-year legislative term were averaged together such that each type of problem has only
one score for each term; the averages were weighted according to sample

---

1. In additional analysis, these categories were collapsed into broader groupings to ensure
that the ranking of important problems was not significantly shaped by the particular categories
used. The rankings of important problems generated using these broader categories did not
result in meaningful differences in the types of problems topping the list each year. I chose to
use the more specific categories in the analysis to facilitate matching the problems people named
to the legislation enacted.

size. Based on these five-year averages, the problems were ranked according to the proportion of respondents who named each issue as the most important. The more respondents who named a problem, the higher this issue was ranked. I used these five-year average rankings to determine the most pressing issues in the country during each five-year legislative term.

Table B.1   Most important problem question wordings

Wording	Years	Firm
In your opinion, what is the principal problem that Venezuela has at this time?	1989–2003	C21
In your opinion, what are the most important national problems of the moment?	1973	Baloyra
What do you think are the most important problems that the new Lusinchi government should resolve?	1983	DATOS
What is the most important issue that the government of Lusinchi should resolve in 1988?	1987	IVAD
Which of the following do you consider the most serious problem confronting the country right now?	1981–82	DATOS
Each country faces its own problems. In your opinion, what is the most serious problem facing the Venezuelan people?	1976–77	DATOS
What are the three principal problems that face the country these days?	1984–88 1992–94 1996, 1999	IVAD
What are the two or three principal problems that face Venezuela these days?	1986	IVAD
What would you say are the principal problems facing the country these days?	1997	IVAD
What are the three principal problems in the country these days, which the current president and his team should resolve?	1998–2002	IVAD
If you were the president of Venezuela, what would be the problem you would attend to before any other?	1998–2001	IVAD

Note: The 1981–82 DATOS question "Which of the following do you consider the most serious problem confronting the country right now?" is close-ended. All other questions are open-ended.

Source: Author's translation and compilation from the listed surveys and firms.

APPENDIX C: LEGISLATIVE OUTPUT CATEGORIZATION AND ANALYSIS

To measure Venezuelan legislative activity, I examined all new laws and reforms of existing legislation passed by Congress and enacted by the executive from 1974 through 2004. I developed a database of legislative activity, using the *Gaceta Oficial de la República (Bolivariana) de Venezuela*, a daily official publication of the Venezuelan government, as well as the legislative archives at the National Assembly's Dirección de Información Legislativa (Legislative Information Directorate). To construct the database, I created a record for each law published in the *Gaceta Oficial*.[1] Each record includes the title of the law, the number and date of the issue of the *Gaceta Oficial* in which it was published, the date Congress passed the law, and the date the president signed it. Then each law was coded according to the major policy areas it addressed as well as its retrospective significance and contemporary importance. I detail these coding processes below.

CODING MAJOR POLICY AREAS

First, to code the major policy areas addressed by legislation, I constructed an exhaustive list of thirty-eight specific policy categories. These are (un)employment, cost of living/inflation, debt, recession/growth, trade, privatization/nationalization, other economic issues, governance/corruption, international relations, the judiciary and justice, crime and security, poverty and scarcity, health, education, housing, public works, transportation, pensions, culture and recreation, family, other social issues, agriculture, business and

1. The database only includes laws and reforms of laws that were passed through Congress. The analysis does not directly include laws enacted by the president under special decree powers. The majority of laws enacted by presidents were implemented based on decree authority granted to them under special enabling laws passed by the legislature. Therefore, these decree laws are incorporated in the analysis indirectly through the inclusion of the enabling laws themselves in the database. However, other decree laws, such as those issued under the president's constitutional powers, are not included in this analysis.

industry, petroleum and mining, the environment, shipping and railroads and airlines, treaties, public credit, government administration and organization, intergovernmental relations, voting and elections, budget, defense and the armed forces, taxes, science and technology, communications, finance, and other (minor laws, such as those that create special government honors or that do not fall into any of the other categories). Because the database of legislative activity was to be used in conjunction with the most important problem data taken from public opinion surveys (as discussed in appendix B), I was careful that this list mirrored all the same policy categories included in the most important problem data. This ensured that effective parallels could be drawn between the legislative activity data and the public opinion data. Other policy categories not mentioned in the public opinion data were also included to account for significant policy areas that citizens did not mention as important but in which government activity is common. Some of these added categories were treaty and public credit laws as well as environment, communications, and science and technology. I created this list of policy areas by consulting the public opinion data and through an initial reading of the laws under analysis. Using this approach, I ensured that the diversity of government policy activity was adequately captured in the coding schema.

Once this list of policy areas was coded, I took a census approach (Neuendorf 2002) to the content analysis by coding each law passed during the period under analysis (1974–2004). I chose to evaluate each law, rather than a sampling of legislation, to fully capture the dynamics of legislative activity during the period. To analyze policy content, each law was read and its major components summarized. In the case of laws that reformed or repealed existing legislation, the new law was compared to the modified law(s) to determine how the new bill changed policy. Based on these summaries, each law was then coded according to the primary policy area(s) it addressed. If significant portions of the law dealt with more than one policy area, it could be coded in multiple categories. Laws are not coded as dealing with a particular substantive area when only a small portion or minor provisions in the law touch on that subject. Both treaty and public credit laws are coded only according to the respective broad type. The substantive content of the public credit or treaty is not coded because in neither case does congressional approval constitute any change in policy. Annual budget laws are likewise coded only as such because the details of all budget laws were not available and the task of analyzing the substance of each budget is a task outside the realm of this project. Furthermore, the Venezuelan legislature has typically possessed little latitude in altering the budget submitted by the executive, minimizing the budget's relevance for understanding policy content as enacted by parties in the legislature.

To assess the reliability of the coding (Krippendorff 2004, 215), I personally coded each law according to its major policy areas before I analyzed the survey data on the most important problems facing the country (thereby avoiding any potential biases toward over- or under-identification of legislative activities in policy areas that Venezuelans identified as important). Then, as a reliability check, I randomly selected 11 percent of all legislation passed between 1974 and 2004; these 125 laws were coded by a secondary coder who followed the same coding process outlined above.[2] I trained this second coder in the coding rules and provided a detailed codebook.[3] This coder, who possesses a Ph.D. in political science and knowledge of Venezuelan politics, followed the same coding process outlined above. After the initial training period, in which the secondary coder and I engaged in consensus coding as part of the coder training, the secondary coder did not receive additional guidance from me, so as to promote the independence of the coding decisions. Using a primary and secondary coder, who each coded following the same procedures and produced independent assessments of legislative content and significance, enabled me to assess the reliability of the coding process. I compared the codes created by the secondary coder to my original codes to evaluate intercoder reliability. In coding the substantive content areas of the legislation, I found 99 percent agreement between the two coders.[4] Agreement coefficients over 0.7 are considered acceptable (Neuendorf 2002, 143), indicating that the coding process was highly reliable. In instances where there was disagreement between coders, I read the original law as well as the summaries generated by both coders and made a final determination concerning the proper code. Slightly more than half the coding disagreements were decided in favor of the primary coder, and the rest followed the secondary coder's decision.

2. For all the reliability checks discussed in this appendix, I follow Neuendorf's (2002) recommendation that intercoder reliability be assessed using at least two coders, where the second coder codes a random sample of at least 10 percent of the material.

3. The guidelines for coding policy areas, as well as retrospective and contemporary importance, are available upon request.

4. To calculate the agreement between coders, I follow Neuendorf's (2002) suggestion to use percent agreement on each type of unit coded. Percent agreement is calculated as the number of agreements divided by the total number of units measured. Percent agreement is the appropriate measure of reliability for nominal coding, which is the type conducted here.

I began the analysis of legislative importance by retrospectively assessing each law's significance. The goal was to identify legislation that was either quite broad in its scope, perhaps by establishing guiding principles for a general policy area, or that constituted an effort to have a profound influence in a narrower policy area. The nationalization of the oil industry would fall into the latter category, while a 1989 housing law that sought to coordinate housing policy and established a variety of housing programs, including housing assistance, preferential mortgage rates, special savings plans, and a lease-to-own program, among others, falls into the former category. To assess a law's significance, I again reviewed the summary of the law to determine its depth and breadth. I then coded the significance of each law based on the intent of the legislation in accord with the text of the law itself and its relationship to existing policy.

The focus is on the content of the law, rather than on any assessment of the policy's implementation or effectiveness. This emphasis on content is appropriate in the analysis of responsiveness because I am concerned primarily with *efforts* made by the parties in the legislature to address important problems. At a basic level, representation entails government action to respond to citizens' concerns. Ideally, government activity would also lead to resolution of the problems facing society. However, oftentimes well-intentioned policy makers fail to create perfect policy solutions for a variety of reasons. Therefore, the coding of retrospective significance centers on the intent of the legislation, rather than its successful implementation.[5]

Several types of laws received automatic codes with regard to their retrospective significance. Given the impact that a budget is likely to have on a wide array of policy areas, I categorized each annual budget law as significant. All treaty and public credit laws were coded as not significant. Treaty laws were coded as unimportant because legislative approval of a treaty does not constitute its enactment; rather it requires further action in the form of either legislation or decrees that align state policy with the treaty. Public credit laws were coded as insignificant for two reasons. The first is that they did not change programs; they only provided additional funding to existing programs. The second reason is more practical. Namely, the legislative

---

5. Furthermore, success in actually resolving serious issues facing the country would most likely be better assessed using direct measures of these problems, such as inflation, unemployment, crime rates, etc.

procedure for approving additional budgetary credits changed significantly over the period under analysis. Up until the 1990s, Congress passed individual laws authorizing government entities to utilize public credits numerous times each year. However, during the 1990s, a change in this type of legislation occurred. An effort was made to include all public credit approvals under a single umbrella public credit law for each budgetary year (*Ley de Paraguas* was the term applied to these laws). These umbrella laws outlined limits on the amount of public credits that could be utilized in the following fiscal year by each government entity. This approach reduced the number of public credit laws from an average of more than ten per year during the end of the Lusinchi administration and the beginning of the second Pérez presidency to only about two public credit laws per year beginning in 1993. Therefore, while there were significant changes in the number of credit laws, the change did not necessarily signify a major shift in policy. Therefore, I elect to retrospectively code all public credit legislation as not significant to avoid biasing the analysis. Furthermore, I discovered in the Phase 2 analysis of contemporaneous significance that the decision to code treaty and public credit laws as insignificant was confirmed by the nearly uniform lack of news coverage of these types of laws. Only a handful of treaty and public credit laws ever received media attention. Those few that were contemporaneously important are captured in Phase 2 of the analysis.

I coded all the laws according to this schema. As an expert in Venezuelan politics and policy, I am particularly qualified to code the retrospective significance of the legislation, and I am confident in the validity of the analysis. However, to assure the reproducibility of the coding, I again used a secondary coder with a Ph.D. in political science and some knowledge of Venezuelan politics to provide a reliability check. This coder coded 125 laws (about 11 percent) following the same guidelines I used. The secondary coder was trained and received a detailed codebook to guide coding. Once the training was complete, the secondary coder carried out the coding without discussing it with me and without knowledge of how I had coded the legislation. This enabled me to examine the reliability of the coding. For the codes of major versus ordinary legislation, the two coders agreed 93.5 percent of the time, which is highly reliable. The same process described above for resolving intercoder disagreement was also utilized here. In this first phase of the importance analysis, we identified 134 laws as retrospectively significant during the 2.5-party system, from the start of Carlos Andrés Pérez's first term in 1974 through the end of Caldera's second term at the beginning of 1999.

To capture laws that Phase 1 may have missed and to include laws that do not seem significant from a retrospective assessment but that were considered important at the time of passage, I extended the analysis of important legislation to a second phase. In Phase 2, I used news coverage of legislation at the time of a law's passage to assess whether it was viewed as important contemporaneously. I examined news coverage of legislative activity in one of Venezuela's most widely read national newspapers, *El Nacional*. Surveys conducted throughout the period under analysis consistently place the newspaper as having more readers than any other paper in the country, and *El Nacional* has traditionally had one of the widest circulations.[6] A major national daily such as *El Nacional* is also most likely to influence people's thinking, to be read widely, and to shape media coverage in other sources (Krippendorff 2004, 120). Furthermore, the major print outlets in Venezuela, while politicized, were generally not partisan, at least not during the period examined in the responsiveness analysis in chapter 5 (Coppedge 1994a).[7] *El Nacional*, therefore, provides an influential and relatively balanced source for determining the importance of a piece of legislation at the time of its passage.

To assess the extent of news coverage for each law, I examined the front page of the paper on six critical days related to each law's passage and enactment. These six days were the day Congress passed the law, the day after the law's passage, the day the president signed the law, the day after the president signed the law, the day the law was published in the *Gaceta Oficial*, and the day after its publication.[8] By analyzing the front page of *El Nacional* on these dates, I was able to determine whether there was coverage of the law at several critical moments of the legislative cycle.

This approach follows other analyses of the importance of government activity. Epstein and Segal (2000) analyze front-page coverage in the *New York Times* on the day after the U.S. Supreme Court passed down a case

6. The only other national newspaper with a readership consistently approaching that of *El Nacional* for the period under analysis is *El Universal*. Occasionally during that period, *El Universal* outpaced *El Nacional* as the most widely read paper, but generally *El Nacional* has had a broader readership.

7. This is historically true. However, in the Chávez era, the media has become more divided along partisan lines.

8. In practice, some of these days overlapped, so the average number of days analyzed for each law was actually about 4.5. Laws that were covered and those that were not had about the same average number of dates analyzed.

decision, thereby determining whether the case was important. In comparing their approach to other measures of importance, Epstein and Segal find that using *New York Times* coverage on this relevant date produces unbiased assessments of case importance and that cases widely recognized as important are consistently captured through this method. In my analysis of Venezuelan legislation, I conducted pilot coding (Neuendorf 2002, 133) with an advanced undergraduate student who used preliminary coding guidelines to help code the front page and the first page of *El Nacional*'s political section for one full year (1976). Through that pretest, we found that the overwhelming majority of laws that received coverage at any point during the year received front-page coverage on at least one of the six days of the legislative cycle identified above. Therefore, by limiting analysis to these six relevant dates, we do not miss much relevant news coverage. And the coding task was much more manageable, increasing its reliability.

Also during the pilot test, we coded complete stories for mentions of laws. We found that when a law was the focus of a story, it was consistently mentioned in either the headline or the lead paragraph. When laws appeared deeper in a story, they were often simply mentioned as other laws that were passed by Congress or signed by the president at the same time as the law that was the focus of the coverage. We decided that such mentions were not signals of importance. In the full analysis, therefore, we only read and coded the headlines and lead paragraphs to assess the coverage of each law on the six relevant dates. This analysis of *El Nacional* mirrors the findings of Althaus, Edy, and Phalen (2001) concerning the *New York Times*, in which they found that using headlines and lead paragraphs as a proxy for analysis of complete stories is an appropriate and unbiased approach to content analysis. Thus, the front-page analysis of headlines and lead paragraphs in *El Nacional* on critical dates in the legislative process follows extant literature as a means of measuring contemporaneous importance. Furthermore, our pilot tests indicated that this approach reliably and validly captured the concept of a law's importance at the time of its consideration, passage, and enactment.

Having established that for each law enacted in Venezuela between 1974 and 2003 we would code the headlines and lead paragraphs of the front page of *El Nacional* on six critical dates in the legislative process, we began the final coding.[9] A political science Ph.D. student with advanced college

---

9. The complete codebook and coding instructions are available from the author upon request. A small number of newspapers associated with various laws' important dates were not available. No papers were missing for the first Carlos Andrés Pérez administration. But at least

Spanish skills coded each law enacted during the period according to this schema. This student did not participate in the developmental pilot testing, but simply applied the coding schema according to the instructions I had developed based on the pretest. For each law, this student coder created a database entry for each of the six legislative dates. If the law was mentioned in a front page headline or lead paragraph on that date, the following information was recorded: the story headline, the number of paragraphs in the story, the number of the first paragraph in which the law is mentioned, whether the law is mentioned in the headline, the total number of story paragraphs that discuss or mention the law, and a brief summary of the story's content. A secondary coder with similar qualifications to the first followed the exact same procedure to code 125 randomly selected laws (about 11 percent), for a total of 551 law dates. A third student coded additional missing data made available later in the coding process as well as relevant dates for about three dozen laws that had also been coded by the primary coder to allow for a reliability check of this third student's codes. The reliability coefficient between the three coders for the contemporaneous significance coding was 0.97, representing high intercoder reliability. In cases of lack of agreement, I personally read the paper for the date of disagreement and, based on my reading, finalized the coding. About 70 percent of the cases of disagreement were resolved in favor of the primary coder's decision, and 30 percent were resolved in favor of the second or third coder.

After coding the news coverage for all of the laws, I constructed a database of laws deemed contemporaneously important according to *El Nacional* coverage. Laws were coded as important if they were mentioned on at least one of the six critical dates in either a headline or a lead paragraph on the front page of the paper.[10] This second phase of the analysis identified 116 contemporaneously important laws during the 2.5-party system (1974–99).

---

one paper was missing for 9 non-treaty laws during the Luis Herrera Campíns administration, for 3 non-treaty laws during the Jaime Lusinchi administration, for 9 non-treaty laws during the second Carlos Andrés Pérez administration, and for 2 non-treaty laws during the second Caldera administration. Given the distribution of these missing papers over the entire time period, it is unlikely that their absence had any systematic impact on the findings.

10. I considered ranking importance by weighting laws that were mentioned multiple times as more significant than those that were only mentioned once. However, such a small proportion of laws were mentioned and even fewer received extensive coverage that distinguishing between levels of importance seemed to ask too much of the data.

COMBINING PHASE I AND PHASE 2

In the final step of the importance analysis, I combined the two measures of significance, creating a single indicator. Any law that was coded as retrospectively significant based on expert assessments or coded as contemporaneously significant based on news coverage is treated as a significant piece of legislation. This combined measure of significance identifies 188 important laws during the 2.5-party system between 1974 and 1999.

REFERENCES

Abers, Rebecca. 1996. From ideas to practice: The Partido Dos Trabalhadores and participatory governance in Brazil. *Latin American Perspectives* 23 (4): 35–53.

Abramson, Paul. 1975. *Generational change in American politics.* Lexington: Lexington Books.

AD. 1993. *Proyecto de bases ideológicas y programáticas de Acción Democrática.* Caracas: Talleres Gráficos de LIBERIL and AD.

———. 1994. *Acción Democrática hacia el siglo XXI: Bases ideológicas y programáticas, documento preliminar para discusión.* Caracas: Fundación Nacional de Estudios Políticos Raúl Leoni.

———. 1996. *Estatutos.* Caracas: AD Secretaria Nacional de Organización. Mimeo.

Alcántara Sáez, Manuel, and Juan Pablo Luna. 2004. Ideología y competencia partidaria en dos post-transiciones: Chile y Uruguay en perspectiva comparada. *Revista de Ciencia Política* 24 (1): 128–68.

Aldrich, Howard. 1999. *Organizations evolving.* Thousand Oaks, Calif.: Sage.

Aldrich, John H. 1995. *Why parties? The origin and transformation of political parties in America.* Chicago: University of Chicago Press.

Alexander, Robert J. 1969. *The Communist Party of Venezuela.* Stanford, Calif.: Hoover Institution Press.

Allum, Felia, and Percy Allum. 2008. Revisiting Naples: Clientelism and organized crime. *Journal of Modern Italian Studies* 13 (3): 340–65.

Almeida, Paul D. 2007. Defensive mobilization: Popular movements against economic adjustment policies in Latin America. *Latin American Perspectives* 34 (3): 123–39.

Althaus, Scott L., Jill A. Edy, and Patricia F. Phalen. 2001. Using substitutes for full-text news stories in content analysis: Which text is best? *American Journal of Political Science* 45 (3): 707–23.

Altman, David, and Rossana Castiglioni. 2006. The 2004 Uruguayan elections: A political earthquake foretold. *Electoral Studies* 25 (1): 147–91.

Alvarez, Elena H. 1995. Economic development restructuring and the illicit drug sector in Bolivia and Peru: Current policies. *Journal of Interamerican Studies and World Affairs* 37 (3): 125–49.

Aragort Solórzano, Yubirí. 2004. La democratización en los espacios de poder local y el clientelismo político. *Fermentum* 14 (41): 533–60.

Arboleda, Jairo, and Elena Correa. 2003. Forced internal displacement. In *Colombia: The economic foundations of peace,* ed. Marcelo M. Giugale, Olivier Lafourcade, and Connie Luff, 825–48. Washington, D.C.: International Bank for Reconstruction and Development and World Bank.

Archer, Ronald P. 1995. Party strength and weakness in Colombia's besieged democracy. In *Building democratic institutions: Parties and party systems in Latin America,* ed. Scott Mainwaring and Timothy Scully, 164–99. Stanford: Stanford University Press.

Archer, Ronald P., and Matthew S. Shugart. 1997. The unrealized potential of presidential dominance in Colombia. In *Presidentialism and democracy in Latin America*, ed. Scott Mainwaring and Matthew Shugart, 110–59. New York: Cambridge University Press.

Arriaga, Irma, and Lorena Godoy. 2000. Prevention or repression? The false dilemma of citizen security. *CEPAL Review* 70 (April): 111–36.

Arrow, Kenneth J. 1974. *The limits of organization*. New York: W. W. Norton.

Artana, Daniel, and Ricardo López Murphy. 1994. *Fiscal decentralization: Some lessons for Latin America*. Buenos Aires: Fundación de Investigaciones Económicas Latinoamericanas.

Auyero, Javier. 2000. *Poor people's politics: Peronist survival networks and the legacy of Evita*. Durham: Duke University Press.

Avilés, William. 2006. Paramilitarism and Colombia's low-intensity democracy. *Journal of Latin American Studies* 38:379–408.

Baccaro, Lucio, Mimmo Carrieri, and Cesare Damiano. 2002. *The resurgence of the Italian confederal unions: Will it last?* Labour and Society Programme Discussion Paper. Geneva: International Institute for Labour Studies.

Baloyra, Enrique, and John Martz. 1979. *Political attitudes in Venezuela: Societal cleavages and political opinion*. Austin: University of Texas Press.

Banks, Arthur S. 2010. *Cross-national time-series data archive* [computer file]. Binghamton: Center for Social Analysis, State University of New York.

Baptista, Asdrúbal. 1997. *Bases cuantitativas de la economía venezolana, 1830–1995*. Caracas: Fundación Polar.

———. 2005. El capitalismo rentístico: Elementos cuantitativos de la economía venezolana. *Cuadernos del Cendes* 22 (60): 95–111.

Barnes, Samuel H. 1974. Italy: Religion and class in electoral behavior. In *Electoral behavior: A comparative handbook*, ed. Richard Rose, 171–225. New York: Free Press.

Barr, Robert R. 2005. Bolivia: Another uncompleted revolution. *Latin American Politics and Society* 47 (3): 69–90.

———. 2009. Populists, outsiders, and anti-establishment politics. *Party Politics* 15 (1): 29–48.

Bejarano, Ana María, and Eduardo Pizarro. 2005. From "restricted" to "besieged": The changing nature of the limits to democracy in Colombia. In *The third wave of democratization in Latin America: Advances and setbacks*, ed. Frances Hagopian and Scott P. Mainwaring, 235–60. New York: Cambridge University Press.

Benton, Allyson Lucinda. 2003. Presidentes fuertes, provincias poderosas: La economía política de la construcción de partidos en el sistema federal argentino. *Política y Gobierno* 10 (1): 103–37.

BID (Banco Interamericano de Desarrollo) and PNUD (Programa de las Naciones Unidas para el Desarrollo). 1993. *Reforma social y pobreza: Hacia una agenda integrada de desarrollo*. Washington, D.C.: BID and PNUD.

Birnir, Jóhanna Kristin, and Donna Lee Van Cott. 2007. Disunity in diversity: Party system fragmentation and the dynamic effect of ethnic heterogeneity on Latin American legislatures. *Latin American Research Review* 42 (1): 99–125.

Blair, Harry. 1996. Supporting democratic local governance: Lessons from international donor experience: Initial concepts and some preliminary findings. Paper presented at the annual meeting of the American Political Science Association, San Francisco, 29 August–1 September 1996.

———. 2000. Participation and accountability at the periphery: Democratic local governance in six countries. *World Development* 28 (1): 21–39.

Blake, Charles H. 1998. Economic reform and democratization in Argentina and Uruguay: The tortoise and the hare revisited? *Journal of Interamerican Studies and World Affairs* 40 (3): 1–26.

Blanco Muñoz, Augustín. 1998. *Habla el Comandante Hugo Chávez Frías: Venezuela del 04F-92 al 06D-98.* 2nd ed. Caracas: Fundación Cátedra Pío Tamayo, Centro de Estudios de Historia Actual, IIES, FACES.

Blondel, Jean. 1968. Party systems and patterns of government in western democracies. *Canadian Journal of Political Science* 1 (2): 180–203.

Bohrer, Robert E., III, and Alexander C. Tan. 2000. Left turn in Europe? Reactions to austerity and the EMU. *Political Research Quarterly* 53 (3): 575–95.

Borges Arcila, Welkis. 1996. El consenso en el modelo político venezolano: Crisis y realidad actual. In *Partidos políticos y crisis de la democracia*, ed. Manuel Vicente Magallenes. Caracas: Consejo Supremo Electoral.

Borja, Jordi, ed. 1989. *Estado, descentralización y democracia.* Bogotá: Foro Nacional por Colombia.

Bottome, Robert. 1997. Severance reform: Congressional re-cap. *Veneconomy,* May, 3–5.

———. 1998. Housing and unemployment insurance bills: Rounding out the reform effort. *Veneconomy,* August, 19–20.

Boudon, Lawrence. 2000. Party system deinstitutionalization: The 1997–98 Colombian elections in historical perspective. *Journal of Interamerican Studies and World Affairs* 42 (5): 33–57.

———. 2001. Colombia's M-19 Democratic Alliance: A case study in new party self-destruction. *Latin American Perspectives* 28 (1): 73–92.

Brancati, Dawn. 2008. The origins and strength of regional parties. *British Journal of Political Science* 38 (1): 135–59.

Brando, Jesús Eduardo. 1990. AD quiere ministros de acción social. *El Nacional,* 15 December, D-1.

Brass, Paul R. 1984. National power and local politics in India: A twenty-year perspective. *Modern Asian Studies* 18 (1): 89–118.

———. 1988. The Punjab crisis and the unity of India. In *India's democracy: An analysis of changing state-society relations*, ed. Atul Kohli, 169–213. Princeton: Princeton University Press.

———. 1994. *The politics of India since independence.* 2nd ed. New York: Cambridge University Press.

Brusco, Valeria, Marcelo Nazareno, and Susan C. Stokes. 2004. Vote buying in Argentina. *Latin American Research Review* 39 (2): 6–34.

Brzinski, Joanne Bay. 1999. Federalism and compounded representation in western Europe. *Publius* 29 (1): 45–70.

Budge, Ian, Hans-Dieter Klingemann, Andrea Volkens, Judith Barra, and Eric Tannenbaum. 2001. *Mapping policy preferences: Estimates for parties, electors, and governments, 1945–1998.* New York: Oxford University Press.

Burgess, Katrina, and Steven Levitsky. 2003. Explaining populist party adaptation in Latin America: Environmental and organizational determinants of party change in Argentina, Mexico, Peru, and Venezuela. *Comparative Political Studies* 36 (8): 881–911.

Burnham, Walter Dean. 1970. *Critical elections and the mainsprings of American politics.* New York: W. W. Norton.

Buxton, Julia. 1999a. Venezuela. In *Case studies in Latin American political economy,* ed. Julia Buxton and Nicola Phillips, 162–84. Manchester: Manchester University Press.

———. 1999b. Venezuela: Degenerative democracy. *Democratization* 6 (1): 246–70.

———. 2003. Economic policy and the rise of Hugo Chávez. In *Venezuelan politics in the Chávez era: Class, polarization, and conflict,* ed. Steve Ellner and Daniel Hellinger, 113–30. Boulder, Colo.: Lynne Rienner.

Calvo, Ernesto, and Maria Victoria Murillo. 2004. Who delivers? Partisan clients in the Argentine electoral market. *American Journal of Political Science* 48 (4): 742–57.

Campbell, Timothy. 1993. *Participation, choice, and accountability in local government: LAC and the U.S.* Washington, D.C.: World Bank.

Canache, Damarys. 2002. From bullets to ballots: The emergence of popular support for Hugo Chávez. *Latin American Politics and Society* 44 (1): 69–90.

———. 2007. Urban poor and political order. In *The unraveling of representative democracy in Venezuela,* ed. Jennifer L. McCoy and David J. Myers, 33–49. Baltimore: Johns Hopkins University Press.

Canache Mata, Carlos. 1997. Por qué sobre vive la democracia. *El Nacional,* 19 March, N-0.

Carrillo, Carmen. 1991. Ortodoxos y sindicalistas rechazen reforma de la Ley de Prestaciones. *El Nacional,* 26 June, D-2.

Carrizo, Carla. 1997. Entre el consenso coactivo y el pluralismo político: La Hora del Pueblo y el Pacto de Olivos (1973–1993). *Desarrollo Económico* 37 (147): 389–418.

Carter, Nick. 1998. Italy: The demise of the post-war partyocracy. In *Political parties and the collapse of the old orders,* ed. John Kenneth White and Philip John Davies, 71–94. Albany: State University of New York Press.

Casanovas, R. 1986. El sector informal urbano en Bolivia: Apuntes para un diagnóstico. In *El sector informal en Bolivia,* ed. Leticia Sáinz, 147–78. La Paz: CEDLA.

CEPAL. 2008. Estadísticas e indicadores sociales. CEPALSTAT: Bases de Datos y Publicaciones Estadísticas. División de Estadística y Proyecciones Económicas, CEPAL. http://www.eclac.org/estadisticas/bases/ (accessed 5 May 2008).

Chandler, William M. 1987. Federalism and political parties. In *Federalism and the role of the state,* ed. Herman Bakvis and William M. Chandler, 149–70. Buffalo: University of Toronto Press.

Chandra, Kanchan. 2004. *Why ethnic parties succeed: Patronage and ethnic headcounts in India.* New York: Cambridge University Press.

Chaudhry, Praveen K., Vijay L. Kelkar, and Vikash Yadav. 2004. The evolution of "homegrown conditionality" in India: IMF relations. *Journal of Development Studies* 40 (6): 59–81.

Chen, Linda. 2004. Corporatism under attack? Authoritarianism, democracy, and labor in contemporary Argentina. In *Authoritarianism and corporatism in Latin America—Revisited,* ed. Howard J. Wiarda, 196–217. Gainesville: University Press of Florida.

Cheresky, Isidoro. 1996. Poder hegemónico y alternativas políticas en Argentina. *Nueva Sociedad,* no. 145:21–32.

———. 1998. Argentina: Posibilidades y obstáculos de la alternancia. *Nueva Sociedad,* no. 153:4–14.

Chernick, Marc W. 1998. Party politics, reformism, and political violence in Colombia. *NACLA Report on the Americas* 31 (5): 38–41.

Chhibber, Pradeep K. 1999. *Democracy without associations: Transformation of the party system and social cleavages in India.* Ann Arbor: University of Michigan Press.

Chubb, Judith. 1981. The social bases of an urban political machine: The case of Palermo. *Political Science Quarterly* 96 (1): 107–25.

Cieza, Daniel, and Verónica Beyreuther. 1996. De la cultura del trabajo al estado de malestar: Hiperdesocupación, precaricazión, y daños en el Conurbano Bonaerense. *Cuadernos del IBAP* 9:1–32.

CISOR. 1975. *Procesamiento especial: Encuesta de hogares por muestreo, primer semestere 1975.* Mimeo.

———. 1982. *Procesamiento especial: Encuesta de hogares por muestreo, primer semestere 1982.* Mimeo.

———. 1997. *Procesamiento especial: Encuesta de hogares por muestreo, primer semestere 1997.* Mimeo.

———. 2001. *Procesamiento especial: Encuesta de hogares por muestreo, primer semestere 2001.* Mimeo.

CNE (Consejo Nacional Electoral de Bolivia). 2010. Elecciones generales. http://www .cne.org.bo/ (accessed 14 September 2010).

CODHES. Various dates. *Boletínes informativos.* Bogotá: CODHES. http://www.codhes .org/ (accessed 12 August 2008).

Colazingari, Silvia, and Susan Rose-Ackerman. 1998. Corruption in a paternalistic democracy: Lessons from Italy for Latin America. *Political Science Quarterly* 113 (3): 447–70.

Collier, David. 1995. Trajectory of a concept: "Corporatism" in the study of Latin American politics. In *Latin America in comparative perspective: New approaches to methods and analysis,* ed. Peter Smith, 135–62. Boulder, Colo.: Westview Press.

Collier, Ruth Berins, and David Collier. 1979. Inducements versus constraints: Disaggregating "corporatism." *American Political Science Review* 73 (4): 967–98.

———. 1991. *Shaping the political arena: Critical junctures, the labor movement, and regime dynamics in Latin America.* Princeton: Princeton University Press.

Colmenares, Maria Magdalena. 2004. Exclusión social y diversidad racial y étnica en Venezuela: Temas claves y acciones prioritarias por una sociedad visiblemente más justa. Paper presented at II Encuentro Nacional de Demógrafos y Estudiosos de la Población: Cambio Demográfico y Desigualdad Social en Venezuela al Inicio del Tercer Milenio, Caracas, Venezuela, 24–26 November 2004. Mimeo.

Colomine, Luisana. 1997a. AD intenta mantener imagen de cohesión ante conflicto. *El Nacional,* 21 May, D-2.

———. 1997b. Buró Sindical ratificó anoche tesis del consenso. *El Nacional,* 24 September, D-1.

———. 1997c. Con propósito de autocrítica los adecos dialogan con el país. *El Nacional,* 9 July, D-1.

———. 1997d. Domingo con César Gil. *El Nacional,* 14 September, D-1.

Combellas, Ricardo. 1997. Evaluación de la descentralización. *El Universal,* April 18.

Conaghan, Catherine M. 1995. Politicians against parties: Discord and disconnection in Ecuador's party system. In *Building democratic institutions: Party systems in Latin America,* ed. Scott Mainwaring and Timothy R. Scully, 434–58. Stanford: Stanford University Press.

Conaghan, Catherine M., and James M. Malloy. 1994. *Unsettling statecraft: Democracy and neoliberalism in the central Andes.* Pittsburgh: University of Pittsburgh Press.

COPEI. 1948. *COPEI: Programa y estatutos.* Caracas: Servicio Editorial de COPEI.

————. 1991. *Estatutos: Aprobados por la XIX Convención Nacional del partido.* Caracas: COPEI.

Coppedge, Michael. 1994a. *Strong parties and lame ducks: Presidential partyarchy and factionalism in Venezuela.* Stanford: Stanford University Press.

————. 1994b. Venezuela: Democratic despite presidentialism. In *The failure of presidential democracy,* ed. Juan J. Linz and Arturo Valenzuela, 396–421. Baltimore: Johns Hopkins University Press.

————. 1999. Venezuela: Conservative representation without conservative parties. Working Paper 268, Helen Kellogg Institute for International Studies, University of Notre Dame.

————. 2001. Political Darwinism in Latin America's lost decade. In *Political parties and democracy,* ed. Larry Diamond and Richard Gunther, 173–205. Baltimore: Johns Hopkins University Press.

————. 2005. Explaining democratic deterioration in Venezuela through nested inference. In *The third wave of democratization in Latin America: Advances and setbacks,* ed. Frances Hagopian and Scott P. Mainwaring, 289–316. New York: Cambridge University Press.

COPRE. 1986. *Propuestas para reformas políticas inmediatas.* Caracas: COPRE.

Corrales, Javier. 2002. *Presidents without parties: The politics of economic reform in Venezuela and Argentina in the 1990s.* University Park: Pennsylvania State University Press.

Cotler, Julio. 1995. Political parties and the problems of democratic consolidation in Peru. In *Building democratic institutions: Parties and party systems in Latin America,* ed. Scott Mainwaring and Timothy Scully, 323–53. Stanford: Stanford University Press.

Cox, Gary. 1997. *Making votes count: Strategic coordination in the world's electoral systems.* New York: Cambridge University Press.

Crisp, Brian F. 1996. The rigidity of democratic institutions and the current legitimacy crisis in Venezuela. *Latin American Perspectives* 23 (3): 30–49.

————. 1998a. Institutional design and compromised legitimacy. In *Reinventing legitimacy: Democracy and political change in Venezuela,* ed. Damarys Canache and Michael R. Kulisheck, 21–38. Westport, Conn.: Greenwood Press.

————. 1998b. Presidential decree authority in Venezuela. In *Executive decree authority,* ed. John M. Carey and Matthew Soberg Shugart, 142–71. New York: Cambridge University Press.

————. 2000. *Democratic institutional design: The powers and incentives of Venezuelan politicians and interest groups.* Stanford: Stanford University Press.

Crisp, Brian F., and Rachel E. Ingall. 2002. Institutional engineering and the nature of representation: Mapping the effects of electoral reform in Colombia. *American Journal of Political Science* 46 (4): 733–48.

Crook, Richard C., and James Manor. 1998. *Democracy and decentralisation in South Asia and West Africa: Participation, accountability, and performance.* Cambridge: Cambridge University Press.

D'Alimonte, Roberto, and Stefano Bartolini. 1997. Electoral transition and party system change in Italy. *West European Politics* 20 (1): 110–34.

Dalton, Russell, Scott Flanagan, and Paul Beck, eds. 1984. *Electoral change in advanced industrial democracies: Realignment or dealignment?* Princeton: Princeton University Press.

Daniels, Philip. 1999. Italy: Rupture and regeneration. In *Changing party systems in western Europe*, ed. David Broughton and Mark Donovan, 71–95. New York: Pinter.

Das Gupta, Jyotirindra. 1988. Ethnicity, democracy, and development in India: Assam in a general perspective. In *India's democracy: An analysis of changing state-society relations*, ed. Atul Kohli, 144–68. Princeton: Princeton University Press.

Dávila Ladrón de Guevara, Andrés, and Natalia Delgado Varela. 2002. La metamorfosis del sistema político colombiano: ¿Clientelismo del mercado o nueva forma de intermediación? In *Degradación o cambio: Evolución del sistema político colombiano*, ed. Francisco Gutiérrez, 319–55. Bogotá: Editorial Norma.

Degregori, Carlos Iván, and Romeo Grompone. 1991. *Elecciones 1990: Demonios y redentores en el nuevo Perú: Una tragedia en dos vueltas.* Lima: IEP.

de la Cruz, Rafael. 1992. *Descentralización, gobernabilidad, democracia.* Caracas: Nueva Sociedad/COPRE/UNDP.

———. 2004. Decentralization: Key to understanding a changing nation. In *The unraveling of representative democracy in Venezuela*, ed. Jennifer L. McCoy and David J. Myers, 181–201. Baltimore: Johns Hopkins University Press.

Delgado, Claudia. 1996. Sancionada ordenanza que regula comercio informal. *El Nacional*, 28 November, C-5.

Delgado, Yeneiza. 1998. Alfaro: El próximo presidente será adeco. *El Nacional*, 6 March, D-1.

della Sala, Vincent. 1993. The permanent committees of the Italian Chamber of Deputies: Parliament at work? *Legislative Studies Quarterly* 18 (2): 157–83.

———. 1997. Hollowing out and hardening the state: European integration and the Italian economy. *West European Politics* 20 (1): 14–33.

de los Ángeles Fernández, María. 2001. Venezuela: De la "ilusión de armonía" a la cuasianomia social. *Estudios Avanzados Interactivos* 1 (1): 1–4. http://web.usach.cl/revistaidea/html/revista%201/html/pdf/fernandez.pdf (accessed 17 January 2009).

de Micheli, Chiara. 1997. L'attività legislativa dei governi al tramonto della Prima Repubblica. *Rivista italiana di scienza politica* 27 (1): 151–87.

Deschouwer, Kris. 1994. The decline of consociationalism and the reluctant modernization of Belgian mass parties. In *How parties organize: Change and adaptation in party organizations in western democracies*, ed. Richard S. Katz and Peter Mair, 80–108. Thousand Oaks, Calif.: Sage.

DeWachter, Wilfried. 1987. Changes in a particratie: The Belgian party system from 1944 to 1986. In *Party systems in Denmark, Austria, Switzerland, The Netherlands, and Belgium*, ed. Hans Daadler, 285–363. New York: St. Martin's Press.

DeWinter, Lieven. 2006. Multilevel party competition and coordination in Belgium. In *Devolution and electoral politics*, ed. Dan Hough and Charlie Jeffrey, 76–95. Manchester: Manchester University Press.

Diamond, Larry. 1999. *Developing democracy: Toward consolidation.* Baltimore: Johns Hopkins University Press.

Diamond, Larry, Jonathan Hartlyn, and Juan J. Linz. 1999. Introduction: Politics, society, and democracy in Latin America. In *Democracy in developing countries: Latin America*, ed. Larry Diamond, Jonathan Hartlyn, Juan J. Linz, and Seymour Martin Lipset, 1–70. 2nd ed. Boulder, Colo.: Lynne Rienner.

Diamond, Larry, with Svetlana Tsalik. 1999. Size and democracy: The case for decentralization. In *Developing democracy: Toward consolidation*, 117–60. Baltimore: Johns Hopkins University Press.

Diani, Mario. 1996. Linking mobilization frames and political opportunities: Insights from regional populism in Italy. *American Sociological Review* 61 (6): 1053–69.

Díaz, Rolando. 2000. Sindicatos y nuevo escenario político en Venezuela. *Nueva Sociedad* 169 (Sept.–Oct.): 153–61.

Dietz, Henry A., and David J. Myers. 2007. From thaw to deluge: Party system collapse in Venezuela and Peru. *Latin American Politics and Society* 49 (2): 59–86.

Dillinger, William R. 1994. *Decentralization and its implications for urban service delivery*. Washington, D.C.: World Bank.

Di Palma, Guiseppe. 1977. *Surviving without governing: The Italian parties in Parliament*. Berkeley: University of California Press.

Dittrich, Karl. 1983. Testing the catch-all thesis: Some difficulties and possibilities. In *Western European party systems: Continuity and change*, ed. Hans Daalder and Peter Mair, 257–66. Beverley Hills, Calif.: Sage.

Dix, Robert H. 1987. *The politics of Colombia*. New York: Praeger.

———. 1992. Democratization and the institutionalization of Latin American political parties. *Comparative Political Studies* 24 (4): 488–511.

Domingo, Pilar. 2001. Party politics, intermediation, and representation. In *Towards democratic viability: The Bolivian experience*, ed. John Crabtree and Laurence Whitehead, 141–59. New York: Palgrave.

Dora Medina, S. 1986. *La economía informal en Bolivia*. La Paz: Editorial Offset Boliviana.

Downs, Anthony. 1957. *An economic theory of democracy*. New York: Harper and Row.

Dugas, John C. 2003. The emergence of neopopulism in Colombia? The case of Álvaro Uribe. *Third World Quarterly* 24 (6): 1117–36.

Durán, Milagros. 1998. Sostiene Pedro Pablo Aguilar, envez de renegar de Irene COPEI debe fortalecerla. *El Nacional*, 30 October, D-2.

Durán López, Milagros. 1996. Responde Héctor Alonso López. *El Nacional*, 19 January, N-0.

Duverger, Maurice. 1954. *Political parties: Their organization and activity in the modern state*. Translated by Barbara North and Robert North. New York: Wiley.

ECB (European Central Bank). 2008. Economic and Monetary Union (EMU). European Central Bank. http://www.ecb.int/ecb/history/emu/html/index.en.html (accessed 16 June 2008).

ECI (Electoral Commission of India). Various dates. *Statistical reports of Lok Sabha elections*. New Delhi: ECI. http://www.eci.gov.in/StatisticalReports/ElectionStatis tics.asp (accessed 15 September 2008).

Eckstein, Harry. 1975. Case study and theory in political science. In *Handbook of political science*, ed. Fred Greenstein and Nelson Polsby, vol. 7, *Strategies of inquiry*, 79–138. Reading, Mass.: Addison-Wesley.

ECLAC. 1987. *Economic survey of Latin America and the Caribbean, 1985*. Santiago, Chile: United Nations.

———. 2009. CEPALSTAT. United Nations. http://www.eclac.org/estadisticas/ (accessed July 23, 2009).

Ellner, Steve. 1988. *Venezuela's Movimiento al Socialismo: From guerrilla defeat to innovative politics*. Durham: Duke University Press.

———. 1993. *Organizing labor in Venezuela, 1958–1991: Behavior and concerns in a democratic setting*. Wilmington, Del.: Scholarly Resources.

———. 1995. *El sindicalismo en Venezuela en el contexto democrático (1958–1994)*. Caracas: Fondo Editorial Tropykos.

———. 1996. Political party factionalism and democracy in Venezuela. *Latin American Perspectives* 23 (3): 87–109.

———. 2003. Organized labor and the challenge of *chavismo*. In *Venezuelan politics in the Chávez era: Class, polarization, and conflict*, ed. Steve Ellner and Daniel Hellinger, 161–78. Boulder, Colo.: Lynne Rienner.

Epstein, Lee, and Jeffrey A. Segal. 2000. Measuring issue salience. *American Journal of Political Science* 44 (1): 66–83.

Erikson, Robert S., Michael B. MacKuen, and James A. Stimson. 2002. *The macro polity*. New York: Cambridge University Press.

Escalante, Ricardo. 1997. AD prohibió campañas de sus precandidatos. *El Nacional*, 28 January, D-2.

———. 1998. En AD cobra fuerza la tesis de escoger candidato. *El Nacional*, 23 February, D-2.

Escobar, Cristina. 2002. Clientelism and citizenship: The limits of democratic reform in Sucre, Colombia. *Latin American Perspectives* 29 (5): 20–47.

Escobar-Lemmon, María. 2001. Fiscal decentralization and federalism in Latin America. *Publius* 31 (4): 23–41.

———. 2003. Political support for decentralization: An analysis of the Colombian and Venezuelan legislatures. *American Journal of Political Science* 47 (4): 683–97.

———. 2006. Executives, legislatures, and decentralization. *Policy Studies Journal* 34 (2): 245–63.

Espíndola, Roberto. 2001. No change in Uruguay: The 1999 presidential and parliamentary elections. *Electoral Studies* 20 (4): 649–57.

Eubank, William Lee, Arun Gangopadahay, and Leonard B. Weinberg. 1996. Italian communism in crisis: A study in exit, voice, and loyalty. *Party Politics* 2 (1): 55–75.

Eulau, Heinz, and Kenneth Prewitt. 1973. *Labyrinths of democracy: Adaptations, linkages, representation, and policies in urban politics*. New York: Bobbs-Merrill.

Fabbrini, Sergio. 2000. Political change without institutional transformation: What can we learn from the Italian crisis of the 1990s? *International Political Science Review (Revue internationale de science politique)* 21 (2): 173–96.

Faguet, Jean-Paul. 2001. *Does decentralization increase responsiveness to local needs? Evidence from Bolivia*. Washington, D.C.: World Bank.

Falleti, Tulia G. 2005. A sequential theory of decentralization: Latin American cases in comparative perspective. *American Political Science Review* 99 (3): 327–46.

———. 2010. *Decentralization and subnational politics in Latin America*. New York: Cambridge University Press.

Fan, David P. 1988. *Predictions of public opinion from the mass media: Computer content analysis and mathematical modeling*. New York: Greenwood Press.

Farneti, Paolo. 1983. *Il sistema dei partiti in Italia 1946–1979*. Bologna: Il Mulino.

Farrell, Michelle L. 2007. Sequencing: Targeting insurgents and drugs in Colombia. Master's thesis, Naval Postgraduate School.

Fernández, Yajaira. 2003. Gasto público social en Venezuela: Respuestas institucionales a las funciones del gasto público y una revisión empírica del gasto social en Venezuela. Working paper, Programa de las Naciones Unidas para el Desarrollo (PNUD) and Cooperación Técnica Alemana and Ministerio de Salud y Desarrollo Social. Mimeo.

Fiorina, Morris P. 1981. *Retrospective voting in American national elections.* New Haven: Yale University Press.

Forno, Francesca. 2003. Protest in Italy during the 1990s. Paper written for the workshop "New Social Movements and Protest in Southern Europe," Edinburgh, Scotland, 28 March–2 April 2003.

Fornos, Carolina, Timothy J. Power, and James C. Garand. 2004. Explaining voter turnout in Latin America, 1980 to 2000. *Comparative Political Studies* 37 (8): 909–40.

Fox, Jonathan. 1994. Latin America's emerging local politics. *Journal of Democracy* 5 (2): 105–16.

Franklin, Charles H., and John E. Jackson. 1983. The dynamics of party identification. *American Political Science Review* 77 (4): 957–71.

Franklin, M. N. 1999. Electoral engineering and cross-national turnout differences: What role for compulsory voting? *British Journal of Political Science* 29 (1): 205–24.

FRL (Fundación Nacional de Estudios Políticos Raúl Leoni). 1997. *Programa nacional para el desarrollo social y económico sustentable: Lineamientos generales.* Caracas: Fundación Nacional de Estudios Políticos Raúl Leoni.

Frognier, Andre-Paul. 1978. Parties and cleavages in the Belgian parliament. *Legislative Studies Quarterly* 3 (1): 109–31.

Furlong, Paul. 1990. Parliament in Italian politics. *West European Politics* 13 (3): 52–67.

Gallagher, Michael, Michael Laver, and Peter Mair. 1995. *Representative government in modern Europe.* New York: McGraw-Hill.

Gamarra, Eduardo A., and James M. Malloy. 1995. The patrimonial dynamics of party politics in Bolivia. In *Building democratic institutions: Party systems in Latin America*, ed. Scott Mainwaring and Timothy R. Scully, 399–433. Stanford: Stanford University Press.

García-Guadilla, María Pilar. 2003. Civil society: Institutionalization, fragmentation, autonomy. In *Venezuelan politics in the Chávez era: Class, polarization, and conflict*, ed. Steve Ellner and Daniel Hellinger, 179–96. Boulder, Colo.: Lynne Rienner.

García-Guadilla, María Pilar, and Carlos Pérez. 2002. Democracy, decentralization, and clientelism: New relationships and old practices. *Latin American Perspectives* 29 (5): 90–109.

Garfield, Elsie, and Jairo Arboleda. 2003. Violence, sustainable peace, and development. In *Colombia: The economic foundations of peace*, ed. Marcelo M. Giugale, Olivier Lafourcade, and Connie Luff, 35–58. Washington, D.C.: International Bank for Reconstruction and Development and World Bank.

Gaviria, Alejandro, and Carmen Pagés. 1999. Patterns of crime victimization in Latin America. Working Paper 408, Inter-American Development Bank, Washington, D.C.

Geddes, Barbara. 1994. *Politician's dilemma: Building state capacity in Latin America.* Berkeley: University of California Press.

George, Alexander. 1979. Case studies and theory development: The method of structured, focused comparison. In *Diplomacy: New approaches in history, theory, and policy*, ed. Paul Gordon Lauren, 43–68. New York: Free Press.

George, Alexander, and Andrew Bennett. 2005. *Case studies and theory development in the social sciences.* Cambridge: MIT Press.

Gibson, Edward L. 1996. *Class and conservative parties: Argentina in comparative perspective.* Baltimore: Johns Hopkins University Press.

Gibson, Edward L., and Ernesto Calvo. 2000. Federalism and low-maintenance constituencies: Territorial dimensions of economic reform in Argentina. *Studies in Comparative International Development* 35 (3): 32–55.

Gilbert, Mark. 1995. *The Italian revolution: The end of politics, Italian style?* Boulder, Colo.: Westview Press.

Gill, Lesley. 2000. *Teetering on the rim: Global restructuring, daily life, and the armed retreat of the Bolivian state.* New York: Columbia University Press.

Goertz, Gary. 2006. *Social science concepts: A user's guide.* Princeton: Princeton University Press.

Goertz, Gary, and James Mahoney. 2005. Two-level theories and fuzzy set analysis. *Sociological Methods and Research* 33 (4): 497–538.

Golbert, Laura. 1996. Viejos y nuevos problemas de las políticas asistenciales. *CECE: Serie Estudios* 12:1–41.

Golden, Miriam. 1986. Interest representation, party systems, and the state: Italy in comparative perspective. *Comparative Politics* 18 (3): 279–301.

Golden, Miriam, and Lucio Picci. 2008. Pork-barrel politics in postwar Italy, 1953–94. *American Journal of Political Science* 52 (2): 268–89.

Goldfrank, Benjamin. 2011. *Participation, decentralization, and the left: Deepening local democracy in Latin America.* University Park: Pennsylvania State University Press.

Gómez Calcaño, Luis. 1998. Redefining the state's social policies: The case of Venezuela. In *The changing role of the state in Latin America*, ed. Menno Vellinga, 213–38. Boulder, Colo.: Westview Press.

Gómez Calcaño, Luis, and Margarita López Maya. 1990. *El tejido de Penélope: La reforma del estado en Venezuela, 1984–1988.* Caracas: CENDES.

González, Luis E. 1995. Continuity and change in the Uruguayan party system. In *Building democratic institutions: Parties and party systems in Latin America*, ed. Scott Mainwaring and Timothy Scully, 138–63. Stanford: Stanford University Press.

———. 1999. Los partidos establecidos y sus desafiantes. In *Los partidos políticos uruguayos en tiempos de cambio*, ed. Luis E. González, Felipe Montesier, Rosario Quierolo, and Mariana Sotelo Rico, 9–18. Montevideo: Fundación de Cultura Universitaria.

Gray-Molina, George. 2001. Exclusion, participation, and democratic state-building. In *Towards democratic viability: The Bolivian experience*, ed. John Crabtree and Laurence Whitehead, 63–82. New York: Palgrave.

Greene, Kenneth F. 2007. *Why dominant parties lose: Mexico's democratization in comparative perspective.* New York: Cambridge University Press.

Grindle, Merilee S. 2000. *Audacious reforms: Institutional invention and democracy in Latin America.* Baltimore: Johns Hopkins University Press.

Grzymala-Busse, Anna Maria. 2002. *Redeeming the communist past: The regeneration of communist parties in East Central Europe.* New York: Cambridge University Press.

Gutiérrez Sanín, Francisco. 2007. *Lo que el viento se llevó? Los partidos políticos y la democracia en Colombia, 1958–2002.* Bogotá: Editorial Norma.

Gwartney, James, Robert Lawson, and Walter Block. 1996. *Economic freedom of the world, 1975–1995.* Vancouver: Fraser Institute.

Hagopian, Frances. 1998. Democracy and political representation in Latin America in the 1990s: Pause, reorganization, or decline? In *Fault lines of democracy in post-transition Latin America*, ed. Felipe Agüero and Jeffrey Stark, 99–143. Coral

Gables, Fla.: North-South Center Press, University of Miami; Boulder, Colo.: Lynne Rienner.

Hale, Henry E. 2007. Correlates of clientelism: Political economy, politicized ethnicity, and post-communist transition. In *Patrons, clients, and policies: Patterns of democratic accountability and political competition*, ed. Herbert Kitschelt and Steven I. Wilkinson, 227–50. New York: Cambridge University Press.

Hannan, Michael T., and Glenn R. Carroll. 1995. An introduction to organizational ecology. In *Organization in industry: Strategy, structure, and selection*, ed. Glenn R. Carroll and Michael T. Hannan, 17–31. New York: Oxford University Press.

Harbers, Imke. 2009. Growing apart or staying together? Multilevel politics and party cohesiveness in Mexico. Paper presented at the annual meeting of the Midwest Political Science Association, Chicago, 2–5 April 2009.

———. 2010. Decentralization and the development of nationalized party systems in new democracies: Evidence from Latin America. *Comparative Political Studies* 43 (5): 606–27.

Hartlyn, Jonathan. 1988. *The politics of coalition rule in Colombia*. New York: Cambridge University Press.

———. 1996. Latin America's parties. Review of *Building democratic institutions: Party systems in Latin America*, by Scott Mainwaring and Timothy R. Scully. *Journal of Democracy* 7 (4): 174–77.

Hartlyn, Jonathan, and John Dugas. 1999. Colombia: The politics of violence and democratic transformation. In *Democracy in developing countries: Latin America*, ed. Larry Diamond, Jonathan Hartlyn, Juan J. Linz, and Seymour Martin Lipset, 249–307. 2nd ed. Boulder, Colo.: Lynne Rienner.

Hausman, Jerry A., and Daniel McFadden. 1984. Specification tests for the multinomial logit model. *Econometrica* 52 (5): 1219–40.

Hawkins, Kirk A. 2003. Populism in Venezuela: The rise of *chavismo*. *Third World Quarterly* 24 (6): 1137–60.

———. 2010. *Venezuela's chavismo and populism in comparative perspective*. New York: Cambridge University Press.

Heisler, Martin O. 1974. Institutionalizing societal cleavages in a cooptive polity: The growing importance of the output side in Belgium. In *Politics in Europe: Structures and processes in some post-industrial democracies*, ed. Martin O. Heisler, 178–220. New York: David McKay.

———. 1977. Managing ethnic conflict in Belgium. *Annals of the American Academy of Political and Social Science* 433 (Sept.): 32–46.

Heller, William B., and Carol Mershon. 2005. Party switching in the Italian Chamber of Deputies, 1996–2001. *Journal of Politics* 67 (2): 536–59.

Hellinger, Daniel. 1996. The Causa R and the *nuevo sindicalismo* in Venezuela. *Latin American Perspectives* 90 (23): 110–31.

———. 2003. Political overview: The breakdown of *puntofijismo* and the rise of *chavismo*. In *Venezuelan politics in the Chávez era: Class, polarization, and conflict*, ed. Steve Ellner and Daniel Hellinger, 27–53. Boulder, Colo.: Lynne Rienner.

Hellman, Stephen. 1988. *Italian communism in transition: The rise and fall of the historical compromise in Turin, 1975–1980*. New York: Oxford University Press.

Herman, Donald. 1980. *Christian democracy in Venezuela*. Chapel Hill: University of North Carolina Press.

Hertog, James K., and David P. Fan. 1995. The impact of press coverage on social beliefs. *Communication Research* 22 (5): 545–74.

Hillman, Richard S. 1994. *Democracy for the privileged: Crisis and transition in Venezuela.* Boulder, Colo.: Lynne Rienner.

Hinich, Melvin, and Michael Munger. 1994. *Ideology and the theory of political choice.* Ann Arbor: University of Michigan Press.

Hochstetler, Kathryn, and Albert Palma. 2009. Globalization, social mobilization, and partisan politics in Latin America. Paper presented at the annual meeting of the Midwest Political Science Association, Chicago, 2–5 April 2009.

Hooghe, Liesbet. 1991. A leap in the dark: Nationalist conflict and federal reform in Belgium. Occasional Paper 27, Western Societies Program, Cornell University.

Hopkin, Jonathan, and Alfio Mastropaolo. 2001. From patronage to clientelism: Comparing the Italian and Spanish experiences. In *Clientelism, interests, and democratic representation: The European experience in comparative and historical perspective,* ed. Simona Piattoni, 152–71. New York: Cambridge University Press.

Hurley, Patricia A. 1989. Partisan representation and the failure of realignment in the 1980s. *American Journal of Political Science* 33 (1): 240–61.

Huther, Jeff, and Anwar Shah. 1999. Applying a simple measure of good governance to the debate on fiscal decentralization. World Bank Policy Research Working Paper 1894, Washington, D.C.

ILO. 1985. *World labour report.* Vol. 2, *Labour relations, international labour standards, training, conditions of work, women at work.* Geneva: ILO.

———. 1987a. *World labour report.* Vols. 1–2. New York: Oxford University Press.

———. 1987b. *World labour report.* Vol. 3, *Incomes from work: Between equity and efficiency.* New York: Oxford University Press.

———. 1997. *World labour report: Industrial relations, democracy, and social stability.* Geneva: ILO.

———. 1998. *OIT informa: Panorama laboral.* Lima: International Labour Organization Statistical Annex.

———. 2001. *Key indicators of the labour report: 2001–2002.* Geneva: ILO.

———. 2009. LABORSTA. http://laborsta.ilo.org/ (accessed 13 February 2009).

IMF. 2004. *Government financial statistics yearbook.* Vol. 28. Washington, D.C.: IMF.

INE (Bolivia). 2008. Indicadores de empleo. http://www.ine.gov.bo/indice/ (accessed 5 December 2008).

INE (Uruguay). 2005. Indicadores de actividad económica. http://www.ine.gub.uy (accessed 15 September 2008).

Iranzo, Consuelo. 1994. Los actores sociales ante la reestructuración productiva en Venezuela: Consecuencias sobre el mercado de trabajo y la acción sindical. In *Nuevo paradigma productivo, flexibilidad y respuestas sindicales en América Latina,* ed. Julio C. Neffa, 25–49. Buenos Aires: Ediciones de Trabajo y Sociedad.

Iranzo, Consuelo, and Thanali Patruyo. 2001. Consecuencias de la reestructuración económica y política en el sindicalismo venezolano. *Cuadernos del CENDES* 18 (47): 233–72.

Isacson, Adam. 2002. Colombia's human security crisis. *Disarmament Forum,* 2002, no. 2:25–40.

Morales Paúl, Isidro. 1996. Los partidos políticos y la democracia. In *Partidos políticos y crisis de la democracia,* ed. Manuel Vicente Magallenes. Caracas: Publicaciones del Consejo Supremo Electoral.

Jones, Mark. 1997. Federalism and the number of parties in Argentine congressional elections. *Journal of Politics* 59 (2): 538–49.

Kada, Naoko. 2003. Impeachment as a punishment for corruption? The cases of Brazil and Venezuela. In *Checking executive power: Presidential impeachment in comparative perspective*, ed. Jody C. Baumgartner and Naoko Kada, 113–36. Westport, Conn.: Praeger.

Kapur, Devesh. 2000. India in 1999. *Asian Survey* 40 (1): 195–207.

Karl, Terry Lynn. 1986. Petroleum and political pacts: The transition to democracy in Venezuela. In *Transitions from authoritarian rule: Latin America*, ed. Guillermo O'Donnell, Philippe C. Schmitter, and Laurence Whitehead, 196–219. Baltimore: Johns Hopkins University Press.

———. 1997. *The paradox of plenty: Oil booms and petro-states*. Berkeley: University of California Press.

Kelley, R. Lynn. 1986. Constitutional forms and realities. In *Venezuela: The democratic experience*, ed. John D. Martz and David J. Myers. 2nd ed. New York: Praeger.

Kelly, Jana Morgan. 2003. Counting on the past or investing in the future? Economic and political accountability in Fujimori's Peru. *Journal of Politics* 65 (3): 864–80.

———. 2005. Failing to represent: The collapse of the Venezuelan party system. Ph.D. diss., University of North Carolina at Chapel Hill.

———. 2006. Party system transformation: Conceptualizing the Venezuelan case. Paper presented at the annual meeting of the Midwest Political Science Association, Chicago, 20–23 April 2006.

Kennedy, Peter. 1998. *A guide to econometrics*. Cambridge, Mass.: MIT Press.

Kenney, Charles. 2000. The collapse of the Peruvian party system: Cleavages, institutionalization, and political elites. Unpublished paper, University of Oklahoma.

Kertzer, David I. 1996. *Politics and symbols: The Italian Communist Party and the fall of communism*. New Haven: Yale University Press.

Key, V. O. 1955. A theory of critical elections. *Journal of Politics* 17 (1): 3–18.

King, Gary, Joseph Honaker, Anne Joseph, and Kenneth Scheve. 2001. Analyzing incomplete political science data: An alternative algorithm for multiple imputation. *American Political Science Review* 95 (1): 49–69.

King, Gary, Robert Keohane, and Sydney Verba. 1994. *Designing social inquiry: Scientific inquiry in qualitative research*. Princeton: Princeton University Press.

King, Gary, Michael Tomz, and Jason Wittenberg. 2000. Making the most of statistical analyses: Improving interpretation and presentation. *American Journal of Political Science* 44 (2): 347–61.

Kirchheimer, Otto. 1966. The transformation of west European party systems. In *Political parties and political development*, ed. Joseph LaPalombara and Myron Weiner, 177–200. Princeton: Princeton University Press.

Kitschelt, Herbert. 1994. *The transformation of European social democracy*. New York: Cambridge University Press.

———. 1995. *The radical right in western Europe: A comparative analysis*. Ann Arbor: University of Michigan Press.

———. 2000. Linkages between citizens and politicians in democratic polities. *Comparative Political Studies* 33 (6–7): 845–79.

Kitschelt, Herbert, Kirk A. Hawkins, Juan Pablo Luna, Guillermo Rosas, and Elizabeth J. Zechmeister. 2010. *Latin American party systems*. New York: Cambridge University Press.

Kitschelt, Herbert, Zdenka Mansfeldova, Radoslaw Markowski, and Gábor Tóka. 1999. *Post-communist party systems: Competition, representation, and inter-party cooperation*. New York: Cambridge University Press.

Kitschelt, Herbert, and Steven I. Wilkinson. 2007a. Citizen-politician linkages: An introduction. In *Patrons, clients, and policies: Patterns of democratic accountability and political competition*, ed. Herbert Kitschelt and Steven I. Wilkinson, 1–49. New York: Cambridge University Press.

———. 2007b. A research agenda for the study of citizen-politician linkages and democratic accountability. In *Patrons, clients, and policies: Patterns of democratic accountability and political competition*, ed. Herbert Kitschelt and Steven I. Wilkinson, 322–43. New York: Cambridge University Press.

Kline, Harvey F. 1988. From rural to urban society: The transformation of Colombian democracy. In *Democracy in Latin America: Colombia and Venezuela*, ed. Donald L. Herman, 17–46. Westport, Conn.: Praeger.

———. 2004. Colombia: Pluralism and corporatism in a weak state. In *Authoritarianism and corporatism in Latin America—Revisited*, ed. Howard J. Wiarda, 173–96. Gainesville: University Press of Florida.

Knight, Alan. 1998. Populism and neo-populism in Latin America, especially Mexico. *Journal of Latin American Studies* 30: 223–48.

Knutsen, Oddbjorn. 2004. Religious denomination and party choice in western Europe: A comparative longitudinal study from eight countries, 1970–1997. *International Political Science Review* 25 (1): 97–128.

Koeneke, Herbert. 1998. Congressional report card: A failure, and little to learn from. *Veneconomy*, September, 15–16.

Kohli, Atul. 1988. Interpreting India's democracy: A state-society framework. In *India's democracy: An analysis of changing state-society relations*, ed. Atul Kohli, 3–17. Princeton: Princeton University Press.

Kondonassis, A. J., and A. G. Malliaris. 1994. Toward monetary union of the European Community: History and experiences of the European Monetary System. *American Journal of Economics and Sociology* 53 (3): 291–301.

Kornblith, Miriam. 1998a. Legitimacy and the reform agenda in Venezuela. In *Reinventing legitimacy: Democracy and political change in Venezuela*, ed. Michael R. Kulisheck and Damarys Canache, 3–20. Westport, Conn.: Greenwood Press.

———. 1998b. *Venezuela en los 90: Las crisis de la democracia*. Caracas: Ediciones IESA.

Kornblith, Miriam, and Daniel Levine. 1995. Venezuela: The life and times of the party system. In *Building democratic institutions: Parties and party systems in Latin America*, ed. Scott Mainwaring and Timothy Scully, 37–71. Stanford: Stanford University Press.

Kothari, Rajni. 1964. The Congress "system" in India. *Asian Survey* 4 (12): 1161–73.

Kreppel, Amie. 1997. The impact of parties in government on legislative output in Italy. *European Journal of Political Research* 31 (3): 327–50.

Krippendorff, Klaus. 2004. *Content analysis: An introduction to its methodology*. Thousand Oaks, Calif.: Sage.

Krishna, Anirudh. 2007. Politics in the middle: Mediating relationships between the citizens and the state in rural north India. In *Patrons, clients, and policies: Patterns of democratic accountability and political competition*, ed. Herbert Kitschelt and Steven I. Wilkinson, 141–58. New York: Cambridge University Press.

Kulisheck, Michael R., and Damarys Canache. 1998. Democratic legitimacy and political change in Venezuela. In *Reinventing legitimacy: Democracy and political change in Venezuela*, ed. Michael R. Kulisheck and Damarys Canache, 39–50. Westport, Conn.: Greenwood Press.

Laakso, Markuu, and Rein Taagepera. 1979. Effective number of parties: A measure with application to West Europe. *Comparative Political Studies* 12 (1): 3–27.

Lalander, Rickard O. 2004. *Suicide of the elephants? Venezuelan decentralization between partyarchy and chavismo.* Helsinki: Renvall Institute for Area and Cultural Studies; Stockholm: Institute of Latin American Studies.

Landé, Carl. 1973. Networks and groups in Southeast Asia: Some observations on the group theory of politics. *American Political Science Review* 67 (1): 103–27.

Lander, Edgardo. 1996. The impact of neoliberal adjustment in Venezuela, 1989–1993. Translated by Luis A. Fierro. *Latin American Perspectives* 23 (3): 50–73.

Langston, Joy. 2009. Party organizational change. In Symposium: Concepts that hinder understanding . . . and what to do about them. *APSA-CP Newsletter* 20 (2): 11.

Lanzaro, Jorge. 2004. *La izquierda uruguaya: Entre la oposición y el gobierno.* Montevideo: Instituto de Ciencia Política.

———. 2007. The Uruguayan party system: Transition within transition. In *When parties prosper: The uses of electoral success,* ed. Kay Lawson and Peter H. Merkl, 117–37. Boulder, Colo.: Lynne Rienner.

LaPalombara, Joseph. 1987. *Democracy, Italian style.* New Haven: Yale University Press.

LAPOP. 2004a. *Auditoria de la democracia: Bolivia 2004.* http://lapop.ccp.ucr.ac.cr (accessed 30 October 2008).

———. 2004b. *Auditoria de la democracia: Colombia 2004.* http://lapop.ccp.ucr.ac.cr (accessed 30 October 2008).

———. 2006. *Auditoria de la democracia: Bolivia 2006.* http://lapop.ccp.ucr.ac.cr (accessed 31 October 2008).

Latin American Weekly Report. 2000. 29 February, 99.

Lawson, Kay, ed. 1980. *Political parties and linkage: A comparative perspective.* New Haven: Yale University Press.

———. 1988. When linkage fails. In *When parties fail: Emerging alternative organizations,* ed. Kay Lawson and Peter H. Merkl, 13–38. Princeton: Princeton University Press.

Lawson, Kay, and Peter H. Merkl, eds. 1988. *When parties fail: Emerging alternative organizations.* Princeton: Princeton University Press.

Leal Perdomo, Adela. 1997a. Claudio Fermín: Acallar a las mayorías es una negación. *El Nacional,* 13 September, D-2.

———. 1997b. Con amenaza de renuncia Alfaro logró total respaldo. *El Nacional,* 9 December, D-1.

Leonardi, Robert. 1980. Political power linkages in Italy: The nature of the Christian Democratic Party organization. In *Political parties and linkage: A comparative perspective,* ed. Kay Lawson, 243–65. New Haven: Yale University Press.

Leonardi, Robert, and Douglas A. Wertman. 1989. *Italian Christian Democracy: The politics of dominance.* New York: St. Martin's Press.

Levine, Daniel H. 1973. *Conflict and political change in Venezuela.* Princeton: Princeton University Press.

———. 1998. Beyond the exhaustion of the model: Survival and transformation of democracy in Venezuela. In *Reinventing legitimacy: Democracy and political change in Venezuela,* ed. Damarys Canache and Michael Kulisheck, 187–214. Westport, Conn.: Greenwood Press.

Levine, Daniel H., and Brian Crisp. 1999. Venezuela: The character, crisis, and possible future democracy. In *Democracy in developing countries: Latin America,* ed.

Larry Diamond, Jonathan Hartlyn, Juan Linz, and Seymour Martin Lipset, 367–427. 2nd ed. Boulder, Colo.: Lynne Rienner.

Levite, Ariel, and Sidney Tarrow. 1983. The legitimation of excluded parties in dominant party systems: A comparison of Israel and Italy. *Comparative Politics* 15 (3): 295–327.

Levitsky, Steven. 2000. The "normalization" of Argentine politics. *Journal of Democracy* 11 (2): 56–69.

———. 2001a. An "organised disorganisation": Informal organisation and the persistence of local party structures in Argentine Peronism. *Journal of Latin American Studies* 33 (1): 29–65.

———. 2001b. Organization and labor-based party adaptation: The transformation of Argentine Peronism in comparative perspective. *World Politics* 54 (1): 27–56.

———. 2003a. From labor politics to machine politics: The transformation of party-union linkages in Argentine Peronism, 1983–1999. *Latin American Research Review* 38 (3): 3–36.

———. 2003b. *Transforming labor-based parties in Latin America: Argentine Peronism in comparative perspective.* New York: Cambridge University Press.

———. 2007. From populism to clientelism: The transformation of labor-based party linkages in Latin America. In *Patrons, clients, and policies: Patterns of democratic accountability and political competition,* ed. Herbert Kitschelt and Steven I. Wilkinson, 206–26. New York: Cambridge University Press.

Linz, Juan J. 1990. The perils of presidentialism. *Journal of Democracy* 1 (1): 51–69.

Lipset, Seymour Martin, and Stein Rokkan. 1967. Cleavage structures, party systems, and voter alignments. In *Party systems and voter alignments: Cross-national perspectives,* ed. Seymour Martin Lipset and Stein Rokkan, 1–64. New York: Free Press.

López Maya, Margarita. 1997. The rise of Causa R in Venezuela. In *The new politics of inequality in Latin America: Rethinking participation and representation,* ed. Douglas A. Chalmers, Carlos M. Vilas, Katherine Hite, Scott B. Martin, Kerianne Piester, and Monique Segarra, 117–43. Oxford: Oxford University Press.

———. 2003. Hugo Chávez Frías: His movement and his presidency. In *Venezuelan politics in the Chávez era: Class, polarization, and conflict,* ed. Steve Ellner and Daniel Hellinger, 73–92. Boulder, Colo.: Lynne Rienner.

López Maya, Margarita, Luis Gómez Calcaño, and Thaís Maingón. 1989. *De Punto Fijo al Pacto Social: Desarrollo y hegemonía en Venezuela.* Caracas: Fundación Fondo Electoral Acta Científica Venezolana.

López Maya, Margarita, and Luis Lander. 2005. Popular protest in Venezuela: Novelties and continuities. *Latin American Perspectives* 32 (2): 92–108.

López Murphy, Ricardo. 1995. *Fiscal decentralization in Latin America.* Washington, D.C.: Inter-American Development Bank.

Lucena, Tibisay. 2003. Las reformas del sistema electoral venezolano y sus consecuencias políticas: 1988–1998. *Revista Alceu* 3 (6): 245–65.

Luna, Juan Pablo. 2004. *La política desde el llano: Conversaciones con militantes barriales.* Montevideo: Ediciones de la Banda Oriental.

———. 2007. Frente Amplio and the crafting of a social democratic alternative in Uruguay. *Latin American Politics and Society* 49 (4): 1–30.

———. 2008. A lost battle? Building programmatic party-voter linkages in contemporary Latin America: A comparative analysis of Chile and Uruguay. In *New voices in the study of democracy in Latin America,* ed. Guillermo O'Donnell,

Joseph S. Tulchin, and Augusto Varas, 153–218. Washington, D.C.: Woodrow Wilson International Center for Scholars.

———. n.d. Party system institutionalization: The case of Chile and why we need to un-pack the concept and its measurement. Unpublished manuscript.

Luna, Juan Pablo, and Elizabeth J. Zechmeister. 2005. Political representation in Latin America: A study of elite-mass congruence in nine countries. *Comparative Political Studies* 38 (5): 388–416.

Lyne, Mona M. 2007. Rethinking economics and institutions: The voter's dilemma and democratic accountability. In *Patrons, clients, and policies: Patterns of democratic accountability and political competition*, ed. Herbert Kitschelt and Steven I. Wilkinson, 159–81. New York: Cambridge University Press.

———. 2008. *The voter's dilemma and democratic accountability: Explaining the democracy development paradox*. University Park: Pennsylvania State University Press.

Machicado, Flavio. 1992. Coca production in Bolivia. In *Drug policy in the Americas*, ed. Peter Smith, 88–98. Boulder, Colo.: Westview Press.

MacKuen, Michael B., Robert S. Erikson, and James A. Stimson. 1989. Macropartisanship. *American Political Science Review* 83 (4): 1125–42.

Madrid, Raul L. 2007. The indigenous movement and democracy in Bolivia. Paper presented at the symposium "Prospects for Democracy in Latin America," University of North Texas, 5–6 April 2007. http://www.psci.unt.edu/Madrid.doc (accessed 30 October 2008).

Magaloni, Beatriz, Alberto Diaz-Cayeros, and Federico Estévez. 2007. Clientelism and portfolio diversification: A model of electoral investment with applications to Mexico. In *Patrons, clients, and policies: Patterns of democratic accountability and political competition*, ed. Herbert Kitschelt and Steven I. Wilkinson, 182–205. New York: Cambridge University Press.

Maheshwari, Shriram. 1976. Constituency linkage of national legislators in India. *Legislative Studies Quarterly* 1 (3): 331–54.

Mahoney, James, and Gary Goertz. 2004. The possibility principle: Choosing negative cases in comparative research. *American Political Science Review* 98 (4): 653–69.

Mahoney, James, and Dietrich Rueschemeyer. 2003. Comparative historical analysis: Achievements and agendas. In *Comparative historical analysis in the social sciences*, ed. James Mahoney and Dietrich Rueschemeyer, 3–40. New York: Cambridge University Press.

Maingon, Thais. 2002. Comportamiento político-electoral del venezolano y construcción de tendencias: 1998 y 2000. *Cuadernos del CENDES* 19 (49): 79–101.

Mainwaring, Scott, Ana María Bejarano, and Eduardo Pizarro Leongómez, eds. 2006. *The crisis of democratic representation in the Andes*. Stanford: Stanford University Press.

Mainwaring, Scott, and Timothy Scully, eds. 1995a. *Building democratic institutions: Parties and party systems in Latin America*. Stanford: Stanford University Press.

———. 1995b. Conclusion: Parties and democracy in Latin America—Different patterns, common challenges. In *Building democratic institutions: Party systems in Latin America*, ed. Scott Mainwaring and Timothy R. Scully, 459–74. Stanford: Stanford University Press.

Mainwaring, Scott, and Mariano Torcal. 2006. Party system institutionalization and party system theory after the third wave of democratization. In *Handbook of party politics*, ed. Richard S. Katz and William J. Crotty, 204–27. Thousand Oaks, Calif.: Sage.

Mainwaring, Scott, and Edurne Zoco. 2007. Political sequences and the stabilization of interparty competition: Electoral volatility in old and new democracies. *Party Politics* 13 (2): 155–78.

Mair, Peter. 1987. *The changing Irish party system: Organisation, ideology, and electoral competition.* London: F. Pinter.

———. 1990. *The West European party system.* New York: Oxford University Press.

———. 1997. *Party system change: Approaches and interpretations.* Oxford: Clarendon Press.

———. 2002. Comparing party systems. In *Comparing democracies 2: New challenges in the study of elections and voting,* ed. Lawrence LeDuc, Richard G. Niemi, and Pippa Norris, 88–107. London: Sage.

———. 2005. Introduction to *Parties and party systems: A framework for analysis,* ed. Giovanni Sartori, xiii-xix. Colchester, UK: ECPR Press.

Malik, Yogendra K., and Dhirendra K. Vajpeyi. 1989. The rise of Hindu militancy: India's secular democracy at risk. *Asian Survey* 29 (3): 308–25.

Malloy, James M. 1991. Democracy, economic crisis, and the problem of governance: The case of Bolivia. *Studies in Comparative International Development* 26 (2): 37–57.

Malloy, James M., and Eduardo Gamarra. 1988. *Revolution and reaction: Bolivia, 1964–1985.* New Brunswick, N.J.: Transaction.

Manor, James. 1988. Parties and the party system. In *India's democracy: An analysis of changing state-society relations,* ed. Atul Kohli, 62–98. Princeton: Princeton University Press.

Márquez, Gustavo, and C. Portela. 1991. *Economía informal.* Caracas: Ediciones IESA.

Marshall, Monty G., and Keith Jaggers. 2009. *Polity IV project: Political regime characteristics and transitions, 1800–2007.* Version p4v2007d [computer file]. Fairfax, Va.: Center for Systemic Peace and Center for Global Policy, George Mason University. http://www.systemicpeace.org/inscr/inscr.htm (accessed 31 July 2008).

Martz, John D. 1966. *Acción Democrática: Evolution of a modern political party in Venezuela.* Princeton: Princeton University Press.

———. 1995. Political parties and the democratic crisis. In *Lessons of the Venezuelan experience,* ed. Louis Wolf Goodman, Johanna Mendelson Forman, Moisés Naím, Joseph S. Tulchin, and Gary Bland, 31–53. Washington, D.C.: Woodrow Wilson Center Press; Baltimore: Johns Hopkins University Press.

———. 1997. *The politics of clientelism: Democracy and the state in Colombia.* New Brunswick, N.J.: Transaction.

Martz, John D., and David J. Myers. 1994. Technological elites and political parties: The Venezuelan professional community. *Latin American Research Review* 29 (1): 7–27.

MAS (Movimiento al Socialismo). 1989. *Estatutos del Movimiento al Socialismo.* Caracas: MAS. Mimeo.

———. 1994. *Documentos normativos del Movimiento al Socialismo: Estatutos.* Caracas: MAS. Mimeo.

Mayhew, David R. 1991. *Divided we govern: Party control, lawmaking, and investigations, 1946–1990.* New Haven: Yale University Press.

Mayorga, René Antonio. 2005. Bolivia's democracy at the crossroads. In *The third wave of democratization in Latin America: Advances and setbacks,* ed. Frances Hagopian and Scott P. Mainwaring, 149–78. New York: Cambridge University Press.

————. 2006. Outsiders and neopopulism: The road to plebiscitary democracy. In *The crisis of democratic representation in the Andes*, ed. Scott P. Mainwaring, Ana María Bejarano, and Eduardo Pizarro Leongómez, 132–67. Stanford: Stanford University Press.

McCoy, Jennifer L. 1989. Labor and the state in a party-mediated democracy: Institutional change in Venezuela. *Latin American Research Review* 24 (2): 35–67.

————. 1999. Chávez and the end of "partyarchy" in Venezuela. *Journal of Democracy* 10 (3): 64–77.

McCoy, Jennifer L., and William C. Smith. 1995. Democratic disequilibrium in Venezuela. *Journal of Interamerican Studies and World Affairs* 37 (2): 113–79.

McDonald, Ronald H., and J. Mark Ruhl. 1989. *Party politics and elections in Latin America*. Boulder, Colo.: Westview Press.

McGuire, James W. 1995. Political parties and democracy in Argentina. In *Building democratic institutions: Party systems in Latin America*, ed. Scott Mainwaring and Timothy R. Scully, 200–246. Stanford: Stanford University Press.

McNeish, John-Andrew. 2006. Stones on the road: The politics of participation and the generation of crisis in Bolivia. *Bulletin of Latin American Research* 25 (2): 220–40.

Medina, Luis Fernando, and Susan C. Stokes. 2007. Monopoly and monitoring: An approach to political clientelism. In *Patrons, clients, and policies: Patterns of democratic accountability and political competition*, ed. Herbert Kitschelt and Steven I. Wilkinson, 68–83. New York: Cambridge University Press.

Mejias Sarabia, Diana Margarita, and Joel Tarazón Rodriguez. 2000. Acción Democrática y Movimiento Quinta República ¿Dos concepciones distintas de hacer política y de conectarse con el electorado? Un análisis comparativo (1974–2000). Thesis, Universidad Central de Venezuela, Facultad de Ciencias Eocnómicas y Sociales.

Miller, Gary, and Norman Schofield. 2003. Activists and partisan realignment in the United States. *American Political Science Review* 97 (2): 245–60.

Miller, Warren E., and J. Merrill Shanks. 1996. *The new American voter*. Cambridge, Mass.: Harvard University Press.

Mishler, William, and Anne Hildreth. 1984. Legislatures and political stability. *Journal of Politics* 46 (1): 25–59.

Molina, José E. 2002. The presidential and parliamentary elections of the Bolivarian revolution in Venezuela: Continuity and change (1998–2000). *Bulletin of Latin American Research* 21 (2): 219–47.

Molina, José E., and Carmen Pérez. 1995. Participación y abstención electoral. In *El proceso electoral de 1993*, ed. CENDES, 29–42. Caracas: CENDES.

————. 1998. Evolution of the party system in Venezuela, 1946–1993. *Journal of Interamerican Studies and World Affairs* 40 (2): 1–26.

————. 2004. Radical change at the ballot box: Causes and consequences of electoral behavior in Venezuela's 2000 elections. *Latin American Politics and Society* 46 (1): 103–34.

Monaldi, Francisco, and Michael Penfold. 2006. The collapse of democratic governance: Political institutions and economic decline in Venezuela. Paper presented at the conference "Venezuelan Economic Growth, 1975–2005," Center for International Development, Harvard University, 27–28 April 2006.

Moreira, Constanza. 2000. La izquierda en Uruguay y Brasil: Cultura política y desarrollo político-partidario. In *La larga espera: Itinerarios de las izquierdas en*

Argentina, Brasil y Uruguay, ed. Susana Mallo and Constanza Moreira, 127–70. Montevideo: Ediciones de la Banda Oriental.

Moreno, Erika. 2005. Whither the Colombian two-party system? An assessment of political reforms and their limits. *Electoral Studies* 24 (3): 485–509.

Morgan, Jana. 2007. Partisanship during the collapse of the Venezuelan party system. *Latin American Research Review* 42 (1): 78–98.

Morgenstern, Scott. 2001. Organized factions and disorganized parties: Electoral incentives in Uruguay. *Party Politics* 7 (2): 235–56.

Morlino, Leonardo. 1996. Crisis of parties and change of party system in Italy. *Party Politics* 2 (1): 5–30.

Morris-Jones, Wyndraeth H. 1978. Parliament and dominant party: The Indian experience. In *Politics mainly Indian*, ed. Wyndraeth H. Morris-Jones, 196–232. Madras: Orient Longman.

Moser, Robert. 2001. *Unexpected outcomes: Electoral systems, political parties, and representation in Russia*. Pittsburgh: University of Pittsburgh Press.

Müller, Wolfgang C. 2007. Political institutions and linkage strategies. In *Patrons, clients, and policies: Patterns of democratic accountability and political competition*, ed. Herbert Kitschelt and Steven I. Wilkinson, 251–75. New York: Cambridge University Press.

Murillo, María Victoria. 2001. *Labor unions, partisan coalitions, and market reforms in Latin America*. New York: Cambridge University Press.

Myers, David J. 1986. The Venezuelan party system: Regime maintenance under stress. In *Venezuela: The democratic experience*, ed. John D. Martz and David J. Myers, 109–48. 2nd ed. New York: Praeger.

———. 1995. Perceptions of a stressed democracy: Inevitable decay or foundation for rebirth? In *Venezuelan democracy under stress*, ed. Jennifer McCoy, Andrés Serbin, William C. Smith, and Andrés Stambouli, 107–37. Miami: North-South Center, University of Miami; New Brunswick, N.J.: Transaction.

———. 2004. Venezuela's Punto Fijo party system: A failed corporatist mediator. In *Authoritarianism and corporatism in Latin America—Revisited*, ed. Howard J. Wiarda, 141–72. Gainesville: University Press of Florida.

Myers, David J., and John D. Martz, eds. 1986. *Venezuela: The democratic experience*. 2nd ed. New York: Praeger.

El Nacional. 1995. AD y COPEI sin recursos para campaña electoral. 22 June, N-0.

———. 1997a. Carlos Navarro disputará presidencia a Álvarez Paz. 17 September, D-1.

———. 1997b. El 2 de deciembre retomarán la discusión. 26 November, D-1.

———. 1997c. Escogencia abierta a toda la sociedad. 12 September, D-4.

———. 1997d. Polaridad Alfaro-Fermín. 8 July, D-2.

———. 1998. Congreso discute hoy Habilitante. 26 August, D-2.

Naím, Moíses. 1993. *Paper tigers and minotaurs: The politics of Venezuela's economic reforms*. Washington, D.C.: Carnegie Endowment for International Peace.

Narain, Iqbal. 1979. India 1978: The politics of non-issues. *Asian Survey* 19 (2): 165–77.

Navarro, Juan Carlos. 1995. In search of the lost pact: Consensus lost in the 1980s and 1990s. In *Venezuelan democracy under stress*, ed. Jennifer McCoy, Andrés Serbin, William C. Smith, and Andrés Stambouli, 13–29. Miami: North-South Center, University of Miami; New Brunswick, N.J.: Transaction.

Nayak, Radhika, N. C. Saxena, and John Farrington. 2002. Reaching the poor: The influence of policy and administrative processes on the implementation of government poverty schemes in India. Working Paper 175, Overseas Development Institute, London.

Neuendorf, Kimberly A. 2002. *The content analysis guidebook*. Thousand Oaks, Calif.: Sage.

Nickson, R. Andrew. 1995. *Local government in Latin America*. Boulder, Colo.: Lynne Rienner.

Noiret, Serge. 1994. Political parties and the political system in Belgium before federalism, 1830–1980. *European History Quarterly* 24 (1): 85–122.

Nuñez, Rafael. 1993. Jefe de finanzas de AD declaró el partido en bancarrota. *El Nacional*, 17 December, D-3.

———. 1994. En AD estudia la posibilidad de postergar processo interno. *El Nacional*, 11 July, D-4.

Oates, Wallace. 1972. *Fiscal federalism*. New York: Harcourt Brace Jovanovich.

OCEI. Various years. *Encuesta de hogares por muestreo*. Caracas: OCEI.

O'Donnell, Guillermo. 1999. *Counterpoints*. Notre Dame: University of Notre Dame Press.

OECD. Various years. *Main economic indicators*. Paris: OECD.

O'Neill, Kathleen. 2003. Decentralization as an electoral strategy. *Comparative Political Studies* 36 (9): 1068–91.

OPEC. 1999. *Annual statistical bulletin*. Vienna, Austria: Organization of the Petroleum Exporting Countries.

———. 2001. *Annual statistical bulletin*. Vienna, Austria: Organization of the Petroleum Exporting Countries.

———. 2003. *Annual statistical bulletin*. Vienna, Austria: Organization of the Petroleum Exporting Countries.

Ordeshook, Peter, and Olga Shvetsova. 1994. Ethnic heterogeneity, district magnitude, and the number of parties. *American Journal of Political Science* 38 (1): 100–123.

Orlando, María Beatriz. 2001. The informal sector in Venezuela: Catalyst or hindrance for poverty reduction. Poverty Project Papers, Universidad Católica Andrés Bello and Asociación Civil para la Promoción de Estudios Sociales, Caracas, Venezuela.

Orlando, María Beatriz, and M. Pollack. 2000. Microenterprises and poverty: Evidence from Latin America. Microenterprise Unit Working Papers, Inter-American Development Bank, Washington, D.C.

Ortega A., Daniel E. 2003. Descripción y perfiles de desigualdad en Venezuela: 1975–2002. Supporting document for *Informe de Desarrollo Humano 2004*. Caracas: PNUD. Mimeo.

Pacek, Alexander C., and Benjamin Radcliff. 1995. The political economy of competitive elections in the developing world. *American Journal of Political Science* 39 (3): 745–59.

Panagariya, Arvind. 2004. India in the 1980s and 1990s: A triumph of reforms. IMF Working Paper 04-43, Washington, D.C.

Panebianco, Angelo. 1988a. The Italian Radicals: New wine in old bottles? In *When parties fail: Emerging alternative organizations*, ed. Kay Lawson and Peter H. Merkl, 110–36. Princeton: Princeton University Press.

———. 1988b. *Political parties: Organization and power*. Translated by Marc Silver. New York: Cambridge University Press.

Panizza, Francisco. 2004. A reform without losers: The symbolic economy of civil service reform in Uruguay, 1995–1996. *Latin American Politics and Society* 46 (3): 1–28.

Park, Richard L. 1975. Political crisis in India, 1975. *Asian Survey* 15 (11): 996–1013.

Pasquino, Gianfranco. 1997. No longer a "party state"? Institutions, power, and the problems of Italian reform. *West European Politics* 20 (1): 34–53.

Pattnaik, Ranjit Kumar, Dhritidyuti Bose, Indranil Bhattacharyya, and Jai Chander. 2005. *Public expenditure and emerging fiscal policy scenario in India*. Mumbai: Reserve Bank of India. http://www.bancaditalia.it/studiricerche/convegni/atti/publ_expe/iii/603-640_pattnaik_bose_bhattacharyya_chander.pdf (accessed 20 October 2008).

Payne, J. Mark, Daniel Zovatto G., Fernando Carrillo Florez, and Andrés Allamand Zavala. 2002. *Democracies in development: Politics and reform in Latin America*. Washington, D.C.: Inter-American Development Bank and International Institute for Democracy and Electoral Assistance.

Pedersen, Mogens N. 1983. Changing patterns of electoral volatility in European party systems, 1948–1977. In *Western European party systems: Continuity and change*, ed. Hans Daalder and Peter Mair, 29–66. Beverly Hills, Calif.: Sage.

Penfold-Becerra, Michael. 1999. Institutional electoral incentives and decentralization outcomes: Comparing Colombia and Venezuela. Ph.D. diss., Columbia University.

———. 2000. El colapso del sistema de partidos en Venezuela: Explicación de una muerte anunciada. Paper presented at the Congress of the Latin American Studies Association, Miami, 16–18 March 2000.

———. 2007. Clientelism and social funds: Evidence from Chávez's misiones. *Latin American Politics and Society* 49 (4): 63–84.

Philip, George. 2000. The strange death of the Venezuelan party system. Paper presented at the Congress of the Latin American Studies Association, Miami, 16–18 March 2000.

Piattoni, Simona. 2001a. Clientelism in historical and comparative perspective. In *Clientelism, interests, and democratic representation: The European experience in historical and comparative perspective*, ed. Simona Piattoni, 1–30. New York: Cambridge University Press.

———. 2001b. Clientelism, interests, and democratic representation. In *Clientelism, interests, and democratic representation: The European experience in historical and comparative perspective*, ed. Simona Piattoni, 193–212. New York: Cambridge University Press.

Pilet, Jean-Benoit. 2005. The adaptation of the electoral system to the ethno-linguistic evolution of Belgian consociationalism. *Ethnopolitics* 4 (4): 397–411.

Piñeiro, Rafael, and Jaime Yaffé. 2004. El Frente Amplio por dentro: Las fracciones frenteamplistas, 1971–1999. In *La izquierda uruguaya: Entre la oposición y el gobierno*, ed. Jorge Lanzaro, 297–319. Montevideo: Editorial Fin del Siglo.

Pitkin, Hanna Fenichel. 1967. *The concept of representation*. Berkley: University of California Press.

Pizarro Leongómez, Eduardo. 2006. Giants with feet of clay: Political parties in Colombia. In *The crisis of democratic representation in the Andes*, ed. Scott Mainwaring, Ana María Bejarano, and Eduardo Pizarro Leongómez, 78–99. Stanford: Stanford University Press.

Pizzorno, A. 1992. Introduzione: La corruzione nel sistema político. In *Lo scambio occulto: Casi di corruzione politica in Italia*, ed. D. della Porta, 13–74. Bologna: Il Mulino.

Policía Nacional de Colombia. Various dates. *Revista de criminalidad*. Bogotá: Policía Nacional de Colombia, Dirección Central de Policía Judicial. http://www.policia .gov.co/ (accessed 20 January 2006).

Portes, Alejandro, and Kelly Hoffman. 2003. Latin American class structures: Their composition and change during the neoliberal era. *Latin American Research Review* 38 (1): 41–82.

Posada-Carbó, Eduardo. 2006. Colombia hews to the path of change. *Journal of Democracy* 17 (4): 80–94.

Powell, John Duncan. 1971. *Political mobilization of the Venezuelan peasant*. Cambridge, Mass.: Harvard University Press.

Prud'homme, Rémy. 1995. The dangers of decentralization. *World Bank Observer* 10 (2): 201–20.

Przeworski, Adam, Pranab Bardhan, Luiz Carlos Bresser Pereira, László Bruszt, Jang Jip Choi, Ellen Turkish Comisso, Zhiyuan Cui, et al. 1995. *Sustainable democracy*. Cambridge: Cambridge University Press.

Przeworski, Adam, and Henry Teune. 1970. *The logic of comparative social inquiry*. New York: Wiley.

Pulgarín, Wilfer. 1997a. Fernández rechaza que Álvarez preside la Convención. *El Nacional*, 15 September, D-2.

———. 1997b. Herrera Campíns and Ramírez controlan mayoría. *El Nacional*, 24 July, D-1.

Ragin, Charles. 1987. *The comparative method: Moving beyond qualitative and quantitative strategies*. Berkeley: University of California Press.

———. 2000. *Fuzzy-set social science*. Chicago: University of Chicago Press.

Ray, Talton F. 1969. *The politics of the barrios in Venezuela*. Berkeley: University of California Press.

Remmer, Karen L. 1991. The political impact of economic crisis in Latin America in the 1980s. *American Political Science Review* 85 (3): 777–800.

Rettberg, Angelika. 2005. Business versus business? Grupos and organized business in Colombia. *Latin American Politics and Society* 47 (1): 31–54.

Reyes Rodriguez, Ascención. 1997. Gobierno debe cambiar el sistema diabólico de bonos compensatorios. *El Nacional*, 14 January, D-5.

———. 1998a. AD es el único partido que escogera por la base. *El Nacional*, 12 January, D-2.

———. 1998b. Domingo con Luis Alfaro Ucero. *El Nacional*, 26 July, D-1.

Rhodes, Martin. 1997. Financing party politics in Italy: A case of systemic corruption. *West European Politics* 20 (1): 55–80.

Richardson, Bradley. 1997. *Japanese democracy: Power, coordination, and performance*. New Haven: Yale University Press.

Riutort, M. 1999. *Pobreza, desigualdad y crecimiento económico*. Documentos del Proyecto Pobreza. Caracas: Universidad Católica Andrés Bello y Asociación Civil para la Promoción de Estudios Sociales.

Roberts, Kenneth M. 1995. Neoliberalism and the transformation of populism in Latin America: The Peruvian case. *World Politics* 48 (1): 82–126.

———. 1998. *Deepening democracy? The modern left and social movements in Chile and Peru*. Stanford: Stanford University Press.

———. 2002a. Party-society linkages and democratic representation in Latin America. *Canadian Journal of Latin American and Caribbean Studies* 27 (53): 9–34.

———. 2002b. Social inequalities without class cleavages in Latin America's liberal era. *Studies in Comparative International Development* 36 (4): 3–33.

————. 2003a. Social correlates of party system demise and populist resurgence in Venezuela. *Latin American Politics and Society* 45 (3): 35–57.

————. 2003b. Social polarization and the populist resurgence in Venezuela. In *Venezuelan politics in the Chávez era: Class, polarization, and conflict*, ed. Steve Ellner and Daniel Hellinger, 55–72. Boulder, Colo.: Lynne Rienner.

————. n.d. *Changing course: Parties, populism, and political representation in Latin America's neoliberal era*. New York: Cambridge University Press, forthcoming.

Roberts, Kenneth M., and Erik Wibbels. 1999. Party systems and electoral volatility in Latin America: A test of economic, institutional, and structural explanations. *American Political Science Review* 93 (3): 575–90.

Roberts, Lia. 2007. Old parties, left parties, and neoliberalism in Latin America. Paper presented at the annual meeting of the Midwest Political Science Association, Chicago, 12–15 April 2007.

Rodríguez-Raga, Juan Carlos. 2007. *Cultura política de la democracia en Colombia: 2006*. Bogotá: Universidad de los Andes, LAPOP, and USAID.

Rokkan, Stein. 1970. *Citizens, elections, parties: Approaches to the comparative study of political development*. Oslo: Universitetsforlaget.

Romero, Aníbal. 1997. Rearranging the deck chairs on the Titanic: The agony of democracy in Venezuela. *Latin American Research Review* 32 (1): 7–36.

Rondinelli, Dennis A., James S. McCullough, and Ronald W. Johnson. 1989. Analyzing decentralization policies in developing countries: A political-economy framework. *Development and Change* 20 (1): 57–87.

Rose, Richard, and Thomas T. Mackie. 1988. Do parties persist or fail? The big trade-off facing organizations. In *When parties fail: Emerging alternative organizations*, ed. Kay Lawson and Peter H. Merkl, 533–58. Princeton: Princeton University Press.

Rotte, Ralph. 1998. International commitment and domestic politics: A note on the Maastricht case. *European Journal of International Relations* 4 (1): 131–42.

Rudolph, Joseph R., Jr. 1977. Ethnonational parties and political change: The Belgian and British experience. *Polity* 9 (4): 401–26.

Rumi, Cecilia. 2005. Ciclo electoral y transferencias federales: Evidencia de Argentina. Paper presented at the conference of the Asociación Argentina de Economía Política, La Plata, Argentina, 2005.

Ryan, Jeffrey J. 2004. Decentralization and democratic instability: The case of Costa Rica. *Public Administration Review* 64 (1): 81–91.

Sabatini, Christopher. 2003. Decentralization and political parties. *Journal of Democracy* 14 (2): 138–50.

Sáinz, Pedro. 2005. La equidad en Latinoamérica desde los años noventa. *Cuadernos del CENDES* 22 (60): 63–93.

Salamanca, Luis. 1995. The Venezuelan political system: A view from civil society. In *Venezuelan democracy under stress*, ed. Jennifer McCoy, Andrés Serbin, William C. Smith, and Andrés Stambouli, 197–214. Miami: North-South Center, University of Miami; New Brunswick, N.J.: Transaction.

Salazar Elena, Rodrigo. 2004. Las elecciones bolivianas de 2002: Los límites del reformismo institucional. *Revista Mexicana de Sociología* 66 (1): 23–56.

Samuels, David. 2003. *Ambition, federalism, and legislative politics in Brazil*. New York: Cambridge University Press.

Sanchez, Alba. 1990. En franca mejoría relaciones AD-Gobierno. *El Nacional*, 6 December, D-1.

Sánchez, Omar. 2008. Guatemala's party universe: A case study in under-institutionalization. *Latin American Politics and Society* 50 (1): 123–51.

Sandholtz, Wayne. 1993. Choosing union: Monetary politics and Maastricht. *International Organization* 47 (1): 1–39.

Santi, Ettore. 1988. Ten years of unionization in Italy (1977–1986). *Labour* 2 (1): 153–82.

Sartori, Giovanni. 1970. Concept misformation in comparative politics. *American Political Science Review* 64 (4): 1033–53.

———. [1976] 2005. *Parties and party systems: A framework for analysis.* Reprint, Colchester, UK: ECPR Press.

Schattschneider, E. E. 1942. *Party government.* New York: Farrar and Rinehart.

Scherlis, Gerardo. 2008. Machine politics and democracy: The deinstitutionalization of the Argentine party system. *Government and Opposition* 43 (4): 579–98.

Schmidt, Steffan. 1980. Patrons, brokers, and clients: Party linkages in the Colombian system. In *Political parties and linkage: A comparative perspective,* ed. Kay Lawson, 265–88. New Haven: Yale University Press.

Schmitter, Philippe C. 1974. Still the century of corporatism? In *The new corporatism,* ed. Frederick C. Pike and Thomas Stritch, 85–131. Notre Dame: University of Notre Dame Press.

Schmitter, Philippe C., and Gerhard Lehmbruch, eds. 1979. *Trends toward corporatist intermediation.* Beverly Hills, Calif.: Sage.

Seawright, Jason. 2003. The demand side of party system collapse in Venezuela and Peru: Economic performance, corruption perceptions, and policy divergence. Paper presented at the annual meeting of the American Political Science Association, Philadelphia, 28–31 August.

———. 2007. Political elites and party system vulnerability. Paper presented at the annual meeting of the Midwest Political Science Association, Chicago, 12–15 April 2007.

Selee, Andrew. 2011. *Democracy close to home? Decentralization, democratization, and informal power in Mexico.* University Park: Pennsylvania State University Press.

Seligson, Amber. 2003. Disentangling the role of ideology and issue positions in the rise of third parties: The case of Argentina. *Political Research Quarterly* 56 (4): 465–75.

Seligson, Mitchell. 2001. *Transparencia y buen gobierno en cuatro ciudades de Colombia 2001.* Nashville: LAPOP and Vanderbilt University. http://www.vanderbilt.edu/lapop/colombia/2001-transparencia.pdf (accessed 9 March 2011).

Seligson, Mitchell A., Abby B. Córdova, Juan Carlos Donoso, Daniel Moreno Morales, Diana Orcés, and Vivian Schwarz Blum. 2006. *Auditoria de la democracia: Informe Bolivia 2006.* Nashville: LAPOP and USAID.

Sen, Amartya. 1993. The threats to secular India. *Social Scientist* 21 (3–4): 5–23.

Shanks, J. Merrill, and Warren E. Miller. 1990. Policy direction and performance evaluation: Complementary explanations of the Reagan elections. *British Journal of Political Science* 20 (2): 143–235.

Shefner, Jon. 2005. Do you think democracy is a magical thing? From basic needs to democratization in informal politics. In *Out of the shadows,* ed. Patricia Fernández-Kelly and Jon Shefner, 241–67. University Park: Pennsylvania State University Press.

Shefter, Martin. 1994. *Political parties and the state: The American historical experience.* Princeton: Princeton University Press.

Siaroff, Alan. 2000. *Comparative European party systems: An analysis of parliamentary elections since 1945.* New York: Garland.

Singer, Matthew M. 2007. The presidential and parliamentary elections in Bolivia, December 2005. *Electoral Studies* 26 (1): 200–205.

Singh, Hoshiar. 1994. Constitutional base for Panchayati Raj in India: The 73rd Amendment Act. *Asian Survey* 34 (9): 818–27.

Sisson, Richard, and Munira Majmundar. 1991. India in 1990: Political polarization. *Asian Survey* 31 (2): 103–12.

Skocpol, Theda. 1984. Emerging agendas and recurrent strategies in historical sociology. In *Vision and method in historical sociology*, ed. Theda Skocpol, 356–91. New York: Cambridge University Press.

Smilde, David. 2004. Popular publics: Street protest and plaza preachers in Caracas. *International Review of Social History* 49 (Dec.): 179–95.

Smith, Gordon. 1979. Western European party systems: On the trail of a typology. *West European Politics* 2 (1): 128–43.

Sridharan, Eswaran. 2010. The party system. In *The Oxford companion to politics in India*, ed. Niraja Gopal Jayal and Pratap Bhanu Mehta, 117–38. Delhi: Oxford University Press.

Stepan, Alfred. 2001. *Arguing comparative politics.* Oxford: Oxford University Press.

Stokes, Susan C. 2001. *Mandates and democracy: Neoliberalism by surprise in Latin America.* New York: Cambridge University Press.

———. 2005. Perverse accountability: A formal model of machine politics with evidence from Argentina. *American Political Science Review* 99 (3): 315–25.

Suárez Molero, Ángel. 1993. AD puede quedar sin luz, agua, ni teléfonos. *El Globo,* 7 July, Política-4.

Swenden, Wilfried, Marleen Brans, and Lieven DeWinter. 2006. The politics of Belgium: Institutions and policy under bipolar and centrifugal federalism. *Western European Politics* (29): 5: 863–73.

Sznajder, Mario. 1995. Italy's right-wing government: Legitimacy and criticism. *International Affairs* 71 (1): 83–102.

Szusterman, Celia. 2007. "Que se vayan todos!" The struggle for democratic party politics in contemporary Argentina. In *Party politics in new democracies*, ed. Paul Webb and Stephen White, 213–42. New York: Oxford University Press.

Tabuas, Mireya. 1995. Buhoneros: Necesidad o facilismo? La calle como oficio. *El Nacional,* 17 January, C-2.

Tanaka, Martín. 1998. *Los espejismos de la democracia: El colapso del sistema de partidos en el Perú, 1980–1995, en perspectiva comparada.* Lima: Instituto de Estudios Peruanos.

———. 2005. Peru, 1980–2000: Chronicle of a death foretold? Determinism, political decisions, and open outcomes. In *The third wave of democratization in Latin America: Advances and setbacks*, ed. Frances Hagopian and Scott P. Mainwaring, 261–88. New York: Cambridge University Press.

Tarrow, Sidney. 1977. *Between center and periphery: Grassroots politicians in Italy and France.* New Haven: Yale University Press.

Ticona, Esteban, Gonzalo Rojas, and Xavier Albó. 1995. *Votos y wiphalas: Campesinos y pueblos originarios en democracia.* La Paz: Centro de Investigación y Promoción del Campesiando (CIPCA).

Tiebout, Charles M. 1956. A pure theory of local expenditures. *Journal of Political Economy* 64 (5): 416–24.

Tilly, Charles. 1997. Means and ends in macrosociology. *Comparative Social Research* 16 (1997): 43–53.

Tocqueville, Alexis de. [1848] 1988. *Democracy in America*. Reprint, New York: Perennial Library.

Torres, Freddy. 1995. Candidatos copeyanos presentarán libros con cuentas electorales. *El Nacional*, 2 September, D-2.

Torres, Gerver. 2000. The torturous road to privatization in Venezuela. In *The impact of privatization in the Americas*, ed. Melissa H. Birch and Jerry Haar. Coral Gables, Fla.: North-South Center Press, University of Miami.

Ulloa, Fernando C., and Eduardo P. Carbó. 2003. The congressional and presidential elections in Colombia, 2002. *Electoral Studies* 22 (4): 785–92.

Urbaneja, Diego Bautista. 1992. *Pueblo y petroleo en la política venezolana del siglo XX*. Caracas: CEPET.

Urwin, Derek W. 1970. Social cleavages and political parties in Belgium: Problems of institutionalization. *Political Studies* 18 (3): 320–40.

U.S. Department of State, Bureau of International Narcotics and Law Enforcement Affairs. Various dates. *International narcotics control strategy report*. Washington, D.C.: U.S. Department of State. http://www.state.gov/p/inl/rls/nrcrpt/ (accessed 2 January 2008).

U.S. General Accounting Office. 2003. *Drug control: Coca cultivation and eradication estimates in Colombia* (GAO-03-319R). Report by Jess T. Ford. Washington, D.C.: GAO. http://www.gao.gov/new.items/d03319r.pdf (accessed 21 January 2008).

Valecillos, Hector. 1992. Mercado de trabajo y redistribución del ingreso en condiciones de reajuste económico: Situación actual y perspectivas. Paper presented to the UNDP National Economic Council Symposium on the Human Development Initiative, Caracas, Venezuela.

Van Cott, Donna Lee. 2000. Party system development and indigenous populations in Latin America. *Party Politics* 6 (2): 155–74.

———. 2003. From exclusion to inclusion: Bolivia's 2002 elections. *Journal of Latin American Studies* 35 (4): 751–75.

———. 2005. *From movements to parties in Latin America: The evolution of ethnic politics*. New York: Cambridge University Press.

Varshney, Ashutosh. 2000. Is India becoming more democratic? *Journal of Asian Studies* 59 (1): 3–25.

Vinogradoff, Ludmila. 1989. AD emitirá bonos para palrar su crisis financiera. *El Nacional*, 30 July, D-4.

Warner, Carolyn M. 2001. Mass parties and clientelism in France and Italy. In *Clientelism, interests, and democratic representation: The European experience in historical and comparative perspective*, ed. Simona Piattoni, 122–51. New York: Cambridge University Press.

Waters, Sarah. 1994. "Tangentopoli" and the emergence of a new political order in Italy. *West European Politics* 17 (1): 169–82.

Weber, Max. 1978. *Economy and society*. Berkeley: University of California Press.

Welsch, Friedrich, and José Vicente Carrasquero. 1989. Las elecciones regionales y municipales de 1989 en Venezuela. *Cuadernos del Cendes*, no. 12:9–29.

Weyland, Kurt. 1996. Neoliberalism and neopopulism in Latin America: Unexpected affinities. *Studies in Comparative International Development* 31 (3): 3–31.

Whitehead, Laurence. 2001. High anxiety in the Andes: Bolivia and the viability of democracy. *Journal of Democracy* 12 (2): 6–16.

Wilkinson, Steven I. 2007. Explaining changing patterns of party-voter linkages in India. In *Patrons, clients, and policies: Patterns of democratic accountability and political competition*, ed. Herbert Kitschelt and Steven I. Wilkinson, 110–40. New York: Cambridge University Press.

Williams, Sue. 1999. The globalization of the drug trade. *UNESCO Sources*, no. 111:4–5.

Williamson, John. 1990. What Washington means by policy reform. In *Latin American adjustment: How much has happened?* ed. John Williamson, 7–20. Washington, D.C.: Institute for International Economics.

Willis, Eliza, Christopher da C. B. Garman, and Stephen Haggard. 1999. The politics of decentralization in Latin America. *Latin American Research Review* 34 (1): 7–56.

Wolinetz, Steven. 2006. Party systems and party system types. In *Handbook of party politics*, ed. William J. Crotty and Richard S. Katz, 51–62. Thousand Oaks, Calif.: Sage.

World Bank. Various years. World Development Indicators. http://data.worldbank.org/data-catalog/world-development-indicators (accessed 12 January 2011).

Wuhs, Steven T. 2008. *Savage democracy: Institutional change and party development in Mexico*. University Park: Pennsylvania State University Press.

Yashar, Deborah J. 1999. Democracy, indigenous movements, and the postliberal challenge in Latin America. *World Politics* 52 (1): 76–104.

Zoco, Edurne. 2008. The collapse of party systems in Italy, Peru, and Venezuela: A cross-regional theory. Ph.D. diss., University of Notre Dame.

INDEX

Page numbers followed by a "t" include the table number after it; page numbers followed by an "f" include the figure number after it.

Alfaro Ucero, Luis
  AD and, 110, 116, 119, 142, 160, 172
  Caldera's alliance with, 117–18, 170–71, 188
  nomination for president, 142, 143–44,
    160–61
Alfonsin, Raúl, 245 n. 3
Alianza Popular Revolucionaria Americana
    (APR, Peru), 31t2.4
Alleanza Nazionale (AN, Italy), 206, 282
Álvarez Paz, Oswaldo, 115, 117
Andreotti, Giulio, 215
appeals. *See also* linkage; programmatic
    appeals
  clientelist, 42, 85 n. 12, 86–88, 89, 137,
    165, 221, 246, 253–54, 267, 286
  conditional, 39–40, 62, 62 n. 15, 82, 87–
    88, 152, 219–20
  direct, 236
  ideological, 41, 49–50, 209, 210, 255
  interest-based, 36, 39, 40–41, 41 n. 3,
    56–57, 64, 82, 88 n. 13, 135, 144, 185,
    207, 211, 233, 258–60, 261, 263, 278,
    279, 285
  substantive, 41 n. 4
  use of term, 39 n. 1
Argentina. *See also* party system survival, in
    Argentina
  parties in, 45, 200, 241–42, 244–46, 248,
    260
  Venezuela compared to, 9, 86, 158, 200,
    241–50, 260, 269, 270, 271, 276
Asamblea por la Soberanía de los Pueblos
    (ASP, Bolivia), 285
Asamblea Uruguay, 259
Asociación Nacional de Industriales (ANDI,
    Colombia), 218 n. 7, 219
authoritarianism, 29 n. 18, 35, 202 n. 8, 242,
    248, 255–56

balance of payments crises, 93, 106–8, 123–
    24, 226, 242, 257–58
Baloyra surveys (Venezuela), 75 n. 3, 76t4.1,
    80 n. 8, 81, 104 n. 13, 114 n. 17, 302
Banco de los Trabajadores de Venezuela
    (BTV), 85
Banzer, Hugo, 225, 229, 230, 232
Batoba surveys (Venezuela), 75 n. 3, 76t4.1,
    80 n. 8, 81, 104 n. 13, 114 n. 17
Belgium. *See also* party system survival, in
    Belgium
  Italy compared to, 200–201, 250–54, 269,
    270, 271
  parties in, 250, 252, 253
  party systems in, 25t2.1, 26t2.2, 252–53

benefits, clientelist, 61–62, 66–67, 281. *See
    also* clientelism; demands, clientelist;
    exchanges, clientelist; resources,
    clientelist
  in Argentina, 243, 247
  in Bolivia, 234–35
  in Colombia, 219, 220–22, 225
  conditionality of, 39–40
  decentralization's effects on, 64–65, 150,
    163
  decreases in, 165, 220–21, 225, 280
  distribution of, 44, 65, 87, 151, 154–55, 159–
    61, 169, 280
  increases in, 257, 276
  in India, 264
  in Italy, 206, 213–14
  used in incorporating linkage, 39, 82, 83,
    88 n. 13, 135, 278
  in Uruguay, 257
  in Venezuela, 78, 88–89, 148–49;
    constraints on, 172–74, 188–89;
    decentralization's effects on, 155–56,
    161–63; employment-based, 82–83, 85,
    134; targeting informal sector with, 88;
    votes exchanged for, 87, 149, 150, 158–
    59, 187
  votes exchanged for, 39–40, 42, 61, 64,
    66–67, 149, 150, 155–56
Berlusconi, Silvio, 5, 206, 282, 286, 287
Bharatiya Janata Party (BJP, India), 262, 263
Blancos (Uruguay), 199t9.1, 201, 254 n. 5,
    254–56, 258, 259, 260, 269, 295
Bolivia, 126, 195, 196. *See also* party system
    collapse, in Bolivia
  constitutions, 196, 230, 292
  electoral system in, 195, 196
  India compared to, 200, 201–2, 202 n. 8,
    241, 260–67, 269–70, 274
  party system institutionalization in, 197,
    202 n. 9
  party system in, 36, 193, 196 n. 2, 225, 227,
    231, 280, 283, 285
  Revolution, 228, 231, 232, 235
bureaucratic rationalization, 65–66, 164,
    169, 172, 249, 271
Burgess, Katrina, 45
Buró Sindical (AD, Venezuela), 84, 141, 142,
    143, 160
business associations, 55, 279. *See also*
    owners, business; FEDECAMARAS
  in Argentina, 242, 243–44, 269
  in Colombia, 218 n. 7
  in Bolivia, 227, 231
  in Italy, 207, 208

in Venezuela, 35, 83–84, 85, 86, 88, 132–33, 139, 144, 269

Caldera, Rafael, 4, 138, 139, 173
  addressing important problems under, 94, 95t5.1, 100, 107–8
  AD's alliance with, 4, 111, 115, 116, 118, 119, 170–71
  Alfaro's alliance with, 117–18, 170–71, 188
  Convergencia Nacional and, 118, 138
  COPEI and, 76, 113–14, 114 n. 16, 119, 167, 170
  decree authority given to, 97 n. 3, 118
  first presidency of, 95t5.1
  MAS and, 113, 118, 119, 158 n. 7
  neoliberal reforms by, 103 n. 12, 107, 111, 116, 118, 124, 130, 139, 177, 188, 258 n. 7
  second presidency of, 95t5.1, 97 n. 3, 103 n. 12, 111–12, 117–19, 139, 173
Cali Cartel (Colombia), 224
Canache, Damarys, 156, 284
Canache Mata, Carlos, 110, 155
Caracazo protests (Venezuela), 4, 75, 102, 135
Catholic Church, 74 n. 2, 207, 211, 218, 250–51
Centrally Sponsored Schemes (India), 265
Centro al Servicio de la Acción Popular (community organization, Venezuela), 137–38
CEPAL poverty estimates, 153
challenges to linkage, 5, 7–8, 9–10, 34, 43–49, 68–70, 204, 271–72, 277–78, 294–96
clientelist, 61–67, 149–50
comparisons of, 197–98, 200, 201–2, 238, 239t10.1, 241, 267–68, 269, 270, 274–80
  in Argentina, 242–43, 244, 247
  in Belgium, 250–51, 253
  in Bolivia, 229, 231–33, 234–36, 237
  in Colombia, 219–20, 220–22, 225
  incorporation, 56–58, 60
  in India, 262–63, 266
  in Italy, 208–9, 211–14, 216
  programmatic, 50–52, 54, 91–92
  in Uruguay, 256–57, 258, 259
  in Venezuela, 90, 92–94, 101, 120–21, 123–28, 151–56, 158–61, 186, 189, 205
change, 8, 9, 21 n. 10, 61, 68, 69–70, 90. *See also* adaptation; party system change; social transformation; structural adjustment policies
charisma, 41 n. 4, 287–88. *See also* personalism

Chávez, Hugo, 161
  consolidation of power by, 3–4, 5, 78, 281–82, 287
  election of, 161, 176, 280–81
  ideology of, 283
  informal sector included by, 44, 273, 284–85, 286
  opposition to, 127–28, 290
  rise of, 30t2.3, 37, 139 n. 5
chavistas (Venezuela), 285, 286, 288, 290
Christian Democratic Party (CVP-PSC, Belgium), 199t9.1, 201, 250, 251–52, 253, 269
Christian Democratic party (DC, Italy), 5, 30t2.3, 193, 201, 206–8, 210–12, 215, 253, 268–69, 280
Christian Democrats (Uruguay), 255
CIEPA surveys (Venezuela), 80 n. 8
class. *See* cleavages, traditional class; middle class; upper class; working class
cleavages, 42, 55–56
  communist-anticommunist, 207, 209, 210
  comparisons of, 201, 202, 203, 269–70
  ethnic: in Belgium, 267; in Bolivia, 193, 231, 233–34, 238, 261, 266–67, 270, 285–86; in Ecuador, 202 n. 8; in India, 199t9.1, 260–61, 261 n. 9, 262–64, 266–67, 270
  ethnolinguistic, in Belgium, 250–53, 254
  formal-informal sectors, 238, 243, 260, 269–70, 284; in Argentina, 243, 270; in Bolivia, 232–33; in Uruguay, 259–60; in Venezuela, 122, 125, 127–28, 132, 147, 238, 243, 270, 284
  newly politicized, 212–13, 216, 250, 254, 264, 270, 281, 285, 293
  regional, 64; in Belgium, 250–51, 251–52; in Italy, 211–13, 212–13, 216, 238, 270, 285
  religious, 5, 201, 207, 211, 213, 216; in Belgium, 201, 250, 251; in Colombia, 218; in India, 261, 263; in Italy, 5, 201, 207, 211, 216, 250, 285; in Uruguay, 255
  traditional class (worker-owner), 5, 55–56, 57, 59, 128; in Argentina, 242–43, 269–70; in Belgium, 201, 250, 251; in Bolivia, 227–28, 231, 233, 234, 237, 261, 270; in Italy, 5, 201, 207, 211–12, 213, 216, 250, 270, 285; in Uruguay, 255, 259, 260; in Venezuela, 83–84, 86, 89, 122, 123, 125, 127–28, 132, 134, 136, 138, 141, 177, 188, 238, 284; lack of, in Colombia, 218
  transformation of, 55–58, 60, 68, 122, 123–28, 126t6.1, 130, 199t9.1, 203–4, 211–13,

cost of living, in Venezuela, 81, 95t5.1, 96,
    108–9, 111–12, 282
Craxi, Bettino, 215
crime
    in Colombia, 222–23
    in Italy, 282
    in Venezuela, 93, 95t5.1, 96, 101, 102 n. 11,
        111, 281, 282
crises. *See also* economic crises; social crises
    as cause of party system collapse, 198,
        199t9.1, 239t10.1, 295–96
    challenges from, 8, 46, 52, 54
    in Colombia, 260
    in Peru, 45
    resources decreased by, 65, 66
    in Uruguay, 255, 259, 260
    in Venezuela, 44, 45–46, 156, 281
Crisp, Brian F., 46, 82 n. 10, 97 n. 3
currency devaluations, 106, 117, 209

data sources
    election results, 186–87
    interviews, 78–80, 297–300
    legislative output, 80, 94, 96–98, 289,
        303–11
    measuring Venezuelan system collapse,
        178–81
    most similar system design, 200
    news reports, 11, 79 n. 5, 80
    party archives, 79 n. 6
    public opinion surveys, 11, 75 n. 3, 80, 88–
        89, 94, 104–6, 114, 146, 173, 176, 292
    socioeconomic statistics, 75 n. 3
DATOS surveys (Venezuela), 75 n. 3, 80 n. 8,
    94, 105t5.2, 146, 176 n. 1
debt, public, 65
    in Argentina, 243 n. 1
    in Bolivia, 226, 227, 228, 231
    in Colombia, 223
    in Italy, 5, 209, 214
    in Latin America, 124
    in Venezuela, 4, 81, 92, 95t5.1, 106, 107,
        109, 130, 134
decentralization, 202
    in centralized party systems, 64, 150, 160–
        62, 212, 237, 271, 276
    clientelist demands increased by, 61, 62–
        65, 67–68
    in Costa Rica, 156
    democratizing potential of, 63
    electoral, 69, 158–61, 250, 271; in
        Argentina, 247–48, 249; in Belgium,
        253, 254; in Bolivia, 235–36; as cause of
        party system collapse, 198, 199t9.1;

clientelist demands increased by, 275;
    in Colombia, 223–25; comparisons of,
    201, 239t10.1; in India, 265 n.10, 265–
    67; in Italy, 213, 214, 215, 216; in
    Uruguay, 255, 256
fiscal, 12, 240, 271; in Argentina, 247–
    48; in Bolivia, 234, 235–36, 237; in
    Colombia, 223, 225, 260; in India, 264–
    65, 266; in Uruguay, 257–58, 260; in
    Venezuela, 150, 156
resources decreased by, 62–68, 155–63
subnational leaders and, 64, 143, 162, 221
as threat to party survival, 62–63, 196 n. 1
in Venezuela, 101, 133, 155–63, 172
Decentralization Law (1989, Venezuela), 157
decision-making, 52, 159 n. 6, 279, 294
deindustrialization, 270
    in Argentina, 243
    in Italy, 211, 212, 213, 216, 285
    in Uruguay, 270
    in Venezuela, 124, 288
deinstitutionalization, 13, 15, 287, 288
Delors Report, 209. *See also* Maastricht Treaty
demands, clientelist. *See also* benefits,
    clientelist; clientelism; elections,
    subnational, clientelist demands
    increased by; exchanges, clientelist;
    resources, clientelist
    comparisons of, 201, 270–71
    decentralization's pressures on, 61, 62–65;
        in Venezuela, 155–63
    failure to meet, 42, 43, 67–69, 277, 280; in
        Venezuela, 167, 176, 188–89
    increases in, 12, 47–48, 58, 61–69, 150,
        238, 240, 271, 275, 276; in Argentina,
        247, 249; in Belgium, 253; in Bolivia,
        226, 234, 235–36; in Colombia, 220,
        221–22, 225; in India, 264–67; in Italy,
        213, 215, 216; in Uruguay, 255, 256–57;
        in Venezuela, 150, 151–55, 165, 172–74,
        175, 177
democracy. *See also* Christian Democratic
    Party (DC, Italy)
    in Argentina, 241, 247, 248
    in Bolivia, 225–26, 235
    Christian, 81, 115, 201
    history of, 29 n. 18
    liberal, 39 n. 1
    oppositions to, 24 n. 16
    pacted, 74, 83, 117
    party systems' relationship to, 5–7, 13, 22
        n. 12
    in Peru, 45
    political parties' relationship to, 3, 63

industrialization, 56, 212, 250, 255. *See also* deindustrialization; import-substitution industrialization (ISI)

inequalities. *See* informal sector; wealth, extremes of poverty and

inflation. *See also* cost of living
  in Argentina, 242
  in Bolivia, 226, 227, 228, 229, 231
  in Italy, 209, 214
  in Latin America, 53, 124
  in Venezuela, 4, 92, 93f5.1, 96, 101, 102, 106, 108–9, 123

informal sector. *See also* cleavages, formal-informal sectors
  in Argentina, 200, 242, 243, 247, 260
  in Bolivia, 226, 229–30, 232, 233, 285
  definition of, 122 n. 1, 125 n. 3
  formal sector's relationship to, 127, 132, 134–35, 140–41
  growth of, 45, 57, 243, 260
  in Latin America, 124, 126
  parties' response to, 88–89, 129–31, 136–38, 140, 144–45, 285, 286
  in Peru, 45
  post-collapse attention to, 281, 284–87, 293
  rejection of traditional parties by, 45, 53, 76, 102, 140, 145–47, 175, 177–78, 187, 258, 279
  instability of employment in, 124, 127–28
  in Uruguay, 259, 260
  in Venezuela: attempts to incorporate, 123, 129–38; clientelist appeals to, 87, 137–38, 179; employment for, 86, 88–89; exclusion of, 85–86, 123, 125, 131, 134, 135, 144–45, 147; growth of, 44, 102–3, 122, 124–28, 126t6.1, 130–31, 135, 140–41, 152, 260; policy making for, 138–40; political parties' neglect of, 136–38, 144–45

instability
  party system, 28, 64
  post-collapse, 13, 289, 290, 294

institutionalization, 193, 196–97
  in Argentina, 45, 241, 249–50
  in Belgium, 250
  in Colombia, 36, 193, 197
  comparisons of, 193, 200–201, 202 n. 9
  in Italy, 36, 197
  of party systems, 4, 6, 9–12, 23 n. 13, 55 n. 13
  in Uruguay, 260
  in Venezuela, 4, 9, 35–36, 37, 46, 73, 75, 82, 196–97

Institutional Pact (Venezuela, 1970), 74 n. 2

Inter-American Development Bank (IDB), 107

interest incorporation. *See* incorporation

interests. *See also* cleavages
  associations of, 219, 234
  class-based, 177, 238
  ethnic, 59, 228, 231, 233, 237
  integration of, 55, 56–60, 67–68, 82–86, 88–89, 123, 127, 207, 227, 250, 260, 276
  representation of, 35, 233
  traditional *vs.* emerging, 133, 134–35, 141–45

International Labour Organization (ILO), 86

International Monetary Fund (IMF), 45, 107, 229, 266, 268

interparty agreements, 17, 25, 219t9.1, 239t10.1, *See also* coalitions, governing
  in Belgium, 278
  blurring ideological distinctions by, 11, 54, 68, 92, 203, 238, 275, 279–80
  in Bolivia, 230–31
  as cause of linkage decay, 198, 199t9.1
  in Colombia, 218, 219
  between Colorados and Blancos in Uruguay, 258, 260
  comparisons of, 24, 239t10.1, 268, 269
  in Italy, 211, 253
  lack of in Argentina, 245, 249
  lack of in Uruguay, 258–59, 260
  undermining programmatic differentiation, 112, 116–20, 258 n. 7, 294–95
  in Venezuela, 74, 83, 117, 119–29, 171–72, 188, 245, 259 n. 7, 268

Italian Confederation of Free Trade Unions (CISL), 207

Italy, 285. *See also* economic conditions, in Italy; party system collapse, in Italy
  Belgium compared to, 200–201, 250–54
  economy of, 5, 208–9
  institutionalization in, 36, 197
  party system in, 36, 195, 196, 201 n. 5, 284

IVAD surveys (Venezuela), 75 n. 3, 80 n. 8, 94, 116

Izquierda Democrática (Ecuador), 18 n. 6

Izquierda Unida (IU, Peru), 31t2.4

Janata Dal (JD, India), 262

Janata Party (India), 261–62, 264

Jefes y Jefas program (Argentina), 243 n. 1

Juntas de Acción Comunal (JAC, Colombia), 218

Justicialist Party (PJ, Argentina). *See* Peronists (PJ, Argentina)

Republican Party of Italy (PRI), 206, 210
research design
  case selection, 29 n. 18
  crucial (or least likely) case, 34–37
  multinomial logit analysis, 181, 182t8.1,
    183, 186, 187
  negative cases, 34, 194, 197–98
  paired comparisons, 12, 194, 197, 200–
    202, 241, 271
  structured, focused comparisons, 202–4
reserves, international, in Venezuela, 92, 107,
  109, 110, 123, 164
resources, clientelist. *See also* benefits,
  clientelist; clientelism; demands,
  clientelist; exchanges, clientelist;
  spending; state, the, clientelist resources
  from
  in Argentina, 247, 248, 249
  in Belgium, 254
  in Bolivia, 226
  in Colombia, 218, 219, 220, 222, 223, 224
  comparisons of, 204, 239t10.1, 240
  decentralization's pressures on, 58, 62–63,
    64–65, 67–68, 155–63
  decreases in, 61–62, 65–68, 69, 150, 204,
    238, 239t10.1, 240, 271, 275, 276, 280;
    in Bolivia, 234, 236, 237; as cause of
    linkage decay, 198, 199t9.1; in
    Colombia, 225, 260; in Italy, 214–15; in
    Uruguay, 255, 256, 260; in Venezuela, 5,
    119, 135, 150–51, 162–63, 164–71, 177,
    188–89, 249
  increases in, 254, 264–67
  in India, 264–67
  in Italy, 208, 213
  maintenance of, 248, 249, 264–65
  post-collapse, 286–87
  in Uruguay, 257–58, 267
  in Venezuela, 152, 158–59, 189; access to
    state supply of, 111, 115, 116, 118, 160–63;
    decreases in, 5, 119, 135, 150–51, 162–63,
    164–74, 177, 188–89, 249
responsiveness, 35, 43, 63. *See also* policy
  responsiveness
  constraints on, 12, 52–53
  decline of, 8, 54, 68, 75
  use of term, 39 n. 1
Roberts, Kenneth M., 7 n. 4, 44
Rokkan, Stein, 55, 279
Rúa, Fernando de la, 245

Saéz, Irene, 144, 161
Salas Römer, Henrique, 120, 143, 161, 163
  n. 7, 176, 283

Samper, Ernesto, 224
Sánchez de Lozada, Gonzalo, 230
Sartori, Giovanni
  party system definition of, 15–16
  party system typology of, 21–22, 23, 24
    nn. 15, 16, 25
Scully, Timothy, 23 n. 13, 36, 200 n. 5, 201
secularization
  in Belgium, 250
  in India, 261, 263, 264
  in Italy, 211, 216, 285
SENIAT (Venezuelan tax administration), 131
service sector, 56, 57, 125, 212
Shefner, Jon, 172–73
Sikhs (India), 263
Siles, Hernán, 226, 227
single-member districts (SMD), 157 n. 4, 159,
  195
social crises
  in Bolivia, 226, 227, 233, 237, 268
  in India, 266
  in Venezuela, 93–94, 119
Social Democratic Party of Italy (PSDI), 206,
  210
Socialist Belgian Workers' Party (BSP-PSB),
  250, 252
Socialist Party of Italy (PSI), 30t2.3, 206, 207,
  210, 215
Socialists (Italy), 5, 193
Socialists (Uruguay), 255, 259
social security system, in Venezuela, 84, 139,
  146
social transformation, 200, 270, 279. *See also*
  change; cleavages, transformation of
  in Argentina, 242, 243, 246
  in Belgium, 250–54
  in Bolivia, 234, 237, 269
  as cause of party system collapse, 198,
    199t9.1, 258, 295
  clientelist demands increased by, 61–62,
    65–68, 69, 150, 256, 275–76
  in Colombia, 219, 220, 222, 225, 260
  comparisons of, 201, 202, 203, 204,
    239t10.1, 269–70, 271
  as incorporation challenge, 11–12, 55–59,
    238
  in India, 266
  in Italy, 5, 208, 213, 215, 216, 269
  as linkage challenge, 8, 46
  in Uruguay, 260
  in Venezuela, 4, 5, 44–45, 46, 122–25,
    126t6.1, 269, 284; cleavage
    restructuring, 123–28; clientelist
    demands increased by, 151–55, 172, 189;

Unión República Democrática (URD,
  Venezuela), 74
unions. *See* organized labor
United States drug policy
  in Bolivia, 230, 286
  in Colombia, 220, 268
universal policy outputs, 81–83
upper classes, 42, 200. *See also* wealth,
  extremes of poverty and
  in Argentina, 244
  in Uruguay, 259
  in Venezuela, 147, 185
urbanization
  in Bolivia, 232, 234–35
  in Colombia, 220, 225
  in Uruguay, 255
Uribe, Álvaro, 280, 282, 283, 286, 287, 288,
  292
Uruguay. *See also* party system survival, in
  Uruguay
  Colombia compared to, 200, 201, 254–60,
  295
  constitution in, 256–57

Velásquez, Andrés, 163 n. 7
Velásquez, Ramón J., 95t5.1, 102 n. 11, 157
Venezuela. *See also* democracy, in Venezuela;
  economic crises, in Venezuela;
  economy, in Venezuela; elections, in
  Venezuela; linkage, in Venezuela;
  linkage portfolios, in Venezuela; oil
  industry, in Venezuela; party system
  collapse, in Venezuela
  Argentina compared to, 5, 45, 86, 156, 200,
  241–50, 260, 269, 270, 271
  constitutions, 77 n. 4, 97 n. 3, 285, 290, 292
  coups in, 4, 74 n. 2, 280, 284, 290
  party system institutionalization in, 4, 35–
  36, 73, 196
  party system in, 3, 5, 25t2.1, 26t2.2, 35–37,
  74 n. 1, 75–77, 176, 195, 196
Viernes Negro (Black Friday, Venezuela),
  106, 117
violence, 51
  in Colombia, 193, 217, 218, 219–20, 221,
  222–23, 225, 239t10.1, 266, 268, 282,
  283
  in India, 262–63, 267
volatility, 6, 202 n. 9, 36
  calculation of, 289 n. 4
  collapse distinguished from, 18 n. 6, 19,
  28–29
  following collapse, 289, 294

in India, 202 n. 9
low in Italian party system, 36, 197, 200
  n. 5, 289
voters/voting. 6, 8, 91, 289 *See also* elections
  appeals to, 36, 39, 42, 47, 88, 176, 179
  in Argentina, 244–45, 247
  benefits exchanged for, 39, 42, 47, 61, 63,
  64, 66–67, 149, 150, 155–56, 166, 221,
  222, 224, 238, 247, 286
  in Bolivia, 233–34, 235–36, 237, 268, 283
  clientelist demands from, 65, 66–67, 150,
  151–52, 179, 201, 221, 271
  in Colombia, 217, 221, 222
  economic theories of, 180, 186
  in Italy, 206, 210–11, 214
  growth of, 47, 61–62, 235, 237
  lack of meaningful alternatives for, 11, 50–
  51, 53–54, 75, 245, 268, 294–95
  parties' monitoring of, 8, 66, 159, 222
  post-collapse, 293
  in Uruguay, 255, 257, 257 n. 6, 258
  in Venezuela, 75, 76, 77 n. 4, 81, 119–20,
  157 n. 4, 183, 185; abstention rates of,
  76, 77 n. 4, 176, 187; choices made by,
  175, 178, 181, 186–87, 280, 283, 284;
  clientelist resources for, 87–88, 150,
  158–59, 172

wages
  in Bolivia, 229, 234
  in Italy, 212
  in Venezuela, 81, 84, 92, 102, 124–25, 128,
  134, 139, 140, 145–46, 152–53, 154f7.2,
  166
Walloon region, Belgium, 250–51, 252–53
wealth, extremes of poverty and, 81, 124–25,
  127, 146–47, 152, 153, 154–55, 253,
  284
welfare state, in Italy, 214
Wilkinson, Steven I., 88
working class. *See also* organized labor
  appeals to, 42, 56, 58
  in Argentina, 242
  in Belgium, 250
  in Bolivia, 227–28
  in Italy, 207, 212
  party support from, 149, 200
  in Uruguay, 256, 259
  in Venezuela, 81, 84, 85–86, 123, 127–28,
  134, 138, 139; weakening of, 122, 124,
  125, 141–42, 239 n. 5
work stoppages. *See* protests
World Bank, 229

www.ingramcontent.com/pod-product-compliance
Lightning Source LLC
Chambersburg PA
CBHW022133020426
42334CB00015B/868